THE
ROMAN EMPERORS

THE
ROMAN EMPERORS

A BIOGRAPHICAL GUIDE TO
THE RULERS OF IMPERIAL ROME
31 BC–AD 476

Michael Grant

WEIDENFELD AND NICOLSON
LONDON

George Weidenfeld & Nicolson Limited
91 Clapham High Street, London SW4 7TA

British Cataloguing in Publication Data
Grant, Michael, 1914–
The Roman emperors.
1. Roman emperors–Biography
I. Title
937'.06'0922   DG274

ISBN 0 297 78555 9

Photoset by Deltatype, Ellesmere Port
Printed and bound in Great Britain by
Butler & Tanner Ltd,
Frome and London

CONTENTS

*From this time onwards the emperors indicated reigned in the west unless otherwise stated.

ACKNOWLEDGMENTS

I should like to thank the following for granting their permission to include copyright material:

The Loeb Classical Library (Harvard University Press: William Heinemann Ltd) for extracts from Dio's *Roman History* VII, VIII and IX; *Scriptores Historiae Augustae* II and III; *Suetonius* II, and *Sidonius* I.

Macmillan Publishers Ltd and the authors for quotations from A. H. M. Jones (ed.), *History of Rome through the Fifth Century*, Vol. II (1970).

Penguin Books Ltd and the translators for short extracts from Suetonius, *The Twelve Caesars* (trans. Robert Graves); Marcus Aurelius, *Meditations* (trans. Maxwell Staniforth) and *Lives of the Later Caesars* (trans. Anthony Birley).

The University of California Press and the translator for passages from *Herodian of Antioch's History of the Roman Empire* (trans. E. C. Echols).

I am very grateful to Dr Walter Hamilton for allowing me to see, and make advance use of, the translation of Ammianus Marcellinus which he is preparing in collaboration with Mr Andrew Wallace-Hadrill for Penguin Classics. I also owe thanks to Mrs Betty Radice, editor of that series, for her good offices in the matter. I have greatly benefited from the perceptive advice of Miss Paula Iley, and record my appreciation of the efficiency of Miss Faith Glasgow, of Weidenfeld and Nicolson Ltd, in steering the volume through the press.

ILLUSTRATIONS

The busts, coins and medallions depicting the emperors included in this book are held in the following collections:

Ancona (Museo Nazionale delle Marche): Augustus
Berlin (Staatliche Museen): Tacitus, Johannes, Leo I, Glycerius
Copenhagen (Ny Carlsberg Glypotek): Gaius
Leningrad (Hermitage): Numerian
London (British Museum): Otho, Gordian II, Valerian, Aurelian, Florian, Carus, Diocletian, Galerius, Constantine II, Constantius II, Julian the Apostate, Jovian, Valentinian I, Valens, Valentinian II, Arcadius, Honorius, Constantius III, Valentinian III, Marcian, Petronius Maximus, Avitus, Libius Severus, Olybrius, Julius Nepos, Zeno, Basiliscus
Milan (Castello Sforzesco): Macrinus, Claudius II Gothicus, Theodosius I, Romulus Augustulus
Munich (Antikensammlungen und Glyptotek): Septimius Severus
Naples (Museo Archeologico Nazionale): Tiberius, Antoninus Pius, Caracalla
Oxford (Ashmolean Museum): Constantine I
Paris (Bibliothèque Nationale): Probus, Gratian
    (Musée du Louvre): Nero, Lucius Verus
Rome (Antiquarium Comunale): Domitian
    (formerly in Piazza del Campidoglio): Marcus Aurelius
    (Museo Capitolino): Galba, Elagabalus, Severus Alexander, Maximinus I, Trajanus Decius
    (Museo del Palazzo dei Conservatori): Commodus
    (Museo Nazionale Romano): Vespasian, Nerva, Clodius Albinus, Gallienus
Sofia (National Museum): Gordian III
Vatican (Musei Vaticani): Titus, Hadrian, Philip
Venice (Museo Archeologico): Trajan
Vienna (Kunsthistorisches Museum): Carinus
Washington (Dumbarton Oaks): Theodosius II

Coins and medallions not listed above are of uncertain location and/or have been taken from sales catalogues. The photographs of busts are from the Alinari and Anderson collections, except for those of Nero, Trajan and Constantius II. I owe gratitude to Messrs Max and Albert Hirmer and to Thames and Hudson Ltd for permission to use a number of photographs of coins which appear in J. P. C. Kent, *Roman Coins* (1978), to the author of which I am also grateful for other assistance.

MAPS AND PLANS

GENEALOGICAL TABLES

xiii

FOREWORD

This book contains brief accounts of the lives and backgrounds of the Roman emperors down to AD 476. They were the rulers, in name and often in reality, of one of the greatest multi-racial states that the world has ever known, a state, moreover, to which we owe many features of our own lives, so that it is worth while to ask what sort of men they were. Admittedly, our own age, because of what we have suffered in the present century, has a distrust of personality cult. This distrust in turn has sometimes been applied in retrospect to the Roman emperors, promoting the suspicion that earlier historians paid rather too much attention to the individual personalities of these rulers and too little to underlying social, economic, political and cultural trends. This is a healthy enough caution. But surely it should only be exercised with moderation. For despite the vast pressures on their time and nerves, by no means all the emperors were just tossed passively upon the surface of events. On the contrary, some of them gave that series of events a sharp impulsion, a formidably decisive turn: who can believe that the course of history would still have been the same if Augustus, Aurelian, Diocletian and Constantine had never existed, or had possessed quite different qualities? Secondly, any man, whatever his faults or deficiencies, who was called upon and agreed to take the helm of the enormous and portentous vessel of the Roman Empire, is an object of legitimate curiosity, and invites further investigation.

My list of emperors includes ninety-two names, in chronological order; the dates indicated at the head of each entry are those of their reigns. I have not given separate headings (though I have generally mentioned them in passing) to about a hundred others whose claim to wear the purple affected too small a geographical area, or was in some other respect too insubstantial. Even in regard to the ninety-two I have included, the information available to us from Greek and Latin authors is often tantalizingly inadequate. At the end of the book appears a list of those writers whom I have cited. I have supplemented their evidence extensively from coins – which show the points of view of the emperors themselves, in contrast to the hostility of many of the writers. Inscriptions, too, and other archaeological and artistic evidence, are drawn upon. I have included a list of Latin technical terms, several genealogical tables and a series of maps and plans. In the index to these maps, the modern equivalents of ancient place-names mentioned in the text are included.

MICHAEL GRANT, 1985

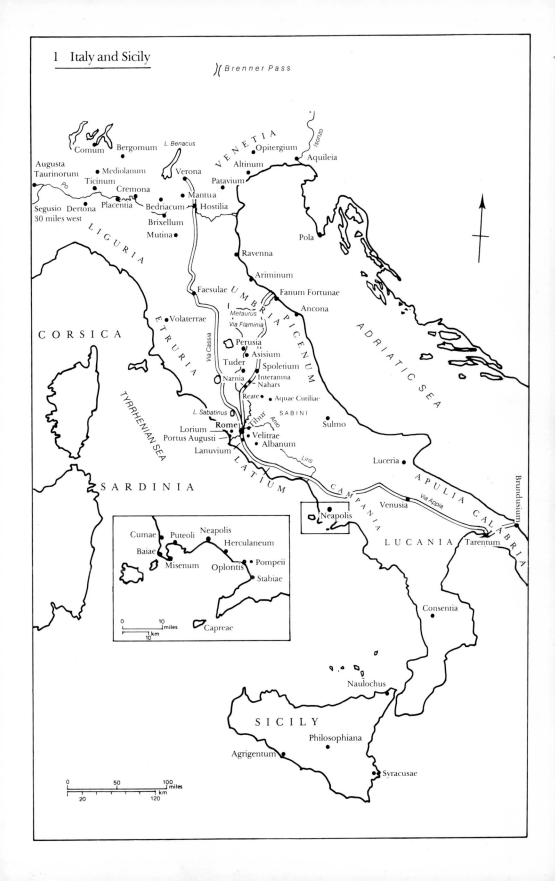

1 Italy and Sicily

Brenner Pass

L. Benacus

Comum
Bergomum
Opitergium
Mediolanum
Altinum
Aquileia
Augusta Taurinorum
Ticinum
Verona
Patavium
Cremona
Po
Mantua
Segusio Dertona
Bedriacum
Hostilia
Placentia
30 miles west
Brixellum
Pola
Mutina

VENETIA

Isonzo

LIGURIA

Ravenna

Ariminum

Faesulae
Fanum Fortunae
Ancona

UMBRIA

Volaterrae
Metaurus
Via Flaminia

ETRURIA

PICENUM

Perusia
Via Cassia
Asisium
Tuder
Spoletium
Narnia
Interamna Nahars
Reate
Aquae Cutiliae

L. Sabatinus
SABINI
Rome
Tibur
Sulmo
Lorium
Anio
Portus Augusti
Velitrae
Albanum
Lanuvium
Luceria

LATIUM
Liris

CAMPANIA

CORSICA

ADRIATIC SEA

TYRRHENIAN SEA

Venusia
Via Appia
APULIA
Brundisium

SARDINIA

LUCANIA
CALABRIA
Tarentum

Neapolis

Cumae
Puteoli
Neapolis
Baiae
Herculaneum
Misenum
Oplontis
Pompeii
Stabiae
Capreae

0   10 miles
10 km

Consentia

Naulochus

SICILY

Philosophiana

Agrigentum

Syracusae

0   50   100 miles
20   120 km

CALEDONIA
Bennachie: 24m WNW of Aberdeen
Clyde
Firth of Forth
PICTS
SCOTS
Solway Firth
Tyne
BRIGANTES
Mona
Eburacum
BRITANNIA
Lindum
FRISIA
Athelstone
Fosse Way
Corinium
Dobunnorum
Verulamium
Camulodunum
Cunetio
Londinium
Colonia
Agrippinensium
Clausentum
Lemanae
Rutupiae
Isca Dumnoniorum
Dubrae
Rhine
SEE INSET
Gesoriacum
MENAPIA
BELGAE
GERMANIA
INFERIOR
AMBIANI
Durocortorum
GERMANIA
SUPERIOR
Rotomagus
Meuse
Main
Seine
Lutetia
Moselle
LUGDUNENSIS
Campi Catalaunii
Aurelianum
Danube
Caesarodunum
Vesontio
Loire
Brigantium
GALLIA
Augustodunum
Brenner
Pass
Augustonemetum
Tinurtium
ALPS
Vienna
Lugdunum
ARVERNI
Culare
Burdigala
Brivas
AQUITANIA
Valentia
Segusio
Rhône
SABAUDIA
Tolosa
Nemausus
Ugernum
Carcaso
Arelate
Pyrenaei
Narbo
Massilia
Bracara
HISPANIA
Augusta
TARRACONENSIS
Cauca
Caesaraugusta
Abula
Tarraco
Barcino
HISPANIA
LUSITANIA
Valentia
Balearic Islands
Corduba
Lucentum
Italica
Uccubi
Baetis
BAETICA
Carthago Nova
Gades
Cartennae
Caesarea (Iol)
Hippo Regius
Carthage
Cirta
TINGITANA
QUINQUEGENTANEI
Hadrumetum
MAURETANIA

0   100   400
          miles
100
      km
      600

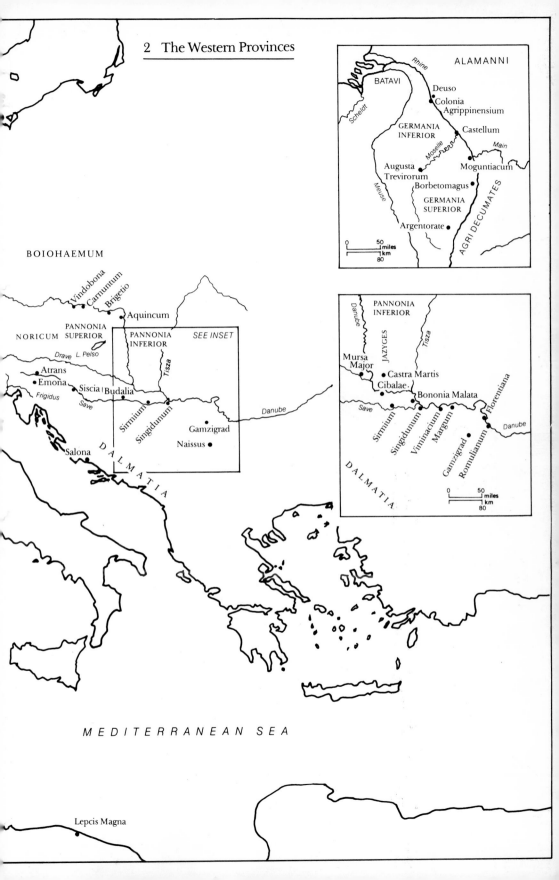

2 The Western Provinces

Inset 1 (top right):

ALAMANNI

Rhine

BATAVI

Deuso
Colonia
Agrippinensium

GERMANIA
INFERIOR

Castellum

Scheldt

Moselle

Main

Augusta
Trevirorum

Moguntiacum

Borbetomagus

Meuse

GERMANIA
SUPERIOR

Argentorate

AGRI DECUMATES

0   50
         miles
         km
         80

Main map:

BOIOHAEMUM

Vindobona
Carnuntum
Brigetio

Aquincum

NORICUM

PANNONIA
SUPERIOR

PANNONIA
INFERIOR

SEE INSET

Drave L. Pelso

Tisza

Atrans
Emona

Siscia | Budalia

Frigidus

Save

Danube

Sirmium

Singdunum

Gamzigrad

Naissus

Salona

D A L M A T I A

Inset 2 (middle right):

PANNONIA
INFERIOR

Danube

JAZYGES

Tisza

Mursa
Major

Castra Martis

Cibalae

Bononia Malata

Save

Florentiana

Sirmium

Singidunum

Viminacium

Margum

Gamzigrad

Romulianum

Danube

D A L M A T I A

0   50
         miles
         km
         80

M E D I T E R R A N E A N   S E A

Lepcis Magna

D A C I A

Iron Gates

MOESIA
SUPERIOR
Ratiaria
Danube
Novae
Serdica
MOESIA
INFERIOR
Nicopolis
ad Istrum
Abrittus
DARDANIA
Balkan Range
Scaptopare
Beroe Augusta
Trajana
BESSI
Philippopolis

Istrus
SCYTHIA
MINOR

B L A C K

Durostorum

Marcianopolis

Anchialus

THRACE

MACEDONIA

Thessalonica

Mt Rhodope

EPIRUS

Nicopolis
Ambracia
Actium

IONIAN
SEA

Hellespont
Lemnos

Ilium

Byzantium
PROPONTIS

MYSIA   *SEE INSET*

BITHYNIA

Pessinus
Ancyra

Gordium

Nacolea

GALATIA

A
S
I
A

I
O
N
I
A

Sardis

Smyrna

LYDIA

PHRYGIA

Eleusis
Athens

ACHAEA

Methone

Ephesus
Aphrodisias

CARIA

Apamea

Cremna

Side

Taurus

ISAUR

Rhodes

CRETE

M E D I T E R R A N E A N

S E A

Thagaste
Carthage

Thamugadi

Thysdrus

M E D I T E R R A N E A N S E A

North Africa

Arsinoe

CYRENAICA

Memphis

Alexandria

Cairo

JUDAEA

A
R
A
B
I
A

Nile
Lycopolis
Coptos

Ptolemais
Thebes

RED
SEA

0   100   500
                              miles
    100   800
                              km

S E A

PONTUS

C A U C A S U S   M T S

Pityus

Trapezus

Euphrates

Kaine Polis

Artaxata

A R M E N I A

M E D I A

CAPPADOCIA

Caesarea

Amida

Elazig

Cucusus

Samosata

OSRHOENE

Tigranocerta

Cilician Gates

Anazarbus

Carrhae

Nisibis

Mts.

Mopsucrene

Tarsus

Issus

Rhesaena

Singara

A S S Y R I A

CILICIA

Cyrrhus

Nicephorium

Seleucia ad
Calycadnum

Antioch

M E S O P O T A M I A

Hatra

Corycus

Salamis

Apamea

Tigris

CYPRUS

Raphaneae

Circesium

Emesa

Zaitha

Dura-Europus

Euphrates

Ctesiphon

Persepolis
400 miles ESE

Caesarea sub Libano

COELE-SYRIA

Seleucia ad Tigrim

S Y R I A

Damascus

PHOENICIA

GAULANITIS

Tyre

GALILEE

TRACHONITIS

Caesarea
Maritima

Bostra

Jamnia

Jerusalem

PERAEA

S A R A C E N I

Ascalon

Bethlehem

Gaza

Bethar

Masada

JUDAEA

Hadrianopolis

0   50   100   200
                          miles
        100   200
              km

Arcadiopolis

Caenophrurium

Tzirallum

Selymbria

Thracian Bosphorus

Heraclea (Perinthus)

Chrysopolis

Byzantium

Chalcedon

Nicomedia

PROPONTIS

Cyzicus

Limnae

Nicaea

Prusa

Hadriani

0   100   300
                                    miles
        100   400
                              km

PART I

THE
JULIO-CLAUDIAN
DYNASTY

The Julio-Claudian Dynasty

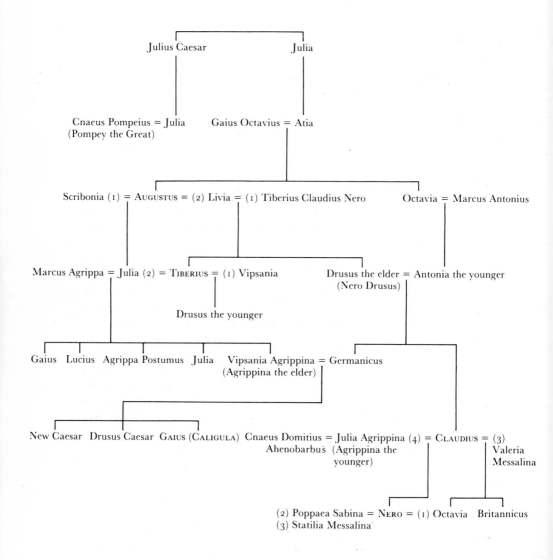

AUGUSTUS
31 BC—AD 14

AUGUSTUS (Gaius Octavius) (31 BC—AD 14) was the first Roman *princeps* or emperor. He was born Gaius Octavius, and changed his name to Gaius Julius Caesar after Caesar's death, but is generally described as Octavian until he was granted the designation of Augustus in 27 BC.

Born in 63 BC, he came of a prosperous family of knights (*equites*) from Velitrae, south-east of Rome. His father Gaius Octavius had been the first of the family to become a senator, rising to the rank of praetor. After his death in 59 BC, his widow Atia was left in charge of the child's upbringing. She was the niece of Julius Caesar, and it was Caesar who launched the future emperor into a Roman public career. When he was twelve, he delivered the funeral speech in honour of his grandmother Julia. At fifteen or sixteen he was appointed a priest (*pontifex*). After accompanying Caesar, now dictator (that is to say absolute ruler, though he is never thought of as the first of the emperors), at his Triumph in 46 BC, the young man, despite delicate health, joined him in his Spanish campaign of the following year. Then, with his friends Marcus Agrippa and Marcus Salvidienus Rufus, he was sent to Apollonia in Epirus to complete his academic and military studies; and it was there, in 44 BC, that he learnt of Caesar's assassination by Brutus and Cassius (who subsequently left for the east).

The publication of the dead man's will disclosed that he had been posthumously adopted as the dictator's son and made his chief heir. Therefore despite his youthful years (he was only eighteen), he decided – against the advice of his stepfather and others – to take up this perilous inheritance and avenge his adoptive father's death. Proceeding to Rome, he tried but failed to persuade Caesar's principal supporter Marcus Antonius (Antony) to hand over the late dictator's assets and documents. Octavius was thus compelled to distribute Caesar's legacies to the Roman public from whatever funds he was able to raise from other sources. At the same time, though, he felt obliged to assert himself against this contemptuous attitude of Antonius. His first step was to celebrate the Games of the Victory of Caesar to win public support. Then, on the initiative of the elder statesman and orator Cicero (who however did not realize the young man's formidable potentialities), the senate granted him, although he was not yet twenty, the status of senator and propraetor; and they enlisted his support in a campaign against Antonius, who was duly defeated at Mutina in northern Italy and forced to retreat into Gaul in 43 BC. Since the consuls who commanded the senatorial forces had both been killed in the battle, Octavian's legionaries compelled the senate, reluctant though it was, to award him one of these vacant posts. It was now that his posthumous adoption by the dictator received official recognition, enabling him to employ the name of Gaius Julius Caesar.

However, because the attitude of the senate remained grudging, he soon came to an understanding with Antonius, and reached agreement, too, with another of Caesar's principal adherents, Lepidus, who had succeeded to his high-priesthood. On 27 November 43 BC, the three men were officially allocated a five-year appointment as 'triumvirs for the constitution of the state', the Second Triumvirate (the first, seventeen years earlier, had been an unofficial arrangement between Pompey, Crassus and Caesar); this endowed them, jointly, with thoroughgoing autocratic powers. When Julius Caesar was recognized as a god of the Roman state (*divus*) at the beginning of 42 BC, Octavian became 'son of a god', but in the subsequent campaign against Brutus and Cassius, which brought about their defeat and death at Philippi in Macedonia, his ill-health obliged him to play a subordinate role to Antonius.

In the division of the Empire that followed, Antonius was allocated the east (and initially Gaul) while Octavian went back to Italy. There, problems arising from the settlement of his demobilized troops involved him in a campaign against Antonius' brother Lucius Antonius and Lucius' vigorous wife Fulvia. The conflict became known as the Perusine War because it culminated in the terrible siege of Perusia of 41 BC. With the aim of conciliating another potential foe, Sextus Pompeius, son of Pompey the Great, who was in control of Sicily and Sardinia, Octavian married Sextus' relative Scribonia. Not long afterwards, however – in October, 40 BC – he reached agreement with Antonius in the Treaty of Brundusium, which jettisoned Sextus, encouraging Octavian to divorce Scribonia and instead to forge a link with the aristocracy by marrying Livia Drusilla, who remained his lifelong partner.

Through the Treaty Antonius retained the eastern imperial territories; Octavian, while keeping control over Italy, was allotted all the western provinces except Africa, which was occupied by Lepidus. The alliance was sealed by the marriage of Octavian's sister Octavia to Antonius. Soon afterwards, however, Antonius abandoned her to return to Cleopatra VII, Queen of Egypt, with whom he had earlier begun a liaison; but Octavian –

plunged into hostilities with Sextus Pompeius – nevertheless confirmed his agreement with Antonius at Tarentum in 37 BC, whereby the triumvirs would remain in power for a further period of more than four years.

In 36 BC Octavian's brilliant admiral Agrippa overwhelmed the fleet of Sextus Pompeius off Cape Naulochus in Sicily. At the same time Lepidus endeavoured to oppose Octavian's authority in the west by military confrontation. But he was disarmed by Octavian, stripped of his triumviral powers and compelled to go into lasting retirement. It soon became clear, however, that Octavian, who was busy founding colonies for his loyal ex-soldiers, would soon be locked in a struggle with Antonius for control of the whole Roman world. Meanwhile, he began to employ the designation 'Imperator' in front of his name, to indicate that he was the unrivalled commander; and between 35 and 33 BC he fought three successive campaigns in Illyricum and Dalmatia which, although laborious and not entirely successful, made the north-eastern borders of Italy much safer than they had ever been before.

With Agrippa's assistance, Octavian spent massive sums on the architectural adornment of Rome. He also did everything he could to stimulate public protest against Antonius' gifts of imperial territory to Cleopatra. Amid ferocious public exchanges, the rift between the two men rapidly widened. By 32 BC the triumvirate had officially come to an end, and Octavian disingenuously denied that he was any longer exercising its powers. Antonius for his part divorced his rival's sister Octavia, whereupon her brother seized Antonius' will and published damaging concessions to Cleopatra that he claimed to have found among its contents. Each of the two leaders administered oaths of allegiance to the populations he controlled: the oath the Italians swore on behalf of Octavian, the *coniuratio Italiae*, became famous. Finally Octavian declared war – not against his compatriot Antonius, since the idea of civil strife was so unpopular, but against the foreign woman Cleopatra who, according to him, had violated her status as a client of Rome.

Antonius, accompanied by Cleopatra, lined the west coast of Greece with his navy and troops. But early in 31 BC, before winter was over, Octavian surprised him by sending Agrippa across the Ionian Sea to capture Methone; then he himself followed, leaving his Etruscan associate Maecenas to look after Italy. Before long, Antony's fleet was trapped inside the Gulf of Ambracia, and when in September he attempted to break out, the battle of Actium ensued. He and Cleopatra, together with a quarter of their ships, forced their way into the open sea and escaped to Egypt, where they committed suicide when Octavian invaded the country the following year.

Octavian's next act was to put to death Cleopatra's son Caesarion, whose fatherhood the Queen had attributed to Julius Caesar. He then annexed Egypt, and preserved direct rule over the country through his personal representatives. The capture of Cleopatra's financial resources also made it possible for him to pay off many of his soldiers and decree their settlement in a large number of colonies throughout the Roman world which now lay wholly in his hands. He gradually reduced his sixty legions to twenty-eight, comprising a hundred and fifty thousand soldiers (mostly Italians, though some were from other Romanized areas), and this force was augmented by approximately the same number of auxiliaries drawn from the provinces (that is to say from regions of the Roman Empire outside Italy). All the legions and auxiliary formations were stationed outside the peninsula: he felt it was too costly, or too tempting to potential rivals, to maintain a central reserve. The officer corps was placed on a far more regular footing than ever before, under his own close supervision, and special attention was devoted to the professional centurions, who constituted its backbone. Towards the end of the reign a military treasury was established to defray soldiers' retirement bounties from taxes. The fleet was also reorganized, with its principal bases at Misenum and Ravenna; and Octavian replaced his former Spanish bodyguard by a German unit. However, this was only supplementary to his principal guard of praetorians which, derived from the bodyguards maintained by earlier generals, was mainly composed of soldiers possessing Roman citizenship, divided into nine cohorts of five hundred infantrymen and ninety horsemen each. The praetorians, whose first joint prefects – of knightly, not senatorial, rank – Augustus appointed in 2 B C, were stationed at Rome and other Italian towns. He also created three city cohorts of a thousand men each (later increased) to serve as the police force of the capital, under the command of the city prefect (*praefectus urbi*).

These measures relating to military and security forces formed just one part, although an essential part, of a prolonged series of tentative and patient steps that created the Roman Principate. Although this was a system over which the ruler himself in effect kept full control, ample lip-service was given to the dignity of the senate, which he had reduced from about a thousand to eight hundred (later six hundred) members. Compliant though it was, and relieved and satisfied by his termination of the civil wars, Octavian however realized – remembering Caesar's fate – that this former ruling class would only welcome him if he ostensibly revived Republican traditions. Accordingly, while retaining continuous consulships from 31 to 23 B C, he made the claim, in 27, that he had 'transferred the State to the free disposal of the senate and people' (a somewhat misleading statement, as by the people he here referred to the Assembly, which now lacked political power). At the same time he was officially awarded, for a period of ten years, the government and command of a province comprising Spain, Gaul and Syria, the regions which contained the bulk of the army, and which he thenceforward governed through his subordinates (*legati*). The remaining areas of the Empire, outside Italy, were to be administered by proconsuls appointed by the senate as of old; for the *princeps* believed that his supreme prestige would ensure that his will was not crossed by these officials, whose selection, by more or less indirect means, he continued to influence.

The emperor's prestige was summed up by the solemn term *auctoritas*, resonant with traditional and religious significance. And linked etymologically with this word, as well as with the ancient cult practice of augury or divination, was the designation of 'Augustus' now conferred on him, which astutely conveyed, without recourse to the constitution, his superiority over other human beings. Aided by the outstanding writers of this literary Golden Age – the historian Livy, and Maecenas' poetical protégés Virgil and Horace, whose endeavours were supplemented by some patriotic verses of Propertius and Ovid – he displayed his veneration of the old Italian religion by resuscitating many of its antique ceremonials, and repairing and reconstructing its broken-down temples. In pursuit of the same aim he celebrated the antique ritual of the Secular Games (Ludi Saeculares) in 17 BC, which marked the transition from one century or epoch to another. He also set up the Altar of Peace (Ara Pacis), adorning it with fine reliefs in the classicizing Augustan style – and very many other important buildings too, religious and secular alike, were erected throughout the Empire. Then on the death of Lepidus in 12 BC Augustus succeeded him as the official chief priest (*pontifex maximus*) of the State religion.

His constitutional settlement of 27 BC had been followed by forceful steps to extend and pacify the imperial frontiers: turbulent Alpine tribes were reduced, Galatia (central Asia Minor) was annexed, and Augustus himself directed part of a campaign to complete the subjugation of Spain. But his health suffered a serious collapse. In 23 BC he seemed at the point of death, and put an end to the continuous series of consulships he had held, assuming instead the *imperium majus*, a power which raised him above the proconsuls and which was separated altogether from office and its practical chores. He was also granted the power of a tribune or *tribunicia potestas*. This award, systematizing earlier, partial conferments, conveniently empowered him to summon the senate. But in particular, because it was the traditional role of the annually elected tribunes of the people (from whom the *tribunicia potestas* took its name) to defend the citizens' rights, the power enveloped him in a 'democratic' aura, all the more needed because the true foundations of his system were, in fact, provided by the support of the established classes. In 19 BC there were further adjustments of Augustus' powers to allow him to exercise authority more conveniently in Italy, and the two following years witnessed social legislation intended, though probably without much effect, to encourage marriage and curb adultery and extravagance.

A few years later the *consilium principis*, an executive or drafting committee, at first unofficial and consisting of those who ranked as his Friends (*amici principis*), was appointed in order to help Augustus prepare the business that the senate conducted. His burden was likewise diminished, and governmental efficiency increased, by the expansion of his own staff – knights, whose careers were made much more attractive, and ex-slaves or freedmen – to form the beginnings of a civil service. Meanwhile, the entire administration of Rome and the Empire was being overhauled. This was made possible by a thoroughgoing reform of the financial structure, in which the central treasury was linked with the treasuries of the provinces, and particularly with those in Augustus' provinces, in an intricate relationship of which the exact nature escapes us. This imperial system was mainly funded by two direct taxes, a poll-tax and a land-tax: the latter was crucial because the economy of the Roman world was still founded on agriculture. The Augustan Peace also provided a marked stimulus to trade; and this was facilitated by a huge expansion and improvement of the Roman coinage, now comprising not only gold and silver pieces but novel token coins of yellow brass and red copper, produced at Rome and Lugdunum and elsewhere.

On all these issues every possible opportunity was taken to proclaim the main publicity themes of the régime; for example, great pride was taken in a triumphant agreement with the Parthians in 20 BC, under which they returned the legionary standards captured from the triumvir Crassus when he had been killed at Carrhae thirty-three years earlier, and acknowledged Rome's protectorate over Armenia. This country now became (precariously) one of the numerous client-states with which Augustus, characteristically extending earlier precedents, ringed the Empire. These client-states were authorized to issue coinages of their own, mainly of bronze, but occasionally of silver (and of gold in the Cimmerian Bosphorus). In many parts of the Empire itself, too, local urban communities were allowed to produce their own bronze money. These regions included Spain (for a time) as well as most territories of the east, where the old city-states, with their Greek institutions and culture, retained varying degrees of autonomy under the loose supervision of the provincial governors and their financial advisers or procurators.

Although the position of *princeps* was not a formal office to which a successor could be appointed, public attention had long been centred on Augustus' plans for the future. His nephew Marcellus, husband of his daughter Julia, died in 23 BC. In the same year Agrippa was dispatched to the east as Augustus' deputy, and four years later he completed the conquest of Spain. But although the widowed Julia had been given to Agrippa in marriage, the senators would never have accepted him as ruler. In 17 BC, therefore, Augustus adopted Agrippa and Julia's children, Gaius and Lucius, aged three and one respectively, as his own sons. Nevertheless, he also gave prominent employment to his adult stepsons TIBERIUS and Nero Drusus (Drusus the elder), who annexed Noricum and Raetia and extended the imperial frontier to the Danube from 16–15 BC.

After Agrippa's death in 12 BC, Augustus obliged his widow Julia to marry Tiberius, though each was reluctant. Both Tiberius and his brother Nero Drusus spent the next few years fighting in the north. But Nero Drusus, after he had advanced as far as the Elbe, died in 9 BC. Three years later Tiberius was elevated to a share in his stepfather's tribunician power, but then he retired from the scene, only to return as Augustus' adoptive son and evident successor following the deaths of Lucius and Gaius in AD 2 and 4 respectively. Tiberius was immediately sent to Boiohaemum to conquer the powerful west German tribal state of the Marcomanni and thus shorten the imperial frontiers. The task was interrupted when revolts broke out in Pannonia and Illyricum in AD 6 and then in Germany, where Arminius, chief of the west German tribe of the Cherusci, destroyed Varus and his three legions in AD 9. Augustus was appalled, and the annexation of Germany and central Europe had to be indefinitely postponed.

Although administrative reforms did not cease, the *princeps* had begun to recognize encroaching age, and in AD 13 Tiberius was made his equal in every constitutional respect. Then Augustus lodged his will and other documents at the House of the Vestal Virgins at Rome. They included a summary of the Empire's military and financial resources and a subtle, never inaccurate but often tendentious political testament known as the *Acts of the Divine Augustus* (or *Monumentum Ancyranum*, since its best-preserved copy is on the walls of the Temple of Rome and Augustus at Ancyra in Galatia). In the following year Tiberius, on his way to Illyricum, was recalled because his stepfather was seriously ill. Augustus died on 19 August and was subsequently deified.

Augustus was one of the most talented, energetic and skilful administrators that the world has ever known. The enormously far-reaching work of reorganization and rehabilitation which he undertook in every branch of his vast Empire created a new Roman Peace, in which all but the humblest classes benefited from improved communications and flourishing commerce. The autocratic régime which (learning from Caesar's mistakes) he substituted for the collapsing Republic – although challenged, from the outset, by a number of conspiracies – was to have a very long life. It brought stability, security and prosperity to an unprecedented proportion of the population for more than two hundred years; it ensured the survival and eventual transmission of the political, social, economic and cultural heritage of the classical world – Roman and Greek alike; and it supplied the framework within which both Judaism and Christianity were disseminated (Jesus Christ was born, and Judaea converted from a client-state into a Roman province, during this reign).

Augustus was a man of some literary ability, the author of a number of books: an exhortation to philosophy, a story of his early life, a pamphlet attacking Brutus, a biography of Nero Drusus and verses of various kinds. All these works are lost, though the subtlety of his *Res Gestae* suggests what he was capable of achieving. As for his character, it was said that he was cruel when young but became mild later on; though this may have been only because the political need for cruelty had diminished, for he was still prepared to be ruthless when this seemed called for. His domestic tastes were simple.

Although unfaithful to his wife Livia Drusilla, he remained deeply devoted to her. His public moral attitudes were strict, and he exiled his daughter and grand-daughter, both named Julia (and the poet Ovid, who perhaps knew too much about the latter's way of life), for offending against these principles. He also banished his grandson Agrippa Postumus, who was regarded as eccentric and recalcitrant. As for the other male relatives who were his helpers, he wrote them kindly letters, some of which have survived. But he drove them very hard.

He drove himself, too, just as relentlessly, though his health suffered from a multitude of persistent ills. His appearance (from which the brilliant sculptors of the day created a memorable and varied series of imperial portraits) is described by the biographer Suetonius:

> Augustus was remarkably handsome and very graceful to look at even as an old man: but negligent of his personal appearance. . . . He always wore a serene expression, whether talking or in repose. . . . His eyes were bright and clear, and he liked to believe that they shone with a sort of divine radiance: it gave him profound pleasure if anyone at whom he glanced keenly dropped his head as though dazzled by looking into the sun. In old age, however, his left eye had only partial vision. His teeth were small, few and decayed; his hair, yellowish and rather curly. . . . Julius Marathus, his freedman and recorder, makes his height 5 feet 7 inches; but this is an exaggeration, although, with body and limbs so beautifully proportioned, one did not realize how small a man he was, unless someone tall stood close to him.

TIBERIUS
AD 14–37

TIBERIUS (AD 14–37) was born in 42 BC. He was the son of the aristocratic Tiberius Claudius Nero, whose names he bore, and of Livia Drusilla. When he was two, his father had to flee from the triumvirs because of his Republican beliefs. When he was four, his parents divorced – shortly before the birth of Tiberius' younger brother Nero Drusus – so that Livia could instead marry Octavian (the future AUGUSTUS).

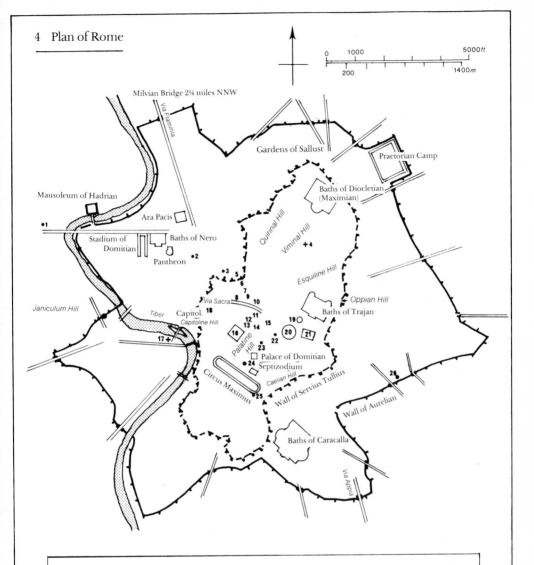

4 Plan of Rome

Milvian Bridge 2¼ miles NNW

Via Flaminia

Gardens of Sallust

Praetorian Camp

Baths of Diocletian
(Maximian)

Mausoleum of Hadrian

Ara Pacis

•1

Stadium of   Baths of Nero
Domitian

Pantheon

•2

Quirinal Hill

Viminal Hill

+4

Esquiline Hill

•3 5
7

Via Sacra 9   10

Janiculum Hill

Tiber   Capitol. 18

Capitoline Hill

Oppian Hill

Baths of Trajan

12 11
13 14   15   19 ○

16   • 22   20   21

Palatine Hill

23

17 +

Palace of Domitian

•24 Septizodium

Circus Maximus

Caelian Hill

Wall of Servius Tullius

25

26

Wall of Aurelian

Baths of Caracalla

Via Appia

1	Basilica of St Peter	14	Arch of Titus
2	Column of Aurelius	15	Temple of Venus and Rome
3	Column of Trajan	16	Palace of Tiberius
4	Church of Santa Maria Maggiore	17	Church of St Chrysogonus
5	Market of Trajan	18	Temple of Capitoline Jupiter
6	Forum of Trajan	19	Baths of Titus
7	Forum of Augustus	20	Colosseum (Amphitheatrum Flavium)
8	Forum of Julius Caesar	21	Golden House (Domus Aurea)
9	Forum of Nerva (Transitorium)	22	Arch of Constantine
10	Forum of Vespasian	23	Circus Maximus
11	Basilica of Maxentius (Constantine)	24	Palace of Severus
12	Arch of Septimius Severus	25	Temple of Sol Invictus
13	Forum Romanum	26	Lateran Basilica

FREE GERMANY

LOWER
GERMANY

BELGICA

LUGDUNENSIS

Rhine

Danube

RAETIA

NORICUM

UPPER
GERMANY

Lugdunum

AQUITANIA

NARBONENSIS

AM

ITALY

TARRACONENSIS

Tarraco

SARDINIA

Rome

LUSITANIA

SICILY

BAETICA

Carthage

AFRICA

AM Alpes Maritimae

——————— Imperial boundary

– – – – – – – Provincial boundaries

0   50   100   200   300
                              miles
              100
                         400 km

5 The Provinces at the Death of Augustus (AD 14)

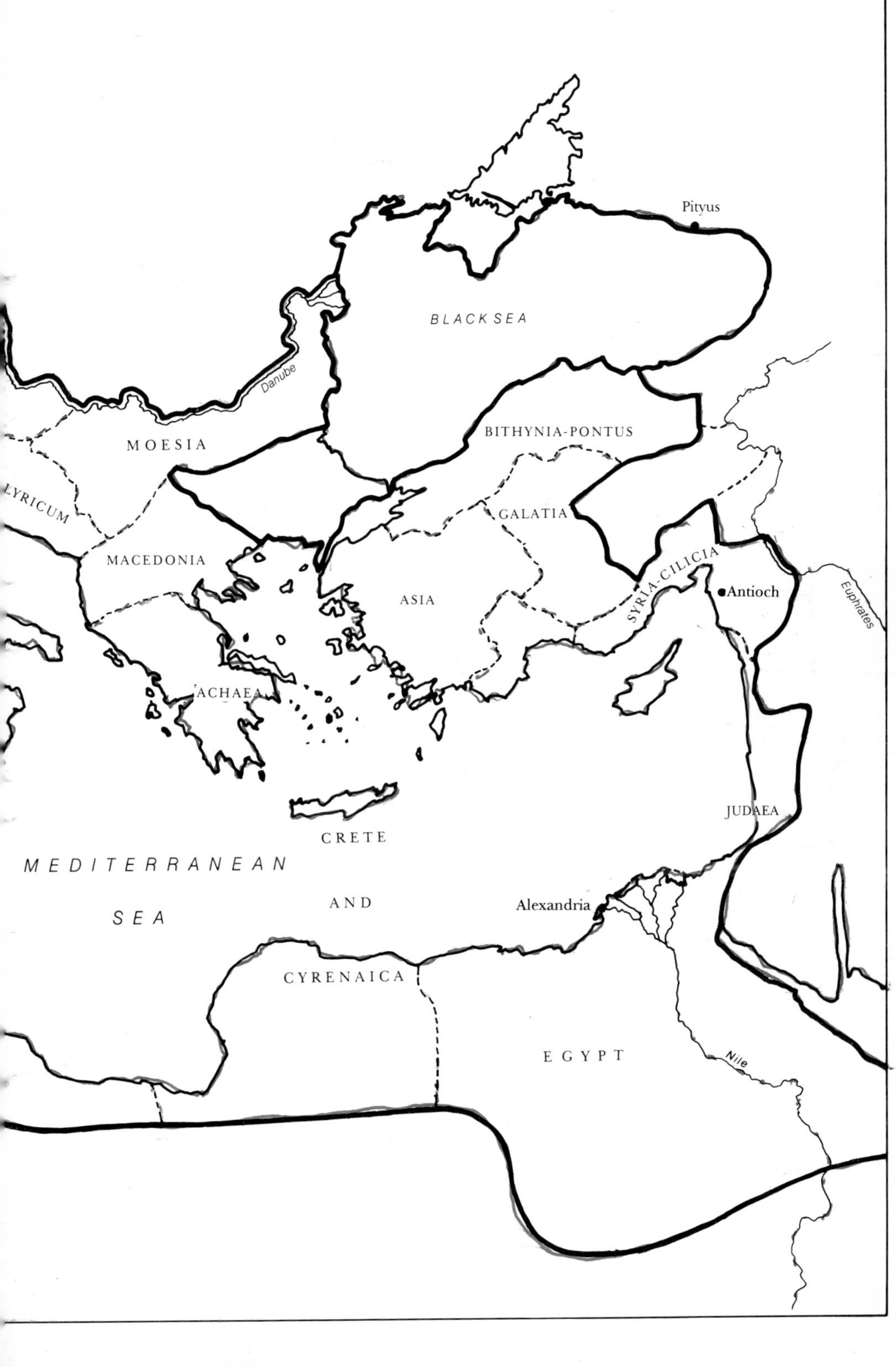
Pityus
BLACK SEA
Danube
MOESIA
BITHYNIA-PONTUS
LYRICUM
GALATIA
MACEDONIA
SYRIA-CILICIA
Antioch
Euphrates
ASIA
ACHAEA
JUDAEA
CRETE
MEDITERRANEAN
SEA
AND
Alexandria
CYRENAICA
EGYPT
Nile

From 20 BC, when he went to the east with Augustus and received back the standards lost to the Parthians thirty-three years earlier, until AD 12 – with a decade's intermission that will shortly be described – Tiberius pursued an intensely strenuous and successful military career. Between 12 and 9 BC he brought Pannonia into the Empire. From 9 BC (when Nero Drusus died) to 7 BC and again from AD 4 to 6, he was fighting in Germany. For the next three years he suppressed major rebellions in Pannonia and Illyricum. Then he returned to restore the Rhine frontier after Arminius the Cheruscan had destroyed Varus' three legions (see AUGUSTUS).

After the death of Agrippa in 12 BC Augustus had compelled Tiberius to divorce Vipsania, mother of Drusus the younger, in order that he should marry Julia, Augustus' daughter and Agrippa's widow. The marriage was unhappy, and Julia was exiled in 2 BC. In 6 BC Tiberius was granted tribunician power but very soon retired to Rhodes, in indignation or embarrassment because Augustus was bringing forward his grandsons Gaius and Lucius. When they died, however, Augustus recognized him – with reluctance it was supposed – as his evident successor; in AD 4 he adopted him as his son, re-awarded him his tribunician power for ten years, and granted him a special overriding command on the Rhine frontier. However, the ruler's surviving grandson Agrippa Postumus was adopted along with him – although later exiled – and Tiberius was simultaneously ordered to adopt his own eighteen-year-old nephew Germanicus, Nero Drusus' son. Nevertheless, it was Tiberius who kept the administration going during these years, introducing unobtrusive but useful improvements. His constitutional powers were renewed in AD 13 on terms of equality with Augustus, which made inevitable his succession after Augustus' death the following year.

The first senatorial business of the new reign made Augustus a god (*divus*) of the Roman State, like Julius Caesar before him, and confirmed bequests to the soldiers. But it fell to the senate also to invest Tiberius formally, despite his show of reluctance, with the status of *princeps* or emperor, as it was now coming to be regarded.

At the very beginning of his reign, the armies beside the Danube (in Pannonia) and the Rhine (in lower Germany) mutinied because their terms of service and demobilization benefits had fallen short of Augustus' promises. Drusus the younger, Tiberius' son, dealt efficiently with the Pannonian disturbances; Germanicus, the emperor's affable and ostentatious nephew and adoptive son, meanwhile handled the German upheaval less effectively, for he made substantial concessions which Tiberius subsequently felt obliged to withdraw. Germanicus then undertook three military campaigns planned to re-annex the territories between the Rhine and the Elbe which had been evacuated after the destruction of Varus by the Germans in AD 9. His imposing expeditions failed in this, although he was awarded a Triumph and received enthusiastic acclaim on his return to Rome.

The relative positions of Germanicus and Drusus the younger with regard to the eventual succession remained ambiguous. Drusus received the Danubian high command and Germanicus was allotted a comparable post in the east. When he arrived there, however, he became involved in a violent dispute with the governor of Syria, Cnaeus Calpurnius Piso, who was reputedly a confidant of Tiberius himself. Then in AD 19, at Antioch, Germanicus died, and his fierce widow Vipsania Agrippina, Agrippina the elder, sailed back to Rome with his ashes. Cnaeus Piso, too, after unwisely attempting to resist those sent to supersede him, returned to the capital, only to face the charge of murdering Germanicus; whereupon he committed suicide. In fact, Germanicus had probably died a natural death. But his popularity gave the whole incident a lurid prominence, stressed by the historian Tacitus, who idolized him. Germanicus' death meant that the emperor's son Drusus the younger would now indisputably become his eventual successor. But in AD 23 Drusus also died. The obvious heirs were now the two eldest sons of Germanicus and Agrippina the elder. Nero Caesar (so called to distinguish him from the emperor Nero) and Drusus Caesar (so called to distinguish him from Nero Drusus and Drusus the younger) were aged seventeen and sixteen respectively; the emperor commended them to the protection of the senate.

Yet Tiberius' relationship with the senators left a good deal to be desired. It was true that he took meticulous care to preserve their traditional dignity, that his methods for influencing the elections to official posts remained discreetly unobtrusive and that he deprecated extravagant flattery addressed to himself. Indeed, two virtues he chose to commemorate on his coins were Moderation and Clemency. Yet his attempt to make the senate an authentic partner of the government came too late, when its impotence could no longer be remedied. Rumour had it that when Tiberius left senatorial meetings, he was heard to comment in Greek: 'Men fit to be slaves!'

The greatest drama and tragedy of his life arose from the elevation of Lucius Aelius Sejanus, who, at the outset of the reign, was made first the colleague and then in AD 15 the successor of his father in the praetorian prefecture. Very soon it became clear that he was the emperor's principal adviser. Sejanus, although the historian Tacitus sneers at his non-senatorial rank, was linked to great families; he was amiable, and a successful seducer of fashionable wives. In about AD 23, no doubt at his own prompting, a step was taken which greatly increased his power. The nine praetorian cohorts previously distributed between Rome and other Italian towns had recently been concentrated in the capital, and now the emperor authorized Sejanus to bring them all into a single new Roman barracks, whose lofty walls are still to be seen today. When Drusus the younger, who did not like the prefect, died, Sejanus became Tiberius' uniquely intimate friend – the 'partner of his labours', as the *princeps* told the senate and Assembly.

From now onwards treason trials multiplied; for Sejanus shared and sharpened Tiberius' fears of plots and revolts, and he used the treason laws to get rid of his own enemies. Nevertheless, his hold over his master was still incomplete. In AD 25, for example, he was refused leave to marry Drusus the younger's widow Livilla (Livia Julia) on the grounds that the union of a mere knight with this princess would be too unpopular with the senate. In the following year, however, Sejanus received a fresh opportunity to enlarge his power when Tiberius decided to withdraw from Rome and take up his residence on the island of Capreae, never to set foot in the city again. It was said that he went in order to get away from his domineering and difficult mother Livia Drusilla, known as Julia Augusta since Augustus had 'adopted' her in his will. Tiberius also wanted to get away from people in general, and particularly from difficult senators; at Capreae he was only accompanied by a very few friends, mostly Greek scholars and astrologers. Furthermore, he was becoming increasingly alarmed for his own personal safety, which magnified the attractions of the inaccessible island, and made his Villa of Jupiter, standing upon its eastern height, seem an attractive refuge.

From there he continued to administer the Empire in his usual conscientious manner. However, his solitary existence inevitably stimulated every kind of damaging rumour, including a rich but unverifiable crop of reports about his alleged sexual deviations. More important, since his direct contact with the senate was now limited to written communications, the authority of Sejanus rose steeply. It was he, in all probability, who had in the first place prompted the move to Capreae; and now he controlled access to Tiberius' person, and provided the guardsmen who transmitted his correspondence with Rome.

Sejanus induced the emperor to believe that the principal dangers threatening his life were presented by Agrippina the elder and her sons Nero Caesar and Drusus Caesar, who had inherited some of the popular appeal of their father Germanicus. In AD 26 Tiberius apparently refused Agrippina leave to marry again. Three years later, following denunciations by Sejanus and then by the emperor himself, legal proceedings were instituted against her and the two young men. The opening moves against Nero Caesar (for sexual perversion) and Agrippina (for treasonable conspiracy) triggered off popular demonstrations in their favour. Both were arrested and banished to islands; Drusus Caesar too was detained, and imprisoned in the capital. They may have plotted or they may not. In any case, four years later all three of them were dead, leaving alive only the third son of Germanicus and Agrippina, the young GAIUS (Caligula).

Meanwhile, in AD 31, Sejanus, although of knightly rank and therefore ineligible for senatorial office, became consul as colleague of Tiberius. When they resigned from their consulships in May, he probably received the same sort of superior power or *imperium* as Tiberius had received from Augustus. He also at last obtained permission to marry Drusus the younger's widow Livilla.

But his downfall promptly followed, on the basis of information which the emperor received from Livilla's mother Antonia. Sejanus was perhaps plotting the elimination of the nineteen-year-old Gaius, whose succession would have meant the end of his own ascendancy; he may have wanted a younger and more malleable heir-apparent, such as Tiberius Gemellus, the twelve-year-old son of Drusus the younger. So the emperor secretly transferred the praetorian command to another of his friends Macro, who, in collusion with one of the consuls and the commander of the fire-brigade, arranged for Sejanus to be arrested during a meeting of the senate. Its members immediately ordered his execution without waiting for specific orders from Tiberius.

Other trials and deaths quickly ensued. Sejanus' widow Apicata committed suicide after informing Tiberius that the death of his son Drusus the younger, eight years earlier, had been caused by her husband and his mistress Livilla. This was probably untrue, but the emperor believed it, and Livilla was starved to death. Tiberius then drew up his will, leaving Gaius and Gemellus as joint heirs, though it was evident that his successor would be Gaius. In March, AD 37, Tiberius was at the Villa of Lucullus at Misenum when, in his seventy-eighth year, he died, seemingly from natural causes, though there were inevitably rumours to the contrary.

Tiberius was a large, strong man, the biographer Suetonius tells us, with an exceptionally powerful left hand, enjoying excellent health until almost the end of his life, though his complexion was sometimes marred by skin eruptions. He had a great fear of thunder. On waking up, he could see for a time in the dark. 'His gait was a stiff stride, with the neck poked forward, and if he ever broke his usual stern silence to address those walking with him, he spoke with great deliberation and eloquent movements of the fingers.' Although irreligious he was interested in myths, and convinced by the astrologers' belief that everything is wholly ruled by fate. He lacked the power of ready communication with other men that Augustus had so abundantly enjoyed. As the historian Dio Cassius later observed: 'Tiberius' words indicated the exact opposite of his real purpose. . . . He thought it bad policy for the sovereign to reveal his thoughts; this was often the cause, he said, of great failures, whereas by the opposite course far more and greater successes were attained.' This failure to make himself intelligible – which continued to be displayed after his withdrawal to Capreae – caused a great deal of trouble. Moreover, his words, spoken and written alike, were often sarcastic and annihilating. Although not inhumane, Tiberius was grim and gloomy. He failed to cultivate popular tastes; for example, he would not even pretend to enjoy gladiatorial Games. Nevertheless, when people misjudged his actions, as they frequently did, he became very upset, and reacted with disconcerting ferocity. He was also profoundly suspicious, and took fright very readily.

The historian Tacitus was obsessed by the figure of Tiberius, and noted a series of progressive deteriorations in the quality of his rule. He was right to detect these, at least as far as the situation of the ruling class was concerned; and in the provinces too, although the general high standard of responsible government was usually maintained, a certain frozen sluggishness took over. Like many other ancient writers, however, Tacitus believed that all human personalities remain unchangeably the same from birth to death, and that if a man's actions did not always exhibit that personality this was only because he was sometimes able to conceal it. Thus in his view Tiberius must be wholly bad (the historian could not help thinking of DOMITIAN, under whom he himself had lived); the many good actions which he manifestly performed could only be attributed to sinister hypocrisy.

The complex and cunningly balanced Principate bequeathed by Augustus must have been more than almost any man could inherit with comfort. Yet Tiberius declared, 'I treat all his actions and words as if they had the force of law', for he knew it was too late for the autocratic machinery to be moved into reverse. His reign was a bridge between the personal system of Augustus and the formally established imperial system of the future; it was a period of cautious consolidation. Nevertheless, Tiberius himself remained permanently uncomfortable, since at heart he was a Republican like his ancestors. He was too honest a man to accept an unwelcome situation with a good grace, and he felt a deep distrust of too many of the senators with whom he had to work.

It was during Tiberius' reign that Jesus Christ undertook his mission in Galilee (part of Herod Antipas' client-princedom of Galilee-Peraea), and was subsequently crucified in Jerusalem (in the Roman province of Judaea). When, according to the Evangelists, Jesus requested that a 'penny' should be brought to him, and, after asking whose image and inscription it bore, pronounced that people should 'Render to Caesar the things that are Caesar's, and to God the things that are God's', the coin must have been a *denarius* bearing the portrait and titles of Tiberius.

GAIUS (CALIGULA) 37–41

GAIUS (Gaius Julius Caesar Germanicus) (37–41), the third son of Germanicus and Agrippina the elder, was born at Antium in 12. While he was with his parents on the German frontier, between the ages of two and four, the miniature military boots or *caligae* that he was given to wear earned him the nickname 'Caligula'.

During his eighteenth and nineteenth years his mother and two elder brothers were arrested, subsequently meeting their deaths. Gaius, however, was appointed to be a priest in 31, and a quaestor in 33; and the emperor TIBERIUS, with whom he lived at Capreae from 32 onwards, appointed him and Tiberius Gemellus (son of Drusus the younger) as joint heirs of his property, while letting it be known that he expected Gaius eventually to succeed him. Gaius was however given no further administrative training. When Tiberius died in 37, there were rumours that Gaius had smothered, strangled or poisoned him, but these stories need not be believed, since his death by natural causes had in any case been imminent.

Supported by the praetorian prefect Macro, Gaius was immediately hailed as *princeps* by the senate. Moreover, as soon as he returned to Rome, the senators seem to have proposed that the Assembly should vote him, in one comprehensive measure, the totality of the imperial powers; and his predecessor's will was declared invalid so that Gaius might inherit the whole of his property, without granting Gemellus a share. But it was the army, above all, that loved the house of Germanicus to which he belonged, and it also pleased the soldiers when he honoured the memories of his relatives who had come to such unpleasant ends. As for Tiberius, the man responsible for these tragedies, Gaius duly celebrated his funeral, but in deference to the general lack of regret for his death quietly dropped an initial request for his deification, and began referring to him in the abusive language which he customarily employed.

His grandmother Antonia the younger, the widow of Nero Drusus, who might have been a restraining influence on the young emperor, died on 1 May. Then in October Gaius fell gravely ill, and according to the Jewish philosopher Philo – who was far from prejudiced in his favour – his popularity throughout the Empire was so extensive that the news caused great public distress and anxiety. He recovered, but Philo may have been right to suggest that he was never the same man again. In 38 he put his principal supporter, the praetorian prefect Macro, to death; and Tiberius Gemellus, who seemed a potential rival, suffered a similar fate. Moreover, Marcus Junius Silanus – the father of the first of Gaius' four wives – was driven to suicide. These developments alarmed the senate, and in January 39, Gaius announced to them that he was going to revive the treason trials, so painfully remembered from the time of Tiberius; the latter's memory, in consequence, enjoyed an official rehabilitation.

Rumours of disloyalty soon began to reach him; and a recently retired governor of Pannonia was compelled to commit suicide. Gaius had been planning to revive the expansionist enterprises of his father Germanicus across the Rhine. But before he left the capital he learnt that, as soon as he reached Moguntiacum, the very influential army commander in Upper Germany, Cnaeus Cornelius Lentulus Gaetulicus, was planning to have him assassinated. Nevertheless, in September 39 the emperor departed suddenly for the north. Among those who accompanied him were a strong detachment of the praetorian guard, his two surviving sisters Julia Agrippina (Agrippina the younger) and Julia Livilla, and Marcus Aemilius Lepidus (widower of his third sister Julia Drusilla and regarded as his likely successor). But soon after they arrived in Germany, Lepidus, as well as Gaetulicus, was put to death, and Agrippina the younger and Julia Livilla were banished, while Gaius seized their property for himself.

Gaius spent the following winter in the Rhine camps and Gaul. But neither his German expedition nor a proposed crossing to Britain (still independent nearly a century after Julius Caesar's two landings) materialized. Tall stories recounted how he bade the troops pick up seashells on the shores of the Channel. But Gaius was no doubt eager to get back to Rome, where the senate, as he knew, had now become dangerously alienated. Even before his arrival in Italy he began harassing them by letter, ordering prosecutions in connexion with Gaetulicus' plot; and when during the summer he arrived in the neighbourhood of the capital, he failed to notify them of his return as courtesy demanded. Meanwhile the senate for their part, after granting him the honour of an Ovation for his imaginary victories, voted that whenever he attended one of their meetings, he should be permitted to introduce a military bodyguard into the building and should be seated upon a lofty, inaccessible platform.

At least three further conspiracies were very soon launched against his life. A group of Romans claiming to be motivated by philosophical, Stoic principles was duly proceeded against. More serious, however, was Gaius' suspicion that the joint praetorian prefects, Marcus Arrecinus Clemens and an unknown colleague, were planning his assassination. Alarmed at being openly taxed with this intention Clemens, and perhaps the other commander as well, joined a party of disgusted and terrified senators in a serious plot. Their agent appointed to perform the act was a senior praetorian officer Cassius Chaerea, whom Gaius had mocked for effeminacy. On 24 January 41, in a corridor underneath the palace on the Palatine Hill, he and two military colleagues fell on the emperor. Some of his German personal guards rushed up, but were too late to save his life. Then a praetorian soldier stabbed Caesonia, his fourth wife, to death, and another smashed their baby daughter's head against a wall.

Gaius' concept of imperial rule had been quite different from the carefully hidden autocracy of his two predecessors. Perhaps influenced by eastern friends, notably a Jewish potentate Julius Agrippa, he was impatient of such concealments, and willing to rule and appear as a despot, like monarchs of the Hellenistic world. Large brass coins issued during the reign name his three sisters, Agrippina the younger, Julia Drusilla and Julia Livilla, who are shown standing with the attributes of goddesses like deified Ptolemaic queens. The first and last-named of these three were later disgraced; but after Julia Drusilla, whom Gaius particularly loved, had died in 38 she was officially deified by the state – the first Roman woman ever to receive this honour.

When Gaius expressed pride in his own inflexibility, his words must have surprised his hearers, who had seen his alarmingly rapid changes of temper and mood. But what he had in mind was this persistent determination to sweep away the Augustan, pseudo-Republican façade. Spectacular gestures demonstrating Gaius' new and more grandiose concept of the imperial office included the construction of a bridge of ships – two or three miles long – across the Bay of Naples, enabling him to claim that, like a new Neptune, he had ridden across the waters. At Rome, too, he came very close to recognition as a god in his own lifetime, though the coinage did not reflect this revolutionary innovation.

The same question of deification created a serious crisis in the east, among the Jews. At Alexandria in 38, members of the large Jewish community had become involved in large-scale, violent fighting against the Greek majority of the inhabitants, who rejected the Jews' claim to full citizenship of the city. This conflict brought about the first serious pogrom known to history, during the course of which pagan gangs forced their murderous way into the synagogues to set up statues of the emperor. In 40, each of the two parties sent a delegation to Rome to plead its case. Philo, who led the Jewish mission, has left us a vivid account of what happened. The Jews tried to explain to the emperor that, although their religious principles made it impossible for them to sacrifice *to* him, they were always very glad to sacrifice *for* him, which indeed they regularly did. Gaius responded with the remark that failure to recognize his divinity seemed not so much criminal as lunatic. But now news reached the capital of ominous events taking place in Judaea itself, among the mixed Greek and Jewish population of Jamnia. The Jews of the town destroyed an altar the Greeks had set up in honour of the emperor, and this prompted Gaius to decree that the country's places of worship should all be converted into shrines of the imperial cult. So instructions were sent to Publius Petronius, the governor of Syria, to commission a statue of Gaius in the guise of Jupiter (Zeus) and to set it up in the Jerusalem temple. Although recognizing that this would lead to a national rebellion and mass-martyrdom, Petronius started to collect a legionary army to enforce the imperial order. Meanwhile Gaius was finally persuaded by his Jewish friend Julius Agrippa to cancel the command; and his assassination followed not long afterwards.

According to the biographer Suetonius, Gaius was very tall and extremely pale, with an unshapely body and very thin neck and legs. His eyes and temples were hollow, his forehead broad and grim, his hair thin and entirely gone from the top of his head, though his body was hairy. Because of his baldness and hairiness, he was said to have declared it a capital offence for anyone either to look down upon him as he passed in the street or to mention goats in any context. He worked hard to make his naturally forbidding features even more repulsive by practising grimaces in front of the mirror. He was passionately devoted to the circus and the stage (and enjoyed the riotous parties they involved), preoccupations which caused him to neglect state affairs to a damaging and perilous extent. The rumours about his sex life suggest startlingly versatile habits, including sadism, homosexuality and incestuous conduct with his sisters. Suetonius diagnosed a case of both physical and mental sickness, noting that the emperor suffered from acute insomnia, was sometimes scarcely able to move his limbs or think, and oscillated wildly between a confident love of vast crowds and a timid hankering after total solitude. He could also get extremely excited and angry. Philo believed that these troubles arose from the illness from which he suffered early in his reign as a result of over-indulgence. He has also been variously described as epileptic, schizoid, schizophrenic and a chronic alcoholic, and his system was said to have been ruined by an aphrodisiac given him by his last wife Caesonia. However, there is not sufficient evidence to enable any of these diagnoses to be accepted.

In spite of his unbalanced personality, Gaius evidently possessed considerable talents. It is true that his frantic energy was not matched by application or persistence; but his powers as an orator, for example, were impressive. His numerous epigrammatic utterances, too, showed a scathing and sceptical lucidity and realism, and his literary criticism displayed similar disconcerting qualities: Homer, Virgil and Livy all became victims of his venomous tongue. So did the philosopher Seneca the younger, described by Gaius as 'mere sand without lime' – who was able to retaliate after Gaius' death by depicting him in the worst possible light.

CLAUDIUS
41–54

CLAUDIUS (Tiberius Claudius Nero Germanicus) (41–54) was born at Lugdunum in 10 BC. He was the youngest son of Nero Drusus (the brother of TIBERIUS) and of Antonia the younger (daughter of the triumvir Marcus Antonius and Octavia). Handicapped by ill-health and alarming uncouthness, which seemed to signify a retarded mind, he received no public distinction from AUGUSTUS except an augurate, and held no official post under Tiberius. His nephew GAIUS, when he became emperor, gave him a consulship as his own colleague in AD 37 but otherwise treated him with disrespect.

After Gaius had been murdered, Claudius fled to an apartment of the palace and hid himself among the curtains of a balcony. But he was discovered by a praetorian guardsman and taken to the praetorian camp, where the men hailed him as emperor, apparently upon the initiative of the joint prefects of the guard, of whom one at least had taken a hand in the assassination of Gaius. At this juncture the senators were still deliberating about what should be done next: even the impracticable idea of restoring the Republic came under discussion. However, they soon fell in line with the praetorians' initiative and granted Claudius all the imperial powers – though he never ceased to resent their initial hesitation, and they for their part never forgave him for having taken the decision out of their hands. It was to be the first of many occasions on which their right to select a new occupant of the throne was brushed aside.

Claudius was also the first emperor to make the praetorian guardsmen a large gift when they proclaimed his accession, thus creating another ominous precedent for the future. Moreover, with a frankness which none of his successors ever equalled, he issued gold and silver coins pronouncing explicitly that it was to the guardsmen and their officers that he owed his throne. One of these series commemorated the oath of allegiance they had sworn him (PRAETORiani RECEPTi in fidem), and another set of issues, even more arrestingly, commemorated his initial entry into their camp (IMPERator RECEPTus). 'Imperator' had now come to mean 'emperor', although like his two immediate predecessors Claudius did not venture to imitate Augustus' use of the title as a special prefix to his personal name. Nevertheless, although he was entirely lacking in military experience the army was very ready to show him good will, since he was the brother of the popular Germanicus who died in AD 19 and whose name he incorporated in his own.

However the atmosphere was soured in 42 by an abortive revolt by the governor of Upper Illyricum (Dalmatia), Marcus Furius Camillus Scribonianus. Although the uprising was quelled before it even began, its instigators had possessed connexions with very influential noblemen in the capital. This shock frightened Claudius into adopting stringent security measures, and it was partly due to these that no success attended any of the six or more further conspiracies which were launched against him during the remaining twelve years of his reign. Their suppression reportedly cost the lives of thirty-five senators and between two and three hundred knights; so it was hardly surprising that the emperor's outward deference to the senate failed to make much impression on its members. On the contrary, his often expressed desire that it should act independently and responsibly fell on deaf ears – especially as he himself controlled its composition more tightly than any of his predecessors, reviving the ancient office of the censorship for this purpose, and holding it in person from 47–8.

As an immediate sequel to Scribonianus' attempted rebellion, Claudius decided to distract attention from these unpleasant happenings by an invasion and annexation of Britain, which Gaius had failed to carry out. Under the command of Aulus Plautius, between 43 and 47, southern and central England were overrun and became the Roman province of Britannia, with its frontier, the Fosse Way, extending from Lindum to a point near Isca Dumnoniorum. Claudius himself came to Britain for the decisive capture of Camulodunum, which had been the royal capital of the defeated Belgae. Meanwhile he had also annexed the two client kingdoms of Thrace, converting them into another new province. The territory became a valuable source for the recruitment of auxiliary troops, to whose terms of service Claudius was attentive. It is from his reign that we begin to find bronze 'diplomas' recording conferments of Roman citizenship upon auxiliaries demobilized after twenty-five years of service, and the grants were extended to their wives and sons as well. This practice may have been introduced by his predecessors, but Claudius did much to convert it into a regular system. He also greatly developed the career structure of military officers, holding out new and favourable opportunities for knights. Another of his achievements was the reorganization of the imperial fleet. In Italy the naval base of Puteoli was supplemented by the initiation of a great new harbour, Portus Augusti, at Ostia, and steps were also taken to establish flotillas in the harbours of Britain and Pontus.

Claudius refused to see the Empire as a predominantly Italian institution, showing a desire, for example, to fill vacancies in the senate not only from Italy and Romanized southern Gaul but also from other, less developed, regions of Gaul. A surviving inscription records a speech on this theme which he delivered to the senate. In this address, he anticipated the objection that he was advocating a revolutionary novelty by pointing out that innovations had always been a feature of the ever-evolving Roman State, and that the step he now suggested did not constitute a departure from tradition but its logical conclusion. 'You ask me,' he went on to say, 'is not an Italian senator preferable to a provincial? . . . I think that not even provincials ought to be excluded, provided that they can add distinction to the senate.' However, his speech, for all its broadmindedness, still made important concessions to Italian superiority; nor were the changes which actually emerged by any means sensational, since the number of non-Italian senators would remain quite small for some decades to come. Yet the emperor's modest suggestions aroused a storm of xenophobia and prompted many bitter jests about his alleged predilection for foreigners.

Claudius' dealings with non-Romans featured again in an edict relating to a problem which confronted him at the beginning of his reign. This was the violent, bloodthirsty and longstanding dispute between the Greeks and Jews of Alexandria (see GAIUS). Both parties sent him deputations immediately after his accession to the throne, and his replies included a strong and impartial admonition:

As for the question which party was responsible for the riots and feud (or rather, if the truth be told, the war) with the Jews. . . . I was unwilling to make a strict enquiry, though guarding within me a store of immutable indignation against whichever party renews the conflict; and I tell you once and for all that unless you put a stop to this ruinous and obstinate enmity against each other, I shall be driven to show what a benevolent *princeps* can be when turned to righteous indignation.

Meanwhile he himself concentrated heavily on the work that had to be done in the capital. In particular, he paid more attention to his judicial functions than any emperor had before. One of the differences between Roman rulers and the heads of modern governments is that the former were expected to serve regularly as judges, not only attending the tribunals that were under the auspices of the senate but also presiding over their own imperial law-court. Claudius performed both these tasks with great assiduity, devoting especial attention to his own court; for example, this court considered treason cases which his predecessors would often have remitted to the senate, so that the range of imperial jurisdiction became substantially increased. Senatorial resentment because of this development no doubt contributed to the rich crop of anecdotes suggesting that Claudius made an eccentric fool of himself as a judge. As a corrective to these tales, however, there is evidence that he instituted valuable reforms in the judicial field, speeding up procedures, creating safeguards for the week and defenceless, and displaying continual willingness to lay aside the letter of the law in order to preserve the spirit behind it. This was just one illustration of the immense industriousness he applied to his duties. A new imperial virtue is celebrated on the coins of his reign, right from the start: it is CONSTANTIA AVGVSTI, the emperor's perseverance.

Yet he could not do everything by himself: like other wearers of the purple, and with the same attendant dangers, he needed helpers. One of the most important of them, despite the distrust he inspired in senators as a whole, was drawn from their own ranks – Lucius Vitellius (father of the future emperor). Although not the son of a senator – his father was a knight from Luceria – he became the most adroit and adaptable politician of the epoch, receiving promotion under Tiberius and Gaius and attaining the rare distinction of a third consulate under Claudius, who also made him his colleague in the censorship. Yet the emperor's burden of work made it essential that he should have other confidential aides, and in consequence he greatly increased the powers and functions of some of his personal staff, of freedman status and mostly near-eastern in origin. Here, as so often, he was only systematizing an existent trend; but under his régime can be found three or four such figures enjoying exceptional and unprecedented influence. Hostile ancient writers, who loathed these non-senatorial orientals, show him feebly submitting to their outrageous whims, but until his last years – when his control over events did begin to weaken – he himself remained the source of all vital decisions. Nevertheless, the proximity of these freedmen to Claudius gave them extraordinary opportunities for patronage and wealth.

One such man was Polybius, the minister *a studiis*; that is to say, it was his duty to arrange for the appointment of the men whom the emperor had earmarked for jobs and promotions, so that his ante-room was thronged by powerful individuals. Callistus, the minister *a libellis* or 'of notes', recommended on petitions received from all over the Empire. But the most important of these state secretaries in the early part of the reign was Narcissus, the *ab epistulis* or minister of letters, who helped the emperor with his voluminous correspondence and knew all his secrets. It was he who in 48 took the necessary action when a crisis arose. It concerned Claudius' twenty-three-year-old third wife Valeria Messalina (grand-daughter of Augustus' sister Octavia), who had taken a rich and noble consul-designate, Gaius Silius (son of a famous general in Germany), as the last of a long line of lovers. While the emperor was away at the port of Ostia they attempted a *coup*, perhaps with the intention of placing the imperial couple's seven-year-old son Britannicus on the throne, with themselves as his regents. Claudius was befuddled by the emergency – perhaps this was the first time that he showed a serious loss of grip – but Narcissus moved decisively, arresting and executing Silius and driving

Messalina to suicide.

Yet paradoxically Narcissus' vigorous intervention accelerated his own eclipse, since the fourth wife whom Claudius proceeded to marry in 49, his niece Agrippina the younger (Julia Agrippina, daughter of Germanicus and Agrippina the elder), was the ally of a rival freedman Pallas. Pallas was the *a rationibus* or finance minister, to whom the senate voted flattering honours. Agrippina was named Augusta, an honour which no living wife of a living emperor had ever received before; and now that Claudius was her husband she had every intention that her twelve-year-old son by a former marriage, later known as NERO, should supplant Claudius' own son Britannicus as the heir to the throne. She duly arranged for Nero to be betrothed to Claudius' daughter Octavia, and a year later the emperor adopted him as his son.

Claudius died in October 54, in his sixty-fourth year. There were conflicting explanations of his death, but the version which secured the widest currency suggested that Agrippina had been his killer, apparently by feeding him with poisoned mushrooms. True, in Italy it is easy to die by choosing mushrooms badly; and it is not at first sight clear why Agrippina should need to take such a step, since her son Nero had manifestly become heir to the throne. But he was already seventeen years of age and perhaps his mother did not like to wait until he felt old enough to dispense with her services as regent.

Claudius, we are told by the biographer Suetonius, was completely heterosexual – a rare phenomenon among Roman rulers. He was tall and well built and had an impressive face and handsome white hair. However, he also stammered, slobbered, ran at the nose, suffered from a persistent nervous tic, and frequently ate and drank himself into a stupor. He slept badly at night, but during the daytime would often nod off while presiding over a lawsuit. Pliny the elder added that the corners of his eyes were covered by hoods of flesh, streaked with small veins and sometimes suffused with blood.

As a boy, he had been the despair of his grandmother Antonia; she described him as a monster whom nature had started work upon, but failed to complete. Later in life, his stomach-aches were so painful that they made him think of suicide – although otherwise his health had become better. All the same, there must have been something fundamentally wrong with him: his complaint has been variously diagnosed by historians as poliomyelitis, pre-natal encephalitis, multiple sclerosis and congenital cerebral paralysis. And paralysis it does seem to have been, of some sort or another, which had afflicted him in his earlier years with such a variety of conspicuous disabilities.

As to the gifts and defects of his character, they are hard to sum up, because senators' hostile feelings have dominated the tradition. Like Augustus, whom he greatly admired, Claudius tried to blend tradition with innovation. His own contribution to the blend was a disconcerting mixture of progressive broadmindedness and antiquarian pedantry. His mind was evidently seething with good ideas. But he found it difficult to coordinate them in a concisely expressed form, and was easily thrown off-course by the suspicion, timidity and fear which were among his most conspicuous characteristics. However, what was most remarkable about Claudius, apart from peculiar appearance and behaviour, was a very high degree of erudition: Pliny the elder, himself phenomenally learned, numbered him among the hundred foremost scholarly writers of the day. In his youth Livy had seen him as a future historian; indeed, advised when young to abandon the delicate project of writing a history of recent Rome, he composed twenty books of Etruscan and eight of Carthaginian history and eight more of autobiographical memoirs – all lamentably lost. He also wrote a historical study of the Roman alphabet, to which he added three letters, though they were removed again shortly afterwards.

Claudius was married four times. His first wife, Plautia Urgulanilla, probably helped to inspire his interest in Etruscan history, since she was an Etruscan herself. After divorcing her he married Aelia Paetina for a short duration, before taking Valeria Messalina, aged fourteen, as his bride in 39, and the thirty-four-year-old Agrippina the younger ten years later.

NERO
54–68

NERO (54–68) was born at Antium in December 37, and at first was named Lucius Domitius Ahenobarbus. His father was Cnaeus Domitius Ahenobarbus, belonging to an extremely noble and ancient family, and his mother was the younger Agrippina, daughter of Germanicus and Agrippina the elder. When he had reached the age of two his mother was banished by GAIUS (Caligula), who seized his inheritance the following year after the death of the child's father.

Under CLAUDIUS, however, the younger Agrippina (his niece) was recalled from exile, and arranged for her son to receive a good education. After she had married the emperor Claudius in 49, the eminent Stoic philosopher Lucius Annaeus Seneca (Seneca the younger) became the tutor of the boy, who was betrothed to Claudius' daughter Octavia (he married her four years later). In 50, Agrippina persuaded her husband to adopt Nero as his son, so that thenceforward he took precedence over Britannicus, the emperor's own younger son by the late Messalina; he now assumed the names of Nero Claudius Drusus Germanicus. On the death of Claudius in October 54, Britannicus' claims were set aside, and, with the support of the praetorian prefect Sextus Afranius Burrus, Agrippina secured the throne for Nero.

Since he was not yet seventeen – far younger than any of his predecessors when they came to the throne – the empire was at first governed by Agrippina, the sister and wife of earlier emperors and now the mother of a third. This unprecedented phase of female rule was underlined by the initial monetary issue of the reign, which displayed the heads of Nero and Agrippina facing one another, with precedence accorded to Agrippina. When the imperial council (*consilium principis*) was in session, she used to listen, people said, behind a curtain; and she employed her power to eliminate possible rivals, notably Marcus Junius Silanus who, like Nero himself, was a great-great-grandson of AUGUSTUS.

But her dominant influence lasted only a very short time: already in 55 her son assumed priority over her on the coinage, and her name and portrait never appeared on any subsequent issue. When early in the same year Britannicus died at a dinner-party in the palace – allegedly murdered by Nero, although this could not be proved – Agrippina was said to have been dismayed, since she wanted to keep the youth in reserve in case her son became too recalcitrant. That remains conjectural; but her power was seen to be waning when the emperor transferred her to a separate residence, thus bringing her impressive Palatine receptions to an end.

The Empire now settled down to a period of sound government under the guidance of Seneca and Burrus. The late Claudius was deified (he was the first emperor since Augustus to receive this honour, which prompted some derogatory jokes), and Nero promised to employ his ancestor Augustus as his model. He also expressed a flattering, if somewhat unrealistic, desire that the senate and consuls should exercise their governmental functions as in ancient times. Steps were taken to improve public order, guard against forgery and reform treasury procedure; provincial governors and their staffs were forbidden to extract large sums of money from the local populations for their gladiatorial shows; and Nero himself, as he grew up, worked hard, particularly at his judicial duties, to which he contributed useful and practical procedural ideas.

He also entertained progressive, liberal feelings; these led him, for example, to try to abolish indirect taxes throughout the Empire (in response to complaints against tax-farmers), to abolish the stationing of praetorian guardsmen in circuses and theatres, and to forbid the killing of gladiators and condemned criminals in public spectacles. All these ideas proved impracticable, the first because it would have meant that direct taxation had to be greatly increased, the second because brawling in the arena soon became intolerable, and the third because public support was not forthcoming. Yet such proposals, even if they came to nothing, suggest that Nero, although easily goaded into ferocity by imagined threats to his personal safety, was basically humane. For example, like his mentor Seneca, he expressed objections to taking life, and this aversion extended to capital punishment. He must therefore have found it intensely disagreeable when the city prefect Lucius Pedanius Secundus was murdered by one of his slaves, with the result that Nero, according to the law, had to have all four hundred slaves of Pedanius' household put to death, despite strong popular pressure in their favour.

Setbacks of this kind gradually dampened such ardour for his administrative duties as he had previously possessed. Eventually they caused him to devote himself more and more to the real interests of his life: horse-racing, singing, acting, dancing, writing poetry and sexual activities of great and indeed almost unlimited versatility, if we are to believe the gossip-writers. Seneca and Burrus tried to canalize these interests so as to prevent them from becoming a scandal, encouraging him, for example, to have a domestic sort of affair with an ex-slave Acte, provided that marriage with her was recognized to be socially out of the question. Agrippina, however, cannot have been pleased that another woman was now in the palace. Moreover, she deplored Nero's un-Roman taste for the arts, not to speak of the effeminate Greek dress that he affected. But when he heard how virulently she was talking against him, in 59, beside the Gulf of Cumae (the Bay of Naples), he arranged for her murder. The historian Tacitus devotes one of his greatest set-pieces to the event, describing how a collapsible ship was provided for her, and how she succeeded in swimming away, only to meet her end on land. The story contains elements of melodrama that can be discounted. Nevertheless, it remains true that he did murder her – and that he reported to the senate that she had plotted against his life, obliging him to have her killed. To posterity, this matricide remained an unforgotten horror. Yet at the time the senators, who had hated her unconstitutional role and arrogant behaviour, did not entirely regret her removal, and Nero was relieved to find that the population and praetorian guard did not seem to mind too much either, even though she had been the great Germanicus' daughter.

In 62, however, an entirely new phase of the reign began, when both Seneca and Burrus disappeared from the political scene. First Burrus was killed by an abscess or tumour of the throat. He was succeeded as praetorian prefect by a pair of colleagues, Faenius Rufus and the far more sinister Gaius Ofonius Tigellinus, a Sicilian who was Nero's evil genius, and encouraged his excesses. Seneca found Tigellinus – and the new self-willed emperor – too difficult to work with; so he resigned, to enjoy the enormous wealth which, despite his critics, he had succeeded in amassing. Soon afterwards Nero showed his new-found independence by changing wives. He divorced Octavia, who, although harmless, was exiled and put to death in 62. Her place was taken by Poppaea Sabina (the wife or mistress of his fashionable friend OTHO), a beautiful amber-haired young woman who, according to rumour, bathed in asses' milk.

But Tigellinus, who connived in these events, perhaps underestimated the senators' unfavourable reaction to Nero's activities in a different field, that of the arts. At first the emperor had limited his stage appearances to private stages, but in 64 he broke out from this restriction and launched his public début at Neapolis. There, to the pleasure of the passionately phil-Hellenic Nero, his audience were Greeks; but in the capital too, in the following year, at the second performance of the Neronian Games which he had instituted on the Greek model, he started to appear before Roman spectators. Tacitus offers a highly coloured and venomous account of these activities, going on to describe how the emperor subsequently instituted Youth Games, attended by every sort of immorality, at which (despite stage fright) he himself performed, escorted by a *claque* of knights known as the Augustiani. He also wrote poetry, stringing together – according to the historian – suggestions thrown out by his drinking companions. Suetonius, less unflatteringly, cited notebooks and papers that prove that Nero did in fact write original verses. He also took quite an expert interest in painting and sculpture.

However, these aberrations, as senators regarded them, did not perturb the peace, prosperity and sound government of the Empire as a whole. Only a few distant frontiers experienced warlike operations. In Britain the expansion of Roman rule, signalled by the fall of the Druid fortress Mona to Gaius Suetonius Paulinus, was temporarily delayed by the revolt of the Iceni in East Anglia. This had been provoked by Roman taxation and British unwillingness to repay a ruinously expensive loan from Seneca. In 60 the tribe's queen Boudicca (Boadicea) overran the Roman settlements at Camulodunum, Londinium and Verulamium, putting seventy thousand Romans or Roman-ized natives to the sword before she was finally defeated near Atherstone. Meanwhile, beyond the opposite extremity of the Empire, the greatest general of the day, Cnaeus Domitius Corbulo, had received an important command whose aim was to detach Armenia from Parthian control. He had nearly completed his task when it was interrupted by the serious defeat of a colleague, Caesennius Paetus, near Elazığ in eastern Turkey in 62. In the following year, however, Corbulo re-established Roman military superiority, concluding an agreement with the Parthians which enabled Tiridates I, their protégé on the Armenian throne, to accept the status of a Roman client. In 66, amid massive celebrations, Tiridates visited Rome as Nero's guest.

During this period, mints in the capital and at Lugdunum in Gaul were issuing the most superb brass and copper coinages ever produced in the Roman world. The emperor's gross, baroque features were depicted with an intriguing blend of magnificence and realism; while an extensive range of designs and inscriptions on the reverses of the coins commemorated, one after another, the benefactions he claimed to have lavished upon the peoples of Rome and the Empire. In addition, some of the pieces even discreetly refer to his interest in the theatre and in horses – tastes which are set within a traditional, creditable framework by allusions to Apollo the lyre-player and to cavalry manoeuvres.

Nevertheless, the situation at Rome was taking a turn for the worse. A crucial event was the Great Fire of Rome in 64, which deprived numerous families of their homes and caused widespread discontent. According to a famous passage of Tacitus, Nero tried to pin the blame for the conflagration on the city's small Christian community (regarded as a dissident group of Jews) and burnt many of them alive; the martyrdoms of Saint Peter and Saint Paul were ascribed to these persecutions. Still, the rumour persisted not only that the ruler had sung his own poem 'The Sack of Troy' (not 'fiddled', as convention has it) while enjoying the spectacle of the flames, but also that he had actually started the fire himself, in order to be able to annex some land he wanted for the erection of his Golden House.

In previous years Nero had constructed an impressive mansion for his own accommodation; this house, under the name of Domus Transitoria, was however now to become the mere entrance hall to the new and vastly greater Golden House, which, together with its grounds, extended over a very large area of Rome, hitherto thickly inhabited by his subjects: never before or since has a European monarch carved out such an enormous area as a personal residence in the very heart of his capital. Designed by Nero's architect-engineers Severus and Celer, the Golden House was a series of separate, graceful pavilions and kiosks set amid the vistas of an alluringly designed landscape, including a large artificial lake stocked with many varieties of fish and animals. The main residential section of the palace, on the Esquiline Hill, is hard to picture today, because it was subsequently built over and now lies far underground. But its domed octagonal hall, lit from a central round opening, was an early and ambitious example of brick-faced concrete construction. The building displayed every sort of technical wonder, including baths flowing with sulphurous and salt waters, the world's largest hydraulic organ, moving panels that showered down flowers and scent on the diners below, and a cupola, surmounting the main banqueting hall, which revolved mechanically 'like the heavens'. When the Golden House was complete, the emperor cried out: 'Good, now I can at last begin to live like a human being!'

Meanwhile, however, his relations with the senatorial class were deteriorating sharply. One of Tigellinus' first actions had been to revive the hated treason law and to liquidate a number of possible suspects. Then the year 65 witnessed what was regarded as a serious plot. Known as the Pisonian conspiracy, its guiding spirit or figure-head, according to one account, was a certain Gaius Calpurnius Piso, an attractive but superficial nobleman. But an alternative version named the leaders as Faenius Rufus – the joint praetorian prefect, resented because his influence had been eclipsed by Tigellinus – and the retired statesman Seneca. The truth will never be known, but nineteen executions or suicides followed, and thirteen banishments. Piso, Faenius and Seneca were among those who died; so did Seneca's nephew the poet Lucan, who had been one of Nero's closest friends; and another victim was a daughter of Claudius.

During the years that followed the government continued to punish suspects. An austerely philosophical personage, Thrasea Paetus, was one of those who succumbed. The eminent commander Corbulo, and the army chiefs of Upper and Lower Germany, likewise met their deaths. They were eliminated by order of Nero himself who had gone to Greece to display his artistic prowess, winning contests in Games (he was granted the prize for the Olympic chariot-race although he fell out of his chariot), collecting works of art, inaugurating a Corinth canal (which was never finished), and ostensibly 'liberating' the Hellenes whom he loved. At Rome, amid continuing executions, a shortage of food caused great hardship, and tension was so acute that the ex-slave Helius, whom Nero had left in charge of the capital, felt obliged to cross over to Greece and summon him urgently back.

Indeed, during January 68 Nero made a spectacular return to the capital. But in March, Gaius Julius Vindex, governor of Lugdunese Gaul, rose in rebellion against him. Galba, in Spain, lent his prestige to the revolt; Lucius Clodius Macer struck out on his own in north Africa; and even the Rhine legions, though they destroyed Vindex at Vesontio, ceased to accept the authority of Nero. The crisis could have been overcome if he had acted with resolution, but all he seemed able to do was to imagine fantastic acts of vengeance or to think of winning back his seditious troops by a dramatic display of weeping. Tigellinus was seriously ill and therefore powerless, and the praetorian prefect of the time, Nymphidius Sabinus, prompted his guardsmen to abandon their allegiance. When Nero heard that the senate, too, had turned against him and condemned him to be flogged to death, he decided, with the assistance of a secretary, to commit suicide on 9 June by stabbing himself in the throat with a dagger. His last words were 'Qualis artifex pereo', 'What a showman the world is losing in me.'

Suetonius offers an impression of his appearance and behaviour:

He was about the average height, his body marked with spots and malodorous, his hair light blond, his features regular rather than attractive, his eyes blue and somewhat weak, his neck over-thick, his belly prominent, and his legs very slender. His health was good: for all his extravagant indulgence he had only three illnesses in fourteen years, and none of them serious enough to stop him from drinking wine or breaking any other regular habit. He was entirely shameless in the style of his appearance and dress, but always had his hair set in rows of curls, and when he visited Greece, let it grow long and hang down his back. He often gave audiences in an unbelted silk dressing-gown and slippers, with a scarf round his neck.

PART II

THE
YEAR OF THE FOUR EMPERORS;
AND THE FLAVIAN DYNASTY

The Flavian Dynasty

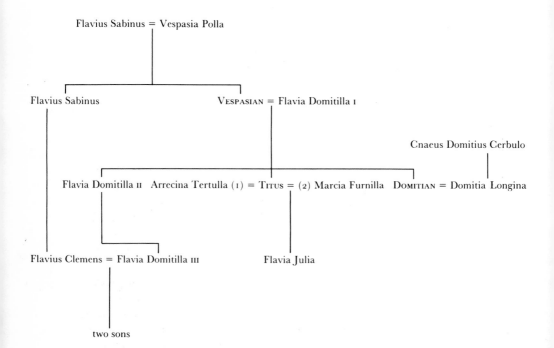

Flavius Sabinus = Vespasia Polla

Flavius Sabinus   Vespasian = Flavia Domitilla I

Cnaeus Domitius Cerbulo

Flavia Domitilla II   Arrecina Tertulla (1) = Titus = (2) Marcia Furnilla   Domitian = Domitia Longina

Flavius Clemens = Flavia Domitilla III   Flavia Julia

two sons

GALBA
68–9

GALBA (Servius Sulpicius) (June 68–January 69) was born in 3 BC, the son
of Gaius Sulpicius Galba, of patrician rank, and of Mummia Achaica who
likewise came of a great family. AUGUSTUS, Livia Drusilla, TIBERIUS,
GAIUS and CLAUDIUS all thought highly of his talents, and he successively
became the imperial governor of Aquitania, in 33 consul, military commander
in Upper Germany, in 45 proconsul of Africa, and imperial governor of Nearer
Spain (Hispania Tarraconensis).

Gaius Julius Vindex, his colleague in central Gaul (Gallia Lugdunensis),
when he revolted against NERO in 68 did not aspire to an imperial role himself,
for he knew he lacked the authority to command widespread support. Instead
he offered Galba the leadership. Galba hesitated, but when the governor of
Aquitania appealed to him for assistance against Vindex, he was compelled to
make a decision. In consequence, on 2 April 68, in a proclamation at Carthago
Nova, he declared himself the representative of the senate and Roman people.
This did not amount to a personal claim to the throne but made him virtually
an ally of Vindex. He was joined by OTHO, the governor of Lusitania; but
Otho possessed no legion and Galba had only one (probably commanded by
his military adviser Titus Vinius), so he now started to mobilize another from
the Spaniards.

At the end of May, however, Vindex was defeated at Vesontio by the general
in Upper Germany, Lucius Verginius Rufus, and committed suicide,
whereupon Galba, in despair, withdrew into the interior of Spain. But some
two weeks later he learnt that Nero was dead, and that he himself had been
pronounced emperor by the senate, many of whose members had already been
secretly in touch with him. The move had the support of the praetorian
guardsmen, whose prefect, Nymphidius Sabinus, bribed his men to abandon
their loyalty to Nero.

With his newly recruited legion Galba moved northwards into Gaul, and at

Narbo, in the first days of July, deputations from the senate and praetorian guard came to visit him. During the autumn he disposed of Clodius Macer – who was taking an independent line in Africa and was suspected of wanting the throne for himself – by arranging for his assassination by the local imperial procurator.

In the capital, however, serious difficulties had already arisen. Galba, although a very wealthy man, did not like spending money and felt that Nymphidius' bribe to the guardsmen had been excessive. Therefore before he even reached Rome he replaced the prefect by his own close friend Cornelius Laco; and Nymphidius' subsequent attempt at subversion ended in his death. Galba replaced the dead man's officers by protégés of his own, and refused to pay the bonuses Nymphidius had promised in his name, remarking: 'I choose my soldiers; I do not buy them.' As a result, the praetorians started to become disaffected. Moreover, as Galba approached the capital his army became involved in a scuffle with discontented marines, who were consequently disbanded, together with the imperial bodyguard. Galba then turned to other attempts at financial retrenchment, which failed to endear him to the population of Rome. The appointment of a commission to recover Nero's gifts again alienated many leading figures who had been among the beneficiaries.

Worst of all, the legionaries in the German camps very soon revolted against Galba. If one legion in Spain could make an emperor, they felt, then seven in Germany could do it better – and could also earn rich presents such as those which Nymphidius had promised the praetorians. So when on 1 January 69 the new commander in Upper Germany, Hordeonius Flaccus, required his troops to renew their oaths of allegiance to Galba, the two legions at Moguntiacum refused to comply and overturned his statues, swearing loyalty to the senate and Roman people instead and demanding that they themselves should appoint a new emperor. On the following day, the troops of Lower Germany similarly rebelled, investing their own new commander, VITELLIUS, with the purple.

Galba was perhaps not aware of this latest news – though he knew what had happened at Moguntiacum – when he decided to adopt a son in order to convey a reassuring impression of dynastic continuity. His choice fell on Lucius Calpurnius Piso Licinianus, a young man of impeccable lineage and character; but the choice so greatly disappointed Galba's earliest supporter OTHO, who had hoped for the adoption himself, that he began to organize a conspiracy among the praetorian guardsmen. And so on 15 January these soldiers – without the connivance of their prefect Laco – murdered Galba and Piso in the Roman Forum, and took their severed heads to Otho in the praetorian camp.

For all the impressiveness of his origins and qualifications – matched by austere features which lent themselves to imposing coin-portraits – Galba had not proved a successful emperor. 'By common consent,' remarked the historian Tacitus, 'he possessed the makings of a ruler – had he never ruled.' His thrifty financial policy, though praiseworthy enough after all Nero's extravagances, was carried out with ham-handed tactlessness. His choice of advisers – Laco, Vinius and the freedman Icelus – was unfortunate, and his selection of a successor proved disastrous. Yet Galba, by selecting a man from outside his own family to become his heir apparent, was at least asserting a new and valuable principle that the throne should go to merit: just as his own elevation had for the first time conferred the Principate upon a man who came from outside the Julio-Claudian house. He was also the first emperor to be raised to power by his legionaries. From this time onwards, therefore, the Roman world was a prize for which any and every commander might compete. Moreover, his death had invested the praetorians with a new and sinister role. Praetorian officers had killed Gaius; abandonment by one of their prefects had caused the death of Nero; but Galba was the first head of the imperial State, though by no means the last, to be brought down by the rank and file of the guard.

OTHO
69

OTHO (Marcus Salvius) (January–April 69) was born in 32 into a family which had been promoted from knightly (equestrian) rank to hold the consulship under AUGUSTUS; his father received patrician status from CLAUDIUS. In the course of a youth devoted to fashionable pursuits at Rome, he became the husband, or perhaps the lover, of the beautiful Poppaea Sabina. But Nero, when he began to take an interest in her (they were later married), sent Otho away to be the governor of Lusitania in 58.

Ten years later, however, after GALBA pronounced his independence of Nero, Otho became his first important adherent. Subsequently, when Galba had been proclaimed emperor and started to move on Rome, Otho went with him and set out to win the favour of the troops, expressing sympathetic concern about the unaccustomed hardships of the march; for it was his intention to secure adoption as Galba's successor. Once in Rome, with the same purpose in mind, he showed the praetorian guardsmen marked generosity, which he could ill afford. Greatly dashed by the proclamation of Piso Licinianus as Galba's heir, he drew a number of praetorians into a plot against the emperor. On 15 January 69 he was warmly welcomed by the soldiers of the guard into the praetorian camp (although their officers at first remained hesitant), where oaths of allegiance were sworn in his name; Galba and Piso were murdered in the Forum and men came to him bringing their heads. The senate, although by now aware that VITELLIUS had been hailed emperor in Germany, acquiesced in Otho's elevation.

Both claimants to the throne set a precedent by having originated from the new aristocracy of office established under the Empire, comprising men of knightly origin. But Otho enjoyed dangerously few links with the army except for the praetorian guard, upon which he depended more completely than any of his forerunners. It was said that he never expected Vitellius to contest his accession, and recoiled from the idea of civil strife (one of his coins hopefully celebrated Universal Peace, PAX ORBIS TERRARVM). Nevertheless, war became unavoidable when Vitellius' generals Valens and Caecina advanced on Italy, crossing the Alps and joining forces at Cremona. Otho achieved little by a naval expedition to southern Gaul; but he was backed by the legions of the Danube and Euphrates, and summoned the former to join him. This was bound to take time, and meanwhile his generals Vestricius Spurinna and Annius Gallus held up the Vitellian advance guard on the River Po.

In Rome, Otho brought Verginius Rufus out of retirement to hold a second consulship, in the hope that his prestige would establish confidence. But the new emperor had to quell disorders among the praetorian guard (eliminating its unpopular commander Laco), and his recruitment of two thousand gladiators set an unattractive precedent. Nor was he wise to divide the command of his troops in the field, though the absence of any potential commander-in-chief seemed to make this inevitable. However, he himself set out for the north on 14 March, attempting to belie his reputation for softness by tramping on foot, unshaven, in front of the standards. As he approached the forces of Valens and Caecina, the Danubian troops on their way to help him were not far away. But the enemy, despite a setback in a minor skirmish, had for their part already received reinforcements and enjoyed a numerical advantage, especially as Otho himself, together with part of his force, remained at his rear headquarters south of the Po at Brixellum.

Nevertheless, and although his best generals Gaius Suetonius Paulinus, Annius Gallus and Marius Celsus advised to the contrary, the emperor and his brother Lucius Salvius Otho Titianus and the praetorian prefect Licinius Proculus determined that the decisive battle must take place immediately – before their troops could melt away, or before Vitellius himself could arrive, or because Otho's personal character proved unable to stand up to the suspense. The decisive engagement took place a little to the east of Cremona, and is sometimes described as the First Battle of Bedriacum. It came to an abrupt conclusion when the Vitellians took Otho's generals in the flank, inflicting a total defeat. Otho himself, when the news reached him at Brixellum, was urged by his counsellors to continue the fight, and the appeal was echoed by a deputation from his Danubian relief army, which had arrived with the news that their advance guard had already reached Aquileia. But Otho rejected this advice and committed suicide on 16 April.

The historian Tacitus offered a gloomy assessment of Otho and Vitellius alike, since he detested civil wars, and saw in this particular struggle no principles or leaders who made it worth while. As for Otho, he ruled for such a short time that it is hard to estimate his qualities as a ruler. He was evidently something of an administrator. In his military capacity, however, he made mistakes, though that was excusable in such a chaotic situation. When he claimed to be the true successor of NERO, this attitude, though quite popular, was felt in responsible circles not to be wholly reassuring; and he was inevitably the servant of the praetorians who had raised him to the throne. He also possessed the unhappy distinction of being the first emperor who had approved in advance – or indeed personally arranged – his predecessors's murder. His own suicide, which seemed premature and left his supporters stranded, could be interpreted (like his over-hasty decision to engage the enemy) as a sign of deficient stamina, or it could be regarded as a praiseworthy move to put an end to the horrors of war.

'Otho', according to Suetonius, 'was of medium height, bow-legged, and with splay feet; but almost as fastidious about his appearance as a woman. His entire body had been depilated, and a toupee covered his practically bald head, so well made that no one suspected its existence. He shaved every day, and since boyhood had always used a poultice of moist bread to prevent the growth of his beard.'

VITELLIUS
69

VITELLIUS (Aulus) (April–December 69) was born in 15. His father was Claudius' principal adviser Lucius Vitellius, three times consul and the emperor's fellow-censor. Aulus became consul in 48 and proconsul of Africa in about 61–2. GALBA appointed him commander in Lower Germany, where the troops were already considering rebellion when he arrived to take charge of them in November 68. On 2 January 69, after hearing that the soldiers in Upper Germany had thrown off their allegiance to Galba, Vitellius' own men, instigated by the legionary commander Fabius Valens and his colleagues, saluted him emperor. The coins he now struck described him as GER-MANICVS, not, like earlier bearers of the title, because of defeats he had inflicted on the Germans, but because he had been nominated by the Roman legionaries in Germany – the largest military concentration in the Empire.

Very soon afterwards this army set out towards Rome, led not by Vitellius himself, who stayed behind to mobilize a reserve force and follow later, but by Valens and another legionary general Aulus Caecina Alienus, each commanding a separate column. Caecina was already a hundred and fifty miles on his way when he learnt that Galba had been killed and OTHO proclaimed in his place. But this did not stop him; on the contrary, he passed rapidly down the eastern borders of Gaul, while Valens followed a more westerly route, quelling a mutiny as he went. Both armies successfully crossed the Alps in March before the winter snows had melted, and effected a junction at Cremona just north of the Po. Not far from that city, in the First Battle of Bedriacum, they launched their Batavian auxiliaries into an attack which routed the enemy force. Otho killed himself on 16 April, and three days later the soldiers in the capital swore allegiance to Vitellius. The senate likewise hailed him emperor.

Vitellius himself, moving southwards, paused at Lugdunum to present his six-year-old son – named Germanicus like his father – to the legions as his eventual successor, thus indicating that he intended to found Rome's second imperial dynasty. His march on Rome, as described by the hostile historian Tacitus, seemed like a conqueror's procession, and was marked by a series of disagreeable incidents. Before his arrival, Vitellius sent instructions to Valens ordering that the entire praetorian guard, which had supported Otho, should be cashiered, and replaced by a much larger body recruited from his own legionaries and auxiliaries. Reaching the city in July, Vitellius appointed new joint praetorian prefects, one a supporter of Caecina and the other an adherent of Valens, whose relations with one another were notably strained and abrasive.

Meanwhile, on 1 July, the armies of the east had declared themselves in favour not of Vitellius but of VESPASIAN, the governor of Judaea, and on his behalf Mucianus, governor of Syria, set out towards the capital with an army. In August the Danube legions, which had supported Otho, joined Vespasian's cause, and one of their legionary commanders, Antonius Primus, made a dash for Italy across the Julian Alps. Valens was ill, and Caecina, now consul, conspired with the prefect of the fleet at Ravenna to betray Vitellius and go over to Vespasian. However, his troops at Hostilia refused to follow him and placed him under arrest; and then they made common cause with the rest of the Vitellian army which was endeavouring to hold the line of the Po at Cremona.

In October, not far from that city, the two forces met in a decisive confrontation known as the Second Battle of Bedriacum. Since Vitellius himself was still at Rome, his troops went into the engagement virtually leaderless, and gravely demoralized. It was a desperately fought struggle, continuing far into the night, until the light of the moon, rising behind the army of Primus, made the Vitellians an easy mark, and they broke and fled in utter defeat. Cremona was brutally sacked by the victors. The fleet at Misenum abandoned Vitellius; Civilis, on the Rhine, led a revolt of Batavian soldiers which spread dangerously to the tribes of Gaul, and became a major Gallo-German rebellion; an attempt by Valens, whose health had recovered, to raise a second army in Gaul failed to make any headway; and Primus, aided by the capitulation of a Vitellian force at Narnia, pressed on towards the capital.

There the city prefect Sabinus, who was Vespasian's brother, nearly persuaded Vitellius to abdicate, which no Roman emperor had ever done before. But troops who were stationed in Rome and still supported his régime joined the civilian population in forcing him to abandon these talks. Sabinus, obliged to take refuge on the Capitoline Hill, was set upon by German troops and killed, and the temple of Jupiter itself, the very symbol of the Roman State, was burnt to the ground. Then Primus entered Rome, overcoming a desperate resistance. On 20 December Vitellius, left alone in the palace, was captured by soldiers, dragged to the Forum, and brutally murdered.

According to Suetonius, he was unusually tall, with an alcoholic flush for most of the time, a huge paunch, and a somewhat crippled thigh from having been run over by a four-horse chariot which the emperor GAIUS was driving. Vitellius is also depicted by ancient writers as cruel, indolent, perverted and absurdly extravagant. Gluttonous he probably was, but the accounts enlarging on the theme are based almost entirely on propaganda by the side that defeated him. It was unfortunate that he lacked military experience and relied on two mutually hostile lieutenants, neither of whom inspired a great deal of confidence. Nevertheless, he himself was by no means unpopular; and brief though his rule turned out to be, it showed signs of constructive moderation and tact. For example, he chose to date his accession from 19 April, the day when he was accepted by the senate, rather than from 2 January, the date when he had first been proclaimed by the army. Moreover, he attended senate meetings scrupulously, permitted the free expression of opposing opinions, and modestly supported his candidates for the consulship in person. At first he would not use the titles 'Caesar' and 'Augustus', associated with such illustrious predecessors; and the former designation —even though his reluctance may have been finally overborne – never appeared on the coinage at all. However, unlike any previous emperor, he accepted a perpetual consulship, no doubt feeling that a ruler who did not belong to the Julio-Claudian house or ancient nobility could not despise such outward forms of privilege and prestige.

VESPASIAN
69–79

VESPASIAN (Titus Flavius Vespasianus) (69–79) was born in 9 at Reate in the Sabine country north of Rome. His father Flavius Sabinus was a tax-collector of knightly (equestrian) rank; his mother Vespasia Polla belonged to a family of the same status, but her brother became a senator. So did

Vespasian himself, together with his elder brother, Sabinus.

Vespasian was praetor in 40, and then gained further preferment through the patronage of CLAUDIUS' minister and freedman Narcissus. As a legionary commander he distinguished himself in Claudius' invasion of Britain in 43–4, earning the insignia (*ornamenta*) of a Triumph and two priesthoods. In 51 he held a consulship, and later, *c*. 63, was proconsul of Africa, where his administration won some praise, for he did not use his tenure of the post to make money. As a result he underwent a period of impoverishment, and indeed was only saved from bankruptcy by his brother, at the price of a mortgage on his house and land.

As a member of the imperial entourage during NERO's tour of Achaea in 66, Vespasian fell into disfavour for falling asleep while the emperor was singing. All the same, in February 67 he was appointed governor of Judaea, with the task of suppressing the First Jewish Revolt, known to the Jews as the First Roman War. Perhaps Nero preferred to have a man of only mediocre reputation commanding such a potentially menacing number of troops; nevertheless, by the middle of 68 Vespasian had reduced almost the entire country to obedience, with the exception of Jerusalem and a few outlying fortresses. On hearing, though, that Nero had killed himself on 9 June, he halted his preparations to storm Jerusalem, and recognized the accession of GALBA.

However, Vespasian was now beginning to be prompted by greater ambitions on his own account. A vital factor in his plans and decisions was the governor of Syria, Gaius Licinius Mucianus. Until recently the two men had not been on good terms, because Mucianus resented the elevation of the Judaean command to a higher status than that of his own governorship. But after Nero's death they made up their differences, and watched the developing political situation together. Galba's murder in the following January caused them to begin considering the possibility of active revolt. The suicide of OTHO in April prompted them to form active plans to that end. While for the moment acknowledging his victor VITELLIUS as emperor, they secretly enlisted the support of Tiberius Julius Alexander in Egypt. Neither Alexander nor Mucianus could claim the throne for themselves, the former since he was a knight, not a senator – and a foreigner as well, a renegade Jew – and the latter because, lacking sons of his own, he could not form a dynasty. Vespasian on the other hand had two sons, TITUS and DOMITIAN (the offspring of his late wife Flavia Domitilla the elder); and the governors now agreed that he should be their candidate for the purple.

On 1 July, therefore, Alexander ordered the Egyptian legions to swear an oath of allegiance to Vespasian, and before the middle of the month the armies in Judaea and Syria had done the same. Their plan was that Mucianus, with twenty thousand troops, should set out for Italy while Vespasian would remain for the time being in the east, where he could control Egypt's grain supply which was vital for Rome. By late August the Danubian armies, too, had declared their support for his cause. Among these troops the initiative was seized by Marcus Antonius Primus, a Gaul from Tolosa who was the commander of one of the legions in Pannonia. Primus moved speedily westwards into the Italian peninsula, apparently without waiting for instructions from the leaders of the rebellion, and on his own account defeated the Vitellians at the Second Battle of Bedriacum.

Primus then marched on Rome itself, which put up a desperate resistance. Shortly before he arrived, Vespasian's brother, the city prefect Sabinus – who had been attempting to secure Vitellius' capitulation – was murdered by the latter's enraged supporters on the Capitol. However, Vitellius himself also came to a violent end, on 20 December. Primus entered the city on the following day and the senate confirmed Vespasian's accession as emperor. Mucianus arrived not long afterwards, and criticized Primus for having acted without orders; he was accused of committing atrocities as well. Primus left for the east to complain to Vespasian, who gave him honours but allowed him to return to his native Tolosa.

Mucianus was now in charge of Rome, where he executed Vitellius' son and other possible malcontents, and kept a suspicious eye on Vespasian's pushing younger son Domitian, who had been with his doomed uncle Sabinus on the burning Capitol before effecting a dramatic escape. Vespasian himself, leaving his other son Titus to capture Jerusalem (an event celebrated by famous coins inscribed IVDAEA CAPTA), returned to the capital in October 70. Mucianus was loaded with distinctions and remained an important adviser of the ruler until his death some six years later, although he was not admitted to any share of the imperial power.

Vespasian's great gift to the Empire was the termination of the civil wars, signalized by his splendid Temple of Peace erected in his new Forum, which was ranked by Pliny the elder as one of the Wonders of the World. His coinage persistently recalled this re-establishment of peace for, his origins being even less glorious than those of his failed predecessors, he needed to make every effort he could to mobilize public opinion in his support.

The principal element in the power structure still remained the army. At one end of the Empire (under Titus) it ended the Jewish revolt (though Masada held out until 73), and on the northern frontier his general Cerealis decisively defeated the Gallo-German uprising and its rebel 'empire' near Augusta Trevirorum, compelling the leader of the revolt, Civilis, to capitulate. Their military tasks done, Vespasian handled his soldiers with an impressive combination of firmness and tact. He did not show them undue munificence, but like Augustus was an expert at delicately precise calculations of what could and could not be done. He regrouped the armies of the Empire so as to ensure that legions which had supported Vitellius should not occupy key positions. Moreover, he began to break up the Rhine and Danube camps, which had been large enough to constitute a political peril; from now onwards, instead, single legions were to be separated one from another, in much smaller camps of their own. They had complained of Vitellius' intention to move them from countries where they had formed ties; and Vespasian allowed them to become more static in character. However, after the shock of the Gallic revolt, auxiliaries were less often employed near their own homes, and Vespasian tended to draft a variety of races into each single unit, so as to deprive these units of their individual ethnic character. Another of his achievements was the annexation of the Agri Decumates which formed the re-entrant between the upper stretches of the Rhine and Danube, with the result that the northern frontier was significantly shortened. In Britain, too, Cerealis shattered the power of the border tribe of the Brigantes, who had become hostile, and pushed the imperial boundary northwards in the direction of Caledonia. But such operations were exceptional, since most of the huge Empire now enjoyed unbroken tranquillity.

Nevertheless, Vespasian did not let the troops underestimate his own military distinction: he allowed them to salute him as Imperator no less than twenty times. And he chose to date his accession not, like Vitellius, from the day when the senate had recognized him as emperor, but from 1 July 69, when he had first been acclaimed by the troops. This was a frank admission that he owed them the job, and a reminder to the senators that it was not themselves but the army which constituted the basis of his power. True, he assiduously attended their meetings and consulted them with scrupulous care, but he had no intention whatever that they should regain any autonomous freedom of action. On the contrary, despite much lip-service to Augustus – the ostensible restorer of the Republic – he went ahead with Claudius' policy of increasing the central imperial authority. Indeed, in 73–4, like that emperor, he revived and himself occupied the office of censor, and used it to exert open control over the membership of the senate. The body that emerged from this operation was less metropolitan and noble, and more municipal and Italian, than it had been before; and there was also a further increase in members from the provinces.

For although Italy still dominated the governmental administration, the provinces, too, encouraged by judicious grants of citizenship and the so-called 'Latin rights', were rising quite rapidly. Vespasian was familiar with their problems, and possessed an Empire-wide standpoint; and it was largely thanks to the durable norm which he thus established that Roman history from now onwards becomes increasingly the story not of a palace but of a vast common civilization.

Yet Vespasian had to act with considerable financial caution, for he had inherited an Empire devastated by civil war. This meant that he was obliged to raise funds by every method he could devise. Oppression, it is true, was by no means what he wanted; for example, he was careful not to burden the provinces with excessive expenses in connexion with the imperial post. But he nevertheless felt it necessary to raise the rates of taxation quite steeply, and showed vigilance in detecting evasions. This was not the public's traditional idea of how a ruler ought to behave, and innumerable jokes about his supposed meanness went into circulation. But these pin-pricks did him no real harm; for he knew where to stop. Besides, the man who built the Temple of Peace, started the building of the Colosseum and endowed the first professorships of Greek and Latin at Rome, could not justly be described as parsimonious.

Although Vespasian allowed himself time off for a daily drive and siesta (which he took in the company of a mistress), he worked extremely hard. Before dawn, he read whatever letters had come in. While dressing and putting on his shoes, he admitted his friends and conversed with them. During the rest of the day he devoted a lot of time to his duties as judge. On his death-bed he tried to struggle to his feet, remarking that 'An emperor ought to die standing.' The man who occupied the imperial throne must always be at his duties, and this involved a remarkably time-consuming level of personal accessibility. At his favoured residence in the Gardens of Sallust, security precautions around his person were greatly relaxed. All this was part of his constant desire to stress his own comparatively humble origins. They are reflected clearly too in a variety of portrait-busts, created by sculptors of great ability and sympathetic insight.

Despite his own incessant labours, Vespasian had to have a helper; and while Mucianus was at first an important adviser, the emperor relied more and more on his elder son Titus. Moreover, it was clearly understood that Titus, his praetorian prefect and colleague in the censorship, would eventually take his place on the throne; for from the very outset Vespasian openly announced (following his less successful predecessor Vitellius) his intention of creating a new Flavian dynasty, and this was explicitly stated on the coinage. However, conservatives still objected strongly to this undisguised assumption that the Principate could be handed down by hereditary transmission, like a personal estate – especially in a family lacking the prestige of the Julio-Claudian house. In consequence, Vespasian incurred a good deal of hostility.

His critics included moralists – describing themselves as Cynic philosophers – who adopted an anarchic, anti-establishment position. But various less philosophical groups of senators, too, were adamant in their objections to Vespasian's dynastic plans. Prominent among them was Helvidius Priscus, an adherent of Stoicism who had married into a family of constitutionalist objectors, being the son-in-law of Nero's victim Thrasea. Priscus had insulted Vitellius in public, and had been a friend of Vespasian; but he changed into such an abrasive critic that the emperor felt obliged to banish him and then in 75 to order his execution, though allegedly with regret. Far more dangerous, however, was the intelligence, received four years later, that two senior senators who formed part of the central imperial establishment, Eprius Marcellus (an intimate counsellor of Vespasian) and Caecina Alienus (who had deserted to Vespasian from Vitellius), were conspiring against his life. By the initiative of Titus, neither survived.

Not long afterwards, Vespasian fell ill of a fever, withdrew to his summer retreat at the spa of Aquae Cutiliae near his birthplace, and died on 24 June 79. Suetonius describes him as a strong, square-bodied man with a curious strained expression on his face. He enjoyed excellent health, which he preserved by fasting one day a month. To his friends, his scurrilous sense of humour proved rather wearing. Much of it centred on the somewhat sordid ways in which he raised money for the state. For example Titus, we are told, complained of the tax which his father had imposed on the contents of the city urinals. In response, Vespasian handed him a coin which had been part of the first day's proceeds: 'Does it smell bad?', he asked; and when Titus had to admit that it did not his father went on: 'Yet it comes from urine.' He also made a final joke on his death-bed: 'Oh dear! I think I am turning into a god' ('Vae, puto deus fio').

TITUS
79–81

TITUS (Titus Flavius Vespasianus) (79–81), the first son of VESPASIAN and Flavia Domitilla the elder, was born in 39. He was educated with CLAUDIUS' son Britannicus, who became his close friend, and when Britannicus died, allegedly of poisoning while at dinner with his step-brother NERO, Titus was reclining at the same table (and, people said, had taken some of the poison himself, which made him very ill). After serving in Germany and Britain as military tribune he became quaestor c. 65 and commanded one of his father's legions in Judaea in 67, where he captured the rebel cities of Taricheae and Gamala (places that cannot be located with certainty today), and had a horse killed under him. Late in the following year he was sent to convey Vespasian's congratulations to GALBA, but at Corinth, on hearing that Galba had been murdered, he turned back.

In the subsequent negotiations between eastern provincial governors which led to the proclamation of Vespasian, Titus played a leading part; and Vespasian's principal backer Mucianus, the governor of Syria, whom he helped to reconcile with his father, was impressed by the young man, not only as a dynastic asset but as an able individual. In summer 69 Vespasian entrusted Titus with the suppression of the Jewish revolt, and in the following year, after a siege of four months, Jerusalem fell to his troops, whose destruction of the temple has reverberated through the centuries. The Jewish historian Josephus, who had come over to the Roman side, declared that Titus had tried to save the sanctuary, but an alternative tradition discounted this view. At all events, his treatment of his Jewish prisoners was ruthless.

His capture of Jerusalem earned him a shower of honours. At Memphis in Egypt he permitted himself to be crowned with a diadem. Eastern coinages, too, gave him the prefix of Imperator, which had hitherto been reserved for emperors. Moreover, the senate at Rome offered him an independent Triumph; but this was soon converted into a joint celebration with his father (later memorably recorded by reliefs on the Arch of Titus at Rome). Titus' success caused suspicions that he might become disloyal to his father, but his fidelity in fact remained undiminished, as he demonstrated when he hastened back to Italy in summer 71.

One motive that inspired his rapid return may have been a desire to counteract Mucianus' influence. If so he need not have been anxious, because Vespasian immediately showed in the most unequivocal fashion that Titus was to be both his deputy and his dynastic heir. 'Either my son', he was reported to have said, 'shall be my successor, or no one at all.' Thus on coins of 71, which display the figures of Titus and his younger brother Domitian in military uniform, Titus is described as Caesar and DES(*ignatus*) IMP(*erator*) – meaning nothing less than emperor-designate. Already joint consul with Vespasian in 70, he soon held the joint tribunician power (in 71) and joint censorship as well (from 73–4). Moreover, he quickly became praetorian prefect. Vitellius' guard had been dismissed, and the unit which replaced it was smaller than before, but the post was more important than ever, and Titus, for all his charm, carried out its duties with harsh rigour.

He had to be on the watch against senators and others who deeply disliked Vespasian's adoption of the dynastic principle. But the most serious potential threat to his position came from his own personal relationship with the Jewish princess Berenice. Titus had by this time been married twice, first to Arrecina Tertulla (whose brother he superseded as praetorian prefect) and then, after her death, to Marcia Furnilla, who bore him his only child Flavia Julia. But they had been divorced since 64 or 65, and in Judaea two years later Titus became deeply attached to the rich, beautiful, capable Berenice, ten years older than himself. She enjoyed powerful connexions at the Roman court, but did not visit the capital until 75 when she and her brother King Agrippa II came and received conspicuous honours. Berenice lived openly with Titus in the palace, but this arrangement provoked criticism and shock – people began talking of the new Cleopatra – and after a time he sent her away.

Among the leading critics of Titus was Eprius Marcellus who, in 79, together with Vitellius' former general Caecina, was thought to be plotting against Vespasian's life (see VESPASIAN). So Titus asked Caecina to dinner and had him stabbed to death, while Marcellus, condemned by the senate, cut his own throat. When Vespasian, too, died shortly afterwards, some people believed that Titus had murdered him; HADRIAN was later to credit the rumour, but even that emperor's secretary Suetonius, a great collector of gossip, did not mention such an improbable allegation when he reported Vespasian's death.

However, when Titus came to the throne he was well aware that the ruthless actions he had taken as praetorian prefect, and, in particular, his suppression of the alleged plotters, had left an unpleasant taste; and now therefore – while quietly retaining some of his father's stringent economic measures – he hastened to present a new and more liberal image. The activities of informers (on whom he had relied considerably) were severely discouraged; the charge of high treason was abolished; a further pair of suspected conspirators was calmly ignored; and when Berenice came to Rome again, he promptly sent her away – to their mutual distress.

The short reign of Titus witnessed three serious calamities. First, only one month after his accession the most famous of all the eruptions of Mount Vesuvius overwhelmed the towns and villas on the Gulf of Cumae: Pompeii, Herculaneum, Stabiae and Oplontis. The event was dramatically described in a letter of Pliny the younger, who was staying with his uncle the elder Pliny, admiral of the fleet at nearby Misenum. After the catastrophe Titus went to the afflicted zone and arranged for a senatorial commission to provide whatever help was possible, though his order to plan the restoration of the obliterated sites was never brought into effect. Next, while he was still in Campania supervising the relief work in 80, a very serious fire broke out in Rome, burning for three days and nights and destroying a large number of important buildings and their valuable contents. Titus again provided generous relief. Yet another catastrophe was one of the worst epidemics of plague on record, which the emperor, according to Suetonius, endeavoured to combat not only by medical remedies but by numerous sacrifices, the latter no doubt intended to allay panic among the population.

The other major event of the reign, however, was an occasion for rejoicing – the completion and opening of the Amphitheatrum Flavium, begun by Vespasian and designed to stage gladiatorial combats and the slaughter of wild beasts as well as imitation sea fights, for which the arena could be flooded. This Colosseum, as the edifice later came to be called after the huge statue or colossus of Nero that stood close by, was the earliest amphitheatre in the city to be made entirely of stone, and became the best-known of all the Flavian dynasty's buildings; it has exercised a vast influence on the architects of later Europe. The travertine-faced exterior, with its blend of solid grandeur and grace, is four storeys high in its final form, the top-most being walled and windowed, and the three others comprising colonnades of arched, concrete-cored piers which bear the weight of the mighty structure, so that the engaged Doric, Ionic and Corinthian columns on their surface serve a decorative rather than a functional purpose.

The Colosseum provided accommodation for forty-five thousand seated spectators and another five thousand standing. They reached their places through seventy-six numbered entrance arches; two others were reserved for gladiatorial processions, and two more for the emperor and his entourage. The crowds could be protected from the summer heat by the erection of a huge awning, supported by masts, which sailors drew across the entire circumference. To grace the dedication of the Colosseum, Titus opened the Baths that bear his name, using ground on the Esquiline Hill, which had belonged to Nero's Golden House. Not much is left of them today, but Renaissance sketches show that they formed an early example of the great, symmetrically planned 'imperial' Thermae, subsequently repeated on a larger scale by TRAJAN, CARACALLA and DIOCLETIAN.

Suetonius was no doubt right to identify many winning features in Titus' appearance, character and habits. Though short and somewhat paunchy, he made a dignified impression. A skilful rider and handler of weapons, he could also sing and play the harp, and could compose – and even extemporize – verses in both Latin and Greek. Yet Suetonius was also aware that, before he came to the throne, the young prince had displayed certain personality defects which for the most part, after becoming emperor, he successfully shed; for example, his infatuation with Berenice had created a bad impression. Moreover, while praetorian prefect he had acted with harshness (his cruelty to the Jewish prisoners the biographer does not mention). Titus also acquired a reputation for greed, and conducted riotous parties with his more extravagant friends far into the night; and he owned a whole troop of sexual inverts and eunuchs. But after his accession, we are told, he 'broke off relations with some of his favourite boys – and although they danced well enough to make a name for themselves on the stage, he never attended their public performances'.

Suetonius was also captivated by Titus' winning epigrams: for example, that perhaps slightly too facile declaration, 'Friends, I have lost a day', when he recalled at dinner that ever since he had woken up in the morning he had done nothing for anyone. Indeed Titus as emperor seemed to the biographer a complete paragon: 'the delight and darling of the human race', 'amor ac deliciae generis humani' (by way of contrast with the brother who took his place). The historian Dio Cassius, however, is more judicious about this two-year reign: the reverse of Augustus, he says – who had started brutally and ended with clemency – Titus 'ruled with mildness and died at the height of his glory, whereas if he had lived for a long time, it might have been shown that he owes his present fame more to good fortune than to merit'. A later poet Ausonius, too, concluded that he was 'happy in the brevity of his reign'.

On the last day of the spectacles celebrating his Amphitheatre and his Baths Titus broke down and wept in public. No one knows why; perhaps he knew he was suffering from an incurable disease. At all events, he remained somewhat inactive thereafter, until in the autumn of the following year his health took a fatal turn. On 13 September, at Aquae Cutiliae where his father, too, had met his end, he died – possibly, as Plutarch said, because the waters were too cold for him, although inevitably there were rumours that DOMITIAN had fed him a poisoned fish.

'I have only done one thing wrong', were his reputed last words. Ausonius, for all his doubts about how the emperor might have turned out, could not believe that he needed to express any such regret; but if he did, nobody knew, or knows, what he meant. Was he remorseful because he had conducted an affair with Domitia, the wife of his brother Domitian? But Suetonius thought that the liaison never took place because, if it had, Domitia would not have kept it quiet. Domitian, for his part, is likely to have agreed that he himself was the cause of Titus' pricking conscience, but for another reason: because he was convinced that their father had intended to bequeath him full partnership in the imperial power, but that Titus, who was known to be a very clever imitator of handwriting, had tampered with the will in order to erase this clause. Dio Cassius, on the other hand, favoured a different explanation altogether. He believed that what the dying man regretted was his failure to prevent Domitian from becoming his successor, which he felt sure would be a national disaster. That may well have been what Titus meant; perhaps, too, it was why he had wept earlier.

DOMITIAN
81–96

DOMITIAN (Titus Flavius Domitianus) (81–96), the second son of
VESPASIAN and Flavia Domitilla, was born in 51. At the time of his father's
uprising in the east against VITELLIUS in the summer of 69 he was at Rome,
and remained there unharmed until 18 December. Then he took refuge in the
Capitol with his uncle Flavius Sabinus, the city prefect; but when the Capitol
was overrun by supporters of Vitellius, Domitian, unlike Sabinus, escaped
(later, he was to arrange for this adventure to be recorded by artists and poets).
After the death of Vitellius he was acclaimed as Caesar by the recently arrived
troops of Primus, who, marching from Pannonia, had won the second Battle of
Bedriacum on Vespasian's behalf; and when Vespasian's representative
Mucianus reached the city shortly afterwards to represent his father, it was
Domitian's name that headed the first official dispatches and edicts of the new
regime from Rome.

But friction between the two men soon arose. Mucianus jealously rejected
Domitian's request that Primus should receive a staff appointment. And with
the co-operation of Cerealis, who was conducting the campaign against
Civilis' German and Gallic rebels, Mucianus also ensured that Domitian's
desire to take over the suppression of the revolt – in the hope of rivalling the
exploits of his elder brother TITUS – was frustrated. During the rest of
Vespasian's reign Domitian received a share of outward privileges, including
consulships, the title of Prince of Youth (*Princeps Iuventutis*) and ample
attention on the coinage; for since Titus had no son it was understood that
brother would eventually succeed to brother. Yet their father never gave
Domitian any position of authority, and never allowed him to pursue any
military glory. The young prince pretended that he did not mind, and took
refuge in poetry and the arts, but he was seething with embittered grievances
and frustrated ambitions.

Nor did matters improve when Titus came to the throne. True, he allotted Domitian additional honours, increased his publicity on the coinage still further, and reiterated that he was his partner and prospective heir. However, the official powers which would have given substance to such a partnership were not conferred. Domitian even believed that Vespasian had intended him to reign jointly with his brother, but that the latter had used his expert handwriting skills to remove this provision from their father's will (see TITUS).

When Titus died – probably not by any act of his brother's – Domitian duly ensured his deification, for, whatever their personal relations had been, it was still necessary to exalt the Flavian house. But the new emperor was determined to remedy the glaring inequality between the military achievements of his elders and his own total lack of such qualifications. His wife Domitia Longina was now elevated to the rank of Augusta, and in keeping with this marriage to the daughter of the great general Corbulo, Domitian's overriding aim was to be a triumphant conqueror. In 83 he therefore completed his father's occupation of the Agri Decumates between the upper Rhine and the upper Danube, suppressing the Chatti, annexing Mount Taunus, and extending the frontier to the rivers Lahn and Main. These campaigns, displaying an ingenious combination of forward offensive actions and defensive fortress construction, enabled him to assume the title of Germanicus – no longer as nominee of the German legions (the sinister significance with which VITELLIUS had endowed the term), but as conqueror of the Germans (the old meaning). Thenceforward he habitually wore the costume of a victorious general, even at meetings of the senate. Shortly after this campaign he also substantially raised the pay of all ranks of the army – not as outrageous a step as his critics later suggested, since inflation had reduced the purchasing power of the currency, but a clear sign, all the same, of the army's central role.

Meanwhile Cnaeus Julius Agricola, governor of Britain, who had already been engaged in military operations in Wales and southern Scotland during the previous reign, launched three further successive advances into Caledonia, winning a battle at Mons Graupius, which is perhaps Bennachie in Aberdeenshire. In about 85 he was recalled to Rome, much to the fury of his passionately partisan son-in-law Tacitus, who came to detest the emperor, perhaps because he was conscience-stricken over the high offices he had accepted from him. But Mons Graupius was evidently not the decisive triumph the historian proclaimed it to be, for no territorial annexation had been achieved.

Domitian's next and most ambitious target was Dacia, which had now, after a century of weakness, risen again as a formidable power under its king Decebalus, who in 85 crossed the Danube and slew Oppius Sabinus, the governor of Moesia. Summoning reinforcements Domitian himself marched to the theatre of war, but returned to Rome the following year. Meanwhile, his armies had suffered another defeat in which this time it was Cornelius Fuscus, the praetorian prefect, who lost his life. Roman superiority, however, was duly reasserted in 88 by a victory by Tettius Julianus at Tapae, not far from the Dacian capital of Sarmizegethusa. After holding the Secular Games at Rome, Domitian staged a Triumph for this success.

It could not however be followed up and converted into something permanent. For in 89, the very year of his Triumph, a threatening military revolt broke out among the Roman troops in Upper Germany under the commander of the legions, Lucius Antonius Saturninus. Saturninus' homosexuality was said to have been the reason for his revolt, since Domitian showed a puritanical disapproval of such tastes. But Saturninus was surely in alliance with other disaffected senators, who disliked and feared the emperor's autocratic behaviour. By seizing the savings banks of the two legions at Moguntiacum, Saturninus induced their men to acclaim him as emperor, and his German auxiliaries joined the rebellion as well. But the commander in Lower Germany, Lappius Maximus, loyally resisted the usurpation, and, in a battle near Castellum, Saturninus was killed. Domitian himself, who had marched with lightning rapidity from Rome, arrived on the scene soon afterwards, and the seditious officers were mercilessly punished (although Lappius Maximus, in the hope of limiting the massacre, destroyed Saturninus' files). Only twenty-four days after the revolt had broken out, priests at Rome were already celebrating its collapse.

Next, Domitian, after overhauling the entire military organization of Germany, became preoccupied with the Danube front, where serious trouble was brewing among the German tribes of the Marcomanni and Quadi and the Sarmatian Jazyges. In order to free his hands to deal with them, he felt he first had to renounce his chance of following up the Roman victory over Decebalus; and when the king made an offer of peace Domitian accepted his proposals. Then he felt free to turn against the Jazyges, and duly defeated them, though not with sufficient completeness, he felt, to justify the celebration of a Triumph. His difficulties in the Danube area had given a foretaste of the crises on this frontier which Germans would precipitate in the following century.

Domitian spent a lot of time with the soldiers, and they liked him. To control their centurions, however, he instituted a new kind of army personnel bureau in which full records relating to every centurion were kept up to date; this enabled him to make personal decisions on all their appointments, promotions and transfers after considering all the evidence. This was only part of much firm and meticulous administrative activity directed by his lucid brain. Even Suetonius, who depicts Domitian as a monster, had to conclude that 'he took such care to exercise restraint over the city officials and provincial governors that at no time were these more honest or just'. As the greatest of all later historians of Rome, Theodor Mommsen, observed, he was one of the best administrators who ever governed the Empire.

However, his régime was characterized by a rigidly austere and somewhat terrifying legal correctness. In 83 Domitian sentenced three Vestal Virgins, convicted of immoral behaviour, to the traditional capital penalty, and seven years later the chief of the same order, Cornelia, condemned to death for a similar offence, was walled up alive in an underground cell while her lovers were beaten to death with rods. These alarming punishments conflicted with the strong aversion to bloodshed which Domitian claimed to feel. But they went together with a strong reverence for the antique Roman religion, which caused him to celebrate ancient rituals with ceremonious pomp. He showed a profound and almost obsessive veneration for the Italian goddess Minerva, worshipped in his family's Sabine Hills. It was she, depicted in no less than four separate guises, who formed the main theme of Domitian's coinage, and whose temple was to be the centrepiece of the new imperial Forum he began to build, the Forum Transitorium (later known as the Forum of Nerva).

For Domitian, in the autocratic tradition, proved to be not only an emperor who staged exceptionally costly public shows (defrayed by severe taxation), but also a builder on a grandiose scale. He completed the restoration of the Temple of Jupiter Optimus Maximus on the Capitol, from whose ruins he had escaped in the civil war. He also built a stadium capable of holding thirty thousand spectators; they crowded in to watch the Capitoline Games which, despite his Roman traditionalism, he inaugurated in the Greek, Olympic tradition, comprising contests in literature, music, athletics and horse-racing. Domitian also ordered the construction of a new and more imposing residence for himself on the Palatine Hill, to express his exalted conception of the imperial role. In addition, he built a magnificent villa outside the city looking down on the waters of Lake Albano; in its grounds were a theatre and an amphitheatre, to which large audiences were invited. Yet another work completed during his reign was the Arch of Titus at the head of Rome's Via Sacra, notable for its simple dignified architectural lines and for its relief sculpture illustrating the Triumph of Domitian's father and brother after the capture of Jerusalem. The Jewish spoils shown on the relief include the table for the shew-bread, the seven-branched candlestick or Menorah and the trumpets for summoning the people.

In Judaea itself, Domitian intensified a policy, initiated by Vespasian, of tracking down and eliminating Jews who claimed descent from the royal house of David. In about 95 Gamaliel II, leader of their principal community (now situated at Jamnia), found it necessary, with three other Pharisee leaders, to make a hurried visit to Rome, probably to ward off further repressive action against their compatriots. Meanwhile the Jews at Rome were running into serious trouble. In particular, the *fiscus Iudaicus*, the tax levied on all Jews by Vespasian, was being collected with the utmost rigour; furthermore, many people who had adopted Jewish practices found themselves condemned for 'godlessness' or 'atheism', which meant that they had refused to sacrifice to the divinity of the emperor.

Such punitive practices came clearly to the public eye because their victims included two of the best-known personages in Roman society. They were Flavius Clemens, consul in this very year (95), and his wife Flavia Domitilla the younger – the emperor's cousin and niece respectively. Clemens and Domitilla were probably sympathizers with Judaism rather than Jews in the full sense of the word. Nevertheless, Clemens was executed and Domitilla banished. It may well be that they owed their downfall not so much to their religious beliefs as to their possession of sons, whom the emperor, suspicious of would-be heirs, wished to remove from the scene: the young men were probably killed.

These savage eliminations were not isolated occurrences but climactic displays of Domitian's progressive and finally almost complete alienation from the ruling class of Rome. As he showed its members all too clearly, AUGUSTUS' polite insistence that the senate was the emperor's partner in a restored Republic only incurred his contempt. Domitian preferred to emphasize that he was an absolute monarch – a conviction which his unprecedented title of 85, Perpetual Censor, served to underline. Aware of the senators' hostile reaction – sometimes framed in the terms of free-thinking philosophy – he viewed its members with rising, unremitting suspicion. This process of estrangement gained impetus after the abortive rebellion of Saturninus. All the unpleasantnesses of treason trials were brought back with harrowing stringency, amid a proliferation of imperial spies and informers. Suetonius estimated the casualties among ex-consuls alone at no less than twelve. Alleged conspiracies came thick and fast; and some of them were no doubt genuine enough, since, as Domitian himself perceptively observed, it was an emperor's unhappy fate that nobody would believe stories about plots against his life until they had successfully taken place.

In this atmosphere the prospect of Domitian's own assassination became more and more imminent. He weakened his position further by dismissing his joint praetorian prefects and bringing charges against them; but the men who took their place, Petronius Secundus and Norbanus, not unnaturally felt nervous, especially when they heard that complaints against them were being made to the emperor. So they decided, out of self-protection, to put him out of the way; and various leading men in the provinces and the German commands were also probably involved in the plot. At the capital the conspirators included Domitian's court chamberlain and one of his state secretaries. Prominent in the project too was his wife Domitia Longina, daughter of Nero's leading general Corbulo, who had been divorced by Domitian but subsequently reinstated, though the coinage previously issued in her name was not revived. A certain Stephanus, an ex-slave of Clemens' banished widow, was mobilized to do the deed, with the help of an accomplice, and after a violent hand-to-hand struggle he succeeded in killing him, though he lost his own life in the process.

Domitian, we are told by Suetonius, was greatly addicted to sexual activity, which he described as bed-wrestling. Although he had been in love with his wife Domitia Longina, he later seduced Flavia Julia, the daughter of his brother Titus, but allegedly caused her death by compelling her to have an abortion. This attachment to Julia may have been one of the reasons why Domitia eventually decided he must die. Suetonius describes him as a large, ruddy man but weak-eyed, spindle-legged, hammer-toed and sensitive about his baldness. Although he remained interested in Greek and Latin culture alike, his initial devotion to poetry (if it was not, as Tacitus suggested, a pose) apparently did not prove lasting. He was cold and cruel: there was a story that he liked catching flies and stabbing them with the point of a pen. He took pleasure in gladiatorial fights between women and dwarfs, Dio Cassius adds, and enjoyed asking senators to dinner-parties at which all the equipment and services were black and funereal, with conversation to match, so that guests were paralysed with fright.

The younger Pliny shows him eating heavily and alone before midday and then sitting down, satiated, to watch his dinner-guests eat, as the dishes were slammed down casually in front of them. Pliny also adds that his nerves were so bad that he could not bear to be rowed on Lake Albano near his country palace because he found the noise of the oars an intolerable irritation; so he had to sit in a separate boat towed by the vessel in which the oarsmen were rowing. He also became a very frightened man, since, despite his popularity with the soldiers, it had already become clear some time before his death that the price of his determination to become an absolute ruler was the increased danger to his life. For the immediate future the more discreet methods of asserting power, formulated by his father Vespasian, promised more success.

PART III

THE
ADOPTIVE AND
ANTONINE EMPERORS

THE ADOPTIVE AND ANTONINE EMPERORS

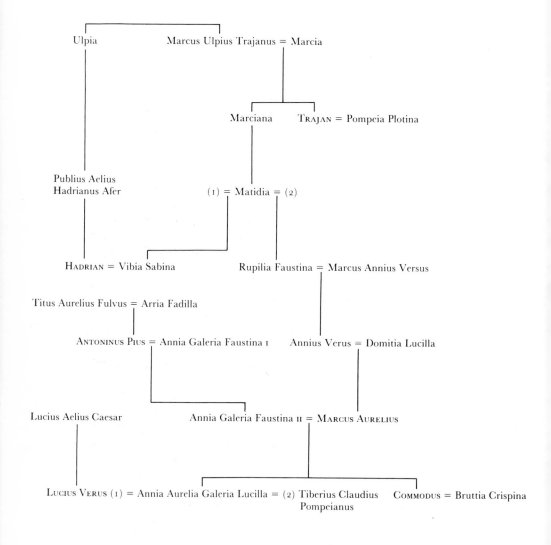

NERVA
96–8

NERVA (Marcus Cocceius) (96–8) was born at Narnia, probably in 30. His grandfather, from whom he took his name, had held the consulship and was a close friend of the emperor TIBERIUS, to whose house the family was also distantly related by marriage. The future emperor, a respected lawyer, was an intimate of NERO, who admired his poetry and rewarded him with triumphal insignia for the part he played in suppressing the conspiracy of Piso in 65. Subsequently Nerva gained high favour with VESPASIAN as well, who chose him as his fellow-consul in 71. In 90 he shared a second consulship with DOMITIAN. But his involvement in the successful plot to assassinate that emperor must be regarded as likely, since he himself was elevated to the throne on the very same day.

Coins and busts depict Nerva as a man with a thin face, a long neck and a long hooked nose. His task as emperor was far from easy, for whereas he was clearly the nominee of the senators, to whom he showed deference – displayed by coins inscribed PROVIDENTIA SENATVS, 'The Foresight of the Senate' – the soldiers violently resented Domitian's murder. Nerva endeavoured to defuse this situation by adopting a genial policy of national reconciliation and useful reform. At the capital, storehouses were built for grain, its distribution was improved, and aqueducts underwent repairs. Exemptions from the inheritance tax were increased, and the unpopular levy of the public post was transferred to the State from the local Italian communities, whose freedom from this burden was proclaimed on the coinage (VEHICVLATIONE ITALIAE REMISSA). Grants of land were made to the poor, and Nerva sold off much of his own private property to pay the cost. Nevertheless, these attempts to gain popularity proved so expensive to the State, as well as to himself, that a five-member commission had to be appointed by the senate in order to recommend reductions of public expenditure.

Moreover, while leaving many of Domitian's measures intact – for example, professional informers still received some encouragement – Nerva also embarked on the task of turning public opinion against the previous régime. Men whom Domitian had banished were brought back, their confiscated property was restored to them, and they were allowed to avenge themselves on those who had supported his régime; while every assistance was given to the blackening of the late emperor's memory. As for the army, it was courted by an accession bonus, recorded by coins which display the unmilitary Nerva addressing them in person (ADLOCVT*io* AV*Gusti*). Another phrase, however, which appeared on the coinage, 'The Harmony of the Armies' (CONCORDIA EXERCITVVM), could not conceal the fact that the soldiers still felt a considerable lack of affection for the new emperor. There was an incipient mutiny at a camp on the Danube; the loyalty of the governor of Syria, commander of a large garrison, was called into question; and it was probably with army backing that the aristocratic Gaius Calpurnius Crassus Frugi Licinianus (related to Galba's heir Piso) reportedly considered forming a plot against Nerva.

The worst trouble arose, however, among the praetorian guard. Pressure from the guardsmen had compelled Nerva to remove their joint prefects, Secundus and Norbanus, because of the part they had played in Domitian's death. But his choice of a partisan and former prefect of Domitian, Casperius Aelianus, to succeed the dismissed prefects was unfortunate, because the new commander associated himself strongly with his soldiers' demand that Secundus and the late emperor's chamberlain, who had likewise been a party to the murder, should be handed over to the guard for execution. When the demonstrators broke into the palace Nerva barred their way; but he was forcibly brushed aside, and the two officials were seized and put to death. Nerva was actually forced to thank the praetorians, in public, for this execution of his friends and supporters. Pliny the younger, an admirer of Nerva who was appalled by these anarchic and humiliating events, felt convinced that the Empire was falling apart, and that the disastrous events of the Year of the Four Emperors (from 68–9) were on the point of being re-enacted.

Nerva also recalled these same events by the measure he took to confront the situation, for, passing over his own well-connected relations, he decided to adopt a man from outside his family as his son and heir. GALBA had done the same; but whereas Galba's nominee Piso had been, except in terms of birth, a nonentity, Nerva selected TRAJAN, the governor of Upper Germany, the most distinguished soldier of the day, giving him powers almost equal to his own. That was in September 97; and in January 98, the emperor died. He had failed to stand up to the army. Yet, on the other hand, he had successfully inaugurated the system of adopting 'the best man' as his heir, a precedent which Galba had tried but failed to institute; and this was the decisive achievement of Nerva's reign. For the four next rulers too, whose remarkable tenures of the imperial office extended over the following eighty years, were peacefully appointed, in every case, by the same means. True, the idea of imperial heredity, as a principle, was not abandoned; but the fortunate chance that one after another of these successive emperors were childless, or were predeceased by their children, meant that the question did not arise.

TRAJAN
98–117

TRAJAN (Marcius Ulpius Trajanus) (98–117) belonged to a family which originally came from Tuder in Umbria, but his ancestors had settled at Italica in Romanized Baetica (southern Spain). His father Marcus Ulpius Trajanus, the first known senator in the family, reached the office of consul, and was governor of Asia and Syria. Nothing is known about the background of the emperor's mother Marcia.

Born probably in about 53, he spent a number of years (as many as ten according to the younger Pliny), as a military tribune (*tribunus militum*), serving in Syria when his father was provincial governor in about 75. After holding the praetorship he commanded a legion, and led it to deal with Saturninus, who had rebelled against DOMITIAN around the year 88; but Trajan's force arrived after the revolt had been put down. Consul in 91, he was governor of Upper Germany in 97 when he learnt of his adoption by NERVA. The choice was likely to be popular with the soldiers, and no doubt enjoyed senatorial and other support at Rome. Nerva died in January 98, and Trajan succeeded to the throne without trouble, duly arranging for divinity to be conferred on his adoptive father.

It was probably soon after his accession that he took certain steps towards evolving a military secret service with the aim of protecting his régime and his person. In particular, the corps of *frumentarii* (couriers in connexion with the grain supply) began to develop significant intelligence duties, operating from a camp (the Castra Peregrinorum) on the Caelian Hill at Rome, and occupying checkpoints on the network of imperial roads far outside the city. Trajan also created a new bodyguard, consisting of mounted soldiers known as the *equites singulares*. Five hundred strong, and later increased to a thousand, they were carefully picked men: mainly Germans and Pannonians from the auxiliary cavalry regiments. Trajan was showing, by this new institution, that he trusted auxiliaries and foreigners no less than he relied upon the mainly Italian praetorian guardsmen.

But these were just preliminary adjustments before he set out on what he believed to be his life's work, the prosecution of conquests that would excel his hero Julius Caesar himself. In the first place, he was determined to go far beyond Domitian's compromise arrangement with King Decebalus of Dacia. Rejecting this sort of peaceful solution, Trajan renewed the war against Decebalus, and in two successive series of operations (101–2 and 105–6) he overran the whole of Dacia and made it into a new province of the Empire. He thus achieved the last major conquest in the history of ancient Rome; and in the process he laid hands on an enormous quantity of plunder, including a great deal of gold.

His troops in action during the campaigns are shown in meticulous detail upon the reliefs spiralling upwards on the Column of Trajan in his Forum at Rome. The imperial army was perhaps 400,000 strong. It included some 180,000 legionaries, forming 30 legions (each larger in size than in earlier times), which were no longer predominantly Italian but consisted almost entirely of conscripted provincials. The auxiliaries were even more numerous, exceeding a total of 200,000. There were also perhaps some 11,000 men in irregular or semi-regular troops, drawn from various nations of the Empire and organized in companies about 300 strong. The creation of these *numeri* (units) or *symmachiarii* (allies), as they were called, represented an attempt to make use of the specialist skills and qualities of particular national groups.

In the east, Trajan rounded off the frontier in 106–12 by creating a new province of Arabia, with its capital at Petra, now in Jordan. But although his contemporary Arrian declared that he at first sought a peaceful solution with Parthia, his overriding purpose was to finish off, once and for all, the problem that country had presented for so long, by nothing short of its total destruction and annexation. In 114 he successfully invaded Armenia and upper (northern) Mesopotamia, and in the following year captured the Parthian capital Ctesiphon and marched on southwards as far as the mouth of the River Tigris on the Persian Gulf. But in 116 the Jews of the Dispersion broke into a wholly unprecedented violent insurrection at a number of centres throughout the near and middle eastern world. In addition to local discontents, Messianic yearnings were a factor, intensified by memories of TITUS' destruction of Jerusalem and the Temple. Moreover, many of the eastern Jews resented the general tax on their communities (the *fiscus Judaicus*), and sympathized with Parthia (under whose rule many of them lived), believing that its eclipse at the hands of the Romans would disrupt their trade. Apparently, however, the initial outbreak occurred among the large Jewish community of Cyrenaica, under a certain Andreas Lukuas (the Lycian?), who first fought the local Greeks and then turned against Roman rule. His rebellion was savagely stamped out, but meanwhile hostilities on a scale that had never before been seen broke out between Greeks and Jews in Egypt as well. A leading general, Quintus Marcius Turbo, who had been sent with a substantial force to crush these disturbances, had to deal, in addition, with a fierce upheaval in Cyprus, where a Jewish leader, Artemion, devastated Salamis. A rising seems also to have started in Judaea itself, though it was quickly and harshly suppressed by Rome's foremost cavalry commander, Lusius Quietus, a Mauretanian.

Meanwhile in the vast, all too sketchily annexed territories of Mesopotamia, Trajan had encountered further and even more serious trouble. In 116 the southern part of the country rose in general revolt. At the same time the Parthian forces rallied, and attacked the Roman base-lines in the north of Mesopotamia, as well as in Adiabene and Armenia. Trajan's lines of communication were menaced and attacked at numerous points. He succeeded, to some extent, in reasserting control, and even set up a puppet Parthian monarch in the palace at Ctesiphon, though this pretender proved unable to establish himself. Before his failure became clear, however, Trajan had set out towards home. But when he had got only as far as Selinus in Cilicia (south-eastern Asia Minor), he became immobilized by dropsy complicated by a stroke, and suddenly died.

During the pauses between his wars he had found time to become an effective civilian administrator. He adhered to traditional constitutional forms and staunchly confirmed the privileges of the senate. The material needs of the people also received his devoted attention. The grain supply was safeguarded and free distributions continued, with more numerous recipients than before. Another of Trajan's achievements was the institution (developed from earlier beginnings) of the *alimenta*, a system of financial subsidies for poor children. Accession gifts, such as Rome's subjects had been obliged to present to previous emperors, were no longer required, and the burden of taxation in the provinces was lightened. Governors of provinces were chosen with particular care – though provincial and local finances, which had in certain areas got out of control, were sometimes entrusted to specially appointed administrators, such as Sextus Quinctilius Valerius Maximus in Achaea, and Pliny the younger in Bithynia. A series of Pliny's surviving letters addressed to the emperor, together with his replies, displays Trajan's humane care for the welfare of the provincials; but this was combined with a suspicious pre-occupation with internal security, and a paternalistic tendency to interfere in the unsatisfactory affairs of the ostensibly self-governing cities. In one of these letters, Pliny enquired how to deal with the sect of the Christians. 'They are not to be hunted out,' Trajan answered. 'Any who are accused and convicted should be punished, with the proviso that if a man says he is not a Christian and makes it obvious by his actual conduct – namely by worshipping our gods – then, however suspect he may have been with regard to the past, he should gain pardon from his repentance.' This reply, tempering firmness with a distaste for excessive severity, shows that he was concerned to cool the temperature rather than add to its heat.

Throughout his reign there was an ever-increasing programme of public works, including a great network of roads and bridges throughout the Empire. His colony founded in 100 for ex-soldiers at Thamugadi in Numidia, designed on camp lines with senate-house, basilica and Forum at the intersection of the two provincial streets, provides the most complete Roman remains to be seen anywhere in Africa. In Italy, his imposing Aqua Trajana, the last of the aqueducts serving the capital, substantially increased its inhabitants' daily supply of water. Fed by springs in the region of Lake Sabatinus, the aqueduct extended to the city's Janiculum Hill, driving the industrial mills in the area, and then passed to the other bank of the river and ended, as recent discoveries have shown, on the Esquiline Hill.

The Esquiline was also the location of Trajan's Baths, built on top of the main residential wing of Nero's Golden House and inaugurated in 109, two days before the Aqua Trajana. Although not much can be seen of the Baths now, their plan can be approximately reconstructed. It is clear that in sheer bulk they exceeded anything that had been seen before; that is to say, they were the earliest of the city's really extensive thermal establishments, of which eleven were eventually constructed. The bathing accommodation which formed the nucleus of Trajan's edifice, adjusted for a variety of different air and water temperatures, was three times the size of the adjoining Baths of Titus. It centred upon an enormous cross-vaulted central hall, surrounded by an outer precinct which housed the manifold social activities of a community centre. This massive, up-to-date, utilitarian and monumental *tour de force* was the work of Trajan's architect Apollodorus of Damascus, a master of the contemporary medium of concrete which made it possible for these soaring arches, apses and vaults to be constructed with such confidence.

Apollodorus was also the planner of the Forum of Trajan, the latest, most complex and most magnificent of the Fora added to the original Forum Romanum by a series of emperors. It occupied an approximate rectangle (182 by 120 yards), created by deeply cutting back the entire lower slopes of the Quirinal Hill. Trajan's Forum included Greek and Latin libraries, which, like most of the Forum, are no longer to be seen. The Column which was erected between the two libraries to celebrate the conquest of Dacia, however, still stands. Nearby was the apsed, colonnaded Hall of the Basilica Ulpia; and the extensive colonnaded open space of the Forum, flanked to north and south by semi-circular recesses, contained an equestrian statue of the emperor himself.

The northern recess formed the curved façade of the Markets of Trajan which lay beyond and above. Covering three levels of terraces, and comprising more than a hundred and fifty shops and offices, the markets were built of concrete faced with durable, kiln-baked, heat-resistant brick, which was now allowed to show itself, uncovered by marble or stone, as the decorative outer surface of the building. The focal point of the precinct was a market hall, consisting of a single cross-vaulted rectangular space, twenty-eight yards long and ten across.

Numerous slogans on Trajan's coins, and the *Panegyricus* written by the younger Pliny, echo the emperor's desire to be the servant and benefactor of humankind, the earthly vicegerent of heaven. His aim was to rule not as *dominus* or lord but as *princeps*, the appellation devised by AUGUSTUS; and the term is united with his special title 'Optimus' (the best) – reminiscent of Jupiter himself, who was known as *Optimus Maximus* – on a great series of coins issued from 103 onwards. His military policy, in the end, had scarcely fulfilled the highest hopes; nonetheless, senators of the later Empire felt justified in voicing the desire that new emperors should be 'more fortunate than Augustus, better than Trajan' *(felicior Augusto, melior Traiano)*. Indeed Eutropius, who relates this, makes it clear that he even ranks Trajan *above* Augustus, admiring him particularly because he respected the prerogatives of the senate. Another historian, Florus, regards his reign as a miracle of Roman rebirth.

Trajan was a tall and well-built man, with an air of serious dignity enhanced by early greyness. 'He was most conspicuous', pronounced Dio Cassius,

> for his justice, for his bravery, and for the simplicity of his habits. . . . He did not envy or slay any one, but honoured and exalted all good men without exception, and hence he neither feared nor hated any of them. To slanders he paid very little heed, and he was no slave of anger. He refrained from taking other people's money, and from unjust murders. He expended vast sums on wars and vast sums on works of peace; and while making very many urgently needed repairs to roads and harbours and public buildings, he drained no one's blood in any of these undertakings. . . . He joined others in the chase and in banquets, as well as in their labours and plans and jests. . . . He would enter the houses of citizens, sometimes even without a guard, and enjoy himself there. Education in the strict sense he lacked, when it came to speaking, but its substance he both knew and applied. I know, of course, that he was devoted to boys and to wine. And if he had ever committed or endured any base or wicked action as the result of these practices, he would have incurred censure. As it was, however, he drank all the wine he wanted, yet remained sober. And in his relation with boys he harmed no one.

Trajan and his family exemplified the rise of the provincial element within the ruling class. His austere-looking wife Pompeia Plotina, who was related to him – and who attended his death-bed – came from Nemausus in southern Gaul (which was as Romanized as his own Spanish homeland, or more so). She and the emperor's sister Ulpia Marciana were both made Augusta in about 105; and when Marciana died later in the year she was deified, and her daughter Matidia (who died in 119) received the title of Augusta in her place. Deification was also conferred on Trajan's father.

HADRIAN
117–38

HADRIAN (Publius Aelius Hadrianus) (117–38) was born in 76 – probably at Rome, though his family lived in Italica in Baetica, to which they had originally come from Picenum in north-eastern Italy. He was the son of Publius Aelius Hadrianus Afer (meaning 'African', perhaps recalling official service in Mauretania) and of Domitia Paulina of Gades; his father's father, a member of the Roman senate, had married TRAJAN's aunt Ulpia. After Hadrian's father had died in 85, he was entrusted to the care of two guardians, Publius Acilius Attianus and the future emperor Trajan himself, whose childless household he joined.

Enrolling in the army, he served as military tribune (*tribunus militum*) of legions stationed in Lower Pannonia, Lower Moesia and Upper Germany. Then, following Trajan's accession, Hadrian accompanied him to Rome, where in 100 he married Vibia Sabina, the daughter of Trajan's niece Matidia Augusta. Next he served as quaestor, staff officer, legionary commander and praetor in the First and Second Dacian Wars respectively, subsequently becoming governor of Lower Pannonia and, in 108, consul. He was appointed governor of Syria during the Parthian War of the following decade, and in 117 was designated for a second consulship to take effect the following year.

Trajan died at Selinus on 8 August; on the 9th it was announced at Antioch that he had adopted Hadrian as his son and successor; but it was not until the 11th that Trajan's death was reported. His widow Pompeia Plotina endorsed the adoption, but there were grave doubts as to whether the dying emperor had ever performed it – doubts not resolved by coinages which were immediately issued to proclaim the event, including one describing Hadrian as Caesar but not yet Augustus (HADRIANO TRAIANO CAESARI).

Whether he had in fact been adopted or not, the army hailed him as emperor, and the senate (although some of its members felt that they themselves possessed superior qualifications) had no option but to do likewise.

Hadrian addressed the senators with respectful tact, swearing that he would never put any of them to death and requesting the deification of his predecessor. Then, however, he struck out on his own, putting into effect an eastern military policy in direct contrast to Trajan's. He was convinced by the recent widespread Mesopotamian disturbances that his predecessor's aggressive endeavours had outrun the Empire's financial and human resources; so he abruptly abandoned Trajan's expansionist ambitions, renouncing his newly created provinces and leaving their territories (insofar as Roman authority prevailed there any longer) in the hands of client-kings. On the northern frontiers, however, to which he next proceeded in person to suppress the Roxolani and other Sarmatian peoples (who were of Iranian origin), he confirmed Trajan's annexation of Dacia, which was subdivided into two provinces and then into three.

Even before his intentions about the eastern frontier were fully known, there had been signs of dangerous internal opposition to his régime. His former guardian Attianus, now praetorian prefect, warned him of three powerful figures who might well become seditious. One of them, Gaius Calpurnius Crassus – who had also been no friend of Trajan's – met his death, it was claimed, without instructions from Hadrian. As for the other two possible conspirators, the emperor preferred to ignore them; but in 118 there were reports of a far more serious plot, which caused Hadrian, spending the winter at Nicomedia in Bithynia, to hasten to Rome. By then, however, the senate itself had dealt with the matter by executing four eminent ex-consuls who had been intimate with Trajan, including the military man Lusius Quietus (removed by Hadrian from Judaea) and the wealthy and well-connected Gaius Avidius Nigrinus, who had been considered a possible successor to Hadrian. It is probable that this group had objected strongly to the new emperor's frontier retreat. Hadrian asserted, once again, that he had never sanctioned or known of their deaths, and put the blame on Attianus, who was replaced but promoted to consular rank. The senators remained sceptical and unforgiving, in the belief that Hadrian had broken his promise never to execute any of their number.

Before long Hadrian began to make journeys round the Empire, and he continued to do so, becoming the greatest of all imperial travellers. Between 121 and 132 he spent an enormous amount of time personally touring the length and breadth of the provinces, discovering the problems of their populations at first hand, gaining their confidence and satisfying their needs and requests. Then, during the next year or so, he issued a varied and unparalleled series of coinages celebrating all these regions of the Roman world by name, and distinguishing them by different designs that personified the salient features of each. The coins refer to his arrival (*adventus*) at the various centres (depicted by scenes of religious sacrifice) or stress his role as their restorer (*restitutor*), raising a kneeling female figure to her feet. On these issues the provinces are represented as women of peaceful or warlike appearance, wearing the costume of their own country and carrying its attributes. Stress is deliberately laid on the local characteristic: the cities of Asia, the games of Greece, the ibis of Egypt, the curved sword of Asia.

Hadrian was the first occupant of the throne to see his territories from any but a purely Roman standpoint. The Empire was to be a living organism not only at its centre but also in all its parts; not merely a collection of conquered, subject lands but a commonwealth in which each individual district and nation possessed its own proud identity. His keen, incessant observation of local conditions was prompted by a desire to show that he appreciated provincial aspirations – of which he himself sought to be regarded as the universal symbol and guide.

Above all else, Hadrian was determined to maintain a constant, expert contact with the armies that he visited, in order to ensure that they remained in a condition of maximum skilled efficiency and readiness. For these armies were now facing a somewhat novel situation. The policy of avoiding external expansion meant an increased reliance on the existing frontiers, which in turn involved a major strengthening of the frontier defences. In consequence, more than ever before the military system of the empire was based on armies permanently located on its borders, along which ever more effective defence works were built. One of the first fruits of this policy, following a minor reverse on the British frontier, was what is today the best-preserved of all the Empire's fortifications, Hadrian's Wall in northern Britain which extends from the Tyne to the Solway – partly of stone and partly of turf, punctuated by towered gates and turrets, fronted by a V-shaped ditch and manned by fifteen thousand auxiliaries watching over the still unconquered Caledonian north. In Germany and Raetia, too, he erected defences wherever no natural barriers, such as rivers, were to be found. These ramparts, including a two-hundred-mile section of the German frontier in the Rhine-Danube re-entrant, consisted of wooden palisades set in steep-sided trenches and fastened together by cross-planking.

Hadrian's concentration on frontier defence created a more and more stationary situation, in which the civilian settlements beside the fortress-camps grew in size and in economic prosperity. Moreover, the peacetime tasks of a non-military nature, which the Roman soldiers themselves undertook as part of their duties, were becoming increasingly varied and extensive: we find them looking after horses, requisitioning clothes, escorting the grain supply, quarrying stones, watching cattle. The growth of these non-operational tasks was encouraged because the legionary forces, which generally stood to the rear of the frontier line fulfilling the role of a reserve, were not normally available for transfer *en bloc* from one territory to another. Hadrian expanded Trajan's regular or irregular units (*numeri*), converting them into permanent units of the Roman army. This evident distinction between mobile and static troops pointed the way to the division between field and frontier forces which was to take place in the later Empire. Nevertheless, mobility was maintained by temporary transfers of smaller detachments (*vexillationes*) from one legionary base to another.

To all these troops Hadrian, on the occasion of his visits, devoted an unflagging personal attention which neglected no possible aspect or detail. He was insistent on military discipline, uniquely celebrating this virtue on his coinage (DISCIPLINA AV*Gusti*); nevertheless, his recurrent presence among his armies, organizing and sharing their manoeuvres and reviews and making himself acquainted with their lives, habits, billets and eating conditions, greatly endeared him to the soldiery. His coinages in honour of the provinces included a unique series commemorating each of his ten principal armies, endowing each with a special character of its own (a numismatic innovation abandoned by his successors, who probably feared it might encourage separatist tendencies).

Fighting during Hadrian's reign was infrequent. But there was one serious war towards the end of his life, a Jewish outbreak – not among the Jews of the Dispersion, as in the previous reign, but a Second Revolt in the homeland of Judaea itself, repeating the rebellion crushed by VESPASIAN and TITUS. For Hadrian, whose cosmopolitan outlook was unsympathetic to Jewish separatism, had established a Roman colony and temple in Jerusalem, now renamed Aelia Capitolina after his own Aelian family;* and this foundation caused great anger among the Jews, who in 132 broke into open insurrection under an inspiring leader, Simeon Bar Kosiba (nicknamed Bar Kochba, 'son of a star'). The rebels took Jerusalem and issued their own coinage, and it took three years to overcome their uprising. During this period the emperor visited Judaea, once if not twice, and he is likely to have been present when Jerusalem finally fell in 134. The surviving militants were rounded up at Bethar the following year, and severe measures of reprisal included a total prohibition of circumcision.

Hadrian's heavy-handed method of dealing with the Jews was untypical, for his imperial administration in general, though not particularly innovative, was careful and helpful. Following on from Trajan's extravagant military expenditure, he took a particular interest in public finance, seeking not so much niggardly retrenchment or confiscation (indeed he burnt the records of huge quantities of bad debts to the treasury) as the elimination of unnecessary costs.

Hadrian was also deeply and beneficially interested in the law, appointing a famous African jurist, Lucius Salvius Julianus, to undertake the collection and

*Or this colony was founded after the revolt.

revision of the successive edicts that the annually elected praetors had for centuries pronounced at the outset of their years of office. Julianus' publication of these edicts helped the poor (*humiliores*), who, although always discriminated against in the courts in favour of the privileged *honestiores*, could at least now achieve some understanding of the legal safeguards to which they were entitled.

Roman law, under Hadrian's initiatives, was entering upon its Golden Age, the most creative and influential period of its history. Jurisdiction, too, displayed significant progress, exemplified by the appointment of four circuit judges to administer law in Italy (a well-meaning measure, despite protests that it weakened the authority of the senate). Moreover, to improve the standard of justice in his own court at Rome, Hadrian gave more formal shape to the group of legal assessors from whom rulers had habitually sought counsel, incorporating them into the imperial council or *consilium principis*. This now assumed a more formal character, in place of the friends whom previous emperors, from AUGUSTUS onwards, had called together less officially for advice. Salvius Julianus, pre-eminent among these advisers of Hadrian, became a leading senator and was elected to a consulship in 175; the assessors also included knights. Nor was this the only important employment Hadrian found for men of this rank, since he often appointed them to the principal secretaryships of the imperial bureaucracy, which took increasingly effective shape. His relations with the senate, on the other hand, unsatisfactory from the outset, became more and more strained as his reign drew to a close, partly, no doubt, because of a deterioration in his health – tuberculosis and dropsy have been conjectured – which affected his temper as well.

The succession was a major problem, for Hadrian, whose relations with his wife Vibia Sabina (who died in 128) were probably cool, had no heir. In 136 the emperor adopted as his son and presumptive successor an elegant, luxurious senator in his mid-thirties, Lucius Ceionius Commodus, thenceforward known as Lucius Aelius Caesar; and he was appointed to the governorship of Pannonia. In the same year, Hadrian ordered the deaths of his aged brother-in-law Julius Ursus Servianus and his grandson, who was being groomed, the emperor suspected, as a rival candidate to Aelius. In January, 138, however, Aelius died. A month later Hadrian adopted ANTONINUS PIUS; and in order to provide for the succession on an even more long-term basis he required Antoninus to adopt two sons in his turn, MARCUS AURELIUS and LUCIUS VERUS (the son of Aelius Caesar), aged seventeen and seven respectively. Then followed the death of Hadrian himself at Baiae, on 10 July. He was buried in the mausoleum which he had erected for the purpose at Rome (and which has survived as the Castel Sant' Angelo). The senate accepted Antoninus' request that he should be deified, but only with reluctance (see ANTONINUS).

The character of Hadrian reflected the key features of the age in an accentuated form. He was an initiate of religious Mysteries, and took a keen interest in astrology and magic. He shared the contemporary tastes not only for indefatigable sightseeing but also for literary activity, with a flavour of archaism: he enjoyed the company of scholars, and was himself something of a writer; a short, moving poem he addressed to his soul still survives. He was also a good painter, and his interest in artistic matters inspired a whole new trend of Greek-influenced Hadrianic Art. From now on imperial portrait-busts have curly beards, and often show a colourful, idealistic style, based on strongly contrasted highlights and shadows. A few portraits succeeded in reproducing the energetic nervousness of Hadrian himself. But more remarkable are the statues and heads of his favourite youth Antinous, whose dramatic death in the Nile in 130 led to an astonishing wave of religious feeling throughout the east – where he was enrolled in the ranks of the gods. For the portrayal of the new deity, the classical Greek tradition which Hadrian so profoundly venerated was summoned up from the past once again to perpetuate Antinous' dreamy gaze and voluptuous contours, expressing sorrow for youth which passes and beauty which perishes.

Hadrian's aesthetic aims and ambitions also found memorable expression in the architecture of his reign, and most of all in the extensive residence he created for himself on the southern olive-clad slopes beside Tibur in the Roman countryside. The group of loosely related or independent buildings which constituted this 'Villa of Hadrian' was intended to recall the sites and buildings which the emperor had admired on his travels, but this was only a modest pretext for a whole collection of bold and original forms. The creations of some gifted and experimental architect, inspired by the emperor's enquiring, restless brain, these adventurous structures ingeniously exploit the potentialities of an uneven site, displaying total technical mastery of their concrete, brick-faced material. Curvilinear shapes of many varieties abound; there is hardly a straight or obvious line anywhere to be seen.

With the building of Hadrian's Pantheon in the Field of Mars at Rome, his architectural revolution reached its zenith. Completely reshaping an earlier temple (erected by Augustus' friend Agrippa), Hadrian's architect erected a circular building; shrines of this shape had been known from very ancient times, but the discovery of concrete had now made it possible to create round structures of infinitely bolder dimensions and design. Behind a huge, rectangular, colonnaded portico stands the rotunda itself, as broad as it is high. Beneath its floating dome, lit by a sun-like central opening and spangled by reliefs of stars, the interior wall is broken by rectangular and semi-circular recesses and vaulted niches, confidently lightening the weight of the concrete framework. The same assurance is displayed by the five ranges of coffering inserted in the dome, which was so strong that it survived, intact, even the removal of its gilded bronze tiles in 663. The Pantheon was perhaps the first major monument ever to be composed as an interior: the decisive factor had ceased to be the solid masonry and was now, instead, the space it enclosed. Unlike the temples of the Greeks, which did not admit worshipping congregations to their interiors, Hadrian's Pantheon was a building for people to assemble in.

In a different part of the capital, near the Forum Romanum, Hadrian erected another spectacular shrine of exceptional size, the Temple of Venus and Rome. He also built a huge temple of the deified Trajan, in Trajan's Forum. And at Athens, too, he was responsible for construction work of major importance, notably the rebuilding, on a massive scale, of the Temple of Olympian Zeus. This exhibited to perfection the thought of Hadrian, who although truly Roman was so markedly phil-Hellenic.

ANTONINUS PIUS
138–61

ANTONINUS PIUS (Titus Aurelius Fulvus Boionius Antoninus) (138–61) was born in 86 at Lanuvium in Latium. His family had come from Nemausus in southern Gaul, but moved to Rome where his grandfather and father (both named Titus Aurelius Fulvus) each attained consulships, the former receiving this honour on two occasions in addition to the office of city prefect. The emperor's mother was Arria Fadilla, whose father Arrius Antoninus, also from Southern Gaul, had likewise twice been consul. When NERVA became emperor, he was said to have offered the new ruler his condolences.

Antoninus spent his youthful years at Lorium, not far from Rome; after his father's early death his education was arranged by his two grandfathers. In his twenties he married Annia Galeria Faustina (Faustina the elder), daughter of Marcus Annius Verus. After holding the quaestorship and praetorship he became consul in 130. Shortly afterwards he was appointed by HADRIAN as one of the four circuit judges whose duty was to administer law in Italy; he acted in this capacity in Etruria and Umbria, where he owned extensive land. As proconsul of Asia (at some date between 133 and 136), he earned an excellent reputation, and on returning to Rome was appointed a member of the reconstituted imperial council. When Lucius Aelius Caesar, Hadrian's adoptive son and heir, died in January 138, the emperor's choice fell on Antoninus, who, after prolonged consideration, accepted the prospect, and was adopted by Hadrian on 25 February, receiving the tribunician power and a post of supreme administrative power (*imperium*) soon afterwards. Coins were issued for him under the name of Titus Aelius Caesar Antoninus. At the same time he himself was required to adopt MARCUS AURELIUS and LUCIUS VERUS, who eventually became his successors. Throughout Hadrian's illness during the months that followed, Antoninus was the virtual ruler of the State, and when the emperor died on 10 July he peacefully ascended the throne.

His reign began with a certain amount of embarrassment, because when Antoninus requested the deification of his predecessor and the ratification of his official actions, the senate proved unresponsive on both counts, re-membering that Hadrian had diminished its authority and executed some of its members. Finally, however, for fear of army intervention if the new régime suffered a setback, the senators complied – in return for the abolition of the unpopular circuit judges in the Italian peninsula. Furthermore, even if some of them regarded Antoninus as no better than themselves in origin and talents, his deferential attitude to their order soon prompted them to confer on him the unusual title of 'Pius', honouring his religious and patriotic dutifulness. In accordance with custom, Antoninus at first thought fit to refuse the title of Father of the Country (Pater Patriae), but in 139 he accepted the appellation, together with a second consulship, followed by a third and fourth in 140 and 145.

The *Historia Augusta* lays great stress on Antoninus' love of peace, and it is true that his reign was largely peaceful – yet not entirely so, for some of the provinces experienced unrest, and sections of the frontiers were uneasy. In northern Britain the suppression of an uprising was followed by the expansion of imperial territory, marked by the construction of a new rampart, the Wall of Antoninus, extending for thirty-seven miles from the Firth of Forth to the River Clyde. The wall was of turf, standing on a cobbled foundation fourteen feet wide, behind a deep ditch. The garrison was stationed in small forts only about two miles apart, instead of the larger and more widely separated forts of Hadrian's Wall. However, trouble fomented by the tribe of the Brigantes in about 154 necessitated the temporary withdrawal of certain troops from Antoninus' defences, a step which resulted in the destruction of forts by raiding tribes. These events apparently prompted Antoninus to evict some or most of the population from between the two walls. Transplanted to Germany, they were settled on either side of the River Neckar and required to assist in the defence of the adjoining frontier, which, as in Britain, was pushed forward and marked by forts, standing behind a palisade equipped with stone watch-towers.

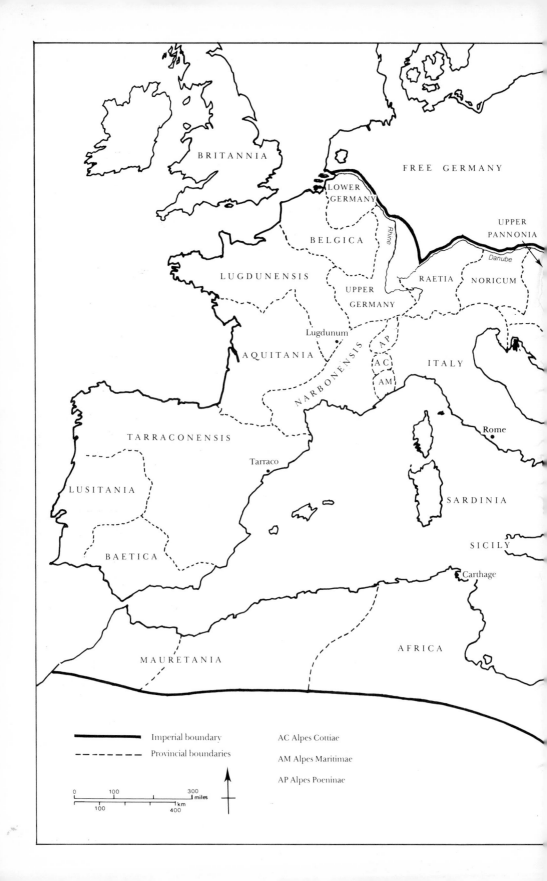

BRITANNIA

FREE GERMANY

LOWER
GERMANY

BELGICA

UPPER
PANNONIA

Rhine

LUGDUNENSIS

UPPER
GERMANY

RAETIA

NORICUM

Danube

Lugdunum

AP

AQUITANIA

NARBONENSIS

AC

AM

ITALY

Rome

TARRACONENSIS

Tarraco

SARDINIA

LUSITANIA

SICILY

BAETICA

Carthage

MAURETANIA

AFRICA

Imperial boundary

Provincial boundaries

AC Alpes Cottiae

AM Alpes Maritimae

AP Alpes Poeninae

0   100   300
                         miles
                         km
   100   400

- Pitvus

LOWER
PANNONIA
POROLISSENSIS
DACIA
UPPER DACIA
LOWER DACIA

BLACK SEA

LOWER
MOESIA

Danube

UPPER
MOESIA

ILLYRICUM

THRACIA

BITHYNIA/PONTUS

GALATIA

CAPPADOCIA

CILICIA

Euphrates

MACEDONIA

ASIA

Antioch
SYRIA

EPIRUS

ACHAEA

LYCIA/PAMPHYLIA

SYRIA-
PALAESTINA

M E D I T E R R A N E A N

S E A

CRETE

AND

Alexandria

A R A B I A

CYRENAICA

Nile

EGYPT

Meanwhile large areas of north Africa were suffering from brigand marauders. They were gradually driven out of Numidia, but in Mauretania reinforcements had to be brought in to launch a large-scale campaign of repression, in the course of which in about 150 the dissident Mauri were driven into the extreme western borders of the country. In Egypt, about four years later, the rigorous imposition of forced labour caused the flight of natives from their homes, followed by an armed uprising which had to be put down; and in 158 a Dacian rebellion was suppressed.

There may also have been trouble in Judaea. There Antoninus Pius soon modified, without completely abandoning, his predecessor's veto on circumcision; that is to say he allowed Jews to circumcise their sons but forbade them to admit converts to the rite, thus weakening Jewish competition with the actively proselytizing Christians. Moreover, the ban debarring Jews from entry into Jerusalem was maintained, and indeed enforced by the construction of a ring of military posts round the city.

As often as possible, however, Antoninus employed diplomacy rather than arms in settling any disputes that arose, notably in dealing with the traditional Parthian foe. And in spite of the various military operations that had to be conducted, the absence of any major emergency enabled him to reduce the privileges of the fleet and auxiliaries, whose children, born in service, ceased to receive Roman citizenship automatically as they had before. Thenceforward, instead, they could only become enfranchised by joining the legions – so that the new restriction was intended to encourage legionary recruiting.

Nevertheless, Antoninus differed markedly from his predecessor, for his interest lay primarily not in the provinces but in Italy, which he intended to confirm and reinstate as the sovereign country of the Roman world. His coinage, although taking due account of provincial interests (for example, BRITANNIA was the prototype of the figure still depicted on Britain's fifty-pence piece), reflected this shift of emphasis strongly. It was reflected again in a series of practical measures within the Italian peninsula. Money was spent, generously but without extravagance, on harbours, bridges, baths and amphitheatres, and the charitable endowments inaugurated by TRAJAN were further developed by a scheme to assist Italian orphan girls, known as the Puellae Faustinianae after Antoninus' wife (she had died in 140 or 141 and, although later tradition questioned her character, received not only deification but an unparalleled mass of commemorative coinage and other honours). Antoninus himself never once left Italy throughout the course of his reign; he enjoyed living the life of a country gentleman in his villa at Lanuvium. Rome, too, was the special focus of his attention, for there he made generous distributions and initiated public spectacles, while the impending nine hundredth anniversary of the traditional foundation date of the city inspired him to issue a series of large brass commemorative medallions paying patriotic honour to the legendary origins of his people.

86

Antoninus' preferential treatment of Italy and the capital was welcome to the senate, with which, having overcome any preliminary hesitations that there may have been among its members, he enjoyed friendly relations (a certain Atilius Titianus showed signs of starting a plot but Antoninus directed that his accomplices should not be sought out). His suppression of the four circuit judges had ostensibly restored full senatorial control over the country. Yet Antoninus was conscious of the senate's essential weakness, and while paying its members every outward respect he reserved for his imperial council the discussion of matters of any real importance. The four successive praetorian prefects who held office during his reign were all members of this council, and it was significant for the future that they were all eminent lawyers as well. The first of them, Marcus Gavius Maximus, held office for twenty years; and provincial governors often stayed where they were for little short of a decade. Antoninus' natural, peaceful death in 161 marked the end of a reign that had been beneficent and not unprogressive, though, quietly, the process of centralization continued – and the Pax Romana, as has been seen, was not quite as ubiquitous as eulogists liked to suggest.

One such eulogist was the Greek popular philosopher Aelius Aristides of Hadriani in Mysia, who was linked with the court because he shared a tutor with the young Marcus Aurelius. Aristides' oration *To Rome* is passionately pro-Roman. 'It is you', he declares to a personification of Antoninus' Rome,

who have best proved the general assertion that Earth is mother of all and common fatherland. Now indeed it is possible for Hellene or non-Hellene, with or without his property, to travel easily wherever he will. . . . Homer said, 'Earth common to all', and you have made it come true. . . . Thus it is right only to feel pity for those outside your hegemony – if indeed there are any – because they lose such blessings.

This roseate view of the second-century world was endorsed by the historian Edward Gibbon in his *Decline and Fall of the Roman Empire* of 1776. 'If', he declared, 'a man were called upon to fix the period in the history of the world during which the condition of the human race was most happy and prosperous, he would, without hesitation, name that which elapsed from the death of Domitian to the accession of Commodus' (AD 96–180). Antoninus Pius can aptly be taken as the symbol and prime exemplar of this imperial Golden Age. If we limit the 'human race' to the Roman Empire, and consider how well many of its inhabitants were faring, Gibbon was probably not too wide of the mark. Yet subsequent historians have queried his assertion, pointing out that the slave population, for example, and the mass of depressed, illiterate agricultural workers, could scarcely be described as 'happy and prosperous', and that the stagnancy and bureaucratic regimentation that were to be so apparent in the following century were already becoming perceptible as early as the time of Antoninus.

Nevertheless there can be no doubt about the lofty nature and intentions of the emperor himself. Panegyrics of these rulers, of which there were many at most epochs, have to be approached with a considerable degree of sceptical suspicion. But the unlimited praise Antoninus received after his death, in the *Meditations* of his adoptive son Marcus Aurelius, does suggest a very attractive character. 'Remember his qualities', urged Aurelius, 'so that when your last hour comes your conscience may be as clear as his.'

MARCUS AURELIUS
161–80

MARCUS AURELIUS (161–80) was born in 121, and given the name of Marcus Annius Verus. His paternal great-grandfather, Annius Verus from Uccubi in Baetica, had established the family fortunes by gaining the rank of senator and praetor. The emperor's grandfather was three times consul, and his father Annius Verus married Domitia Lucilla, whose wealthy family owned a tile factory (inherited by Marcus) in the neighbourhood of Rome. In his earlier years he bore the additional names of Catilius Severus in honour of his step-grandfather on his mother's side, consul in 110 and 120.

As a boy he attracted the favourable attention of the emperor HADRIAN, who nicknamed him 'Verissimus', made him a priest of the Salian order when he was only eight years old, and entrusted his education to the best teachers of the day, including the famous Fronto, who taught him Latin literature. When Hadrian adopted Lucius Aelius Caesar in 136, Marcus was allocated Aelius' daughter as his future bride; but after Aelius had died, ANTONINUS, whom Hadrian adopted in his place in 138, jointly adopted two sons in his turn. One was the young Marcus, who was the nephew of Antoninus' wife Faustina the elder, and now assumed the names Marcus Aurelius Caesar (Aurelius being one of Antoninus' names); the other youth was LUCIUS VERUS (as he was later called), the son of the late Aelius.

Following the accession of Antoninus Pius, Marcus Aurelius' engagement to the daughter of Aelius was broken off and in 139 he became betrothed instead to Antoninus' own daughter Annia Galeria Faustina the younger, whom he married six years later. He held the consulship in 140 and 145 as the colleague of his adoptive father, and in 146 was invested with powers indicating his position as heir to the throne (tribunician power – *tribunicia potestas* – and a proconsular post of superior authority or *imperium* outside Rome). At about the same time, much to the disappointment of Fronto, he abandoned rhetoric for Stoic philosophy (taught him by Junius Rusticus), which thenceforward exerted a dominant influence on his life. On his death-bed in 161 Antoninus Pius transferred the imperial authority into his hands. The new ruler, already named Aurelius after him and now assuming the name Antoninus as well, requested the senate to appoint Verus as his full colleague, thus introducing a novel concept (see below, LUCIUS VERUS). Trouble soon appeared on several frontiers. In the east a major crisis arose when the Parthian king Vologeses III (148–92) marched into Armenia and defeated two imperial armies in turn. After a large relieving force had been sent out under the titular leadership of Lucius Verus, from 163–4 Armenia was overrun by Roman generals and made a protectorate; and thus were revived TRAJAN's claims to control territory beyond the Euphrates. To celebrate the Triumph of the joint emperors in 166 the two young sons of Aurelius, COMMODUS aged five and Annius Verus aged three, received the title of Caesar and took part in the procession.

By this time on the northern frontier, however, the most formidable German tribes ever seen had broken across the Danube, which now had a garrison of ten Roman legions, compared with four on the Rhine. This migration caused a series of events which permanently transformed the Empire. It was the first time that the Romans had been forced to confront tribesmen determined to settle in their own territory; and furthermore, these frontier peoples were now themselves under pressure from convulsive population movements far to the north. First, in 162 the west German tribe of the Chatti burst into Upper Germany. They were dealt with, but about four years later a far more serious situation developed when the comparatively Romanized Marcomanni of Boiohaemum, together with the Langobardi and others, flooded across the Danube, while a branch of the Sarmatians collusively moved to the attack between the Danube and Tisza. These onslaughts were not unexpected, but because of the war in the east too little had been done to avert them.

In 167 both emperors moved to the northern frontier. Then, after the death of Lucius Verus two years later (see LUCIUS VERUS), Aurelius felt obliged to return to the Danube to meet the challenge more decisively. The fighting was more serious than anything of the kind that had occurred before, and it continued, under the emperor's personal direction, for most of the remaining fourteen years of his life. The chronology of the campaigns is disputed, but they included two disastrous setbacks in about 170, or somewhat earlier. One was inflicted by the Marcomanni and Quadi, who broke through into the flat lands south of the upper and middle Danube, burnt Opitergium and besieged Aquileia. At almost the same time the Costoboci, a band of marauders from the Carpathian region, overran the lower Danubian area and penetrated deep into Greece, where they plundered Eleusis. Aurelius' armies, weakened by an epidemic brought back from the east (see LUCIUS VERUS), slowly and laboriously re-established control in a prolonged series of campaigns.

The emperor envisaged two main solutions to the German problem. One, in 171, was to allow large numbers of these tribesmen to settle in the Empire as they wished. This had been done before, but Aurelius systematically developed the process in a wide variety of territories – Dacia, Pannonia, Moesia, Germany and Italy itself – assigning the settlers to Roman proprietors or to the tenants of imperial properties and tying them legally to the land they thenceforward occupied and cultivated. The policy was censured, then and later, as a barbarization of the Roman world; yet it relieved the pressure on the frontiers, and provided cultivators and soldiers whom later rulers would need in order to survive. Aurelius' other major intention was to push the northern border forward and create two new provinces: Sarmatia, centred upon the long Danube–Tisza re-entrant, and Marcomannia, comprising Boiohaemum and parts of what are now Moravia and Slovakia. These measures, which might eventually have led to even more extensive advances, would have shortened the frontier, based it for much of its length on mountains rather than rivers, and brought many potentially dangerous Germans under imperial control.

However, Marcus Aurelius' expansionist plans proved no more successful than the similar attempts made earlier by AUGUSTUS. His first series of campaigns had to be cut short because of a perilous revolt in the east. This was led by Avidius Cassius, a Syrian rhetorician's son, who, after winning distinction in the Mesopotamian War, had been granted special powers in all the eastern provinces in 172 and now, in 175, claimed the throne for himself. He seems to have believed that Marcus Aurelius, far away on the Danube, had died – and was apparently supported by the empress Faustina the younger, who was with her husband and thought he was so ill that he would not survive. All the eastern provinces except two (Cappadocia and Bithynia) joined the rebellion. When, however, it was learnt that Aurelius not only still lived but had returned from the Danubian area to Rome – and was on his way to the eastern provinces – the rising collapsed, after less than a hundred days, and Avidius Cassius was killed by his own men.

Nevertheless, the emperor felt obliged to set out for the east. Moreover, Faustina accompanied him. She had already been his companion for four years during his northern campaigns, and was hailed on the coins issued in her honour as 'Mother of the Camp' (*mater castrorum*); if she was suspected of complicity in Avidius' rebellion, Aurelius, who was very fond of her, took no notice. She died, however, in south-eastern Asia Minor, and was deified at the emperor's request. He himself returned to Rome late in 176, and celebrated a Triumph. In the following year he set out for the north for the second time, to resume his operations against the Germans, and one of his generals gained a decisive victory over the Marcomanni in 178 which brought the annexation project almost, but not quite, within reach. But then Aurelius fell seriously ill once again, and after sending for his son he died peacefully in his sleep on 17 March 180.

In civil affairs Marcus Aurelius had pursued the principles of just dealing inherited from Antoninus Pius. Like his predecessor he was deeply interested in legal affairs, and benefited from the advice of a distinguished jurist, Quintus Cervidius Scaevola, who not only enjoyed popular demand as a consultant but was also the author of voluminous learned works. Yet Aurelius' government, like that of his predecessor, was characterized by detailed reform rather than innovation. Perhaps the most distinctive feature of his reign was a further elaboration of the imperial bureaucracy, due to the increasing complexity of the administrative, financial and military structure of the Roman world.

He carried out all his duties with unremitting care, and treated the senate with an honourable show of deference. Yet the costs of prolonged warfare, together with seven large distributions of cash (deemed necessary to keep up public morale) subjected the national financial reserves to an almost intolerable strain – as emergency auctions of imperial property, and tell-tale debasements of the silver coinage, clearly revealed; while the appointment of commissioners for non-Italian communities threatened with bankruptcy was symptomatic of a loss of municipal initiative that was characteristic of the epoch. Beneath the façade of genuinely high-principled government this combination of economic stress and bureaucratic intervention continued to point the way, all unconsciously, to the grim authoritarianism of the following century.

During the later years of his life Marcus Aurelius gradually brought forward his son COMMODUS, who was appointed Caesar in 166 and joint Augustus in 177 at the age of sixteen, and became sole emperor three years later. Owing to his defects Aurelius, in retrospect, was greatly blamed for this reversion to the hereditary doctrine, bringing eighty-two years of adoptive succession to an end. However, unlike his forerunners he was fatally handicapped by the absence of any other candidate who might have been more generally acceptable; the elevation, for example, of Tiberius Claudius Pompeianus, husband of his daughter Lucilla since 169, would only have provoked rivalries and civil wars. This at least was avoided, since the changeover passed off smoothly.

It is ironic that an emperor who spent so much of his reign at war was the nearest approach to a philosopher-king that the western world has ever known. Marcus Aurelius was one of those rare rulers whose actions have been outdone and outlived by what he wrote. This intimate revelation of his profoundest thoughts, addressed (according to its editors) 'to himself' and later known as his *Meditations*, is the most famous book ever composed by a monarch. It is in Greek, and framed in literary shape, but was originally intended as a series of private notes; Aurelius had no intention that these highly personal self-scrutinies and self-exhortations should ever be published. But published they were, and his beliefs, thus disclosed, display a lofty and bracing austerity. We must all just struggle onwards to the best of our ability, he concludes, with patient long-suffering endurance. To gain the necessary strength for these efforts, we have to turn inwards upon ourselves, and draw out of our profoundest resources the courage to carry on our day-to-day lives. And Aurelius – who warned himself not to be 'too deeply dyed with the purple' – found his own life, with all its unique and massive burdens, almost too much to bear. However, he reminds himself and the reader, our existence upon this earth is only a fleetingly short and transitory affair, a brief visit paid to an alien land. At least while we are engaged upon this journey we can rise above the squalid material things that encumber us (sex, eating and other bodily functions) and behave as responsibly, decently and co-operatively as we can to our fellow-travellers.

Many of these insistences on self-reliant endeavour are traditional Stoic philosophy, but none of its previous exponents had communicated their hard creed in such poignant and urgent language. Nor is Aurelius' message entirely without comfort. For, he insists, although so many happenings in our lives are predestined there is much that can be changed for the better, if only sufficient will-power and discipline are mobilized and applied; and then 'no man has the power to hold you back. . . . Be like the headland against which the waves break and break. . . . Try to see, before it is too late, that you have within you something higher and more godlike than mere instincts which move your emotions and twitch you like a puppet!' Stoics had long been saying that all men and women have a share of this divine spark, so that they are, in the last resort, brothers and sisters, members of one and the same world-community: 'Men exist for each other', as Aurelius expressed it: 'then either improve them or put up with them!'

The sculptors of the epoch, benefiting from an increasingly free employment of the drill to produce contrasting effects of light and shadow, manage to catch this heartfelt concern for the inner life in some of their portraits of Aurelius. The pensive Hellenic idealism that emerges gives further definition to a spirituality seen in slightly earlier portrait styles of Asia Minor and Greece: a gold head of the emperor reminded its recent discoverers of 'a saint in church'. Members of the Christian Church, however, found him by no means sympathetic. They were persecuted in Gaul during his reign, and their subsequent writers, notably Orosius, described the plagues of the time as a punishment for this treatment. But Aurelius saw Christians as self-dramatizing martyrs who perversely refused to participate in the common life of the

Roman Empire which, for all its imperfections, seemed to him the most complete earthly expression of the ideal Stoic cosmopolis that he always held before his eyes.

LUCIUS VERUS
161–9

LUCIUS VERUS (joint emperor, 161–9) was born in December 130 as Lucius Ceionius Commodus – the name of his father whom HADRIAN adopted as his heir in 136 (and was thenceforward known as Lucius Aelius Caesar). When Aelius died in 138, Hadrian adopted ANTONINUS PIUS with the requirement that he in turn should adopt MARCUS AURELIUS and the boy Ceionius (renamed Lucius Aelius Aurelius) Commodus. His advancement was less rapid than that of the older Marcus Aurelius; however, he became quaestor in 153 and consul in 154 and 161. On the death of Antoninus Pius, Marcus Aurelius made him his imperial colleague, under the name Lucius (Aurelius) Verus. He was proclaimed Augustus and granted the tribunician power; indeed, he held equal powers to Marcus Aurelius in every respect, except that Aurelius alone was chief priest (*pontifex maximus*). Thus the two men reigned jointly, creating a novel precedent which was to be very often followed in the later centuries of the Empire.

In 162, Verus was entrusted with the supreme command in a major eastern war provoked by the Parthian king Vologeses III who had placed his own nominee, Pacorus, on the throne of the contested client-state of Armenia. Also, a Parthian general defeated the Roman governor of Cappadocia at Elegeia on the Armenian border, and the governor of Syria suffered an equally decisive setback. It was the task of Verus and his generals to remedy this situation. It took him at least nine months, however, to reach Antioch; this was partly attributable to illness, but people also ascribed the delay to his indolent, pleasure-loving temperament. Nevertheless, his subordinate commanders, their forces strengthened by reinforcements from Europe, displayed great energy. Statius Priscus invaded Armenia and captured and destroyed its capital Artaxata. The designation 'Armeniacus' was conferred on Lucius Verus in 163, while Aurelius, so as not to encroach on his colleague's glory, delayed his own acceptance of the title until the following year. A Roman protégé, Sohaemus, was crowned King of Armenia, and in 165 Gaius Avidius Cassius, after taking over the governorship of Syria and retraining its legions, collaborated with Publius Martius Verus in eastward moves, penetrating deeply into Mesopotamia. The cities of Edessa, Nisibis and Nicephorium capitulated, and Lucius Verus was hailed as 'Parthicus Maximus' (while Aurelius again postponed the acceptance of a similar honour until a year later). In 166 the campaign was brought to a successful conclusion by the capture of the two great cities of Seleucia on the Tigris and Ctesiphon. No steps were taken to annex Mesopotamia, but the country was returned to a Roman client-prince, and operations in the highlands of Media earned the joint emperors the title 'Medicus' (though it was soon dropped from the coins).

Verus returned to Rome; in October 166 he and his colleague, whose daughter Annia Aurelia Galeria Lucilla he had married two years earlier, celebrated a magnificent Triumph, and both assumed the title 'Father of their Country' (Pater Patriae). But Verus' troops had brought back with them from the east a serious epidemic or plague, which was said to have first infected them at Seleucia. Its character is uncertain: it may have been smallpox, or exanthematous typhus, or bubonic plague. At any rate the scourge spread, with devastating results, into Asia Minor and Greece. Next it penetrated into the Italian peninsula – already suffering from several years of bad harvests – and struck Rome even before Verus himself got back to the city. Very soon, the epidemic was carrying desolation as far as the Rhine. It left many districts almost totally depopulated, and contributed substantially to the future weakening of the Empire.

Moreover, at just about the time when the two Augusti were celebrating their Triumph, a barbarian storm burst over the Danube frontier. Aurelius declared in the senate that 'both emperors were needed for the German war'. Their departure for the north, however, was delayed by the pestilence and by shortages of food, and it was not until the late autumn of 167 that they could leave the capital. When they reached Aquileia, the invaders withdrew and asked for a truce, and Verus suggested that he and his colleague should immediately return to Rome. However, Aurelius felt that a show of force across the Alps was still required, and after it had taken place the emperors stayed on at Aquileia for the following winter. When plague broke out again among the soldiers, however, they set out for Rome, in the spring of 169. But at an early stage in their journey, at Altinum, Verus was stricken by an apoplectic fit and died. His body was taken to Rome and buried in the Mausoleum of Hadrian, and he was pronounced a god of the Roman State.

'Lucius Verus', we are told by the *Historia Augusta*,

was a tall, good-looking man with a genial face and projecting forehead, who let his beard grow almost to a barbarian amplitude and sprinkled gold dust on his blond hair. He spoke haltingly, but was quite an accomplished orator all the same, and something of a poet as well, benefiting from the company of learned men, which he enjoyed. He was also addicted to the pleasures of hunting and wrestling and other athletic sports.

When he left his skilled generals to do the work for him in the east, perhaps he acted wisely, for, although not the idle fool he was sometimes made out to be, he seems to have been something of an agreeable lightweight. Aurelius meticulously gave him credit and awarded him honours. Yet Verus was by no means the partner needed to deal with the grim emergencies of the time. The first experiment in joint rule had not been an unqualified success.

COMMODUS
180–92

COMMODUS (Lucius Aurelius) (180–92) was born at Lanuvium in 161. He was the elder son of MARCUS AURELIUS and the younger Faustina, and was given the name of Commodus which Aurelius' colleague LUCIUS VERUS had originally possessed. He was proclaimed Caesar in 166 (see MARCUS AURELIUS). When Avidius Cassius rose against Aurelius in the east in 175, the rebel intended to march on Italy in order to seize the boy, but was killed before he could do so. In association with his father, Commodus received the titles Imperator, Germanicus and Sarmaticus, and was granted the tribunician power and the appellation of Augustus in 177. A brass medallion of the time is dedicated to father and son alike as dynastic founders (PROPAGATORIBVS IMPERII). Upon the death of Aurelius in 180 he became sole emperor, changing his name to Marcus Aurelius Commodus Antoninus – the first man for nearly a century to succeed his father on the throne.

After an initial declaration to the contrary, Commodus, perhaps acting on the advice of his Bithynian court chamberlain Saoterus, abandoned all his father's schemes for territorial expansion. He judged that they would overstretch the resources of the Empire, and he may have been right. At the same time he came to an agreement with the Marcomanni – incorporating various conditions for their peaceable behaviour – which proved more satisfactory than conservatives were willing to admit.

Commodus then returned promptly to Rome. There he claimed to have detected a conspiracy in which his own sister Annia Lucilla (as well as her eminent cousin, the ex-consul Marcus Ummidius Quadratus) was allegedly involved: since the death of her husband Lucius Verus, she had been married to Tiberius Claudius Pompeianus of Antioch, twice consul and a possible rival to the throne. Pompeianus' nephew Quintianus was designated to strike the fatal blow but he was overpowered, sword in hand. He and Quadratus were executed, and Lucilla was banished to Capreae and put to death soon afterwards. Commodus was also informed that a leading military jurist, Tarrutenius Paternus – joint praetorian prefect since the previous reign – had been involved in the plot, so he too was dispatched.

In taking this action the new emperor was prompted by Paternus' fellow-prefect Tigidius Perennis, who now became the sole commander of the guard and the most powerful man in the Empire, for Commodus willingly relinquished the complete control of the government into his hands. Never before had a praetorian prefect held such vast authority; and he retained his position for three years. About the quality of the man and of his rule there were sharply divergent opinions. Dio Cassius approved of him strongly, but that may have been because the historian, a young public servant at the time, owed him advancement: the *Historia Augusta*, on the other hand, saw him as an avaricious despot.

Perennis tried to safeguard his position by having Commodus' chamberlain Saoterus murdered; and he appointed two of his own sons to the key military governorships of Pannonia. In the end, however, an army deputation from Britain told Commodus that the prefect had designs on the throne, whereupon Perennis' own guardsmen were induced to strike him down, killing his wife, sister and sons at the same time. To celebrate his 'escape', Commodus assumed the title of 'Felix'. An imperial freedman, Marcus Aurelius Cleander, was believed to have been behind the *coup*, and after two years of rapid changes in the prefectship it was Cleander who emerged as the most influential of the emperor's advisers. His two fellow-prefects ranked as his juniors, and the emperor bestowed upon him the unprecedented title of the Dagger (*a pugione*), that is to say minister of security or protection. Elevated to this unique status, Cleander speedily outdid even Perennis in the extent of his power. Finally, however, he was brought down by the director of the grain supply (*praefectus annonae*), who first deliberately created an artificial food shortage in the capital and then (in 190) succeeded in inciting the metropolitan garrison and crowd to lay the blame for this deficiency on Cleander and put him to death. Commodus did nothing to save him, and may even have encouraged his downfall.

Near the beginning of Commodus' reign, the Caledonians broke through the Antonine Wall – not for the first time. They destroyed a Roman force and overran southern Scotland. Commodus sent a former governor of Britain, a stern disciplinarian named Ulpius Marcellus, to put down the revolt, which he successfully achieved in three campaigns, temporarily re-manning the breached fortifications. Before long, however, mutiny broke out in the garrison of the British province. In Spain and Gaul, too, guerrilla disturbances occurred, fomented by a deserter named Maternus.

These were difficult times for the army, since its soldiers were increasingly seen throughout the Empire as military secret police and oppressors. At Rome itself, too, the abrupt and lethal shifts of power behind the throne created a nerve-racking situation for senators. The emperor subjected them to increasingly heavy attacks, seizing their property to replenish the treasury which his extravagance had denuded. Meanwhile he himself was showing increasing signs of megalomania, even going so far as to rename Rome as his own personal colony, under the title of Commodiana; and the same designation was conferred upon the legions, a new African grain fleet, the city of Carthage and even the cowed Roman senate.

Finally a new praetorian prefect, Quintus Aemilius Laetus – the first North African, it seems, to hold the post – decided that Commodus had become insupportable; and the emperor's mistress Marcia and court chamberlain Eclectus agreed with him. In case the army might react unfavourably to the termination of the Antonine dynasty, however, supporters of their proposed *coup* also had to be enlisted from among leading figures in the provincial administrations. Two of Laetus' African compatriots, SEPTIMIUS SEVERUS and CLODIUS ALBINUS, were appointed to the governorships of Upper Pannonia and Britain respectively, and another of the prefect's confidential friends, PESCENNIUS NIGER, became governor of Syria; but it was the city prefect PERTINAX, according to the plan which now took shape, who was designated to become the next emperor. Finally, on the last night of the year 192, plans for the assassination of Commodus were complete; and an athlete, Narcissus, whom he employed as a wrestling partner, succeeded in strangling him. While senate and people condemned the late emperor's memory, pulled down his statues and erased his name from inscriptions, Laetus – although probably responsible for the murder – saved the body from a traitor's grave and gave it secret burial.

The plot had been precipitated by the emperor's shocking proposal that when he assumed the consulship on the following day, 1 January 193, he should celebrate his inauguration by leading a procession from the gladiators' barracks – himself wearing gladiatorial uniform. Commodus was obsessed by his prowess in the arena. Dio Cassius, as a member of the senate, had to attend such displays, and gives an account of the ludicrous pleasure his slaughter of animals inspired in the emperor, so that Dio himself and his senatorial colleagues could hardly prevent themselves from laughing. It was their duty, on such occasions, to shout repeatedly: 'Thou are lord and thou art first, of all men most fortunate! Victor, thou art, and victor thou shalt be! From everlasting Amazonian, thou art victor!'

For like Alexander the Great, and many a Persian and Parthian monarch as well, Commodus fancied himself as the Royal Huntsman. A coin which shows him attacking a lion is inscribed 'to the Courage of the emperor' (VIRTVTI AVGVSTI), for the ruler's bravery in the hunt symbolized military victory, and the slaughtered animals represented the powers of evil and enemies of the Empire. Moreover, their killing had been a traditional occupation of Hercules, a popular hero who, after his death, had supposedly risen to heaven because of his mighty achievements and was seen by court philosophers as embodying many of the chief concepts of enlightened monarchy. Commodus identified himself passionately with Hercules. Indeed, according to the historian Herodian, 'he issued orders that he was to be called not Commodus, son of Marcus, but Hercules, son of Jupiter. Abandoning the Roman and imperial mode of dress, he donned the lion-skin, and carried the club of Hercules . . . most of his own names and titles actually referred to Hercules, describing him as the manliest of men.' This information is confirmed by Commodus' coinage, on which he and the hero appear as interchangeable figures (HERCVLES ROMANVS AVGVSTVS, HERCVLES COM-MODIANVS), and Hercules is described as founder of the 'Colonia Commodiana' that Rome had now become. The terms 'conqueror' and 'unconquerable' (*victor*, *invictus*), which from this time onwards became official designations of Roman emperors, again imply a comparison with Hercules, and with Alexander the Great as well.

And yet, by what might seem a contradictory process of thought, Commodus not only saw himself as the new Hercules but also called Hercules his 'Comrade' or 'Companion' (HERCVLI COMITI). Henceforward, Roman coins and medallions increasingly display the gods in this light – that is to say, not as autonomous beings so much as protectors and comrades of successive Roman emperors. In this capacity they are almost forerunners of the Christian saints; and the resemblance was not fortuitous, for Commodus, who revived Antoninus' title of 'Pius', stood for an age in which the old traditional Olympian gods and goddesses were coming to be regarded as branches or aspects or symbols of a single transcendent divinity. Thus a coin of Commodus describes Jupiter as *Exsuperator* or *Exsuperantissimus*, the chief god; but the meaning is more emphatic than that: the world was approaching the time when monotheistic Christianity would fulfil such growing popular needs.

This new spiritual character of the age, which seems in such contrast to Commodus' personal behaviour, is echoed by contemporary works of art. In particular, the Column of Marcus Aurelius, which is still to be seen at Rome, was completed at this time, and reflects a marked change in the atmosphere;

for the sculptors of its spiralling reliefs, discarding the extrovert pictures of conquest on the Column of Trajan, instead tell a tale of humanity and pathos. No longer do Rome's wars appear simply as triumphant, exciting adventures, but scenes of tragic and harrowing suffering are dwelt upon too – and there is even sympathy for the fates inflicted upon the barbarian enemy. This is a world of fear and horror; and the sculptor of the Column gives haunting shape to the supernatural in his depiction of the Miracle of the Rain which, on one occasion, had supposedly saved the imperial army from disaster.

The sculptors of Commodus' portraits once again show a novel approach, but in this case by offering amusing baroque treatments of the emperor's dead-pan but slightly supercilious and sinister good looks; their preference for polished satiny surfaces shows a new, sensuous appreciation of the texture of flesh. Commodus, we are told by Herodian, was an extremely handsome man, whose blond and curly hair gleamed in the sunshine as if it were on fire, inspiring flatterers to detect a heavenly light. But he was guileless and simple, added Dio Cassius, and this made him the slave of his companions, who seduced him into cruel and lecherous habits.

PART IV

THE
HOUSE OF SEVERUS

The House of Severus

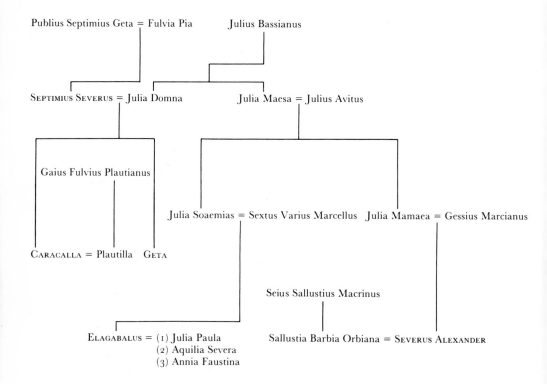

PERTINAX
193

PERTINAX (Publius Helvius) (January–March 193) was born in Liguria in 126. His father was a freed slave, Helvius Successus, who allegedly named his son Pertinax to celebrate his own perseverance in the timber trade. After teaching in a school Pertinax entered the army, rising to the command of units in Syria, Britain and Moesia. Then, temporarily, he reverted to civilian life in order to hold two procuratorships of knightly rank, first in Italy – a welfare post concerned with allowances to the poor (*alimenta*) on the Via Aemilia in 168 – and then in Dacia. Subsequently he was called back to the army as a commander of legionary groups (*vexillationes*) in Pannonia, where he fought against the Germans and took part in MARCUS AURELIUS' measures to protect Italy against their invasions. Promoted to senatorial status with the rank of praetor, Pertinax distinguished himself as a legionary commander in Raetia (from 171 onwards), became consul in 174 or 175, helped to put down the rebellion of Avidius Cassius in Syria, and held governorships in Upper and Lower Moesia and Dacia and Syria.

Under COMMODUS he fell from favour because of connexions with alleged conspirators in 182 but was brought out of retirement to command the mutinous army of Britain from 185–7. In 188 he went to Africa as proconsul, and subsequently (at a time of crisis) became city prefect of Rome, gaining a second consulship in 192. He is not likely to have been wholly unaware of the plot to murder Commodus on the last night of that year; for after it had been carried out, Laetus, the praetorian prefect, called upon him to accept the throne, whereupon Pertinax hurried to the praetorian camp, promised the guardsmen a large bonus, and received their acclamation as emperor.

Before the night was over he also visited the senate, whose members greeted him warmly, as one of their number, Dio Cassius, confirms. Pertinax was careful to show the senators respect and courtesy, 'for he was easy of access, listened readily to anyone's requests, and in answer gave his own opinion in a kindly way'. Disclaiming any suggestion that, at his advanced age, he felt eagerness to assume the imperial purple, he declined the senate's proposal that his wife Flavia Titiana (daughter of the city prefect Titus Flavius Sulpicianus) should be given the title of Augusta, and also turned down their offer to raise his son Pertinax the younger to the rank of Caesar – though inscriptions from Egypt and Arabia, and coins issued by the governor of Egypt, belie these modest refusals, or indicate that they were not taken seriously. The Roman coins of Pertinax display a novel dedication to 'Praiseworthy Good Sense', *Bona Mens* (MENTI LAVDANDAE). Yet his policy of financial retrenchment, though necessary after the excesses of Commodus, inevitably included unpopular features. The sale of the late emperor's extravagant possessions was reasonable enough. But Pertinax's general policy of rigorous· economy resulted in a decline of the general standard of living, while unkind· people at the same time asserted that he himself had somehow managed to· become rich. And they recalled, too that before coming to the throne he had· allegedly sold exemptions from service and military appointments, gaining a reputation for greed.

Pertinax soon lost the support of the praetorians, since he failed to pay them more than fifty per cent of the bonuses that he had promised. While he was temporarily absent from Rome there seems to have been a plot to set one of the consuls, Quintus Sosius Falco, on the throne in his place. Pertinax returned in time to prevent the senate from condemning Falco, but the praetorians' dissatisfaction with his régime was increased by the execution of some of their fellow-soldiers on the evidence of a slave. Finally, on 28 March, a group of soldiers broke into the palace; and the praetorian prefect Laetus, when ordered by Pertinax to confront them, went away to his own home instead, for it was he himself, disillusioned with the emperor's refusal to accept his guidance, who had instigated their hostile move. When they reached the inner part of the palace, the emperor, accompanied by his court chamberlain Eclectus, harangued them in a long and serious speech. But their spokesman, a certain Tausius who was a member of the imperial bodyguard, hurled his spear at Pertinax, and he fell transfixed in the chest. Eclectus managed to stab two of his assailants but then succumbed as well. Next, the soldiers charged through the streets of Rome displaying the head of the ruler they had proclaimed eighty-seven days earlier.

'Pertinax', reports the *Historia Augusta*,

was an old man, of an appearance that commanded respect, with long beard and hair brushed back. In figure he was rather stout and his stomach projected somewhat, but his stature was that of an emperor. As an orator he was mediocre. He possessed charm rather than kindliness, but he was never regarded as straightforward. While affable in conversation, in reality he was ungenerous and rather mean – to the extent of serving half-portions of lettuce and artichoke at banquets while a private citizen. . . . Even as emperor, if he ever wanted to send friends something from his meal, he would send a couple of scraps or a piece of tripe, occasionally chicken-legs.

Dio Cassius adds that he had retained his physical strength but suffered from a slight impediment in walking because there was something wrong with his feet.

Dio was also well qualified to offer a general estimate of his brief reign:

> Pertinax was formidable in war and shrewd in peace. . . . When advanced to preside over the destinies of the world he remained unchanged absolutely from first to last. . . . He at once reduced to order everything that had previously been irregular and confused; for he showed not only humaneness and integrity in the imperial administration, but also the most economical management and the most careful consideration for the public welfare. . . . But he undertook to restore everything in a moment. . . . Though a man of wide practical experience, he failed to comprehend that one cannot safely reform everything at once, and that for the restoration of an entire state, both time and wisdom are needed.

And so the events of the Year of the Four Emperors seemed to be repeating themselves – the career and fate of Pertinax had a good deal in common with GALBA's 124 years earlier. He was later deified by Septimius Severus.

DIDIUS JULIANUS
193

DIDIUS JULIANUS (Marcus Didius Severus Julianus) (28 March – 1 June 193) was born in 133, and came from one of the most prominent families of Mediolanum; his mother, a north African, was a close relative of Salvius Julianus, the outstanding lawyer of HADRIAN's reign.

Brought up in the household of Domitia Lucilla, the mother of MARCUS AURELIUS, Didius Julianus embarked on a long and distinguished public career. Praetor in about 162, he subsequently commanded a legion at Moguntiacum, and then governed Gallia Belgica from about 170–5. Next, after holding the consulship in about 175 (with the future emperor PERTINAX as his colleague), he became governor of Illyricum from 176–7 and of Lower Germany in about 178. He was subsequently appointed director of the child welfare system (*alimenta*) of Italy. At that time he was accused of having joined his relative Publius Salvius Julianus (the son of the jurist) in a conspiracy against the life of COMMODUS in 182; but he was acquitted and appointed proconsul, first of Pontus and Bithynia, and then from about 189–90 of Africa, where he succeeded Pertinax.

Then Didius Julianus returned to Rome, and after the brief reign and murder of Pertinax he decided to make his own bid for the throne. But there was a competitor, Titus Flavius Sulpicianus, the late emperor's father-in-law. There followed a notorious scene. 'Didius Julianus', according to Dio Cassius,

was an insatiate amasser of money and a wanton spendthrift – and always eager for revolution. So when he heard of the death of Pertinax, he hastily made his way to the camp, and standing at the gates of the enclosure, made bids to the soldiers for the imperial throne. Then ensued a most disgraceful business and one unworthy of Rome. For, just as if it had been in some market or auction-room, both the city and its entire empire were auctioned off. The sellers were the ones who had slain their previous emperor, and the would-be buyers were Sulpicianus and Didius Julianus, who vied to outbid each other, one from the inside, the other from the outside. They gradually raised their bids up to twenty thousand *sestertii* for each soldier. Some of the soldiers would carry word to Julianus, 'Sulpicianus offers so much; how much more do you make it?' And to Sulpicianus in turn, 'Julianus promises so much; how much do you raise him?' Sulpicianus would have won the day, being inside and being prefect of the city and also the first to name the figure twenty thousand, had not Julianus raised his bid by a whole five thousand at one time, shouting the sum out in a loud voice and indicating the amount with his fingers. So the soldiers, captivated by this excessive bid and at the same time fearing that Sulpicianus might avenge Pertinax (an idea that Julianus put into their heads), received Julianus inside and declared him emperor.

'It was on the occasion of their shameful auction', adds Herodian, 'that the character of the praetorians was corrupted for the first time; they acquired their insatiable and disgraceful lust for money and their contempt for the sanctity of the emperor.' Edward Gibbon made the most of this 'auction of the Empire' and it has passed into history as all that is known about the reign of Didius Julianus. But the incident, though picturesque, must be seen in context. We are told that Didius Julianus finally offered twenty-five thousand *sestertii* a head, and gave thirty thousand. But even the saintly Marcus Aurelius and his colleague LUCIUS VERUS had given twenty thousand *sestertii* when they came to the throne, and since then the currency had undergone considerable inflation. All the same, the undignified manner in which the two rivals bid for the throne created a lamentable impression, and revived in the frontier armies the competitive idea that emperors could be made outside the capital just as well – or a good deal more effectively.

A praetorian contingent conducted the new ruler to the senate house, where the cowed members ratified the guard's choice. Julianus' wife Manlia Scantilla and daughter Didia Clara were both declared Augusta and had coins issued in their names. Clara was given in marriage to a certain Cornelius

Repentinus, who was made prefect of the city. Julianus declared that he wished to honour the memory of Commodus, and in consequence he had Laetus, the praetorian prefect involved in his murder, put to death.

He himself was declared Father of his Country (Pater Patriae). But his elevation to the purple aroused instant anger among the populace of the capital, who on the day immediately following his accession – despite promises that they, too, would receive substantial sums of money – assailed him with violent menaces. Such incidents throw a lurid light on the coins upon which we find his novel self-description as Ruler of the World (RECTOR ORBIS). Even more ironical was another type celebrating the Harmony of the Soldiers (CONCORDIA MILITVM); for within a very short time PESCENNIUS NIGER and SEPTIMIUS SEVERUS, governors of Syria and Upper Pannonia respectively, each declared himself emperor in Julianus' place. Indeed Severus, after conciliating another possible rival, CLODIUS ALBINUS, the governor of Britain, set out from Carnuntum late in April and crossed the undefended Julian Alps, penetrating deep into Italy, where Ravenna and its fleet went over to his side.

Julianus tried to convert Rome into an armed camp by building walls and ramparts; according to rumour, he even mobilized the elephants of the Circus, in the hope of causing a panic among Severus' Danubian legionaries. But his ability to put up any effective resistance proved negligible. The praetorians were disaffected because he had failed, after all, to pay the price he had bid for the Empire; and they were not very impressed by belated distributions now. The marines, too, whom he had summoned from Misenum, proved undisciplined and useless. Julianus declared Severus a public enemy, but when he sent a senatorial deputation to recall the Danubian troops to their allegiance many of the envoys preferred to defect. At a meeting of the senate he proposed that a mission consisting of Vestal Virgins should be dispatched to implore Severus' mercy, but then, in the face of remonstrations, he took this defeatist suggestion back – requiring the senate, however, to pronounce his rival joint emperor with himself. Severus, when he heard of the suggestion, rejected it and had the envoy who conveyed him the offer killed (the unhappy messenger was the joint praetorian prefect Tullius Crispinus).

Julianus then dispatched a message to the guardsmen granting them their lives if they handed over the murderers of Pertinax and remained otherwise inactive. They gave this proposal a favourable hearing, and thus, in effect changed sides. When one of the consuls, Silius Messalla, learnt what they had done, he summoned a meeting of the senate, which deposed Julianus and proclaimed Severus emperor in his place. Julianus made a desperate attempt to enrol the aged Tiberius Claudius Pompeianus (widower of the empress Annia Lucilla) as his own imperial colleague; but when this offer, too, was refused, he sought refuge in the palace, accompanied by his son-in-law Repentinus and the remaining praetorian prefect, Titus Flavius Genialis.

However, hostile senators introduced a soldier into the palace, who, on 1 June, put the emperor to death. Severus handed over his body to his wife and daughter, but the latter lost her title of Augusta and her inheritance.

Dio Cassius states that a salient feature of Julianus' short reign was the assiduous court he had paid to members of the senate and other men of influence, laughing and joking with them, and organizing one dinner-party after another. The *Historia Augusta* even gives an account (probably fictitious) of the food he provided on these occasions. It also, more convincingly, blames him for allowing too much authority to fall into the hands of his subordinate officials.

SEPTIMIUS SEVERUS
193–211

SEPTIMIUS SEVERUS (Lucius) (193–211) was born in 145 at Lepcis Magna in Tripolitana. His father Publius Septimius Geta was obscure, but had two first cousins who rose high in the senate. The future emperor was given the names of his paternal grandfather. His great-grandfather, who was probably of Punic (Carthaginian) extraction, had moved from Lepcis Magna to Italy towards the end of the first century A D, rising to knightly (equestrian) rank. Severus' mother Fulvia Pia may have been descended from an Italian family which immigrated to north Africa.

Severus entered the senate in about 173, became governor of Gallia Lugdunensis and Sicily, and then in the last years of COMMODUS, consul in 190 and governor of Upper Pannonia. After the brief reign of PERTINAX and the accession of DIDIUS JULIANUS in 193, he was saluted emperor by his legions at Carnuntum, while PESCENNIUS NIGER was similarly acclaimed in the east. The praetorian guard in the capital proved susceptible to Severus' approaches, and Didius Julianus, sentenced to death by the senate, was murdered in his deserted palace. Severus advanced rapidly on Rome, entering the city after insignificant resistance. On arrival he disbanded the entire praetorian guard, replacing it by a force twice the size drawn from the legions and, in particular, from the Danubian units which had accompanied him on his march. Severus also trebled the numbers of the city cohorts and doubled the watch (*vigiles*), who were now regarded as part of the regular army.

After taking these steps he devoted himself to the elimination of rivals. The governor of Britain, CLODIUS ALBINUS, was a powerful figure who possessed many supporters in the senate. Severus did not need him as an heir, since he and his wife Julia Domna, daughter of an eminent priestly personage from Emesa in Syria, had two young sons of their own, CARACALLA and GETA (who were then five and two years old respectively). Nevertheless, he felt it diplomatically necessary to promote Albinus to the rank of Caesar – which seemed to imply eventual succession to the throne (see CLODIUS ALBINUS). Then Severus set out for the east, and in 194 crushed Pescennius Niger at the battle of Issus, near the junction between Asia Minor and Syria. In the following year, punitive expeditions were launched against the Osrhoeni of Mesopotamia and other Parthian vassals who had supported Niger's cause; and in order that future governors of Syria should not imitate his defeated rival's imperial ambitions, the province was divided into two, Coele-Syria and Phoenice (Phoenicia).

Soon afterwards Severus felt himself strong enough to turn against Albinus, whom he openly rebuffed by declaring his own elder son Caracalla his heir after all. Albinus, however, was proclaimed emperor by his soldiers, and moved from Britain into Gaul, with Rome as his target. Meanwhile Severus, after a brief visit to Rome in 196–7, marched through Pannonia, Noricum, Raetia, Upper Germany and Gaul, collecting troops on the way; and, after a first successful engagement at Tinurtium, destroyed Albinus and his army at the battle of Lugdunum in 197. Britain, like Syria, was then divided into two provinces, Britannia Superior and Inferior, with Londinium and Eburacum as their respective capitals.

The civil wars of 193–7 had lasted much longer than those of 68–9, and the damage that they caused was far greater. At Rome twenty-nine senators and many knights lost their lives because they had supported the enemies of Severus.

It was not only Romans and Parthian clients who had helped his enemy Niger; for the Parthians themselves had felt the same. At this juncture, therefore, Severus moved east once again in order to punish them, mobilizing three new legions, which he assigned to the command of knights rather than the senators who had normally monopolized such appointments – for the senators were regarded by Severus with considerable suspicion. The ensuing warfare culminated in the fall of the Parthian capital Ctesiphon in 197–8; and the annexation of Mesopotamia, first proclaimed more than three decades previously, was declared to have taken place again. However, Severus' further attempts to capture the desert fortress of Hatra, which would have made it possible to expand the imperial frontier into what is now southern Iraq, twice ended in failure.

After he had returned to the west he created a precedent by stationing one of his new legions inside the Italian homeland itself, at Albanum, very close to the capital. This measure appears to have been prompted by the need to have a central military reserve, which the armies of the emperors had hitherto lacked. Combined with his previous expansion of the metropolitan units (praetorian and city cohorts), this meant that the troops in Italy were multiplied by Severus at least threefold, amounting to a total of at least thirty thousand men. Moreover, the army throughout the whole Empire now included no less than thirty-three legions, as against thirty and twenty-five at the deaths of TRAJAN and AUGUSTUS respectively. And Severus also substantially expanded what had previously been regarded as 'irregular' troops (*numeri*) – notably the mounted archers from Osrhoene and Palmyra, who were distributed to all fronts and frontiers of the Roman world.

It seems surprising that even a monarch endowed with the strong-minded determination of Severus became, at the very height of his powers, as wholly dependent on a praetorian prefect as any ruler before him. The prefect in question was Gaius Fulvius Plautianus – his fellow-townsman and a relative of his mother – who from 197 onwards exercised comprehensive authority over almost every branch of the imperial administration. Moreover, Plautianus' daughter Plautilla became the wife of the emperor's elder son Caracalla. But the marriage proved unhappy, and both Caracalla and his mother Julia Domna turned against Plautianus. Severus' brother, too, on his death-bed in 205, denounced the prefect for allegedly planning a revolt; whereupon Caracalla arranged for his assassination. However, the pair of prefects who succeeded him – the outstanding lawyer Papinian was one of them – received even more far-reaching powers over the civilian administration, and served as the emperor's personal representatives on his council.

The imperial territory which most pressingly needed Severus' personal attention now appeared to be Britain. The Antonine Wall, from Forth to Clyde, had never completely fulfilled its allotted role, and by the end of the second century its defences seem to have been more or less abandoned, leaving the provincial territory vulnerable to invasion from the north. In consequence, Severus set out for Britain in 208, accompanied by his wife and two sons and Papinian. The massive expeditions that followed penetrated Caledonia as far as the Moray Firth, but did not achieve any durable result. No attempt was made to reoccupy the Antonine Wall as a permanent borderline; instead, Hadrian's Tyne–Solway wall was reconstructed and revived to mark and defend the frontier. Meanwhile, in 211, Severus fell fatally ill at Eburacum and summoned Caracalla and Geta to his bedside; and shortly afterwards, at the age of sixty-six, he died.

'Keep on good terms with each other,' was believed to have been his death-bed counsel to his sons, 'be generous to the soldiers, and take no heed of anyone else!' Already at the outset of his reign Severus had shown how highly he estimated the soldiery by issuing a large series of coins (like Marcus Antonius more than two centuries earlier) commemorating the individual legions one by one. Moreover, he had come to the logical conclusion that if all these soldiers, on whom everything depended, were to be expected to display loyalty and efficiency, then they would have to be better paid. So the legionaries, despite conservative laments, had their pay raised from three hundred to five hundred *denarii* a year; and in addition, because of the diminution of the currency's purchasing power, they increasingly received payments in kind as well as in cash – and parts of the bonuses that supplemented their salaries were paid to them in gold. Furthermore, legal recognition was granted to the soldiers' unions with native women, and garrisons and troops were assigned allotments of land to employ for farming, and facilities to engage in commercial enterprises as well.

Particular favour was also shown to their officers, including centurions, who received greatly improved emoluments and a variety of privileges and amenities. Moreover, army service now became an alluring preliminary to a considerable range of careers; Severus had created a new military aristocracy, regularly replenished from the ranks, which thenceforward provided the Empire with its administrative élite (and with most of its future emperors as well). Severus tied all these officers and soldiers very closely to his own person. He habitually wore a sumptuous military uniform, and at the various legionary headquarters worship of the ruler became intensified, increasingly eclipsing the traditional cult of the standards. To counteract this powerful, warlike, autocratic emphasis, Severus also proclaimed himself the heir of the high-minded ANTONINUS PIUS and MARCUS AURELIUS, asserting his retrospective adoption into their family and giving his son Caracalla their names. In accordance with this desire to maintain the Antonine heritage, there was also continued progress in the development of Roman law: under the influence of the emperor himself, who had been taught by the jurist Cervidius Scaevola, the work of pre-eminent legal experts, notably Papinian and Ulpian, consolidated the administrative and legal practices, norms and ideals that had been formulated in earlier epochs. And cultural life, too, by no means stagnated. In particular, Severus' Syrian empress Julia Domna, whose influence gained her the titles of Mother of the Camp and the Senate and the Country, possessed intellectual gifts which earned her the nickname 'the philosopher'; and she gathered around herself a coterie of learned men, including the philosopher Philostratus and the physician Galen – who did much to bring Greek and Roman thought closer together. Moreover, Severus himself wrote his autobiography, which unfortunately has not survived.

He also made his mark as one of the outstanding imperial builders. His native north Africa benefited especially from this intensive activity; it can still be admired today at his home town Lepcis Magna, upon which he bestowed a

Forum, a Basilica, a great new temple and a colonnaded street leading to the harbour, which was ambitiously reconstructed. He also erected a four-way triumphal arch on the occasion of his visit to the city in 203. The reliefs that adorned it display styles indicating that a new, less classical artistic epoch is well on its way. One scene depicts a siege in a map-like fashion reminiscent of oriental textiles. Another panel, depicting the ruler in his chariot, introduces an almost medieval technique, two-dimensional rather than plastic, which concentrates on rhythmical repetitive symmetry and offers a novel, frontal presentation of the emperor, who is shown as a potent centre-piece and talisman, resembling the images of Parthian kings or a Boddhisatva gazing at his worshippers. And upon Severus' great arch in the capital itself, beside the Forum Romanum, bird's-eye perspectives and rows of figures flanking his chariot once again indicate a renunciation of the old humanistic formulae and look forward to the artistic concepts of late antiquity.

Severus also constructed the Septizodium, a fanciful magic castle of fountains on the Palatine Hill; it was demolished in 1588, but engravings show what it was like: an elegant cumulation of three tiers of porticos, one upon another. His own statue stood in the building among the Seven Planets of astrology, in the guise of the Sun-god. Under the family of Severus solar worship almost took control of the entire Roman pantheon. The pagan religion, that is to say, was changing. But so were the social lives of the peoples of the Empire. For although Severus gave his elder son the name 'Antoninus', and great lawyers remained eager to perpetuate all that was best in the past, there were reasons why any authentic or universal return to the Antonine golden age could hardly be envisaged. For Severus believed that the repetition of the terrible civil wars from which his régime had emerged could only be prevented by a vast expansion of the military basis of his own power; and this in turn meant that civilians (although many of them still lived well) were increasingly subjected to requisitions, exactions and exploitations by imperial officials, in collusion with landlords. These grimmer elements of the reign were by no means underplayed by the two senatorial historians who were Severus' contemporaries, Herodian and Dio Cassius. Indeed (unlike a later historian Victor, an African himself, who greatly admired him), they probably treated his memory with excessive harshness, because they had known and regretted the happier days of old, and believed that the series of disasters that came after Severus were due to his policies. But that was only another way of saying that his reign was the bridge between two epochs – between the stability of the second century and the crises of the third.

John Malalas, writing four centuries later, observed that Severus was dark-skinned, and African history-books today depict him as black. But, dark though his complexion may well have been, Malalas should not be too much relied upon: for example, another of his statements, that Severus had a long nose, is unmistakably wrong, for portraits show that his nose was short and slightly *retroussé*. His hair and beard were curly. He was small of stature, but strong and energetic. The *Historia Augusta* remarks that he retained a trace of a north African accent for the whole of his life, and this may well be true. But to speak of him as the founder of a 'Semitic' (or 'African') dynasty, or as the deliberate barbarizer of the army, is erroneous. He belonged to a cosmopolitan élite imbued with Roman ideas and ideals, and so did the Africans whom he promoted around him.

PESCENNIUS NIGER 193-5

PESCENNIUS NIGER (Gaius) (rival emperor in the east, 193–5) was born in about 135, of a family of Italian knights. Brought into the senate by COMMODUS, he fought against the Sarmatians in Dacia in 183 (together with another future claimant to the throne, CLODIUS ALBINUS), and obtained a consulship. Then in 190, through the favour of Narcissus, the athlete who subsequently strangled Commodus, Niger became governor of Syria, where he was admired for his munificent sponsorship of public spectacles. When he learnt, in about the middle of 193, of the murder of PERTINAX and unpopularity of his successor Didius Julianus, he allowed himself to be hailed emperor by his troops at Antioch – at about the same time as Septimius Severus was proclaimed in Pannonia.

The whole of the east, with its nine legions, declared for Niger, hailing him as a new Alexander the Great; and the King of Parthia, Vologeses V, likewise expressed sympathy for his cause, although too preoccupied with his own internal troubles to send him troops, other than contingents from client-princes. On the European side of the Bosphorus, Niger obtained the support of Byzantium, from which he hoped to gain control of the two principal inter-continental land routes. To this end it was necessary to occupy another city, Perinthus. But meanwhile Severus, although worried by the considerable support Niger enjoyed in the capital, had left Rome and started out for the east; and despite a modest initial rebuff, his advance guard gained control of

Perinthus, whereupon he placed Byzantium under siege. As for Niger, after his commander-in-chief, Aemilianus, had suffered a setback near Cyzicus, he withdrew into Asia Minor, but was decisively defeated again near Nicaea in 194. With the remnants of his army he retreated across the Taurus mountains to Antioch, only to learn very shortly afterwards that Egypt had revolted against his rule: a papyrus shows that already on 13 February an Egyptian town, Arsinoe, was celebrating its adherence to Severus' cause.

Nor was it long before his triumphant generals, overcoming the resistance of Niger's rearguard, broke through the Cilician Gates, placing Antioch in peril. To meet the threat Niger advanced to Issus, on the borders of Asia Minor and Syria. There once again – perhaps not before the middle of 195 – his army was routed. He was able to get back to Antioch, but when news came that Severus was approaching he evacuated the city and fled towards the Euphrates. Before he could get across the river, however, he was overtaken by pursuers and put to death. His head was brought to Severus, who in turn sent it on to Byzantium as a warning that further resistance would provoke similar punishment; and indeed, after its siege had dragged on for two and a half years, the city fell to him, and the threatened reprisals were ruthlessly carried out.

The extensive and interesting silver coins which Niger had issued at Antioch (and perhaps other mints as well) pay tribute to the normal Roman tradition, but also betray their eastern origin by reverse inscriptions and designs of an exotic character. Thus Apollo is SANCTVS, a term which is used to translate a title of Syrian deities, and refers here to the great god of Daphne beside Antioch; Jupiter 'who presides over the world' (PRAESES ORBIS) is a blend between the Roman deity and a Syrian Baal; Fortuna (much emphasized) is Atargatis, *dea Suria*, the greatest of Syrian goddesses; and BONVS EVENTVS, the emperor's good luck, is the Greek Agathodaimon, a favourite deity of Alexandria. But Niger's own chosen epithet or surname for himself is IVSTVS, for he claimed to be guided by Justitia (Astraea), the spirit of the Golden Age, a theme that runs steadily through his coinage. It also claims numerous victories; but these were for the most part only hopeful aspirations, not facts, for his Syrian legions did not fight as well as Severus' Danubian army.

'Pescennius Niger', records the *Historia Augusta* (with dubious reliability once more),

was tall in stature and handsome of person, his hair being brushed back gracefully towards the crown. His voice was raucous but resonant, so that when he spoke on the parade-ground he could be heard a mile away if the wind was not against him. His face was dignified and always ruddy, his neck was so black that according to what many say he got the name of Niger from that, the rest of his body being white and rather fat. He was very fond of wine, a sparing eater, and absolutely unacquainted with sex other than for begetting children.

His coin portraits show a long narrow head with distinctive features and a pronounced beard. But as to the extent of his abilities, the questionable assertions of the literary sources – including a predictable torrent of abuse derived from Severus' autobiography – make it hard to come to a decision. Was he a good general, as is sometimes said – or rather, would he have been, if he had possessed better troops? Was he a disciplinarian and reformer? Was he too much inclined to procrastination? Almost all that remains, finally, is the unusual and idealistic programme outlined by his coins, and that does not, of course, prove anything about his character, since it may have been the brainchild of a propagandist – either himself or one of his advisers. Perhaps the last word should remain with Dio Cassius: 'Pescennius Niger was remarkable for nothing, good or bad.'

CLODIUS ALBINUS 195–7

CLODIUS ALBINUS (Decimus Clodius Septimius Albinus) (rival emperor in the west, 195–7) was probably born between 140 and 150. He came from a wealthy family of Hadrumetum in north Africa. The *Historia Augusta* suggests that he began his public career as a knight (*eques*) and entered the senate in the later years of MARCUS AURELIUS, to whom, as governor of Bithynia, he remained loyal during the revolt of Avidius Cassius in 175. Under COMMODUS, in 182–4, he was fighting in or 'beyond' Dacia, and then, perhaps, governed one of the German provinces. Consul before or after 190, he subsequently became governor of Britain in about 191, where he had to deal with serious discontent among the garrison. When DIDIUS JULIANUS came to the throne in 193, it is likely that Clodius Albinus supported him, since Didius' mother came from his own home town.

SEPTIMIUS SEVERUS, on asserting his claim to the imperial office after Didius' murder, decided to free his hands for the prospective war against his eastern rival PESCENNIUS NIGER by offering Clodius Albinus the title of Caesar. That this implied the prospect of succession to the Empire is confirmed by inscriptions on Severus' coins issued from 194 in Albinus' name, notably 'The Foresight of the Emperor' (PROVIDENTIA AVGVSTI) and 'Fortune which will bring [Albinus] back to Rome' (FORTVNA REDVX). It may seem strange that Albinus trusted the offer of the Caesarship enough to accept it and co-operate when Severus had two sons, CARACALLA and GETA, whom he would obviously wish to become his heirs; his offer to Albinus, therefore, looked like the piece of temporary opportunism that it was, designed merely to safeguard his rear for the eastern war. However, Caracalla was only five years old, and Albinus, even if sceptical, presumably hoped he might succeed to the throne before the boy became old enough to anticipate such a step.

In 194 he was granted a second consulship *in absentia*; but in the following year he broke with Severus. He had not timed this step very cleverly, since Severus' attention was no longer distracted by his other rival Pescennius Niger, whom he had just overthrown. But there was now, it appears, unmistakable evidence that Severus – encouraged by his victory over Niger – had decided to make it clear that his heir was, after all, Caracalla (who was duly made Caesar in the following year). So Albinus, throwing off his allegiance to Severus, had himself proclaimed Augustus; and in consequence Severus' government pronounced him an enemy of the State. Nevertheless, Albinus enjoyed considerable favour in senatorial circles, and his supporters included Lucius Novius Rufus, the governor of Hispania Tarraconensis.

Encouraged therefore by this backing, Albinus sailed across the Channel, leading an army of legionaries and auxiliaries whose removal left Hadrian's Wall dangerously unprotected from the north. Once established in Gaul, he set up his headquarters at Lugdunum. There he proceeded to issue coinage bearing the full imperial titles. A tactful dedication to the Genius of Lugdunum (GEN. LVG.) is the only provincial note in a series that is otherwise entirely Roman in character. The type CLEMENTIA AVG(usti) is intended to show that, once he was victorious, the capital would have nothing to fear from him. Albinus' final issue honours 'the Loyalty of his Legions' (FIDES LEGIONum).

This loyalty was indeed an urgent and difficult requirement; for despite an early victory by a section of his army over Virius Lupus, the governor of Lower Germany, the German legions remained loyal to Severus. Moreover, Albinus' plan to invade Italy was forestalled by his opponent, who sent a detachment to block the Alpine passes and then, in mid-winter 196–7, himself arrived in Gaul. After an initial clash at Tinurtium, which went in Severus' favour, the decisive confrontation took place near Lugdunum in February 197. Dio Cassius' statement that one hundred and fifty thousand men were engaged on either side may be exaggerated, but the rival forces were large, and the battle historic. Severus' left wing suffered an initial setback, in which he himself lost his horse, but after two days of fighting one of his generals, Julius Laetus, won the battle with his cavalry. During the flight, Albinus stabbed himself to death, or was stabbed; his head was sent to Rome as a warning to those who had supported him. His sons at first received a pardon but were later beheaded, together with their mother. A lasting result of the war was the destruction of Lugdunum, which never again recovered its position as the principal city of Gaul.

It is difficult to discover the truth about Albinus' character, because Severus' autobiography effectively damned his enemy as drunken, effeminate, crafty, shameless, dishonourable, greedy and extravagant – a man better suited for the stage and its male choruses than for the battlefield. Herodian saw him as a rather conceited and naïve person who had been stupid to accept Severus' assurances of friendship at their face value. The *Historia Augusta* also tells us, with how much justification we do not know, that Albinus was a writer of erotic stories, an indefatigable womanizer and a brutal master of soldiers and slaves. But however this may have been, the senators, at least, accepted his assurances that in dealing with themselves he would be mild. They were also impressed by his blue blood. 'By the senate', the *Historia* even goes so far as to observe, '*he was loved to an extent that none of the emperors had been*'; for he was the candidate of the aristocracy of the Latin-speaking west – in contrast to Niger who had the support of the Greek-speaking east and its garrison, and Severus who had the backing of the Danubian army (which proved decisive).

CARACALLA
211–17

CARACALLA (more correctly Caracallus) (211–17) was the nickname of the elder son of SEPTIMIUS SEVERUS – a nickname taken from the long Gallic cloak which he made fashionable at Rome. When he was born in 188, his original name was Julius Bassianus, after his Syrian maternal grandfather, the father of his mother Julia Domna.

In 195 his father made him Caesar and changed his name to Marcus Aurelius Antoninus. He became Augustus in 198, and in 208 accompanied his family to Britain, leading the last Caledonian campaign in person because his father was ill; and meanwhile he devoted himself to gaining the good will of the soldiers. After the death of Severus in 211, he and GETA succeeded as joint emperors, following the collegiate model of MARCUS AURELIUS and LUCIUS VERUS half a century earlier. Putting an end to the British campaign – in a more satisfactory manner than the strictures of his expansionist critics would suggest – the two new rulers both returned to Rome. But they disliked one another intensely (see GETA); and Julia Domna's efforts to bring them together were unsuccessful. It was not long before Caracalla had Geta assassinated. This murder, however, was by no means universally popular among the praetorian guardsmen, some of whom remained conscious that they had sworn an oath of allegiance to both emperors alike. At first they showed signs of serious recalcitrance. But then, according to the historian Dio Cassius, who was a senior senator at the time, Caracalla addressed them with vigorous assurances:

Rejoice, fellow-soldiers, for now I am in a position to do you favours! I am one of you, and it is because of you alone that I care to live, in order that I may confer upon you many favours. For all the treasuries are yours. I pray to live with you, if possible, but if not at any rate to die with you. For I am not afraid of death in any form, and it is my desire to end my days in warfare. There should a man die, or nowhere!

But Caracalla appreciated that the praetorians wanted material advantages as well as fighting words, and consequently proceeded to grant them bonuses of 2,500 *denarii* each, at the same time enlarging their ration allowance by fifty per cent. In addition, he increased legionaries' pay from the 500 *denarii* fixed by his father to 675 or 750, with proportionate rises for other troops as well. Moreover, since by this time inflation was so steep that such salaries did not amount to much more than pocket-money, Caracalla went on to arrange that the soldiers' payments in kind – foodstuffs and the like – should be substantially raised.

At the same time there were sweeping changes in the high command, resulting from the elimination of officers who had supported Geta or tried not to take sides. The casualties included the praetorian prefect and lawyer Papinian. The intelligence service too, and the couriers who served it, came under two new directors, Ulpius Julianus and Julianus Nestor: they were probably commandants at the secret police headquarters. Caracalla also arranged that not one single province of the Empire should contain a garrison of more than two legions, his purpose being to ensure that no governor could ever control a force formidable enough to launch a rebellion. Twenty-four legions were allotted in pairs to twelve provinces, the remaining nine (including the legion in Italy) being distributed one by one elsewhere.

In 213 the emperor left for Germany, where at that time the loose confederation of tribes known as the Alamanni are first mentioned as enemies of Rome, threatening the Agri Decumates, the 'duck's beak' re-entrant between the upper Rhine and the upper Danube. Caracalla defeated the

Alamanni near the Main, though his critics claimed that he bought them off, and it is true that he adopted a policy of pacification through subsidies. This practice was deplored by traditionalist Roman opinion, but it cost less than fighting and staved off the German peril for two decades to come. A psychological factor, too, was involved; Caracalla was a new kind of emperor who felt no distaste for the Germans, and indeed liked them, and himself wore a wig of golden hair arranged in the German style.

Caracalla's taste for this non-Roman fashion (like the flowing Gallic cloak which gave him his nickname) was part of a wider phenomenon characteristic of the age, namely a gradual breakdown of Roman and Italian exclusiveness. This was symbolized by the most famous legal measure of antiquity, promulgated by the same emperor and named after him, the Constitutio Antoniniana. With the exception of slaves, this enactment bestowed upon virtually the entire population of the Empire the status of Roman citizens, which had hitherto been restricted to Italians and a relatively small élite body of provincials. As far as the army was concerned, the measure wiped out the traditional distinction between citizen legionaries and non-citizen auxiliaries, establishing a principle of egalitarian uniformity instead, although the change also made it harder to attract ambitious men in the legions. But the principal aim of the regulation was probably fiscal: it seems to have been designed to augment the number of people who had to pay the indirect dues on inheritance and on the emancipation of slaves – these being taxes for which only Roman citizens were liable. For financial anxieties were very much on Caracalla's mind (he debased the coinage, for his own profit, by issuing what we call the *antoninianus* – after his name Antoninus – which weighed 1½ *denarii* but was valued as 2). As for the differentiation between citizens and non-citizens, this had already become more and more blurred during recent generations, as the great lawyers revealed in their ever-increasing employment of an alternative distinction between the two main social classes, that between the *honestiores* and the *humiliores*. So Caracalla's measure, though historic and dramatic in its sweeping completeness, must also be seen within its context as one step in a gradual, well-advanced process in which the privileged status of citizenry was being eliminated.

Egalitarianism at a more material level was displayed by the amenities he provided for the general population, notably the stupendous Baths at Rome – by far the largest yet created – which bear his name but which had been begun by Severus. Surrounded by an enclosure containing gardens and open-air gymnasiums and art collections, the main building of the Baths of Caracalla was equipped with complex hydraulic, heating and draining services, designed to cater for one thousand six hundred bathers. The central feature was a hall which contained a swimming-pool and was roofed by intersecting concrete cross-vaults resting upon four enormous piers of the same material. The hall itself was so large (185 by 79 feet) that the human beings whom it served were dwarfed by its size; for this was a new epoch in which the individual was one of a mass.

Caracalla thought large. Indeed, as the sculptors of his baroque portrait-busts took pains to indicate, he liked to see himself not only as an incarnation of the Sun-god but as a new Alexander the Great – bestower of universal citizenship and victor over the whole world. With this aim he planned to conquer the Parthian east, as even TRAJAN had failed to do. In 214, in the Danube camps, he mustered a great army for this oriental expedition, including a phalanx of sixteen thousand men, clothed and equipped like the Macedonians of old. In the following year the emperor moved onwards into Parthian territory, and the frontiers of his father's province of Mesopotamia were successfully pushed forward; but an attempt to overrun Armenia proved fruitless. In 216 he invaded Media, but then once again returned behind his new Mesopotamian borders. There, however, MACRINUS, one of his joint praetorian prefects, took fright, since his inspection of the emperor's correspondence (which he controlled) had led him to conclude that his own life was imperilled. So while Caracalla, travelling on horseback between Edessa and Carrhae (to visit the temple of the Moon-god in the latter city), dismounted to relieve himself, he was stabbed by a soldier and finished off by guards officers, at Macrinus' instigation.

Dio Cassius reflects the highly critical opinions of Caracalla held by the senators. He was shrewd, we are told, and capable of expressing himself with force, having been given a very thorough intellectual training by his father. However, as time went on he showed a marked preference for physical activity, energetically riding and swimming and engaging in blood-thirsty sports. It was his habit to blurt out recklessly whatever came into his head, and he would not ask advice, regarding experts, and indeed people who were good at anything at all, with strong aversion. Dio Cassius believed he was both physically sick and mentally deranged. Yet if a soldier had been called upon to write a character sketch of Caracalla, his judgment would no doubt have been a great deal more favourable.

GETA
211

GETA (Publius Septimius) (joint emperor, February–December 211 or possibly the beginning of 212) was the younger son of SEPTIMIUS SEVERUS and Julia Domna, being born in 189. In 197 he accompanied his father, mother and elder brother CARACALLA to the Parthian War. In the following year, after Severus' victory at Ctesiphon, he was named Caesar, at the same time as Caracalla became Augustus.

During the years 199–202 Geta travelled extensively, first in the east and then in Thrace and Moesia and Pannonia. In 203–4 he went with Severus and Caracalla to their native north Africa. In 205 he shared the consulship with Caracalla (his second, Geta's first); but relations between them were already hostile. Caracalla's father-in-law, the prefect Plautianus, did his best to keep their enmity within bounds, but after his murder the two young men, according to Dio Cassius, 'went to all lengths in their conduct'.

They outraged women and abused boys, they embezzled money, and made gladiators and charioteers their favourite companions, emulating each other in the similarity of their deeds, but full of strife in their rivalries; for if the one attached himself to a certain faction, the other would be sure to choose the opposite side. Finally, they were pitted against each other in some sort of contest with teams of ponies, and drove with such fierce rivalry that Caracalla fell out of his two-wheeled chariot and broke his leg.

In the hope of reconciling his two sons, Severus made them spend the greater part of the years 205–7 together in Campania, in his own company. With a similar purpose, the brothers were again appointed joint consuls in 208. In the same year they left with their parents for Britain. Geta stayed with his mother at Eburacum but in 209 took over the administration of the British provinces, and received the designation of Augustus in addition to the other imperial titles – eleven years after Caracalla, who was only one year older than himself. Geta's full style was now 'Imperator Caesar Publius Septimius Geta

Pius Augustus', and the victorious surname 'Britannicus' was added in the following year.

Before Severus died in 211 he was reported to have urged his two sons to come to terms with one another; but of this, when they became joint Augusti after his death, there was not the slightest hope. In the further deterioration of their relationship that followed, Caracalla seems to have taken the initiative by persistently acting without reference to his brother. He at once made peace with the Caledonians, so as to be able to return to Rome and consolidate his position. At the same time he got rid of Severus' advisers, who would have been likely, out of respect for their late master's wishes, to have offered Geta some support. The army, too, was likely to take the same view, especially as Geta bore a physical resemblance to his father.

Taking Severus' ashes with them, and accompanied by Julia Domna, the two youthful co-emperors set out for Rome. Such was their mutual hostility that they refused to stay at the same inn or join each other for meals, for fear of poisoning. Both were eager to reach the capital, where they felt they would be safer. Once they had arrived, after celebrating the funeral and deification of Severus they chose to reside in different parts of the palace, where each lived under heavy military guard. A scheme was put forward – anticipating later epochs – for the territorial partition of the Empire, according to which Geta should take Asia and Caracalla Europe. But Julia Domna opposed this idea, reputedly declaring: 'You may divide the Empire, but you cannot divide your mother.' The scheme might have provided at least a temporary solution; but Domna was no doubt afraid that it would diminish her own influence.

Caracalla apparently intended to murder his brother at the festival of the Saturnalia, but failed to carry out the plan because the news of what he had in mind leaked out. Geta increased his guard, keeping soldiers and athletes on duty day and night; so Caracalla adopted a new strategy. He suggested to Julia Domna that she should invite them both, unattended, to her apartment, in the hope of effecting a reconciliation. But when Geta entered the room, a group of Caracalla's centurions broke in and cut him down. It was afterwards asserted, in melodramatic style, that Geta clung to his mother, begging for her help, whereupon the officers slew him in her arms. At all events, once the deed was done Caracalla declared that his brother had been plotting against his life, and, despite initial reluctance on the part of the legion at Albanum, he secured the support of the praetorian guard and the senate. Geta's name – as can still be seen today – was erased from inscriptions, and his supporters were eliminated.

Despite Dio's description of his youthful excesses, a later historian, Victor, declared that he had been a courteous young man and, according to one reading, even-tempered – as Caracalla surely was not. 'Always hated by his brother,' reports the *Historia Augusta*, he was mindful of his father's opinions, and was more affectionate than his brother towards their mother. He had a resonant voice, with a slight stammer. He was very fond of elegant clothing; so much so that his father used to make fun of him. If he got anything from his parents he used it for his external appearance, and never gave anything to anyone. . . . He was regarded as a good companion even in his youth. . . . In his study of literature he stuck to the old writers. . . . His funeral is said to have been fairly elaborate for one who appeared to have been killed by his brother.

MACRINUS
217–18

MACRINUS (Marcus Opellius) (April 217–June 218) was born in 164 to a poor family at Caesarea (Iol) in Mauretania, and the *Historia Augusta* offers the information, unconfirmed from elsewhere, that as a young man he worked successively as a gladiator, huntsman and courier. Subsequently he moved to Rome, where he gained a reputation as a jurist, becoming the legal adviser of SEPTIMIUS SEVERUS' praetorian prefect Plautianus, who died in 205. Then he served as director of traffic on the Via Flaminia and financial administrator of Severus' private estates (*procurator thesaurorum*).

In 212 CARACALLA appointed him to the praetorian prefecture, which he occupied jointly with Oclatinius Adventus, who had been promoted from the ranks. In 216 Macrinus took part in the emperor's Parthian expedition, and in the following year received consular status (*ornamenta consularia*). In the spring of the same year, however, while stationed in Mesopotamia, he detected that a message denouncing him as a security risk had been sent (allegedly by an astrologer) to Caracalla, whom he consequently caused to be assassinated, on 8 April. The agent he enlisted to commit the crime, a certain Martialis, was arrested and killed by the imperial bodyguard. This convenient disappearance, and Macrinus' pretended sorrow for his master's death, enabled him to conceal his own leading role in the murder. During the two days that followed Oclatinius Adventus was offered the purple and declined the honour on grounds of age – or it may be that he made a bid for it in vain. At all events, the soldiers then hailed Macrinus as emperor.

He was not only the first Mauretanian but also the first non-senator to occupy the throne. Moreover, his indebtedness for his accession exclusively to the army – without any consultation of the distant senate – foreshadowed the long line of 'soldier emperors' whose elevation was to take place in a similar way. Yet Macrinus remained all too conscious that his popularity with the troops might not last, especially if they began to suspect his responsibility for the death of Caracalla, whom they had greatly liked; so instead of denigrating his predecessor and victim, he arranged for his deification. He also called himself Severus on his coinage – whether this had been one of his original names is uncertain, but it seems unlikely. In addition, hopeful of establishing a new imperial house, he placed the portrait of his own nine-year-old son Diadumenianus on the coinage, naming him Antoninus and Caesar and 'Prince of the Youth' (PRINCEPS IVVENTVTIS) and 'the Hope of the State' (SPES PVBLICA).

Although Macrinus had assumed the imperial office without first consulting the senate, its members were predisposed to accept him because of their hatred of Caracalla, and rapidly confirmed his titles and privileges. Macrinus tactfully apologized for his non-senatorial origin and promised to rule like MARCUS AURELIUS and PERTINAX. And even if the senators were not very pleased by his appointment of Oclatinius Adventus as city prefect, the cancellation of certain of Caracalla's tax increases, the restriction of the (revived) powers of circuit judges in Italy, and an amnesty to political exiles, met with their marked approval.

However, all this proved beside the point, because Macrinus was unable to hold the loyalty of the army. This failure was due in the first place to unpopular political solutions of the eastern question. The granting of the crown of Armenia to Tiridates II, son of a monarch whom Caracalla had imprisoned, meant that in practice that country passed out of Roman control. Macrinus' prestige also suffered from his failure to check the Parthian monarch Artabanus V, who had invaded Mesopotamia, refusing the emperor's initial offer of peace. Despite the claims of 'Parthian victory' on Roman coins, it appears that a three-day battle near Nisibis did not turn out well for Macrinus and that, uncertain of his troops, he then proceeded to patch up an inglorious peace, agreeing early in 218 to surrender prisoners and pay a substantial indemnity. His veterans, unimpressed, clamoured for a return to their native countries, while new recruits too became rapidly discontented when they found that a new and lower pay rate discriminated against them.

The circumstances were appropriate for a *coup*, and it was launched by a Syrian woman, Julia Maesa, the sister of Septimius Severus' late wife Julia Domna. Enlisting local army support in the eastern garrisons, she had her fourteen-year-old grandson Varius Avitus Bassianus (ELAGABALUS), priest at Emesa, taken to the headquarters of the legion at Raphaneae in Phoenicia and proclaimed emperor on 16 May.

The revolt was well-timed because the threat from Parthia, which might have been as disastrous to the rebels as to the emperor, had been removed; and Macrinus was not given time to call in the troops from the Danube and Rhine. He reacted by dispatching the joint praetorian prefect Ulpius Julianus, with a cavalry force, to put the insurrection down, but the soldiers murdered Julianus and went over to the pretender. Then Macrinus moved his headquarters to Apamea where he asserted the stability of his dynasty by declaring his son Diadumenianus joint Augustus, and issuing coins in his name at Antioch which celebrated 'the Bliss of the Age' (FELICITAS TEMPORVM). He also sought to ingratiate himself by cancelling his earlier pay reductions and promising the soldiers an enormous bonus.

Nevertheless, in the battle that followed, a whole legion deserted Macrinus' cause and he had to retire precipitately to Antioch. The governors of Phoenice and Egypt remained loyal, but could not provide help quickly enough; for a considerable force under Varius Avitus' eunuch Gannys now proceeded to march against him, and in a confrontation twenty-four miles from Antioch inflicted a decisive defeat upon the emperor, who, after varying fortunes, had by 8 June been abandoned by most of his troops. Disguised as a spy from the military police, he fled and made for Europe on horseback, but at Calchedon on the Bosphorus a centurion identified him, and he was placed under arrest. So he had to make the long journey back to Antioch; and there he was put to death. Diadumenianus, who had tried to escape to Parthia, met with a similar fate.

There are two quite distinct coin-portraits of Macrinus. One, displaying a short profile and a slight beard, is scarcely modified from the latest portraits of Caracalla, and was composed at Rome by artists who had little knowledge of what the new emperor looked like. The other, which originated at Antioch, seems much more realistic: it displays a long profile, heavy features and a considerable beard. As to his personal qualities, much of our tradition derives from the slanders of those who were opposed to him. We are told by the *Historia Augusta*, for example, that he ate and drank much too much, and used to flog his servants mercilessly in the name of discipline. Dio Cassius, a well-informed contemporary, on the other hand concedes that Macrinus had some good points. He was a faithful observer of legal precedents, we are told, even though he did not know the law any too well; and during his service as praetorian prefect he acted with good sense, whenever he was allowed to use his own judgment. Thereafter, Dio concludes that all would have been well if only, instead of seeking the throne for himself, he had let a senator have the job. There speaks the voice of senatorial bias; and it speaks accurately insofar as, having no such background behind him, Macrinus did not possess the administrative experience an emperor needed. Nor did the army, once it had elevated him to the throne, think much of his qualities. Perhaps his best hope would have been to return rapidly to Rome in order to confirm the not unfavourable view the senate had taken of the *fait accompli* of Caracalla's death. This however he was prevented from doing, first by the Parthian War and then by Julia Maesa's revolt. From each of these two campaigns, it emerged that he was a less than adequate general, and this was his most fatal disadvantage.

ELAGABALUS
218–22

ELAGABALUS (218–22) was born in 204. Soon after the assassination of CARACALLA in 217 his Syrian mother Julia Domna committed suicide, but her sister Julia Maesa, widow of a consul Julius Avitus, decided to overthrow MACRINUS. He had ordered her to retire to her home at Emesa in Syria, but this provided an excellent base for a rebellion. Her daughter Julia Soaemias was married to a fellow-Syrian, Varius Marcellus, who, after a distinguished career as a knight, had been elevated to senatorial rank. Their fourteen-year-old son Varius Avitus Bassianus (this last name being the family's *cognomen*, which Caracalla too had borne) held the hereditary priesthood of the Sun-god El-Gabal at Emesa (a manifestation of the chief Semitic deity El), and possessed attractive looks which enabled him to fulfil the bejewelled ceremonial of the cult with spectacular panache.

The Roman legionaries in the garrison of Raphaneae were won over by a large-scale outlay of Julia Maesa's wealth. The boy was taken to their camp at night by the legionary commander Publius Valerius Comazon, and on 16 May 218, at sunrise (the auspicious hour for a priest of the solar deity), he was proclaimed emperor as Marcus Aurelius Antoninus, the names of Caracalla, whose natural son he claimed to be. Following desertions from the unpopular Macrinus to his cause, an army commanded by Gannys, one of the eunuchs who formed Julia Maesa's entourage, decisively defeated the imperial forces near Antioch on 8 June. Shortly afterwards Macrinus was killed; but Elagabalus reckoned the beginning of his reign from the date of the battle that had brought him victory.

In letters written from Antioch to Rome his advisers, like those of his predecessors, assumed his possession of the imperial titles without waiting for a senatorial decree, but were careful, at the same time, to offer conciliatory gestures. The senate duly acquiesced and accepted his claim to be the son of Caracalla, whom they deified (although they had hated him). Coins were issued in honour of the new god (DIVO ANTONINO MAGNO – 'Great', like Alexander the Great) and in memory of the likewise deified Julia Domna (DIVA IVLIA AVGVSTA), as well as in the names of those who had now seized control of the State, the new emperor and his two Augustae, Julia Maesa and Julia Soaemias.

In August, the three sailed to Bithynia, where they spent the winter at the city of Nicomedia. There Elagabalus' bizarre oriental religious rites caused dismay, and amid angry demonstrations Gannys was killed. Slowly moving on towards the west, the imperial family reached Rome in early autumn 219. Once they were there, many Syrian henchmen and partisans (some of them far from respectable, in the belief of outraged senators) received important posts. One of their number, Comazon, became joint praetorian prefect (and subsequently city prefect) and directed the government in collaboration with Julia Maesa – who was now the most influential woman the Empire had ever known.

Theirs was a difficult and delicate task, since the youthful emperor displayed an alarming degree of independence, in both his personal and religious inclinations and activities. His sexual tastes, above all, earned him everlasting notoriety, for he was evidently a passive homosexual. Roman public opinion was accustomed to emperors who associated with young boys – usually as a sideline to their heterosexual activities – and it had been widely believed that Nero took an interest in men older than himself, although he was fond of women as well. But Elagabalus appears to have been a complete invert, and one who was determined to indulge his taste to the uttermost. While the lavish details provided by the *Historia Augusta* need not all be taken too literally, Dio Cassius, a contemporary senator and historian, deserves some credence when he identifies the emperor's favourite 'husband' – Hierocles, a blond Carian slave. But also, according to Dio, Elagabalus used to 'stand nude at the door of his room in the palace, as harlots do, and shake the curtain which hung from gold rings, while in a soft and melting voice he solicited passers by'. Herodian commented that it was a pity he appeared in public with painted eyes and rouged cheeks, because this spoilt his naturally handsome appearance.

Such eccentricities prompted Julia Maesa's advisers, eager for counter-propagandist measures, to provide Elagabalus with a series of legitimate brides – all women of impeccably Roman, aristocratic origin. According to one report he married and divorced, in the course of his short reign, no less than five wives, one after the other. The coinage displays as many as three, all granted the rank of Augusta and honoured by designs in which 'Harmony' (CONCORDIA) plays a prominent part. His first wife, from 219–20, was Julia Cornelia Paula. The second was Aquilia Severa – extracted, shockingly, from the ranks of the Vestal Virgins. Very soon, however, he repudiated her and married Annia Faustina, of the house of MARCUS AURELIUS. However, this union only lasted briefly, from 220–1, and was followed by his return to Severa. These continuous matrimonial changes suggest that his own veering personal affections played some part in the sequence. But the rapid succession of empresses could not conceal the fact that the boy's personal sexual interests were wholly engaged with men.

Far greater anxiety, however, was caused by Elagabalus' religious activities. From the reign of Septimius Severus onwards, solar worship had increasingly taken charge of the entire Pantheon. But Elagabalus swept aside all tradition and caution in his haste to incorporate a peculiar version of sun worship into the Roman imperial theology. For this unusual Roi Soleil imported his own eastern, local solar cult into the centre and summit of the state religion of Rome – in which it ranked even above the worship of Jupiter. His marriage to the Vestal Severa (from which he was understood to have expressed a hope for 'god-like children') had been intended to demonstrate the alliance of the two faiths, and for the same reason he gave the Roman goddess Minerva to El-Gabal as his wife. For this Unconquerable Sun deity (*Sol Invictus*) of Emesa, a black phallic meteorite, a resplendent temple was built on the eastern spur of Rome's Palatine Hill. The huge platform of its rectangular porticoed enclosure can still be seen; and medallions of the following reign (after the shrine had been adapted for other purposes) display a grandiose gateway and monumental flight of steps.

It was because of this cult that the emperor himself came to be known, from his deity, as Elagabalus, after the eastern custom of identifying the priest with the god whom he served. To consecrate his priesthood he had himself circumcised, and made his friends undergo the same rite. We are also told by Herodian how he danced round the altars dedicated to El-Gabal, while Syrian women played on cymbals and drums, and senators and knights had to stand and watch. And on midsummer day every year, the deity assumed the central part in what now became Rome's greatest annual festival. 'He placed the sun god', continues Herodian,

in a chariot adorned with gold and jewels and brought him out from the city to the suburbs. A six-horse chariot carried the divinity, the horses huge and flawlessly white, with expensive gold fittings and rich ornaments. No one held the reins, and no one rode in the chariot; the vehicle was escorted as if the god himself were the charioteer. Elagabalus ran backward in front of the chariot, facing the god and holding the horses' reins. He made the whole journey in this reverse fashion, looking up into the face of his god.

This picture is implicitly confirmed by the imperial coinage, which defines the young ruler as the 'Unconquered' and 'Supreme Priest', 'the priest of the Sun-god El-Gabal' (SACERDos DEI SOLIS ELAGABali); and another coin, issued at Antioch, shows the triumphal chariot to which Herodian referred, drawn by four horses, surrounded by four parasols, and carrying the sacred conical stone, surmounted by a Roman eagle.

Whether the juvenile emperor was also as cruel and treacherous as hostile tradition reported is uncertain. But his personal aberrations and, above all, his religious activities, were giving Julia Maesa such cause for alarm that she decided he had been a bad risk, and had to be liquidated. His mother Julia Soaemias, who had encouraged his solar indulgences, seemed equally damaging, and instead Maesa turned to her second daughter Julia Avita Mamaea, who had a thirteen-year-old son, Alexianus. The two women succeeded in persuading Elagabalus to appoint Alexianus as Caesar, so that he himself would be able to devote more time to his religious duties. Thus Alexianus was duly elevated to the rank of Caesar, under the name of ALEXANDER.

When, Elagabalus, soon afterwards, changed his mind and attempted to eliminate him, Maesa and Mamaea thwarted his moves, and a judicious distribution of their wealth prompted the praetorian guard to take action. On 11 March 222, Elagabalus and his mother Soaemias were murdered in the camp. Their bodies were dragged through the streets of Rome and thrown into the Tiber, and a large number of their henchmen likewise met their deaths. The Emesan god, the black stone, was sent back to his native city, where his worship continued with undiminished fervour after the strange interlude of his four years at Rome.

SEVERUS ALEXANDER
222–35

SEVERUS ALEXANDER (222–35) was born in 208 in the Phoenician city of Caesarea sub Libano; he was originally known as Marcus Julius Gessius Alexianus. His father was Gessius Marcianus and his mother Julia Avita Mamaea, daughter of Julia Maesa and niece of Julia Domna, the wife of SEPTIMIUS SEVERUS. Like his cousin and predecessor ELAGABALUS, Alexianus was a priest of the Sun-god at Emesa.

When Maesa concluded that Elagabalus had to be supplanted, she successfully persuaded him – with the connivance of Mamaea – to adopt Alexianus as his heir; the thirteen-year-old boy, granted the titles of Caesar and 'Prince of Youth', assumed the names of Marcus Aurelius Severus Alexander in 221, and coinage was issued in his and his mother's names. In the following year he and the emperor held the consulship together. Noting with displeasure the popularity of his amiable cousin, Elagabalus soon began to insult him and wanted not only to revoke his promotion but to have him put to death. However, these plans were frustrated by the vigilance of his grandmother and aunt, who arranged to have Elagabalus and his mother Julia Soaemias murdered by the guard. Thereupon Severus Alexander ascended peacefully to the throne. The government was first in the hands of Maesa and Mamaea, and then, after the former's death in about 223, it was Mamaea who exercised control.

However, Mamaea did not find it easy to assert her authority. During a three-day-long outbreak of street fighting, praetorian guardsmen clashed with their own commander, the great lawyer Ulpian (Domitius Ulpianus), who was Mamaea's Syrian compatriot and principal counsellor. Ulpian seems to have held the position of praetorian prefect in chief, presiding over two other prefects (Flavianus and Chrestus) as their superior officer. Both these men, however, died shortly afterwards, whereupon the guardsmen turned against Ulpian – holding him responsible for the deaths of his two subordinates, or disliking his old-fashioned disciplinary ideas. At all events they attacked him, and so in 223 he lost his life. Mamaea and Alexander, with whom he took refuge, had found it impossible to save him, and were even compelled to award his principal murderer, Marcus Aurelius Epagathus, the governorship of Egypt – though they subsequently procured his assassination. Ulpian's death ended the series of great jurists who served as praetorian prefects; from then onwards the civil duties of the prefecture became, for the time being, less prominent, owing to the succession of military emergencies that followed thick and fast.

In 225 Mamaea, who exercised a careful supervision over the mild, civilized and docile young emperor, selected for him, from a patrician family, a wife named Cnaea Seia Herennia Sallustia Barbia Orbiana, who was given the title of Augusta and displayed on the coinage. Her father, Seius Sallustius Macrinus, seems to have been awarded the rank of Caesar. Before long, however, he and his daughter fell out of favour with the jealous and suspicious Mamaea, who compelled Alexander – against his own wish, we are told – to exile Orbiana to Africa; while her father, fleeing to the praetorian camp, was seized and put to death as a rebel in 227 or 228. Thenceforward Mamaea, honoured with the title 'Mother of the Emperor and the Camp and the Senate and the Country', tolerated no potential rival at court. But the praetorians, whom the collapse of Sallustius had deprived of the chance to show their power, were still restless. One of the principal targets of their hostility was the historian and senator Dio Cassius, on the grounds (according to his own version) that while governor of Upper Pannonia he had 'ruled the soldiers with a strong hand'. The guardsmen had already protested against Dio in Ulpian's time, and when he became consul for the second time in 229 the emperor advised him to spend his two months of office in unobtrusive safety outside the capital.

The *Historia Augusta* insists, at flattering length, that this reign was a Golden Age of re-established senatorial authority. But such elaborate assertions, forming the nucleus of a biographical essay that is, in other respects, almost unrelievedly fictitious, appear to be unwarranted. The writer of the *Historia* has arbitrarily chosen to build up the harmless youth into an ideal prince, blessed with a wide (and conflicting) range of virtues, and supposedly the author of administrative reforms that were dear to the heart of the historian (or his source). As for the restoration of senatorial power, it is possible, at most, to accept Herodian's report that the insecure Maesa and Mamaea –understandably anxious to create a new and welcome image after the catastrophic reign of Elagabalus – established a committee of sixteen senators (perhaps part of a larger senatorial council) to advise his successor during the years of his minority. But the historian's further comment that such measures restored the dignity of the senate rather than its power is clearly very much to the point. As Dio Cassius made Augustus' minister Maecenas remark – in an imaginary speech to his master – the senate received sufficient honour if it was allowed the *appearance* of supremacy. In fact, however, the inexorable trend towards military absolutism continued, without any marked discontinuity. Even Elagabalus' chief minister Comazon survived, to hold the prefecture of the city for the third time; and Mamaea and Alexander did all they could to cultivate the good will of the army – with much less insistence on strict, old-fashioned military discipline than the *Historia* wants readers to believe.

Progress was however made in criminal law: the tendency to mitigate legal harshness, in this field at least, does represent a contrast to the greater severity of Elagabalus' reign. But unfortunately the new régime soon began to acquire a reputation for meanness. This was not altogether fair, since five distributions of grain were made to the Roman populace, and an active programme of public works was pursued in various parts of the Empire. This was particularly noticeable at Rome, where Nero's Baths, for example, were enlarged, and equipped with a new aqueduct and library, under the new name of the Baths of Alexander. Moreover, taxes were cautiously diminished, and the consequent losses in revenue replenished by duties on luxury goods. Nevertheless, the State still had to watch its expenditure closely in order to recover from the financial extravagances of the previous reign. The youthful Alexander, we are told, was thrifty in his personal expenditure, while his mother displayed notable avarice; and this, according to Herodian, disgusted her son – though he was too subservient to take effective counter-measures, with the result that her greedy and acquisitive behaviour prevented the reign from being really successful.

It also endangered her own position, at a time when the Empire's external military situation had changed dramatically and permanently for the worse. This was because the old Parthian administration, across the Euphrates, had been replaced by a quite different Persian régime. The recurrent wars with Rome had for some time gradually weakened the hold of the Parthians over their feudal dependencies. Among these was the princedom of Persepolis, whose ruler Ardashir from 223–30 proceeded to invade Parthia and overthrow its last monarch, setting up through the entire kingdom his own Sassanian dynasty, named after his grandfather. This new government was far more formidable and dangerous to Rome than the Parthians had ever been. Presiding over a strongly centralized and nationalistic government, its rulers were also aggressively interested in territorial expansion, asserting their desire to restore the ancient Persian frontiers as far as the westernmost shores of Asia Minor.

In 230 news reached Rome that Ardashir, in pursuit of this aim, had overrun Mesopotamia and was threatening Syria and the other Asian provinces. In the following year, therefore – after negotiations had proved futile – Mamaea and Alexander departed for the east, accompanied by a considerable army. A second diplomatic approach was once again rebuffed, and indeed countered by an ultimatum from Ardashir commanding the Romans to evacuate all the territory he claimed. Alexander's coinage hopefully proclaimed 'the Loyalty of the Army' (FIDES EXERCITVS, FIDES MILITVM); but at the same time there were mutinies, an attempted usurpation among the officers in Mesopotamia, and trouble among the contingents summoned from Egypt. Nevertheless, in 232 the Romans were ready to launch a simultaneous three-pronged campaign, in which Armenia, the northern reaches of Mesopotamia, and the southern areas of the same country, were simultaneously invaded. It seems that while the first column was successful, and pressed on into Median territory – though suffering severely from the winter cold on its return journey – the second, under the emperor's personal command, failed to get moving (perhaps because of the torrid climate), and the third was annihilated on the Euphrates. All the same, the Roman province of Mesopotamia was recovered; and Ardashir made no further move for four years. So when Alexander and Mamaea returned to Rome in autumn 233, the former celebrated a grandiose triumph as 'Persicus Maximus'.

But the Roman government had for some time been anxiously aware of serious unrest upon the Rhine and Danube frontiers as well; thus the two imperial leaders, already preoccupied with the Persian crises, found themselves confronted with a second menace, heralding a new, grim epoch, in which the Empire was to be almost perpetually assailed on these two frontiers at once.

In particular, news of a dangerous threat from the Alamanni had already arrived before the emperor and his mother departed from the east. When it became known, the Danubian legions which they had taken on the Persian campaign (already jealous of the rulers' preference for the troops of their native east) clamoured to go back home to the European frontiers so as to defend their own countries if they came under attack; and Alexander and Mamaea, when they returned to Rome, sent them direct to the north. In 234 they too moved in that direction, to join the legions on the Rhine, at Moguntiacum.

A pontoon bridge was thrown across the river, but when Alexander, who was evidently no general, attempted to buy off the Germans, his troops felt humiliated and transferred their loyalty to a senior officer of their own Danubian stock, MAXIMINUS by name. In March 235 they invested him with the purple, and the soldiers that Alexander and Mamaea had brought from the east failed to come to their help. On the contrary, when Maximinus advanced against them they set upon the imperial pair at Vicus Britannicus, and put them to death.

During his reign the emperor and his mother had made a careful attempt to guide the sun worship into less exotic channels than those favoured by Elagabalus. True, Sol, the quasi-monotheistic deity of the age, is still to be seen repeatedly on the coinage. At this date, however, he appears no longer in Syrian guise, but wearing the traditional radiate crown of the Roman god – and Elagabalus' temple was transformed into a shrine of Jupiter the Avenger. The *Historia Augusta* depicts the religious tastes of Alexander as tolerant and eclectic:

> First of all, if it were permissible – that is to say, if he had not slept with his wife – in the early morning hours he would worship in the sanctuary of the Lares, in which he kept statues of the deified emperors (of whom, however, only the best had been selected) and also of certain holy souls, among them Apollonius of Tyana, and, according to a contemporary writer, Christ, Abraham and Orpheus, and others of this same character, and, besides, the portraits of his own ancestors. . . . Alexander the Great, too, he enshrined in this sanctuary along with the most righteous men and the deified emperors.

This reference to a statue of Jesus is not altogether implausible, for at the time there must have been an increasing number of Christians in the imperial household.

PART V

THE
AGE OF CRISIS

MAXIMINUS I
235–8

MAXIMINUS I (Gaius Julius Verus) (235–8) was stated (although this cannot be verified) to have been the son of a peasant Gothic father and a mother belonging to the Alan tribe (related to the Sarmatians, from the Black Sea area). He was known as 'the Thracian' (Thrax) but probably came from a more northerly region, not far from the Danube. Zonaras' report that he was born in 172 or 173 is improbable; the date should perhaps be a decade or more later.

Attracting attention by his legendary strength and size, he rose from the ranks – the first Roman emperor to do so – and moved rapidly up the military ladder. In 232 he may have commanded a legion in Egypt, and subsequently became governor of the reconquered province of Mesopotamia. In 235 he was in charge of a force of Pannonian recruits on the Rhine, and it was they who slew Severus Alexander and Julia Mamaea and awarded the Empire to Maximinus, whose record contrasted so favourably with his predecessor's military ineffectiveness. The senate was obliged to confirm his elevation, though no doubt with considerable reluctance, since they had not been consulted, nor did they by any means regard him as one of themselves.

Maximinus I judged the German war his most important task. But, before taking it in hand he had to deal with two threatened internal rebellions. First, while he was campaigning across the Rhine, a group of officers planned to break down the bridge, thus stranding him on the other side of the river, after which they proposed to elevate a senator named Magnus to the throne in his place. But word of the conspiracy leaked out, and Maximinus put to death all the suspects. Secondly, the important corps of archers from Osrhoene, devoted to the memory of Severus Alexander, invested one of his friends, Quartinus, with the purple. But their leader Macedo changed his mind and murdered Quartinus instead, though this did not avail to save his own life. After these menacing disturbances, Maximinus remained suspicious and embittered. All officers of senatorial rank were removed from the army, and replaced by professional soldiers whom he himself had promoted.

Once these incipient revolts had been stamped out, the new emperor crossed the Rhine and pushed deep into Germany. Plundering the country and burning its villages, he compelled the Germans – and especially the Alamanni who were his principal enemies – to take refuge in their forests and marshes. Before long, however, an important battle was fought, in a swamp near the borders of northern Württemberg and Baden. The emperor, riding chest-high in the water, displayed personal courage, and despite high Roman losses inflicted a crushing defeat which re-established peace for some time. A painting of the battle was sent to Rome for display in the senate-house; and Maximinus, accepting the victorious title of Germanicus Maximus for himself, elevated his son Maximus to the rank of Caesar and Prince of Youth, issuing coins in his name and that of his own deceased, deified wife Caecilia Paulina.

Although Maximinus next made moves to strengthen the frontier defences, he may also have intended, at a later date, to follow up his victory by further campaigns beyond the Rhine border. If so, the plan had to be abandoned owing to threats from tribes on the Danube. After spending the winter of 235–6 at Sirmium, a road junction which had become a major military centre, Maximinus moved against these hostile tribesmen, subsequently assuming the titles Sarmaticus Maximus and Dacicus Maximus. To judge from his earlier successes in Germany, there is no reason to suppose that such triumphant claims were fictitious. His headquarters were still at Sirmium in the spring of 238 when news came of the revolt of the aged GORDIANUS AFRICANUS, governor of Africa, assisted by his son of the same name. Although the senate and most of the Empire supported the insurgents, they were destroyed after only twenty-two days, when the governor of Numidia, Capellianus, who remained loyal, killed the younger Gordian in battle, and his father committed suicide. But then the senate immediately appointed two new emperors from their own order, BALBINUS and PUPIENUS, in continued defiance of Maximinus.

When he learnt of the revolt of the Gordians, Maximinus had decided upon an early invasion of Italy. On reaching Emona, however, he found the city evacuated, and its stores removed or destroyed, much to the disappointment of his soldiers, who began to show mutinous tendencies. Moreover, determined resistance was encountered at Aquileia; and even after improvising a pontoon bridge over the flooded River Sontius (Isonzo), the emperor failed to take the city by storm. The heavy losses thus incurred, combined with a shortage of food for the troops and severe treatment meted out to unsatisfactory officers, caused a general lowering of discipline and morale in the imperial forces – as a result of which, on 10 May, the soldiers belonging to a particular legion which had an additional reason for disaffection (because their families and possessions were in enemy hands at Albanum) fell upon Maximinus and his son as they were taking their siesta after the midday meal, and put them to death. Their heads were sent to Rome under cavalry escort.

The features of Maximinus on his busts and coins confirm Herodian's assertion that he had a frightening look. 'His body, too,' adds the historian,

was huge; not easily would any of the skilled Greek athletes or the best-trained warriors among the barbarians prove his equal. . . . He used his power savagely to inspire great fear. He undertook to substitute for a mild and moderate rule an autocracy in every way barbarous, well aware of the hostility directed towards him because he was the first man to rise from a lowly station to the post of the highest honour. His character was naturally barbaric, as his race was barbarian. He had inherited the brutal disposition of his countrymen. . . . His actions, however, would have enhanced his reputation, if he had not been much too ruthless towards his associates and subjects.

These critical observations, echoed by the *Historia Augusta*, reflect the attitude of the senate, since its members detested Maximinus. And this was a feeling that he strongly reciprocated, being an uneducated man who barely spoke Latin, and who felt little sympathy for the traditional upper class and middle ranks of Roman society. Not once, for example, during the three years of his reign, did he find time to visit the capital. Moreover, it appears that under his rule the more prosperous sections of the population, beset by a host of tax collectors, agents and military spies, were obliged to contribute more heavily than ever before to the defence of the Empire; and they had to pay not in the steadily deteriorating imperial currency, but in bullion and kind. Among upper-class sufferers, these exactions earned Maximinus a name for extortionate greed.

Nevertheless, his harshness was founded on a realistic assessment. The Empire was desperately hard-pressed. New and ruthless ways of thinking and acting were demanded in order to keep it from total disintegration – and only a novel type of emperor, prepared to subordinate everything to military needs, could provide these radical methods. For the same reason, he reversed his predecessor's clement attitude to the Christians, since any influences that might undermine the national patriotic effort could not, in his opinion, be tolerated.

Despite his failure at the end – partly due, as Herodian said, to excessive severity – Maximinus I had shown himself to be a highly competent commander. He deserves to be regarded as the first of the imposing line of Danubian emperors – sprung from the finest fighting peoples in the Roman world – who during the half-century that lay ahead managed to rescue the Empire from chaos, although the price paid in material comfort was devastating.

GORDIAN I
238

GORDIAN I (Marcus Antonius Gordianus Sempronianus Romanus) (joint emperor with his son GORDIAN II, March–April 238) was born in 159 or a year or two later. His parents were stated by the *Historia Augusta* to have been called Maecius Marullus and Ulpia Gordiana, though the name 'Maecius' sounds suspiciously like an anachronism, because it was a name characteristic of the later fourth century when the *Historia* was written. The name 'Ulpia' ascribed, no less dubiously, to Gordian's mother recalls the pretence that, through her, he was descended from TRAJAN; on his father's side his ancestors were stated to be those idealistic Republican reformers, the Gracchi. More probable than any of these assertions is a link between the name Gordianus and the town of Gordium in Asia Minor. Modern writers have conjectured that he only assumed the name of Romanus on his accession, but the existence of a woman named Sempronia Romana, attested by an inscription, suggests instead that it was part of his original nomenclature.

Gordian I was a wealthy landowner of a literary turn of mind. Philostratus dedicated a book to him (or his son), and there was a family connexion with the famous Athenian sophist Herodes Atticus, who was consul in 143. After holding the various senatorial offices the older Gordian reached the consulship at the comparatively advanced age of sixty-four. He also governed a number of provinces, including Lower Britain, and in 237/8, when approaching eighty, he found himself appointed by MAXIMINUS I to the governorship of Africa. In that province one of the emperor's agents was undertaking the collection of the imperial taxes in an oppressive fashion, with the particular aim of confiscating the possessions of rich, landed proprietors. In self-defence a number of young nobles formed a conspiracy against the procurator, and, mobilizing their tenants and domestic staffs, cornered him at Thysdrus and put him to death. After this rebellious action, their only means of saving their own lives was to rouse the whole province to revolt – and to proclaim a rival emperor to Maximinus.

For this purpose they approached Gordian I. At first, it was said, he seemed reluctant, but on about 19 March 238, he accepted acclamation as Augustus, and a few days later, escorted by soldiers and the tallest youths in the city, he made a ceremonial entry into the provincial capital, Carthage, together with his son of the same name whom he appointed as his imperial colleague. 'For a brief period,' declared Herodian, 'Carthage was Rome in appearance and prosperity,' and it was not long before both Gordians assumed the additional name of Africanus. Their first step was to dispatch a deputation to Rome, headed by the father's bold and physically powerful aide, who delivered the Gordians' proclamation to the senate and people. The envoys also took private letters addressed to various senators. One of the principal aims of these delegates was to eliminate the praetorian prefect Vitalianus, who was a firm adherent of Maximinus. By claiming that they were engaged upon a secret mission on Maximinus' behalf, they contrived to obtain an introduction to the prefect and murdered him.

Next, the Gordians published their programme, promising the suppression of informers and the restoration of exiles, and a bonus for the troops. On 2 April the senate (although it had not apparently been a party to the rebellion) confirmed their imperial titles. Severus Alexander was deified, and Maximinus declared a public enemy; his supporters, including Sabinus the city prefect of Rome, were hunted down and slain. Moreover, acting with an unusual degree of energy, the senators next proceeded to appoint a committee of twenty ex-consuls, allotting to each of them a different part of Italy with instructions that they should defend it against Maximinus' expected invasion. At the same time emissaries were dispatched to the provincial governors, calling upon them to declare allegiance to the Gordians, and (as milestones confirm) with the exceptions of Pannonia and Dacia and Spain the recipients seem to have complied.

However, events in Africa itself, from which the Gordians had still not departed, now proved ruinous to their cause. As a result of a lawsuit, they were on bad terms with Capellianus, the governor of neighbouring Numidia, and tried to remove him. He refused to recognize their régime and moved his regular troops against them. The younger Gordian was killed in battle, and his father hanged himself (according to another source he had already done so before the engagement). They had only worn the purple for twenty-two days, and the inscription on their coins, 'The Security of The Emperors', proved bitterly ironical. Yet their reign remained memorable, despite its brevity, because the cowed and dejected senate had once again, after so many years, placed itself in the front of the picture, and assumed an independent political role.

Gordian I, according to the portraits on his coins, was an old man with thin features. Although determined to portray him, misleadingly, as an ideal

Antonine emperor, the *Historia Augusta* may have been drawing on a reliable source when it offered a personal sketch. He was impressive-looking, we are told, elegantly dressed and fond of his relations; and he greatly enjoyed bathing. However, the writer goes on to remark, 'there is nothing you can say that he ever did passionately, immoderately or excessively. His love of sleep was enormous; he would doze off even at table, if he was dining with friends, and without any embarrassment.'

GORDIAN II
238

GORDIAN II (Marcus Antonius Gordianus Sempronianus Romanus) (joint emperor with his father GORDIAN I, March–April 238) was born in about 192. He became governor of Achaea and then consul, and when his aged father was appointed proconsul of Africa accompanied him to Carthage as his deputy. After GORDIAN I, at the request of the local nobility, had accepted the purple at Thysdrus in March 238 the old man made his son his imperial colleague with the title of Augustus, or emperor in every respect except that he did not share the high-priesthood; both appointments were ratified and welcomed by the senate. When, almost immediately, Capellianus, the governor of Numidia, acting on behalf of Maximinus, marched against Carthage (the provisional capital of the new régime), Gordian II moved out to oppose his advance.

'Capellianus', reported Herodian,

was at the head of a huge army of young, vigorous men equipped with every type of weapon and trained for battle by military experience gained in fighting the barbarians. . . . The younger Gordian was chosen to command the crowd of civilians that opposed him. . . . When the battle was joined, the Carthaginians were superior in numbers, but they were an undisciplined mob, without military training; for they had grown up in a time of complete peace and indulged themselves constantly in feasts and festivals. To make it worse, they were without arms and proper equipment. Each man brought from home a dagger, an axe, or a hunting spear; those who found hides cut out circles of leather, arranged pieces of wood as a frame, and fashioned shields as best they could. The Numidians, by contrast, were excellent javelin men and superb horsemen. Scorning a bridle they used only a stick to guide their mounts. They easily routed the huge Carthaginian mob; without waiting for the Numidians' charge, the Carthaginians threw down their arms and fled. Crowding and trampling one another underfoot, more Carthaginians were killed in the crush than fell by enemy action.

One of the casualties was their commander, Gordian II himself; his body was never discovered. His father committed suicide before or after the battle (see GORDIAN I). Capellianus entered Carthage and instituted a reign of terror, repeated elsewhere in the African province. The operation had shown that any rebellion or *coup* launched without the support, or against the wishes, of the regular army was doomed to failure.

On his coins the younger Gordian bears the same titles as his father, but his portrait is distinguished by plumper features and a high bald forehead. The *Historia Augusta*, perhaps embroidering the facts, declared him to have been

a man of huge size. . . . He had a craving for cold drinks and passed the summer with great difficulty unless he drank a great many of them. . . . There are still in existence various things written by him both in prose and in verse, which are often quoted by his kinsmen today. These are neither good nor yet very bad, but rather mediocre. They seem, in truth, the work of one who was really talented but gave himself over to pleasure and wasted his genius. . . . He had taken his studies very seriously. And not only was he remarkably good-looking but his memory was extraordinary. (He was also very kind-hearted – when any of the boys was flogged at school he could not restrain his tears.)

His tutor Serenus Sammonicus, the *Historia* continues,

a great friend of his father's, when he died left the young Gordian all the books that had belonged to his own father (after whom he was named), and these were estimated at sixty-two thousand. . . . Gordian II lived a life of revelry – in gardens, in baths, and in most delightful groves. . . . He was very fond of women; indeed, it is said that he had twenty-two mistresses formally attached to him, from all of whom he had three or four children apiece.

This description gave Edward Gibbon the opportunity for one of his best-known epigrams: 'Twenty-two acknowledged concubines, and a library of sixty-two thousand volumes, attested the variety of his inclinations; and, from the productions that he left behind him, it appears that the former as well as the latter were designed for use rather than for ostentation.' Gibbon concludes that 'his manners were less pure, but his character was equally amiable with that of his father.'

BALBINUS
238

BALBINUS (Decimus Caelius Calvinus Balbinus) (joint emperor with PUPIENUS, April–July 238) cannot have been born as late as 178, as indicated by Zonaras; *c.* 170 or *c.* 165 are more probable dates. The son, by birth or adoption, of a certain Caelius Calvinus, he was of patrician status, since the Salian priesthood, of which he became a member, was reserved for men of that rank. Balbinus was consul in 203 and again in 213. The *Historia Augusta* also credits him with the governorships of Asia and Africa following on five similar tenures of other provinces, but this detailed record is open to suspicion, although no doubt he held some such posts.

The senate had publicly committed itself to the revolt of GORDIANS I and II against Maximinus, and after their deaths became known, it could not turn back. When its members recognized the Gordians, they had appointed a committee of twenty to supervise the defence of Italy, and now, meeting in the temple of Jupiter on the Capitoline Hill, they elevated two of the twenty to become the next Augusti. Balbinus was one of them and the other was PUPIENUS. The position of these two emperors was something new in the history of Rome. Whenever there had been joint emperors before – such as MARCUS AURELIUS and LUCIUS VERUS, and the two Gordians – one had been regarded as superior to the other, and it was he alone who became chief priest. But neither Balbinus nor Pupienus enjoyed precedence over his colleague, and even the hitherto indivisible dignity of the high priesthood was bestowed upon each of them.

Their close relationship to the senate, which had appointed them, was reflected in the retention of the committee of twenty; and coins were issued hailing the new emperors as 'the Fathers of the Senate' (PATRES SENATVS). However, the régime was greeted with grave unrest at Rome – mainly because Pupienus (*q.v.*) was unpopular – and the imperial colleagues therefore decided to stress their political continuity with the late-lamented

Gordians: first by announcing their deification, and secondly by raising MARCUS ANTONIUS GORDIANUS (III), grandson of Gordian I and nephew of Gordian II, to the rank of Caesar. These measures were influenced by the consideration that his family wealth would now be at their disposal – indeed, it soon proved possible to distribute a cash bonus to the Roman population.

But it had now become imperative to deal with MAXIMINUS, whose invasion of Italy was imminent. Accordingly, while Balbinus remained in Rome, Pupienus marched off to collect an army in the northern part of the peninsula. At this juncture the two emperors enjoyed an enormous stroke of luck; for the ex-consuls Crispinus and Menophilus, members of the committee of twenty, displayed a successful resistance to Maximinus at Aquileia, with the result that he and his son were murdered by their own discouraged soldiers. The population of Aquileia hung portraits of Balbinus, Pupienus and Gordian III upon its walls, and invited the besieging troops to do them homage. The men duly responded, and were allowed to stave off famine at a market provided by the defenders on the outskirts of their city.

Not long afterwards, they sent envoys to express allegiance to Pupienus, who visited Aquileia and then returned to Rome, where he was met at the gates by Balbinus and Gordian III. But in the meantime Balbinus had been encountering grave difficulties in the capital. The trouble had started when two senators, Gallicanus and Maecenas, arranged for a small group of praetorian guardsmen, who had made their way into the senate-house, to be set upon and killed. This alarmed and infuriated the rest of the guard, who in any case disliked being governed by nominees of the senate; fighting broke out, as Gallicanus mobilized a troop of gladiators and the praetorians murderously retaliated. Balbinus, who had remained at Rome throughout this tense period, issued an edict in which he sought to calm the people, and promised the praetorians an amnesty. But neither side listened, and the soldiers started a fire which did enormous damage.

When, therefore, Pupienus returned to the capital in jubilation, Balbinus was all too well aware that he for his part had suffered a serious loss of prestige. Their coinage reflects their elaborate efforts to assert that they were still on good terms: the type of clasped hands was used not only to indicate their joint rule as Fathers of the Senate but to demonstrate their personal friendship, emphasized by a number of different inscriptions; in particular Balbinus celebrates their mutual dutifulness and trust (PIETAS MVTVA AVGG. [Augustorum], FIDES MVTVA AVGG.). These protestations however rang increasingly hollow, since their relations rapidly and sharply deteriorated.

The common task of repelling external enemies might have patched matters up, and plans to this end were duly formed: Balbinus was to move against the Goths, who had crossed the Lower Danube, while Pupienus would proceed against the Persians. But the praetorians decided otherwise. Already disaffected and violent, they feared supersession by Pupienus' German body-guard, and, upon the conclusion of the Capitoline Games, moved on the palace in order to take it by storm. This brought the two rulers' disagreements to a head, because Balbinus refused to allow the Germans to be summoned to their help, fearing that they would oust him in favour of his colleague. While he and Pupienus were arguing, the praetorians rushed in, seized them, tore off their clothes and dragged them through the streets to their own camp, beating and torturing them as they went. Their German bodyguard, it was rumoured, was on its way to rescue the prisoners. Learning of this, their captors put them to death, and left their bodies lying in the street. They had reigned for ninety-nine days.

Balbinus was described by Herodian as a man who possessed a more frank and open nature than his colleague; he had earlier proved himself, the historian added, a useful provincial governor. His portraits, especially on coins, are highly individual, displaying smooth, plump features and a ponderous jowl. The *Historia Augusta* attributed to him not only many amiable literary and oratorical talents but also an aristocratic taste for wine, food, love-making and elegance of dress; but its writer may have been exaggerating, for his aim was to point a rhetorical contrast with the alleged uncouthness of Pupienus.

PUPIENUS
238

PUPIENUS (Marcus Clodius Pupienus Maximus) (joint emperor with BALBINUS, April–July 238) was, according to Zonaras, seventy-four at the time of his accession. Independent evidence however suggests that he was only in his early sixties – younger, perhaps, than BALBINUS, over whom he nevertheless took precedence on papyri and inscriptions. As to their background, the *Historia Augusta*'s dramatic contrast between the noble family of Balbinus and the humble birth of Pupienus appears to be fictitious. It is preferable to believe Herodian's report that both men were of equally upper-class origins; indeed, Pupienus seems to have held patrician rank, to judge by the careers of one or both of his presumed sons. Other eminent figures bearing the names of Pupenius and Pupienius may have been his relations, and the name of the emperor's daughter Sextia Cethegilla suggests noble marriage connexions. She was honoured by two freedmen named Pupienus at Volaterrae in Etruria, and the family was evidently Etruscan (although an Athenian who became consul also bore this rare name).

Even if the early military career and governorships of the future ruler, as recorded by the *Historia Augusta*, seem to form a series of imaginative inventions, Herodian's statement that he had been governor either of Upper or Lower Germany may be accepted. He also held the governorship of Asia. He was twice consul, in about 217 and in 234, and became prefect of the city in the 230s. Like Balbinus, he was serving as one of the committee of twenty appointed to repel MAXIMINUS I from Italy at the time when, following the deaths of the GORDIANS, the senate called them both to the throne, with exactly equal powers (see BALBINUS). Pupienus' elevation was far from popular, for as city prefect he had displayed considerable severity, particularly in dealing with criminal elements. In consequence, the two new emperors had to surround themselves with an improvised guard before they could force their way out of the Capitol, where the senate had been meeting. It was because of this deterioration of public order that they felt obliged to nominate the young grandson of Gordian I as Caesar (GORDIAN III), a decision which placated the crowd sufficiently to allow the new emperors to get to the palace.

Pupienus then had the task of repelling Maximinus' invasion of Italy; but while endeavouring to collect an army in the north of the peninsula the welcome news reached him at Ravenna that his enemy, together with his son and heir, had been killed by his own men while engaged in an unsuccessful siege of Aquileia. Thereupon Pupienus himself proceeded to the recently beleaguered city. Its people eventually opened their gates to him, and Maximinus' troops were sent back to their homes. Accompanied by a bodyguard of Germans – who felt loyal to him after his earlier governorship of their country – Pupienus returned to the capital and received an ovation from the senate and people.

Yet Balbinus was jealous, and to judge from the coins, with some reason: they show that his colleague began to call himself 'Pupienus Maximus' instead of 'Marcus Clodius Pupienus'. Admittedly 'Maximus', as inscriptions confirm, had always been one of his family names. However, the word also means 'the Greatest', and it can hardly be fortuitous that he began to stress this appellation at the time of his triumphant return to the capital, where his colleague, by way of contrast, had been suffering some unpleasant experiences. Pupienus echoed Balbinus' propagandist assertion of their excellent relations by likewise stressing their mutual affection and love (CARITAS MVTVA AVGG., AMOR MVTVVS AVGG.). Nevertheless, relations between the two emperors remained manifestly unfriendly; and it was particularly unfortunate, in this situation, that the praetorians entertained a profound hostility towards Pupienus' bodyguard, whom they suspected of planning to supersede them. Before long, therefore, a group of praetorian soldiers broke violently into the palace – where the joint emperors were, at the time, engaged in furious argument. The story of their subsequent deaths has been told in the life of Balbinus (above).

Like him, Pupienus was an experienced administrator, and it was Pupienus, rather than his colleague, whom the senate selected to command the military resistance to Maximinus I. Yet about his personal qualities very little can be said, because the *Historia Augusta* follows up its fraudulent contrast between the joint emperors' pedigrees by an equally fictitious rhetorical distinction between the aristocratic amiability of Balbinus and the just but stern peasant virtues of Pupienus. It may have been true that Pupienus was stern, since his city prefecture had been marred by that reputation. But the only historically certain contrast to Balbinus (apart from their obvious temperamental incompatibility) relates to their personal appearances; for in sharp distinction from Balbinus' chubby physiognomy an equally realistic series of coin-portraits of Pupienus depicts his thin features and long nose and beard. The *Historia Augusta*, not implausibly, declares that he looked morose and gloomy, but its further assertions that he was a sparing drinker, continent in affairs of love and unwilling to accept anyone's opinion except his own, cannot necessarily be trusted.

The administrative capacities of Pupienus and Balbinus are on the whole favourably treated by our literary tradition – though this would naturally be prone to speak well of senatorial nominees. Their catastrophically short reign, however, immediately following upon the equally transient régime of the Gordians, confirmed once and for all that the senate could not effectively appoint emperors: only the army was able to do this with any measure of success.

GORDIAN III
238–44

GORDIAN III (Marcus Antonius Gordianus) (238–44) was born in 225. The names of his parents as recorded in the *Historia Augusta* are imaginary. However, his mother was evidently a daughter of GORDIAN I and sister of GORDIAN II. When these men were murdered in 238, their successors BALBINUS and PUPIENUS, in order to stave off hostile rioters (and to gain some control over the Gordians' large resources), raised the young Gordian III to the rank of Caesar, issuing coins in his name; and after their assassination later in the same year, the soldiers elevated Gordian III to the throne.

Initially (whether the *Historia Augusta*'s reports of his mother's powerful eunuchs and court favourites are accurate or not), the new administration remained under the control of the senate. Yet it was obliged to be careful how it handled the soldiers, since it was they who had nominated Gordian III, and who still regarded him as their protégé. Nevertheless, his government ventured to cashier the legion which had supported Capellianus' successful attempt to overthrow his grandfather and uncle; for their memory was scrupulously honoured, with a dutifulness for which the new boy-emperor assumed the designation 'Pius', which henceforward appeared regularly on his coinage. This action against the legion however left the African province dangerously denuded of troops, so that when its governor, Sabinianus, rebelled in 240, his rising had to be put down by units summoned from Mauretania.

Meanwhile, however, there had been far more serious threats from external enemies, probing the northern river frontiers. Already during the reign of Balbinus and Pupienus the Goths had broken into Lower Moesia and pillaged the city of Istrus, while the Dacian tribe of the Carpi crossed the Danube farther to the west. Menophilus, governor of Lower Moesia, intervened at the head of a large body of troops, and offered annual subsidies which induced the Goths to hand over prisoners they had captured – refusing, however, a similar demand from the Carpi, once his army had been sufficiently reinforced. In 239 bronze coins issued at Viminacium in Upper Moesia recorded the beginning of a new provincial era, bearing witness to a general programme of reorganization throughout the region, including the strengthening of its defences.

In 241 the régime changed character, when the praetorian prefecture passed into the hands of a man who rapidly acquired complete influence over Gordian III. He was Gaius Furius Sabinus Aquila Timesitheus, a man of culture and eloquence, who had earlier risen from the ranks by way of the centurionship into the order of knights. Thereafter he occupied an impressive series of administrative posts in one reign after another, weathering the storms that accompanied so many abrupt changes of régime. After appointing him praetorian prefect, Gordian III married his daughter Tranquillina, celebrating the event by coins displaying her portrait and honouring VENVS VICTRIX, the victorious goddess of love. The *Historia Augusta* calls the prefect 'Misitheus' (Hater of the Gods), yet invents an inscription acknowledging him as Father of the Emperor and Protector of the Empire.

It was fortunate that Gordian III, still in his teens, had lodged the government in such capable hands, for it was during his reign that the full, unprecedented burden which would thenceforward be imposed on the Roman armies by the Persians first became apparent. This threat was foreshadowed when their new ruler Shapur (Sapor) I (239–70) arranged to be hailed, on his coronation, by the provocative title of 'King of Kings of Iran and non-Iran'. Next to Hannibal, Shapur was the most dangerous enemy whom the Romans ever had to confront. His predecessor Ardashir, in the reign of MAXIMINUS I, had captured Carrhae and Nisibis in Mesopotamia, and now it was learnt that Shapur was invading Syria and threatening Antioch itself. An immediate Roman military response proved impossible, since the Danubian frontier had to be re-established first, but in spring 243 the main Roman army, supported by the fleet, was ready to march to the east. There, in the course of a series of successful operations directed by Timesitheus, Antioch was relieved (becoming an imperial mint); Carrhae and Nisibis returned into Roman hands; and the Persian army, in full retreat, was overtaken and severely defeated at Rhesaena (although Shapur afterwards chose to represent Gordian III in a prostrate position on a relief).

The young emperor intended to follow up these victories by an advance on the Persian capital Ctesiphon, but this plan was suspended when Timesitheus fell ill and died in the winter of 243. His deputy, PHILIP the Arab, took his place. Some believed he had poisoned his predecessor; at all events, he wanted not only the prefecture but the imperial throne for himself, and worked up the soldiers against Gordian. The latter for his part, according to one report, offered to resign and to become Philip's Caesar or accept any other subordinate post. Philip left the decision in the hands of the soldiers, who declared that they needed an adult man as a ruler, and not a child. Thereupon, near Zaitha on the Euphrates, Gordian met his end, on 25 February 244. The senate was informed that he had died a natural death, and a cenotaph was erected in his honour at the place where he died; but he was probably assassinated at Philip's instigation.

He had inherited an unhappy Empire, and there are certain signs that he, or rather his counsellors, tried to improve the situation, at least up to a point. Inscriptions found at Aphrodisias reflect the correct aims of his provincial administration. A decree published in 238 commands governors to ensure that nothing was done which was not in keeping with the principles of the age. Unwarranted decisions by military judges concerning civil issues were forbidden, and precautions were taken against stretching the law in favour of State officials. An inscription from Scaptopare in Thrace shows its inhabitants complaining to the emperor about their oppression by soldiers and others, who had been insisting on the provision of hospitality free of charge. The villagers presented their petition through one of their number who was a member of the praetorian guard, hoping that this might earn their plea special attention. But the spokesmen for Gordian III, like those of other rulers, replied that the Thracians must air their grievance through the usual and proper channels – and thus it no doubt followed the same useless path as innumerable other complaints during this period of widespread oppression and excessive taxation.

Nothing is known for certain about the character of the youthful Gordian III, so we have to turn to the *Historia Augusta* – taking the usual pinch of salt. 'He was a light-hearted lad,' we are told, 'handsome, winning, agreeable to everyone, merry in his life, eminent in letters; in nothing, indeed, except his age was he unqualified for empire. Before Philip's conspiracy he was loved by the people, the senate and the soldiers as no prince had ever been before.'

PHILIP I
244–9

PHILIP I (Marcus Julius Verus Philippus) (244–9) was born in about 204. He was the son of an Arab chieftain named Marinus, holding Roman knightly rank, from a town in Trachonitis. He became known as Philip the Arab – the first man of that race to occupy the imperial throne. Accompanying GORDIAN III on his eastern campaign, he held the office of deputy praetorian prefect. Then late in 243, in place of Timesitheus (whom he was accused of having murdered), he became prefect, and inflamed the soldiers against the emperor by blaming him for a scarcity of food due to the non-arrival of grain ships. The subsequent death of the young ruler seems attributable to Philip's prompting. Nevertheless, he reported to the senate that it had been due to natural causes and insisted on Gordian's deification. The senators, with whom Philip immediately established a friendly relationship, concurred and recognized his claim to the throne.

The initial act of the new reign was the conclusion of an agreement with the Persians. Philip's desire to get to Rome – a journey which MAXIMINUS I had, so mistakenly, never found time to do – meant that the treaty was arranged with some haste. However its terms were not unfavourable, for although the Romans only kept a nominal supervision over Greater Armenia, Lesser Armenia and Mesopotamia (as far as Singara) remained under imperial control, so that Philip felt entitled to adopt the appellation 'Persicus Maximus'.

Philip showed a strong dependence upon his own family, appointing his brother Gaius Julius Priscus and his father-in-law or brother-in-law Severianus to the governorships of Mesopotamia and Moesia (the combined Upper and Lower provinces) respectively. He was also determined to found a new dynasty. His son Philip the younger was immediately declared Caesar and Prince of the Youth, and decrees were published in his name as well as his father's; the emperor's wife Otacilia Severa was quickly granted the title of

Augusta; and wife and son alike figured prominently and continually on the coinage. Moreover, in order to endow his régime with additional legitimacy, Philip deified his late father Marinus, whose head appeared on local bronze issues of their home town, now raised to the rank of a colony under the name of Philippopolis (which was also the designation of another new colony in Thrace).

Not long after the beginning of the reign the Dacian Carpi once again crossed the Danube. Neither Severianus nor his subordinate general in Lower Moesia were able to make any headway against the invaders, and at about the end of 245 Philip himself set out from Rome to confront them himself. His presence in Dacia in 246 is confirmed by the inauguration of coinage in the region, announcing that a new provincial era was dated from his visit. There must also, in this year, have been fighting against the Germans (presumably Quadi), for the emperor assumed the title 'Germanicus Maximus'. The additional designation of 'Carpicus Maximus' in 247 bears witness to an impressive victory over the Dacian Carpi, who failed to break out of their principal fortress and were compelled to sue for peace. Returning to Rome, the emperor took advantage of his enhanced prestige to raise his son Philip the younger to the rank of Augustus. The youth, Philip II, was also made joint chief priest, so that his powers were exactly equal to his father's, and a double principate, like that of BALBINUS and PUPIENUS, was once again created, at least in constitutional terms – although in view of the younger Philip's immature years it had no immediate practical effect.

In 248 the two Philips became consuls together, the father for the third time and the son for the second. It was in this year that the outstanding event of the reign occurred: the celebration of what, in keeping with the calculations of the learned Varro (d. 27 BC), was the thousandth birthday of Rome, the end of its tenth century and the beginning of its eleventh. The occasion was commemorated with great magnificence, reflected on an abundant issue of coins (SAECVLARES AVGG., SAECVLVM NOVVM). In addition to the traditional religious ceremonies, lavish Games were held in the Circus Maximus, in which a varied array of wild beasts, collected by Gordian III for his proposed Persian Triumph, were brought into the arena: the coinage depicts hippopotami, lions and deer. After years in which rigid economy had been necessary, no expense was spared. A bonus was distributed to the people of Rome, who were exhorted to see the eternity of their city reflected in the everlasting future of his dynasty, summed up by the coin inscription AETERNITAS AVGG. (*Augustorum*) and symbolized by a picture of the long-living elephant.

But all this cheerful optimism was premature and misplaced. In the very same year as the Secular Games, at least three separate military pretenders assumed the purple in various provinces, inaugurating a period in which the tendency for individual army garrisons to set up their own generals as emperors began to assume alarming and almost uncontrollable proportions. First a unique coin found in Lorraine shows the brief emergence and usurpation of a certain Silbannacus. Secondly, in the early summer news reached Rome that some of the legions on the Danube, all too well aware of their pre-eminent position in the Roman army, had awarded the throne to one of their officers named Pacatianus – perhaps because he had comported himself well against the frontier tribesmen. Coins issued in Pacatianus' name at some centre in Moesia commemorate the recent imperial millenary with an inscription celebrating 'the thousand and first year of eternal Rome' (ROMAE AETER [nae] AN [no] MILL [esimo] ET PRIMO). This rebellion had the predictable effect of inciting the Goths – who had been refused the annual tribute Gordian III had promised them – to break across the Danube into Lower Moesia; other Germans, and the Carpi, did the same. These apparently unending waves of invaders, however, were held up by a stout Roman defence of Marcianopolis, made possible by the enemy's ignorance of siege-craft.

At about the same time, trouble broke out in the eastern provinces. There Philip's brother Gaius Julius Priscus had been promoted from the governor-ship of Mesopotamia to the post of supreme commander in the entire area, with the unusual title of 'praetorian prefect and ruler of the east'. His oppressive administrative measures, however, including a particularly rigorous enforcement of taxes, caused the soldiers to proclaim a certain Iotapianus as emperor, apparently in northern Syria. Iotapianus, who was perhaps related both to Severus Alexander and to the former ruling house of Commagene on the Syrian border (in which princesses were often named Iotape), assumed the titles that Philip had awarded to Priscus – adding the rebellious designation of Augustus. This appears on his coinage, which also proclaims a military victory (VICTORIA AVG.), though nothing is known about it.

Convinced that the rising of Pacatianus and Iotapianus heralded the breaking apart of the Empire, Philip proceeded to lose his nerve. Addressing the senate in tones of deep alarm and depression, he offered to step down from the throne. The suggestion was received in silence, until the city prefect DECIUS expressed the opinion that such despair was uncalled for, as Pacatianus had no qualifications for imperial office, and would soon be killed by his own men. Indeed, this was precisely what happened shortly afterwards; and Iotapianus was murdered as well. But Philip remained deeply worried by the situation in the Danubian provinces, and arranged that Severianus – many of whose soldiers were deserting to the Goths – should be superseded by Decius, who thus became commander-in-chief in Moesia and Pannonia. Before the end of 248 he had impressively restored order and discipline; and six months later his troops were so attached to him that they hailed him as emperor. Unimpressed by Decius' protestations that he had no desire to accept this honour, Philip marched northwards against him. But he was in poor health, and not much of a general: in the battle that followed at Verona his army, although superior in numbers, was totally defeated. He himself met his death in battle – and so did his son, unless (as was also reported) the praetorians took him back to their camp and killed him there.

According to gossip recorded by Eusebius, Philip was the first Christian emperor of Rome. But the tradition is untrue. It arose from an apparent contrast with his vanquisher and successor, Decius, who launched a campaign of severe persecution of the Christians. All that can be said of Philip in this connexion is that he may have been tolerant towards the Christians. This was the view of Dionysius, the contemporary bishop of Alexandria; and it was at least true that Pope Fabianus found it possible to return the bones of his predecessor Pontianus, who had died in exile in Sardinia, to the capital.

In accord with a contemporary pamphlet *To the Monarch*, which pronounced Philip's rule to be based on the virtues of the Stoic philosophers, he appears to have done what he could to palliate injustices and improprieties in the machinery of government. He intervened to prevent abuses in the treasury administration, and a number of his rulings which later found their way into Justinian's Codex reflect vigilant protection of civil rights. He disliked homosexuality and castration and passed laws against both those practices. He was also a munificent provider of public works, furnishing the trans-Tiberine areas of Rome with a much improved water supply. Yet he could do little or nothing to mitigate the extortionate demands rendered inevitable by the maintenance of a large army. Thus a petition addressed to the emperor by the tenants of his estates at Aragüe in Phrygia protests against unprecedented ill-treatment at the hands of imperial officers, soldiers and civil servants, not to speak of municipal functionaries. Philip may well have done more than his predecessor Gordian III to remedy such abuses. Yet his reign took place under a shadow, for it had only been made possible by Gordian's highly suspect death; and the emergencies that followed thick and fast during his final years were evidently more than his mental and physical condition could deal with. The court artist catches the highlights of his character in a superb portrait: he depicts a new and non-Roman type, with a highly charged expression – eloquent of suspicion and repressed turbulence – flickering over his tense and mobile features.

TRAJANUS DECIUS 249–51

TRAJANUS DECIUS (Gaius Messius Quintus Decius) (249–51) was born in about 190. He came from the village of Budalia near Sirmium, not far from the Danube. He was probably of local extraction, though not a simple soldier but member of a family which enjoyed Italian connexions and possessed extensive lands; his wife, Herennia Cupressenia Etruscilla, was an Etruscan of distinguished origin. Decius was a rare example of a Danubian who became a senator and gained the consulship. He may well be the governor of Nearer Spain and Lower Moesia, named on inscriptions as Quintus Decius Valerinus in the former of those provinces and as Gaius Messius Quintus Decius Valerianus in the latter.

When PHILIP, in 248, was beset by usurpers and proposed to abdicate, Decius, by this time city prefect, dissuaded him on the grounds that the pretenders in question would soon succumb, a forecast which proved accurate; and then he accepted a special command in Moesia and Pannonia, where he repelled the Gothic invaders and restored the discipline of his troops. Later historians idealized his behaviour. One of them, Zosimus, declared that Decius warned the emperor in vain of the inevitable sequel: what he feared was that the soldiers would transfer their allegiance from Philip to himself, and that is just what happened, in June 249. He then wrote a letter to Philip, Zonaras adds, promising that once he had returned to Rome he would lay down the imperial insignia he had been compelled to assume. But the 'reluctant usurper' was a familiar, romantic literary theme, and there is no good reason to credit Decius with any such high-minded unwillingness.

After his decisive victory over the superior forces of Philip at Verona, resulting in the deaths of that emperor and his son, Decius returned to Rome, where the senate, early in October, confirmed his proclamation and loaded him with honours. These included the award of the name of Trajan, which appeared on all his coins. It had been conferred, in part, to celebrate the friendly attitude which, it was hoped, the emperor would maintain towards the senate, following TRAJAN as his model. Yet Trajan had also, above all else, been a conqueror, and Decius, never forgetting this precedent, immediately began to issue a series of coins unequivocally celebrating not only his own Danubian origin and the provinces to which he owed his elevation (PANNONIAE, GENIVS ILLVRICI) but also the armies of that region, which, at this time, formed the nucleus of the imperial forces (GENIVS EXERCITVS ILLVRICIANI).

The first year of his reign was devoted to various measures of reorganiz-ation, at home and abroad. The emperor showed a particular concern to rally the pagan spiritual forces of the Empire behind his embattled régime, earning the title, as a recently discovered inscription has disclosed, of 'Restorer of Cults'. As polytheism, however, showed signs of becoming unfashionable, or changing its character, it was not so much the Olympians as the *divi*, the deified Roman rulers of earlier times, upon whom such an endeavour had to be focused. At almost all periods of the empire coins were issued with the heads of one or more of them. But on a few occasions the government, looking into the past even more assiduously than usual, produced a series of coins honouring a whole range of these imperial divinities at one and the same time. The most ambitious of these multiple 'consecration' issues is one which, from stylistic considerations and the evidence of hoards, may be ascribed to the reign of Trajanus Decius. The coins are of base silver, and attributable to the mint of Rome, while local bronze pieces of similar types were minted at Philippopolis in Thrace. Decius, standing in the line of militant Danubian emperors, believed and maintained that he stood for the survival of *Roma Aeterna*, and this numismatic array of deified former rulers displayed how, in a time of supreme external and internal crisis, he sought to close the ranks behind patriotic tradition.

This was also the motive underlying the most remembered feature of his régime: a systematic persecution of the Christians. Although their community was still relatively small, its efficient and self-contained administrative structure, distancing itself from the State, seemed a provocation to the beleaguered Roman authorities. In consequence, Decius, reversing the tolerant policy of Philip, singled out the Church directors for removal, with more determination than any of his predecessors. After executing Pope Fabianus he is said to have remarked: 'I would far rather receive news of a rival to the throne than of another bishop in Rome.' At a time of harrowing troubles and miseries, when confidence was totally breaking down, it seemed to him that the Christian leaders tempted his other subjects away from paying reverence to the pagan religion which was the backbone of the State and of its welfare. He did not order Christians to give up their faith, but would not tolerate any refusal to participate in communal corporate observances. He demanded from them only one pagan religious observance. When this act had been duly undertaken, one of the local Sacrificial Commissions established round the empire handed over to its performer a Certificate of Sacrifice, of which examples have come to light in Egypt. The Church, being mainly concentrated in the cities, was dangerously vulnerable to police pressure, so that many believers momentarily lapsed, agreeing to do what they were told. Others contrived to evade compliance – and not all the commissioners were above accepting bribes. But a considerable number of Christian men and women flatly refused to obey, and were put to death.

Meanwhile Decius' régime was plunged into yet another external emergency by an unprecedentedly large-scale crossing of the Danube by the Goths under their gifted monarch Kniva, in collusion with the Carpi who simultaneously broke into the Dacian provinces. After crossing the ice-bound river, the Goths divided themselves in two armies. One pushed on as far as Thrace and besieged its governor Titus Julius Priscus in Philippopolis, while Kniva himself moved eastwards against Novae. TREBONIANUS GALLUS, the governor of Upper and Lower Moesia, forced him to withdraw. But then Kniva turned into the interior and besieged Nicopolis ad Istrum, where large numbers of people had taken refuge.

Decius then decided that the time had come for a great imperial expedition led by himself, in order to drive the invaders out. First, however, he made certain arrangements at Rome, where a senator named PUBLIUS LICINIUS VALERIANUS (the future emperor) was given a specially created office in charge of the central administration (during the course of the war he had to put down a pretender, Valens Licinianus; while other rebels arose in Gaul and the east). But Decius also clearly indicated his intention of founding an imperial dynasty. His wife Herennia Etruscilla had been elevated to the rank of Augusta, and in early summer 250 their elder son Herennius Etruscus was made Caesar and Prince of the Youth.

Although still in his teens, Herennius was at once sent with the vanguard of the army to Moesia. Soon afterwards Decius himself set out in the same direction, and succeeded in relieving Nicopolis ad Istrum, from which Kniva recoiled with heavy losses. The emperor also cleared Dacia of the Carpi, and was honoured as its restorer and as Dacicus Maximus. However, while in hot pursuit of Kniva he suffered a severe setback at Beroe Augusta Trajana, which prompted Titus Julius Priscus, still blockaded in Philippopolis and beset by his own mutinous troops, to declare himself emperor as an act of despair, and join the besieging Goths. But this treasonable action did not save the city from capture and savage destruction at their hands, and of Titus Priscus no more is heard.

Unable to prevent the Goths from devastating Thrace, Trajanus Decius, with what was left of his army, fled back to Oescus, where Trebonianus Gallus' troops were still intact; and the two armies took up positions on the Danube in order to trap the invaders as they returned home. In the following year, at some point north of the Balkan range, Decius apparently engaged them with some distinction, since both he and his son Herennius Etruscus celebrate a 'German victory' on their coins. It was at this moment of comparative success that Herennius was proclaimed Augustus and joint ruler with his father, while Decius' younger son Hostilianus, who had been left in Rome, was appointed Caesar. But the decisive battle came when Kniva, on his return journey, reached Abrittus in Scythia Minor (the Dobrogea). There, in about July 251, he was confronted by the main army of Decius, who defeated two of his divisions but then allowed himself to be trapped, whereupon first of all his son Herennius Etruscus met his death, and then he himself was killed, together with almost the whole of his army.

It was the first time that an emperor of Rome had ever fallen in battle against a foreign foe. But Decius' admirers put the blame not upon any failure on his own part but upon betrayal by his lieutenant and successor Trebonianus Gallus; whereas the fate suffered by Decius evoked in the minds of these same eulogists heroic memories of two warriors of the same name, in legendary times, who had immolated themselves for the sake of the Roman Republic. It was this consoling interpretation of the catastrophe, combined with an idealized view of the circumstances acccompanying Decius' accession, that inspired Edward Gibbon to compare him and his son 'both in life and death, with the brightest examples of ancient virtue'. That is praise which Decius does not deserve. All the same, to assess his qualities more accurately remains a difficult task. His patriotic religious policy was enforced by an iron hardness which is reflected in his coin-portraits – though a marble bust, which has also survived, is chiefly notable for its anxious (and strangely asymmetrical) gaze. As a general he was no doubt competent, but evidently not quite competent enough; indeed few men could claim to be in this epoch when one shattering crisis rapidly followed another.

TREBONIANUS GALLUS
251–3

TREBONIANUS GALLUS (Gaius Vibius Afinius) (251–3) was an Etruscan, belonging to an old family from Perusia, who was born in about 206 and became consul in 245. In 250, as governor of Upper and Lower Moesia, he compelled Kniva and his Goths to retreat from Novae, and was joined by the emperor DECIUS at Oescus after the latter had suffered a defeat. When the two commanders subsequently manned the Danube to prevent Kniva from getting back to the north, Gallus' post was at the river mouth. Decius' defeat and death at Abrittus were later blamed on his treachery, but without justification as far as we know.

It is true, however, that after the catastrophe the soldiers proclaimed him emperor. His first act was to make a highly unfavourable peace treaty with the Goths, who were allowed to return home not only with their plunder but also with the Roman prisoners (including many of high rank) whom they had captured at Philippopolis; they were also promised annual subsidies in the hope of persuading them not to return to Roman provincial territory. Gallus then hastily marched back to the capital, hoping to safeguard his position by a display of respect for the senate; he was also careful to treat the memories of the fallen Decius and his elder son with due reverence, ensuring that they were deified by senatorial decree. Decius' younger son Hostilianus, who had remained in the capital, was raised to the rank of Augustus and co-emperor with Gallus; and in order not to infringe on the prerogatives of Decius' widow Etruscilla, Gallus did not honour his own wife, Baebiana, with the title of Augusta. However, he gave his son Volusianus the rank of Caesar and Prince of Youth, and when Hostilianus died shortly afterwards Volusianus was made Augustus in his place.

The brief reign of Gallus was a period of continuous disasters. Most damaging of all was the outbreak of a terrible pestilence (which was blamed for the death of Hostilianus). For a decade and a half it was to rage through the entire Empire, inflicting incalculable losses and gravely crippling the army. The military threats on the frontiers, too, had become more perilous than ever, despite the wildly over-optimistic revival of the coin inscription PAX AETERNA. Gallus was unable to prevent the Persians from taking over Armenia – where they murdered the local monarch and expelled his son – and early in 253 their king, Shapur I, began a Persian offensive against Rome's eastern provinces, which was to continue for nearly a decade; his troops swarmed into Mesopotamia and Syria, overran Antioch and took away with them a vast amount of loot and numerous prisoners. Meanwhile a mixed mass of marauders coming from across the Danubian frontier – Goths and others – not only burst into the European provinces but even made an expedition by sea to Asia Minor, which they devastated as far as Ephesus and Pessinus.

To distract attention from these misfortunes, Gallus revived Decius' persecutions of the Christians, imprisoning Pope Cornelius, who died while under arrest. From a military point of view, the only encouraging feature was provided by MARCUS AEMILIUS AEMILIANUS, governor of Lower Moesia, who launched a successful attack on the Goths north of the Danube. Declared emperor as a result by his soldiers in July or August (or, according to some authorities, earlier), he immediately advanced into Italy, perhaps penetrating as far as Interamna, only twenty miles north of Rome. Gallus and Volusianus, taken by surprise, declared him a public enemy; and they also took the precaution of summoning PUBLIUS LICINIUS VALERIANUS (who had represented Decius in the capital, and was now on the Rhine) to come to their assistance. Pending his arrival, however, they were only able to raise an army of much inferior dimensions to that of the invader. In consequence their troops, to avoid hazarding a hopeless battle, murdered them both and swore allegiance to Aemilianus.

Even if Gallus is cleared of treachery to Decius, his conduct during his reign seems listless and ineffective. A portrait bust displays grotesque anxiety and strain – and failure to cope. It is surprising that he allowed such a portrait to be made and, presumably, put into circulation; but it may be that he lacked artistic sense, or had no inclination or time to share the interest shown by so many of his predecessors in the publicity value of these duplicated images.

AEMILIAN
253

AEMILIAN (Marcus Aemilius Aemilianus) July/August (?)–September/ October 253) was born in Mauretania. Aemilian became governor of Lower Moesia in 252. In spring of the following year the Goths under Kniva, who had been promised subsidies by TREBONIANUS GALLUS, became restive again and demanded that the sums should be increased. Aemilian, however, exhorting his troops to be mindful of the greatness of Rome and promising them liberal bonuses if they fought with success, put such Goths as remained in his province to death, and then moved across the Danube into their own territory, where the suddenness of his onslaught proved extremely effective.

This unexpected triumph, following upon so many Roman setbacks, prompted his soldiers to declare him emperor in July or August 253 in place of Gallus. Without waiting to clear Thrace of the hostile Goths, Aemilian moved rapidly into Italy and proceeded southwards, whereupon the army of Gallus and his son Volusianus murdered their masters and accepted Aemilian. The senate, which had only a little earlier pronounced him an enemy of the State, confirmed his elevation, and coins issued in his name show that he was recognized in Egypt and throughout the east. A certain Cornelia Supera, who appears on other pieces with the title of Augusta, seems to have been his wife.

Meanwhile VALERIANUS, whom Gallus had summoned from the Rhine, did not, when he heard of his death, abandon his advance into Italy, and on the way his soldiers declared him emperor; his army was large, for it had been strengthened to fight the Alamanni. As Aemilian began to move up the peninsula to meet him, the history of his own recent accession to power repeated itself, for he fell to the daggers of his own soldiers near Spoletium or Narnia, not far from the place where his predecessors had met their deaths. His men felt that Valerian's forces were stronger than their own, that he himself was a more impressive personage than Aemilian, and that the unpleasantness of further civil war had better be avoided.

VALERIAN
253–60

VALERIAN (Publius Licinius Valerianus) (253–60; see also his son and colleague in the west, GALLIENUS) had been consul in the time of SEVERUS ALEXANDER and played a part in inducing the senate to support the rebellion of the two elder Gordians against MAXIMINUS in 238. TRAJANUS DECIUS nominated him to a new and important office at Rome, intended to involve responsibility for the affairs of the capital and the maintenance of liaison with the senate when the emperor was absent at the front. He may also have served under Decius against the Goths. In the reign of TREBONIANUS GALLUS, from 251–3, he held a command on the Upper Rhine and was summoned to bring his forces to help resist AEMILIAN. But he started too late to save Gallus, who succumbed to his own troops after a battle at Interamna.

Undaunted, however, by the news of Gallus' death, Valerian continued with his plans for the invasion of Italy, and in Raetia, during the course of his journey, was hailed emperor by his own troops. On hearing this news the soldiers of Aemilian murdered him, swearing allegiance to Valerian; and their decision was ratified by the senate. In autumn 253, Valerian proceeded onwards to Rome, and upon his arrival adopted his son GALLIENUS as full partner in the imperial power. Coinage was issued in both their names, as well as for their respective wives, the late Mariniana (who was deified) and Cornelia Salonina.

While plague and civil strife raged within the provinces of the Empire, Valerian also inherited some fearsome military situations on its northern and eastern borders, and these problems speedily worsened still further. Groups of German tribesmen invaded the provinces in ever greater and more efficiently organized numbers, and across an increasingly wide range of fronts, so that for a time it was quite impossible to withstand them. Goths and other east German tribal groups, including the Burgundians, devastated Thrace and penetrated as far as Thessalonica, which in c. 254 they failed, however, to capture. Asia Minor, too, recently ravaged overland, was now further threatened by the raiders' acquisition of ships, forcibly commandeered from the Roman client-kingdom of the Cimmerian Bosphorus. These craft were first obtained by the tribe of the Borani, who crossed over to the east coast of the Black Sea and attacked the Roman frontier town of Pityus in about 256. But owing to the vigorous resistance of the local governor Successianus, they were driven off with great losses, and, seizing what ships they could (for the Bosphoran flotilla had gone home), sailed back the way they had come. In the following year however, grabbing yet another fleet, they made a second attempt on Pityus, which this time – in the absence of Successianus, now promoted to praetorian prefect – proved successful. Next, conscripting skilled oarsmen locally, they sailed westwards to Trapezus, which fell to a surprise night attack and was burnt to the ground. Then the assailants returned home, laden with enormous plunder. At some stage Panticapaeum in Tauris (the Crimea) was also sacked, with disastrous effects on the Roman grain supply from the region.

Very soon afterwards it was the turn of the Goths to renew the onslaught on these rich and defenceless territories. They selected a different route, moving their fleet down the west coast of the Black Sea, while their land army marched down as far as the Propontis. There it embarked and crossed over to Chalcedon, which was captured without a fight. The invaders then captured, one after another, some of the greatest cities of Bithynia. The fleeing inhabitants managed to get much of their wealth away, but Nicomedia and Nicaea went up in flames.

Meanwhile, since a single emperor could not put up a defence to north and east at the same time – and Valerian's son and colleague Gallienus (q.v.) was already fully occupied on the northern frontiers – he extended the principle of collegiate rule in 256/7 by dividing the provinces and armies between the two of them on a territorial basis, in anticipation of the divisions between western and eastern realms in subsequent centuries. Taking the east as his own responsibility, Valerian, in the face of the Gothic naval invasion, sent an officer to take charge of the defences of Byzantium, while he himself moved over to Asia Minor in the hope of bringing relief to Bithynia. But the enterprise came to nothing, partly because his army was immobilized by the renewal of a plague epidemic, and partly because an even graver threat now manifested itself further to the east.

The threat was provided by Shapur (Sapor) I of Persia. He had launched his first attack on the Roman frontiers in the early 240s, and his second onslaught came at the beginning of the reign of Valerian, or may have started slightly earlier. A certain Uranius Antoninus, chief priest of El-gabal at Emesa, managed to hold out against him, issuing his own gold coins as a token of independence. But it was Shapur's third invasion that proved most disastrous to the Romans. His boast that he had captured thirty-seven cities, announced in a trilingual inscription at Naksh-i-Rustam near Persepolis, is probably justified. Among the Mesopotamian centres lost to him at different times were Carrhae, Nisibis (in about 254), Dura-Europus (between 255 and 258), and Hatra (of late a Roman ally). His armies also overran Armenia and Cappadocia, and in Syria he even seized the provincial capital Antioch (possibly in 256), setting up a puppet Roman emperor Mareades or Cyriades in the city; but when the Persians withdrew he was left without support and burnt alive by the returning Romans.

Shapur plundered all these regions with a harsh disregard for public opinion which suggests that, despite his far-reaching claims, he was primarily interested in loot and did not have permanent annexation in mind. However, he soon decided to make yet another attack on imperial territory, and in about 259 Valerian had to take an army into Mesopotamia in order to drive him back from the besieged city of Edessa. Since, however, the Romans had suffered serious casualties – not least because of a recurrence of the plague – the emperor first decided to attempt negotiation. Envoys sent to Shapur I, in April or May 260, returned with a request for a personal meeting, and Valerian, accompanied by a small staff, set out to discuss terms of peace; but instead he was made prisoner by Shapur, and taken back to Persia. There are various divergent accounts telling how he was captured by treacherous tricks and traps. But it is also not impossible that he was deliberately taking refuge from his own army, which may have turned mutinous.

Gibbon quotes a tradition that 'when Valerian sank under the weight of shame and grief, his skin, stuffed by straw, and formed into the likeness of a human figure, was preserved for ages in the most celebrated temple in Persia; a more real monument of triumph than the fancied trophies of brass and marble so often erected by Roman vanity. The tale is moral and pathetic, but the truth of it may very fairly be called in question.' Even so, the solemn moralizing is scarcely out of place; for the capture of an emperor by a foreign foe was an unparalleled catastrophe, the nadir of Roman disgrace.

Valerian was apparently an honest and well-intentioned man, who had gained the confidence of the senate and seems to have done something to restore discipline in the army. But it was his misfortune to inherit an Empire that was now almost completely out of control. Christian writers later exaggerated his personal defects, because he had revived the persecution of Christianity in order to divert attention from the catastrophes that beset the Roman world, enforcing recognition of the State religion as a remedy for these ills. He may previously have assisted Trajanus Decius in his measures against the Christians; then, when he became emperor himself, he issued two further edicts on his own account. The first, in August 257, ordered the higher Christian churchmen to sacrifice to the gods of the State, although they were not prohibited from worshipping Jesus Christ in private. The second and harsher edict was drawn up in the east during the following year and

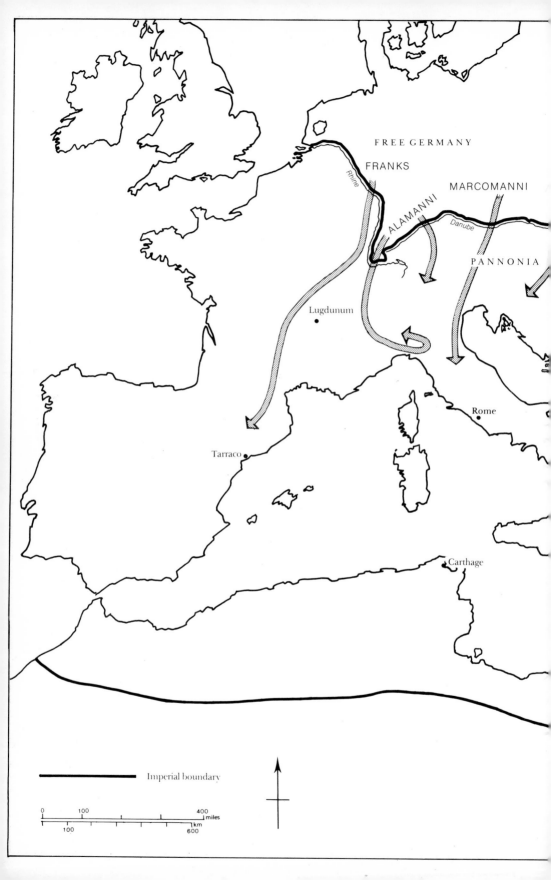

FREE GERMANY

FRANKS

MARCOMANNI

ALAMANNI

Rhine

Danube

PANNONIA

Lugdunum

Rome

Tarraco

Carthage

━━━━━━━━ Imperial boundary

0   100   400
└┴┴┴┴┴┴┴┴┴┴┴┴┘ miles
  100   600
  └─────────────┘ km

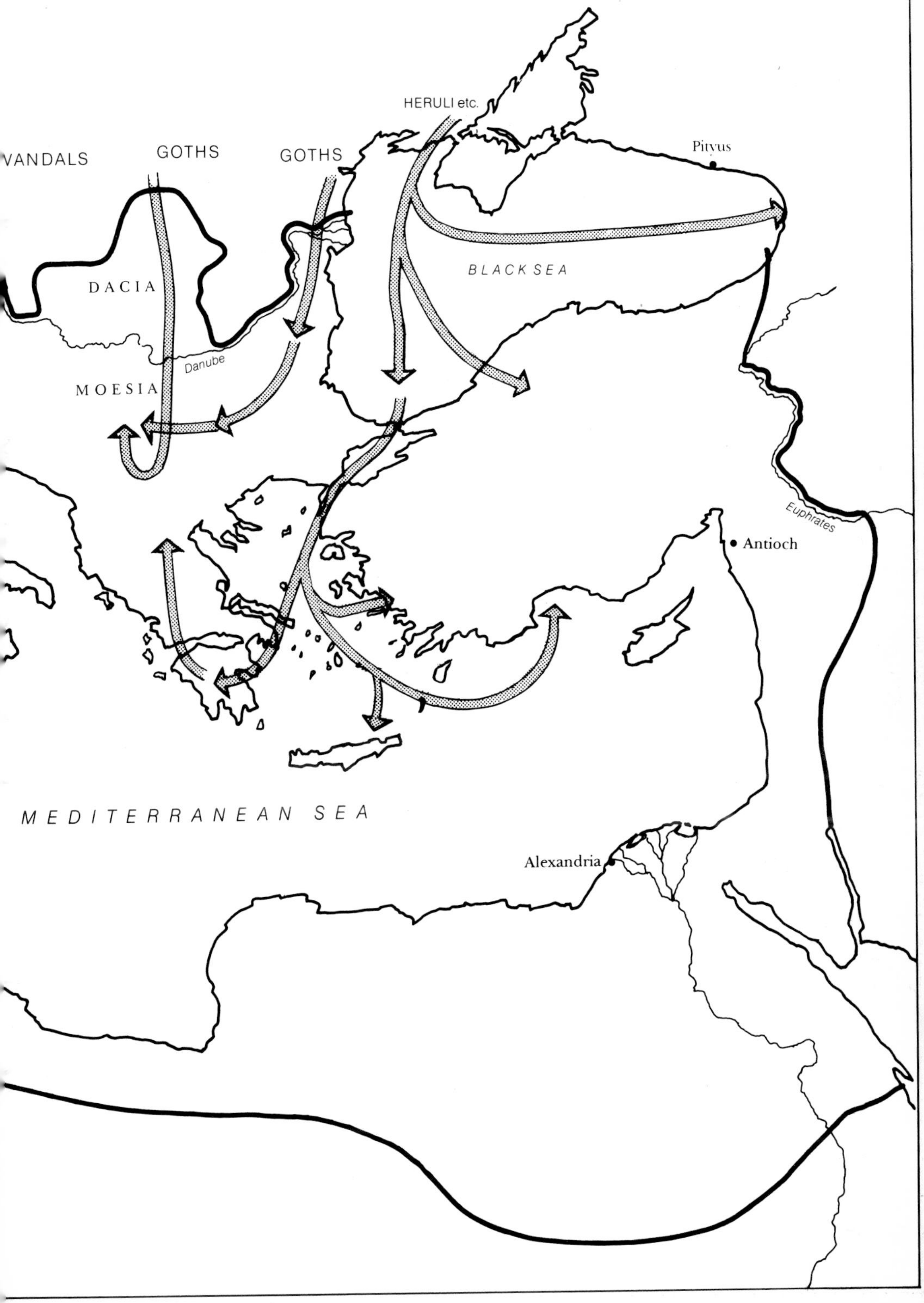

VANDALS   GOTHS   GOTHS   HERULI etc.   Pityus

DACIA

BLACK SEA

Danube

MOESIA

Euphrates

Antioch

MEDITERRANEAN SEA

Alexandria

circulated by the senate to provincial governors. It made clergy liable to capital punishment; notable Christians who thus became martyrs included Pope Xystus (Sixtus) II and St Lawrence – burnt to death in Rome – and St Cyprian, executed at Carthage. The edict went on to decree penalties for Christian laymen as well, with special reference to senators and knights, whose property was confiscated; while tenants of imperial estates who embraced the faith were condemned to the mines.

GALLIENUS
253–68

GALLIENUS (Publius Licinius Egnatius) (joint emperor, 253–60; sole central emperor, 260–68) was the son of VALERIAN. When his father was proclaimed emperor by his troops in Raetia in 253, and the soldiers in Rome murdered AEMILIAN, Gallienus, who was in the capital, was declared Caesar by the senate. When Valerian reached Rome, he raised his son to the rank of Augustus, thus returning to the dual collegiality instituted by MARCUS AURELIUS and LUCIUS VERUS. Gallienus played a very full part in their joint reign that followed.

Almost immediately, in 254, when major unrest was reported among the German tribes, he set out for the Rhine frontier. During the first three years of his command his coins record several victories: it appears that forces of German tribesmen were prevented from reaching the Rhine, and others were defeated as they tried to cross the river. A number of Roman fortresses on or behind the left bank were strengthened at this time; and Gallienus opened a new mint at Augusta Trevirorum. His assumption of the title Dacicus Maximus in 257 also suggests that he was involved with the Carpi who were invading Dacia – although not, apparently, with quite the success that he claimed, for Rome's hold over at least part of that country seems to have become weakened at this period.

Early in 256, in order to safeguard the future of the dynasty, Valerian gave the title Caesar to Gallienus' oldest son Valerianus the younger; when he died (and was deified) about two years later, his brother Saloninus was promoted in his place. It was in 256 or 257 that the emperors Valerian and Gallienus, faced with shattering crises on the European and Asian frontiers alike, divided up the Roman world between themselves on a territorial basis, Valerian taking the east and Gallienus the west. The autonomy of Gallienus' command, in a practical if not in a constitutional sense, was emphasized by coins depicting him 'with his own army' (GALLIENVS CVM EXERcitu SVO).

However, the situation with which Gallienus was now faced was a daunting one. German tribes were joining in a mass onslaught along the entire length of the northern frontier. Particularly threatening were the Franks, now heard of for the first time: a confederacy formed from various smaller groupings which convulsive population movements around the lower Elbe had precipitated against the Rhine border. Launching repeated attacks by compact forces of about thirty thousand men, they punctured the Roman defences and overran Gaul and Spain, destroying the Spanish capital Tarraco and raiding as far as the coast of Tingitana in north Africa. Meanwhile another powerful group of German peoples, the Alamanni, were continually harassing the Raetian frontier fortresses, and in 258 invaded Italy by way of the Brenner Pass. Gallienus moved out of Gaul to attack them and seems to have won an important victory near Mediolanum, where a mint was established in about 259. But he also took certain non-military steps to deal with the German peril. Thus the Marcomanni of Boiohaemum were permitted to form a state, or an extension of their existing state, to the south of their homeland on the Roman bank of the Danube; and Gallienus himself reportedly contracted a secondary marriage with the daughter of their ruling prince. At about the same time, however, the Agri Decumates, the strategically vital re-entrant zone between the Upper Rhine and the Upper Danube, was overrun by another German people, the Suevi, and lost to Rome for ever.

These events may have occurred or reached their climax in 260, which indeed became, as misfortunes accumulated, the most disastrous year in all Roman history. The capture of Valerian by the Persians – unrescued, as critics noted, by Gallienus, who became sole ruler – was followed by a series of usurpations on the part of generals who proclaimed themselves emperor in various provinces. Some of the accounts describing the period as an 'Age of the Thirty Tyrants' are of uncertain authenticity and significance. Other such reports, however, are reliable enough. Thus it is certain that in the Danube lands two such pretenders arose in quick succession (very probably during this single year 260). First Ingenuus, governor of Pannonia, made a bid for the throne, supported by the troops stationed in Moesia. He set up his headquarters at Sirmium; but not far away, at Mursa Major, he was attacked and defeated by Gallienus and his general Manius Acilius Aureolus. Ingenuus attempted to flee, but was captured and put to death. However, his troops remained seditious, and next invested Regalianus, the governor of Upper

Pannonia, with the purple. He issued coinage at Carnuntum (overstriking earlier pieces) in his own name and that of his wife Sulpicia Dryantilla, who belonged to a powerful senatorial family. But within a few weeks Gallienus returned to the area, and crushed him as well, opening a new mint at Siscia in 262 (after an invasion of Upper Pannonia by the Sarmatian Roxolani had been driven back).

While Gallienus was engaged in these operations he had entrusted the Rhine command to a general named POSTUMUS, leaving his own son and heir Saloninus Caesar at Colonia Agrippinensium under the care of the praetorian prefect Silvanus. But Postumus quarrelled with Silvanus and marched on the city. While the siege was still in progress, Saloninus, as a unique gold coin indicates, was defiantly proclaimed joint Augustus with his father. But not long afterwards the garrison surrendered, and the young man, together with Silvanus, was put to death. Postumus' troops proclaimed him emperor, all the western provinces seceded in his wake, and Gallienus, severely wounded in recent fighting, failed to take any effective counter-measures.

Meanwhile in the east, the capture of Valerian left Rome's provinces at the mercy of the Persians. They stormed Antioch and Tarsus and the cities of Mesopotamia; and Caesarea in Cappadocia, despite a gallant defence, was betrayed into their hands. Macrianus, the imperial quartermaster-general in the east, endeavoured to rally what remained of the Roman army at Samosata – aided by a general called Callistus (nicknamed Ballista, 'catapult'), who surprised and defeated Shapur at Corycus on the Cilician coast and compelled him to retreat to the Euphrates. After this success Macrianus, too old and lame to claim the throne for himself, had his sons Macrianus the younger and Quietus proclaimed joint emperors, and Syria, Asia Minor and Egypt joined their cause. Leaving Quietus in Syria, the two Macriani ambitiously advanced into the Balkans, only to be defeated and killed by Domitianus, a subordinate of Gallienus' general Aureolus. Gallienus also mobilized the help of Odenathus, the extremely powerful hereditary prince of Palmyra in Syria, making him supreme commander of the Roman armies in the east. Quietus, attacked by Odenathus at Emesa, was put to death by the townspeople.

Then, during five successive years from 262–7, Odenathus launched a series of attacks on the Persians, recapturing much of Mesopotamia (though their capital Ctesiphon eluded him) and probably occupying Armenia as well. Gallienus rewarded the victorious general with the title of Imperator; he had done much to prevent the loss and fragmentation of the eastern provinces, and remained formally loyal to the central Roman authority, though in fact he himself was undisputed master of the entire region. In 267, however, he and his eldest son were murdered, and his widow Zenobia inherited his position. Gallienus then decided that the time had come to put a stop to the independent power of Palmyra. But repressive efforts by his praetorian prefect Heraclianus proved unsuccessful.

Shortly afterwards the east was faced with a massive threat from the Goths. Drawing their sailors from the ranks of the Heruli – recent arrivals in the region of Lake Maeotis – they mustered unprecedented numbers of men and ships at the mouth of the River Dniester in 267–8. This great fleet set sail, and Greece and Asia Minor were once again subjected to violent devastations, though the historian Dexippus himself beat back an attack on Athens. But it was Gallienus, it would seem (though hostile critics, followed by many modern writers, preferred to ascribe the triumph to his successor CLAUDIUS GOTHICUS, over-praised because Constantine claimed him as an ancestor), who intercepted the invaders as they were returning homewards by the Balkan land route. Falling upon their straggling column, the Roman army fought the bloodiest battle of the century at Naissus, gaining a complete victory and killing thirty or even fifty thousand of the enemy. After the Herulian chief had capitulated, however, Gallienus reverted to a diplomatic, conciliatory policy by awarding him consular insignia. This military success meant that the tide had begun to turn: a start had been made in the huge task of pushing the Germans back, in the face of all historical probability.

Amid all these convulsions, Gallienus somehow found time to give new shape to his military organization. The Romans had long employed mounted archers and javelin-men, and for a hundred years and more they had also been relying upon units of mailed horse. But now, the heavy cavalry which the Persians and some northerners (notably the Sarmatians, themselves of Iranian origin) were so formidably deploying demonstrated that this branch of the imperial army needed extension on a major scale. Accordingly, in about 264–8 or a little earlier, Gallienus created an impressive cavalry corps of armoured horsemen. This group of formations – though very dear, for a horse's feed cost as much as a soldier's rations – was designed to constitute not only a striking force but a central military reserve, which had scarcely existed before, though SEPTIMIUS SEVERUS may have made a start in that direction. As the principal base of the new army Gallienus selected Mediolanum, conveniently equidistant from the frontiers and Rome; from now onwards it was linked to the other main cities of north Italy in a new defensive and offensive system. These developments were rendered especially necessary because the recent loss of the Agri Decumates, between the upper Rhine and the upper Danube, meant that the Germans had come much nearer to the Italian peninsula itself.

The coinage of Gallienus celebrated various virtues attributable to this new élite cavalry force, including its speed (ALACRITATI); and a particular appeal was made to its loyalty (FIDEI EQVITVM). Moreover, one of the large gold medallions, which it had become customary to distribute to senior officers as personal gifts and rewards, was now inscribed, with revealing candour, 'Because you have remained loyal' (OB FIDEM RESERV-ATAM). In order to ensure that these officers did not abandon this desirable fidelity, Gallienus enrolled a number of them in a carefully selected staff unit of household troops or *protectores*, most of whom, led by 'the protectors of the divine flank', were encamped in the vicinity of the emperor, and attached to his own person.

However, it was precisely in this matter of loyalty that the new cavalry corps proved most inadequate. For although Gallienus, in 268, hopefully appointed his third son Marinianus consul, as his destined successor, the commanders of the new corps turned out to be as addicted to plots and uprisings as the generals of earlier epochs. This meant that Gallienus was not in a position to follow up his victory over the Goths at Naissus, because of news that his cavalry commander Aureolus, whom he had left in charge of the defences of Italy, had revolted. Gallienus marched straight back to Italy and succeeded in penning the rebellious general into the city of Mediolanum, to which he laid siege – although, at the same time, Aureolus was defiantly proclaimed emperor by his garrison.

At this juncture, however, a conspiracy was launched against the life of Gallienus, and he was assassinated. The leaders of the *coup* were Heraclianus, who was now praetorian prefect, Marcianus, who had conducted operations against the Goths, and Cecropius, the commander of a Dalmatian division of cavalry; and the two next emperors, Claudius Gothicus and AURELIAN, seem to have been accomplices in the deed. All these men came from the Danube area, like most of Rome's other best generals and best troops, and these Danubian leaders felt strongly that the ruler should be one of themselves.

Besides, Gallienus, although popular enough with the soldiery, was a very different person from the military emperors who came before and after him. The difference can be clearly seen from his surviving portraits, which do not depict a crew-cut tough, like them, but something of an intellectual; for he was a man of enthusiastic Greek tastes, interested in literature, art and philosophy. He was initiated into the Eleusinian Mysteries – survivals of the most antique classical tradition. Moreover, encouraged by his wife Cornelia Salonina (known also as Chrysogone, 'begotten of gold'), it was he who inspired the great neo-Platonist Plotinus with the hope of founding a philosophers' state in Campania. And yet, for all his pagan intellectual allegiances, Gallienus also decided to abandon his father's militant campaign against the Christians, in order to secure the sympathy of their eastern communities against Sapor.

Although grappling to the best of his ability with a constant series of public emergencies, Gallienus was censured because he found time, now and then, for cultural pursuits as well. However, these and other criticisms directed against him were unfairly motivated, first (as already mentioned) by the tendency of later writers to favour his successor Claudius Gothicus instead, and secondly by the resentment of senators because Gallienus mistrustfully excluded them from high commands.

The military and political crises of the reign were matched by an economic situation closely approaching complete chaos; and this too may have influenced the conspirators who decided to put an end to him. As an example, the debasement of the coinage had descended to its worst point in all Roman history. Not only was the weight of the standard gold coin, the *aureus*, sharply decreased, but the so-called silver pieces now contained almost no silver at all, except a superficial wash which soon vanished. When this deterioration became clear to the public – which expected the currency to contain their money's worth of precious metal – they and bankers and traders would no longer accept the vast mass of intrinsically almost worthless pieces at its face value, so that prices suffered inflations of many hundred per cent – which meant virtual government bankruptcy and untold personal hardship.

POSTUMUS
260–8

POSTUMUS (Marcus Cassianius Latinius) (260–8), ruler of the Gallo-Roman empire, may himself have been a Gaul. When Ingenuus – probably after learning of VALERIAN's capture by the Persians in 260 – revolted against his son GALLIENUS in Pannonia, the latter left Postumus, at that time governor of Upper or Lower Germany, in command on the Rhine. But while Gallienus was absent (he also had a second usurper, Regalianus, to deal with), his praetorian prefect Silvanus came under attack from Postumus, who compelled his garrison at Colonia Agrippinensium to surrender and had him killed, together with the emperor's son Saloninus, assuming the purple himself. He was recognized not only by the German legions but also by the armies and populations of Gaul and Spain, and after a time Britain, which he visited in person.

Postumus set up a new Roman State, entirely independent of the central government. Its machinery included a separate senate and separate pairs of annually elected consuls; Postumus himself occupied the office on five different occasions. He also possessed his own praetorian guard, stationed at Augusta Trevirorum, the city which he chose for his own residence – anticipating the imperial capital of later decades – and embellished with important buildings. Nevertheless, in his relations with Rome he at first proceeded with some caution, declaring that he would shed no drop of Roman blood, and that his only intention was to protect Gaul – which was the task, after all, that Gallienus had assigned to him.

This programme was announced by coins describing him as 'The Restorer of the Gauls', RESTITVTOR GALLIAR (*um*), and referring to institutions of local interest, such as the cult of Hercules at Deuso (HERC*uli* DEVSONIENSI). Other coin types, displaying Neptune and a warship, recall Postumus' successful efforts to protect the coastline from pirates. Moreover, he made good his claim to be the protector of the land frontier as well. It is true that the detachment of the Agri Decumates from the Empire (see GALLIENUS) was largely due to his secession. Nevertheless, he managed to reoccupy and re-fortify some of the advanced posts within that territory (in the Neckar valley), and in 261 drove back the Franks and Alamanni who had crossed the Rhine, so that his proclamation of 'Victory over the Germans' (VICT*oria* GERM*anica*) was not wholly unwarranted.

Gallienus however felt that this breakaway Empire could not be tolerated. In 263, taking advantage of his control of the Alpine passes, he crossed into Gaul to attack Postumus. After an initial setback he gained an important success, but the pursuit of the defeated pretender was not pressed by his cavalry general, Aureolus. Postumus was consequently able to collect a new army – including Germans mobilized from across the Rhine; yet, even so, he was beaten by the imperial forces once again, and forced to barricade himself inside a town. But Gallienus, after starting to besiege him there, was wounded and had to be taken home.

The attempt to eliminate Postumus' secessionist Empire had failed. Indeed, there may have developed, at this juncture, a tacit agreement that thenceforward the pretender would be left alone: that seems to be the meaning of Postumus' coin type of 265 describing Mercury as the 'Messenger of the Gods' (INTERNVNTIVS DEORVM) – the intermediary, that is to say, between himself and Gallienus. At all events, Postumus was reprieved, and his coins show that he began to form new and grandiose ambitions extending far beyond the territories he actually ruled. He is now no longer the 'Restorer of the Gauls' but champion of ROMA AETERNA and 'Restorer of the World' (RESTITVTOR ORBIS) – potentially including the east as well, which is imaginatively added to his dominions (ORIENS AV*Gusti*); there is also a comprehensive, Empire-wide reference to the 'Welfare of the Provinces' (SALVS PROVINCIARVM). His religious policy, too, underwent corresponding expansions. No more do we hear of the local Hercules of Deuso but of Hercules the Roman – with whom Postumus is implicitly linked, as emulator of the hero's glorious achievements. The association is seen more strongly still upon coins which unite portraits of Postumus and Hercules, who are made to look significantly similar.

In 268 Gallienus' general, Aureolus, the cavalry commander who had failed to pursue Postumus' retreating forces five years earlier, openly changed sides. The emperor Gallienus, while absent in eastern Europe, had placed him in command of his forces in north Italy, with the aim of preventing an expected invasion of the peninsula by Postumus. But now Aureolus declared for Postumus instead, and issued a group of coins in his name at Mediolanum. Postumus' own attitude to the *coup* is unknown; but in any case he proved unable to come to the help of Aureolus – now besieged by Gallienus in Mediolanum – because a rebel had risen against his own rule on the German frontier. This was one of his own senior officers, Laelianus, who declared himself emperor at Moguntiacum, and was joined by other leading garrisons in the area. Postumus took Moguntiacum by siege and put Laelianus to death, but then refused to allow his soldiers to sack and plunder the city: a decision which infuriated them, so that his assassination followed shortly afterwards.

In the absence of a sound literary tradition, it is fortunate that the coins of Postumus are so varied and informative: a scrutiny of thirteen thousand base metal pieces found at Cunetio in England, and now located in the British Museum, has proved particularly revealing. This abundant currency formed part of a deliberate plan to revive commercial activity. Its only certain mint is Colonia Agrippinensium, named on an issue of 267; such an unusual specific mention is probably intended to record the inauguration of the new mint after its transfer from some other centre, probably Postumus' capital Augusta Trevirorum. His gold coinage was much more precisely regulated in weight than the *aurei* of Gallienus, bearing witness to his economic efficiency; and it was also greatly superior in workmanship and design. Its portraits of Postumus display vigorous curly beards, and often depict elaborate cuirasses and helmets; some heads, exceptionally, are not shown in profile but facing. Although other evidence is not available, these ambitious compositions suggest that the court of the breakaway Empire may not have been inferior to the entourage of Gallienus in artistic pretensions.

Deprived of Britain and Spain, which returned to central allegiance after Postumus' death, the shrunken remains of his Gallo-Roman dominions were inherited by Marius (for about two months in 268), Victorinus (c.269–71) and Tetricus (271–4), who succumbed to AURELIAN.

PART VI

MILITARY RECOVERY

CLAUDIUS II GOTHICUS 268–70

CLAUDIUS II GOTHICUS (Marcus Aurelius Valerius Claudius) (268–70) was born in about 214, probably in Dardania (Upper Moesia). The *Historia Augusta* quotes letters indicating that he served as military tribune under TRAJANUS DECIUS and VALERIAN, who then appointed him commander-in-chief in the Illyrian region; the documents are fictitious, but there may be some truth in what they profess to report. At the time of the assassination of GALLIENUS outside Mediolanum in 268, in which Claudius seems to have been a participant, he was deputy chief commander in the region. The selection of the next emperor lay between Claudius and another senior officer, AURELIAN, who had also been privy to the plot; we do not know why the army chose Claudius, though Aurelian's reputation as a martinet might have had something to do with his rejection. In any case, the story was put out that Gallienus, as he lay dying, had formally appointed Claudius as his successor.

However, the murder of Gallienus had angered the soldiers, and a mutiny immediately ensued, which was only put down by the time-honoured promise of a bonus payment, amounting to twenty gold coins per head. The senators at Rome, on the other hand, welcomed the death of Gallienus, because of resentment against their exclusion from high commands; and now they proceeded to put his friends and relations to death, including his brother and his surviving son Marinianus. But Claudius sent the senators a plea for clemency, insisting, moreover, that the late emperor should be deified, in order to placate the army.

After Claudius' accession, the siege of the rebel general Aureolus in Mediolanum, upon which Gallienus and his assassins had all been engaged, continued without a break. On learning of the change of ruler, Aureolus tried to come to terms, but when his approaches were rejected he decided to capitulate to Claudius instead, presumably on the understanding that his life would be spared. But very soon afterwards he was put to death, because the soldiers resented his disloyalty to Gallienus. Despite his removal, Claudius' presence in north Italy was still urgently required, because of a grave threat from the Alamanni. Either on the invitation of Aureolus, or because the Raetian garrison had been weakened because of his troop transfers to Mediolanum, these Germans had broken through the Brenner Pass and penetrated as far as Lake Benacus. There Claudius encountered them, inflicting such a heavy defeat that only half their number managed to get back to the north; thus he was able to assume the title Germanicus Maximus.

The secessionist Empire set up by POSTUMUS in the west was going through difficult times, and in the hope of weakening it further Claudius sent an exploratory force to southern Gaul under Julius Placidianus; camping near Cularo, he opened up communications with Spain, bringing it back under the control of the central government. Claudius did not lead the expedition in person because he had decided that his first priority must be a further confrontation with the Goths in the Balkans. Gallienus had not been able to follow up the victory he seems to have won against them at Naissus in 268, but his general Marcianus continued to harass the invaders, and now Claudius himself appeared, to complete the operation. When the Goths, suffering from lack of provisions, felt obliged to come down from their camp on Mount Gessax in order to seek food in Macedonia, Claudius savaged them badly, apparently in the neighbourhood of Marcianopolis. These successes were celebrated on the coinage (VICTORIAE GOTHICae) and earned the emperor the title of Gothicus, by which he was henceforward habitually known. Fresh bands of Goths crossed the Danube to help their compatriots, but with little success; while others, transported on Herulian ships, who tried to force their way into the cities of the Aegean, likewise found their assaults defied, and suffered reverses from a Roman fleet commanded by Tenagino Probus, governor of Egypt. Many Germans who were captured or surrendered during these various campaigns were drafted into the Roman army, or settled as colonists in the northern Balkans; and milestones bear witness to a considerable amount of road construction in the area.

Claudius was still engaged in rounding up the Goths on Mount Haemus when dispatches reported that the tribe of the Juthungi, hitherto kept quiet by subsidies from Rome, had crossed the upper Danube in search of new lands and placed Raetia in peril, while another powerful German people, the Vandals, were preparing to invade Pannonia. So Claudius, after entrusting the Gothic command to Aurelian, marched to Sirmium in order to supervise these new theatres of war. But plague broke out in his army and in January 270, Claudius himself succumbed to the scourge.

Although he had reigned for less than two years he was sincerely mourned by soldiers and senate alike, and his deification promptly followed. Moreover, his memory later received a further extraordinary impetus when CON-

STANTINE THE GREAT asserted that his grandmother had been Claudius' daughter or niece. The claim was fictitious, but retrospectively transformed the literary accounts of Claudius' reign into panegyrics of an exaggerated nature. Even so, it remained true that he had been a commander of unusual distinction, a fine example of the Danubian military skill and valour to which the Empire owed its very survival. But he had no time or opportunity to deal with its economic woes; for example, the silvered bronze coinage reached a new low level of debasement and shabbiness, with unfavourable effects on the already massive inflation of prices. The coins show portraits of a typical Danubian military man of the period, short-haired, unshaven and formidably grim.

QUINTILLUS
270

QUINTILLUS (Marcus Aurelius) (January–March/April 270) was the brother of CLAUDIUS GOTHICUS and apparently commanded those of his troops that were concentrated at Aquileia to protect north-east Italy against German invasions. When the news of Claudius' death reached the camp he was hailed as emperor, first apparently by his own soldiers and then, with some enthusiasm, by the senators, who were afraid (like sections of the army) that the more obvious candidate for the throne, AURELIAN the commander-in-chief on the Lower Danube, would not treat them with sympathy. Quintillus was also, evidently, accepted in the provinces, since coins were issued in his name not only in Rome and Mediolanum but at Siscia and Cyzicus as well – though not at Antioch, now under the control of Zenobia of Palmyra (see AURELIAN), who had just decided, or was planning, to break away openly from the Empire. There were also fears of an attack from Victorinus, ruler of the Gallo-Roman secessionist state founded by POSTUMUS.

At Quintillus' request the senate awarded his late brother his deification, which was recorded on coins issued at Rome and Mediolanum. Quintillus was especially eager to gain the favour of the vitally important armies in the Danubian area, from which he himself originated; and personifications of the Pannoniae – the Upper and Lower provinces of that country – appeared on his issues from Mediolanum. But there was renewed unrest in the Balkan peninsula, where Goths, on their return journey to their homes across the Danube, would have sacked Anchialus and Nicopolis ad Istrum if they had not been effectively repelled. In this resistance, local initiative reportedly played a part, but the intervention of Aurelian was decisive. After successfully completing these operations, Aurelian proceeded to Sirmium, where the garrison acclaimed him emperor – and he himself declared that Claudius Gothicus had intended him to be his successor; although the *Historia Augusta*, on the other hand, was of the opinion that he had designated Quintillus, who was not, like Claudius himself, childless, but had two sons. When Quintillus learnt the news of Aurelian's proclamation he was still at Aquileia, for he had failed to move down to the capital. This was a mistake since, once in Rome, he could have taken steps to consolidate his power, for example by distributing to the populace the bonuses he had promised them. For a few days he attempted to contest Aurelian's claims, but then, deserted by his soldiers, committed suicide by opening his veins.

How long his reign had lasted is hard to determine. Eutropius and Zonaras gave it a length of seventeen days (modified by the *Historia Augusta* to nineteen), but this figure may be a mistake for seventy-seven, the duration quoted by the compiler known as the 'Chronographer of 354'. Zosimus, too, suggests that he ruled for a few months; and his coins are sufficiently abundant for this to seem reasonable. It is likely, therefore, that he met his end in March or April 270. A papyrus dated 25 May indicates that it was known in Egypt, by that time, that he had ceased to be emperor.

Eutropius, echoed by the *Historia Augusta* and Orosius, ascribes him the virtues of outstanding moderation and courtesy. This was no doubt partly because by the time when he wrote, Quintillus' brother Claudius Gothicus had been retrospectively pronounced the ancestor of the Constantinian royal house. Yet Eutropius even goes on to say that the qualities of Quintillus were not only comparable to those of Claudius but superior. The reason for this is the recollection that Quintillus had been the senate's nominee. In fact, however, he could clearly not compete in experience, leadership or reputation with the talents either of his brother or of Aurelian, before whose resistance he so promptly collapsed.

AURELIAN
270–5

AURELIAN (Lucius Domitius Aurelianus) (270–5) came not from Sirmium, as one account suggests, but from the more easterly Danubian region of Lower Moesia. He was born of poor parents in 214. His early career as reported by the *Historia Augusta* is a series of inventions. But in 268 he evidently held a cavalry command in north Italy, at the time when Aureolus rebelled against GALLIENUS. Aurelian, together with his compatriot CLAUDIUS GOTHICUS, suppressed the revolt but then, almost at once, plotted to murder Gallienus, whereupon Claudius, his successor, appointed him Master of the Horse.

When Claudius died of the plague in 270, Aurelian quickly finished off the Gothic war by relieving the sieges of Anchialus and Nicopolis, and then contested the imperial claims of QUINTILLUS, the late emperor's brother, by accepting his own elevation at Sirmium, enforced by the assurance that he himself, not Quintillus, had been Claudius' intended successor.

It was now imperative for Aurelian to set out against the German Juthungi, who had traversed the Brenner Pass and moved into Italy. On hearing of his approach they began to withdraw, hoping to be able to take home the rich plunder they had collected; but Aurelian intercepted their retreat and severely mauled them on their passage across the Danube. They then dispatched envoys requesting a renewal of the peace treaty and of the financial subsidies which the Romans had paid them earlier. Dexippus describes how the delegation was received by the emperor, seated on a dais and robed in a purple cloak, in front of his assembled army. Their proposals were rejected, but permission to return to their own country was duly conceded.

Aurelian next moved on to Rome, where the senate, without great enthusiasm (since he was not their own choice), awarded him the customary powers. Almost immediately afterwards, however, he was summoned to the north again, this time because another German people, the Vandals, had crossed the Danube. After ordering the governors of Upper and Lower Pannonia to move all food supplies into the towns so as to deny them to the enemy, the emperor himself arrived on the scene and won a decisive military victory. The Vandals sued for peace, and Aurelian placed the issue before his troops, who agreed that their request should be granted. So the tribesmen were allowed to go back to their homeland, on condition that they surrendered their sons as hostages and supplied two thousand horsemen to the Roman cavalry. Five hundred of their number, however, proved disobedient and were annihilated.

The Vandals had not yet withdrawn across the Danube when another and even more formidable German invasion was announced. This time it was the German Alamanni and Marcomanni (together, perhaps, with a new wave of Juthungi) who had broken through into the Italian peninsula. Aurelian hastened back from Pannonia and came upon them in the neighbourhood of Placentia. There, blocking their lines of retreat across the Alps, he suggested they should surrender; but they caught him in an ambush and inflicted a severe defeat. Alarmist rumours began to circulate at Rome, and bloody disturbances broke out. It seems that they were initiated by Felicissimus the mint-master (*rationalis summae rei*) – or another possibility is that they arose because Felicissimus had been killed. At all events the rioting was started by moneyers who had lost their jobs, apparently because they had increased the debasement of the coinage, without authority and for their own gain. However the disorders spread with sinister rapidity, encouraged by certain senators who were not sorry to see Aurelian's authority weakened.

Meanwhile, Aurelian himself had been preserved from the worst consequences of his defeat by the Germans, because, in their eagerness for plunder, they had split up into a number of separate, scattered bands. These he was able to defeat one by one in a series of crushing victories, upon the River Metaurus and at Fanum Fortunae and near Ticinum; and few of the invaders survived to return across the Alps. The emperor did not trouble to pursue them, because of the problems that awaited him at Rome. There, the mint-workers and their supporters, amid heavy casualties, were overpowered on the Caelian Hill, and a number of senators suffered the confiscation of their properties, or lost their lives.

The whole incident, however, had been merely the by-product of a far greater danger, the continuous menace of barbarian invasions from central Europe. With this peril in mind, Aurelian began to build a new wall round the capital in 271. Covering a circumference of twelve miles (far longer than the old Wall of Servius Tullius), his rampart was twelve feet thick and, for the most part, twenty feet high, and contained eighteen single or double gates, surmounted by protective towers to house heavy artillery. The wall did not, however, constitute a massive fortification, but was only intended to meet a sudden barbarian attack, unsupported by siege apparatus. Moreover, simplicity of design was essential, since the construction was undertaken by civilian labour: no soldiers could be spared for the task, as they were urgently needed for other duties.

For in addition to pressures from outside, the Empire inherited by Aurelian was beset by internal usurpers – Septimius in Dalmatia, Domitianus in southern Gaul (probably the general who had defeated the Macriani under Gallienus), and a certain Urbanus elsewhere. But these were only transient pretenders; much graver was the truncation of the Empire by major secessionist states in east and west alike. The eastern provinces were ruled by Zenobia of Palmyra and her son Vaballathus Athenodorus as an independent dominion, in which they had proclaimed themselves Augusta and Augustus during the first half of 271; and Tetricus reigned on the Rhine over the breakaway Gallo-Roman state which had been inaugurated by POSTUMUS and still survived in substantial, if diminished, form. Aurelian intended that both these independent régimes should be stamped out, and set about this formidable dual task without further delay.

His first target was the Palmyrene state, and in 271 Aurelian set out for the east to suppress it. On the way, he paused to clear marauders out of Thrace and the territories adjoining the Danube; and he also crossed over to the northern bank of the river, where Gothic raiders were pursued and rapidly crushed in a series of major engagements, in the course of which the enemy leader Cannabaudes lost his life. These successes won the emperor the designation of Gothicus Maximus, which was fully earned, for thereafter the Goths remained quiescent for many years. And yet, triumphantly victorious though he was, it was at this very juncture, apparently, that he decided to move out of Rome's trans-Danubian territorial protuberance of Dacia – leaving it to the Goths – with the result that this very large region, Rome's last important conquest, now became the first (after the Agri Decumates) to be abandoned. This was because the projecting borders of Dacia were almost impossible to defend: the country had been overrun time after time, and, indeed, a major part of its legionary garrison had already been removed. So Aurelian, no doubt wisely, withdrew the frontier to the river, and resettled the evacuated inhabitants on its right bank, where two new provinces perpetuating the name of Dacia (Ripensis and Mediterranea) were created out of Moesian and Thracian territory.

This done, the emperor continued his march against the secessionists based on Palmyra. His recovery of Asia Minor was unchallenged, except for a brief resistance by the city of Tyana, which he would not allow his victorious soldiers to plunder. This restraint encouraged other Greek cities to give him a favourable reception, and Egypt, too, surrendered to his general PROBUS (the future emperor), without striking a blow. In Syria, Aurelian was met by the main Palmyrene force under Zabdas, whose armoured heavy cavalry, in a clash beside the Orontes, proved no match for his light horsemen. Welcomed by the population of Antioch and strengthened by reinforcements from various parts of the east, Aurelian won another victory on the Emesan plain and then pursued Zenobia to Palmyra itself, where the town prepared for a siege but was captured while seeking Persian help; put on trial by Aurelian, Zenobia blamed the rising on her learned chief adviser Cassius Longinus, who was executed in consequence. Palmyra duly capitulated, but after Aurelian had returned to Europe it renewed its revolt, in defiance of Marcellinus whom he had left as governor-general of the east; while a certain Firmus showed signs of disobedience in Egypt. Aurelian, however, moved east once again with the utmost speed, captured and sacked Palmyra, and compelled Firmus to commit suicide.

He was now free to complete the reunification of his Empire by proceeding to Gaul and eliminating Tetricus, who in the middle of a battle on the Campi Catalaunii came over to his side, deserting his own troops (274). His Gallo-Roman empire came to an end, and he and his son, together with Zenobia, were compelled to parade in a magnificent Roman Triumph. After this procession, however, all three were spared; the elder Tetricus was made governor of Lucania in south-western Italy, and Zenobia was settled at Tibur and given a Roman senator as a husband. Such was the end of the woman whom Edward Gibbon admired as a unique heroine of the ancient world.

One of the next tasks to which Aurelian addressed himself was a reorganization of the national coinage, whose increasingly degraded debasement contributed largely to the uncontrollable price inflation of the times. Commercial confidence might have been revived by the restoration of a true silver coinage or of reasonably extensive gold issues of adequate weight, but neither of these steps was regarded as practicable, no doubt because of a lack of sufficient precious metals. Nevertheless, Aurelian's new base-silver coins at least presented a better appearance than the wretched pieces they superseded. Moreover, they bore marks specifying the denominations they represented, and their values were firmly fixed in terms of gold.

Such cautious measures were possible because the recovery of the eastern provinces had placed the imperial revenue on a more solid basis. Making use of these additional resources, Aurelian was also able to adopt other measures calculated to bring back financial stability. He cancelled all arrears to the treasury and vigorously suppressed embezzlers and informers. At Rome he instituted measures to control the price of bread, reorganized its free distributions (on a hereditary basis), and added pork, oil and salt to the ration. The food supply was further ensured by measures to clear the bed of the Tiber and repair its banks; and elsewhere in Italy steps were taken to reclaim waste land – perhaps with a view to cheapening the price of wine. State centralization and regimentation were promoted by the conversion of certain food and shipping guilds into bodies of an official, quasi-military character.

Aurelian also introduced important religious innovations. Sun worship had long been on the increase in the Empire, reflecting the monotheistic ideas which now increasingly dominated pagan worship and thought. The conclusive step was now taken by Aurelian, who established a massive and strongly subsidized cult of the Unconquerable Sun (Sol Invictus), endowing the deity with a splendid temple in the capital, staffed with a new College of Priests on the model of the ancient priestly colleges. His birthday was to be celebrated on 25 December (which was eventually a bequest of the solar cult to Christianity, converted into Christmas Day). Aurelian's Danubian homeland was deeply devoted to the veneration of the sun, and in the course of his campaigns against Zenobia he himself had visited Emesa and Palmyra, both leading centres of solar theology. Elagabalus had sought to supersede the traditional cults of Rome by his Emesan sun worship, but it was Aurelian's intention not to overturn these ancestral rituals but to add to them, so that Sol now stood at the head of the pantheon, weaving together the main religious strands of east and west into a united, cosmopolitan universal faith. In unprecedented fashion, the head of the Sun himself was placed on the obverse of bronze Roman coins, described as 'Master of the Roman Empire' (SOL DOMINVS IMPERI ROMANI) and served by Aurelian as its priest. The cult was now officially prescribed for the army, and its symbols were added to military insignia.

Late in 274 Aurelian was called to the north to suppress disorders at Lugdunum and to repel a barbarian invasion of Raetia. But his ambitions were centred once again upon the east, where the reconquest of Mesopotamia from the Parthians had still not been achieved. So in the summer of 275 he set out towards Asia. But when, in October or November, he had got as far as Thrace – to Caenophrurium, between Perinthus and Byzantium – a minor incident had catastrophic effects. Aurelian detected his confidential secretary Eros in a lie and threatened to punish him. In self-defence Eros informed a number of senior praetorian officers that the emperor had marked them down for execution, together with himself. As he had hoped, the officers, afraid of Aurelian's iron discipline – or perhaps, in some cases, afflicted by a guilty conscience – accepted the warning as authentic, and one of them, a Thracian named Mucapor, struck the emperor down.

The achievement of his five-year reign, against internal and external enemies alike, had been colossal, setting the seal upon the Empire's recovery from the chaos which had threatened to bring about its disintegration. Aurelian's large and varied coinage was issued at the mints of Rome, Mediolanum (replaced by Ticinum), Lugdunum (after the suppression of Tetricus), Cyzicus, Antioch (retaken from Zenobia), Siscia and Serdica. At Serdica, a new mint established for the evacuees from Dacia and the army that protected them, some of the issues are dedicated to the emperor as 'born God and Master' (DEO ET DOMINO NATO). This was unaccustomed hyperbole. But it was reasonable enough that other coinages should hail him as 'Restorer of the Army' (RESTITVTOR EXERCITI), and even as 'Restorer' and 'Pacifier of the World' (RESTITVTOR, PACATOR ORBIS). And he, for his part, paid tribute to his stalwart Danubian compatriots who provided the nucleus of his troops (VIRTVS ILLVRICI, GENIVS ILLVRici, PANNONIAE).

The *Historia Augusta* records that Aurelian was known as 'Sword-in-hand' (*manu ad ferrum*), and sums him up, with rather unusual felicity, as an emperor who was necessary rather than good. The senate were frightened of him, and he was said to have snubbed his own wife, Ulpia Severina (in whose name he issued coins); for 'when she asked him if she might keep a single roll of purple silk, he replied: 'God forbid that a fabric should be worth its weight in gold!'

TACITUS
275–6

TACITUS (Marcus Claudius) (October or November 275–*c*. June 276) was of disputed origins: about these, as about his reign, some of the literary sources – and not only the *Historia Augusta* as might be expected, but Eutropius and Victor as well – are singularly misleading. The ascription of his birthplace to Interamna in Italy is based on a fable; he probably came from the Danubian area, like so many other emperors in this epoch. The assertion that he claimed a relationship to the historian Tacitus is, once again, unlikely to be well-founded; and the belief that his proclamation as emperor followed a six-month interregnum is based upon a confusion with the actual duration of his reign. Furthermore, the statement that Tacitus was seventy-five when he came to the throne is founded on nothing more factual than the desire to portray a venerable senator; he was probably a good deal younger. The belief of the ancient writers that his elevation to the throne constituted a revival of senatorial influence and rule is likewise founded on a series of wishful, romantic and edifying fictions. In fact, as Zosimus and Zonaras recognized, he was proclaimed not by the senate but by the army: he was a military emperor, like those before and after him. It is true, however, that at the time of

AURELIAN's murder he was not with the troops, but was residing at his house at Baiae in Campania. From there, once he had been hailed by the soldiers, he came to Rome to witness the senate's confirmation of his imperial powers, which he received, it was said, with appropriate modesty.

His request that the senators should deify Aurelian was granted. Tacitus was interested in the foundation of a dynasty of his own, as he had sons to succeed him; and he made his brother or half-brother FLORIAN his praetorian prefect. The Germans were launching one of their most formidable attacks: the Franks crossed the Rhine, while in the south the Alamanni, and another German tribe, the Longiones (Lugii), penetrated through the Neckar valley and likewise burst into Gaul. Although many unfortified cities succumbed to these assaults, Tacitus and Florian decided that an acute eastern crisis needed their prior attention, and so they set out to deal with it. For other Germanic groups, including the Heruli and Maeotidae (Goths from Lake Maeotis), who claimed to have been commissioned by Aurelian to assist in his campaign against the Persians, proceeded, after his murder, to invade Asia Minor from the Caucasus, penetrating as far south as the sea coast of Cilicia. Tacitus and Florian took the field against them, and the latter won a victory which Tacitus celebrated on his coinage (VICTORIA GOTHIca), assuming the title Gothicus Maximus.

Another of the emperor's relatives, Maximinus, whom he had appointed to the governorship of Syria, was only briefly of assistance, since before long he was murdered. Shortly afterwards it was learnt that Tacitus himself had died, at Tyana in Cappadocia. There were two conflicting explanations of how he had met his death. According to one version he was murdered by Maximinus' killers, who had subsequently moved up from Syria into Asia Minor. But it was alternatively asserted that Tacitus had fallen ill of a fever and died a natural death: a phenomenon that was so unusual among third-century emperors that the story may well be true.

The coinage of Tacitus' short reign displays the usual optimistic patriotism in abundant and varied forms. One portrait uniquely identifies him with Courage (VIRTVS) itself. The Sun-god still appears as the sponsor of the imperial forces, raising his hand to bless a goddess described as the Divine Foresight (PROVIDENTIA DEORum), who carries two standards. But in general the emphasis falls much more upon the ancient divine protectors of Rome, and especially upon ROMA AETERNA herself. One notable theme, the Clemency of the Times (CLEMENTIA TEMPorum), is illustrated by a figure of the emperor receiving a globe from the hands of Jupiter; and on another piece, the same inscription is unexpectedly accompanied by a figure of Mars – holding not only the usual spear and shield, but also the olive-branch of peace.

The *Historia Augusta* adds certain personal particulars to which can be attached as much credence as desired. 'In his manner of living,' the writer

assures us,

Tacitus was very temperate, so much so that in a whole day he never drank a pint of wine, and frequently less than a half-pint. Even at a banquet there would be served a single cock, with the addition of a pig's jowl and some eggs. In preference to all other greens he would indulge himself without stint in lettuce, which was served in large quantities, for he used to say that he purchased sleep by this kind of lavish expenditure. . . . He took baths rarely, and was all the stronger in his old age. He delighted greatly in varied and elaborate forms of glassware. . . . He was fond of marbles.

FLORIAN
276

FLORIAN (Marcus Annius Florianus) (*c.* April–June 276) is variously described in the *Historia Augusta* as the emperor TACITUS' brother and half-brother (the son of the same mother); the difference in their family names suggests that the latter is more likely. Tacitus appointed him prefect of the praetorian guard and then took him to the east to confront the Goths who had invaded the peninsula from across the Black and Azov Seas, penetrating as far south as Cilicia. Florian carried on the war with success, and had cut off the tribesmen's retreat when he learnt that Tacitus had died at Tyana. He then declared himself emperor without awaiting the proclamation of the soldiers or confirmation by the senate. It seemed for a brief moment that Florian's *coup* had been successful, since the western mints (Rome, Lugdunum, Siscia and Ticinum) coined in his name and he was apparently recognized throughout the Empire – except only in Syria and Egypt, which after two or three weeks came out openly in support of the eastern commander PROBUS instead. On learning of the defiance from Probus, Florian decided to march against him, believing that the numerical superiority of his own forces would prove decisive. The armies confronted each other near Tarsus, but Probus avoided a pitched battle. During this period of suspended action, the health of Florian's European soldiers became so seriously undermined by the hot climate that they decided they had had enough of civil war and put him to death, probably with the complicity of Probus (though the latter's admiring biographer avoids any suggestion that this may have been so).

The coinage of Florian, considering the brevity of his reign, was remarkably varied. Its designs and inscriptions particularly concentrate on the military courage (VIRTVS FLORIANI AVG*usti*) which he had displayed while serving under Tacitus and which he continued to manifest with the aid of a united army (CONCORDIA MILIT*um*, EXERC*itus*); thus Florian, supported by Mars the Bringer of Peace, would become the Pacifier of the World (PACATOR ORBIS) and Restorer of the Age (RESTITVTOR SAECVLI). His victories would go on forever (VICTORIA PERPETVA). Indeed, the peculiar and distinctive feature of this over-optimistic coinage is its preoccupation with stability and permanence: PERPETVITATE AVG(*usti*), AETERNITAS AVG(*usti*), PAX AETERNA, SECVRITAS AVG(*usti*), SECVRITAS SAECVLI. These were fatally empty and elusive desiderata, and Florian and his proclaimed hopes came and went without making the slightest impact on the events and crises of the age.

PROBUS
276–82

PROBUS (Marcus Aurelius Equitius) (276–82) was born at Sirmium, perhaps in 232 (though this may have been a historian's guess, based on a rough estimate that he was fifty at the time of his death). Whether his father Maximus was, as stated, a market-gardener named Dalmatius is also uncertain; he may instead have been a minor state functionary or a soldier.

Probus' early career, as reported in the eulogistic *Historia Augusta*, seems largely fictitious. But he was apparently the most distinguished of the generals serving under AURELIAN, on whose behalf he defended the German frontier against Alamannic incursions. Next, in the reign of TACITUS, he held a high post in Syria and Egypt – according to one source, the supreme eastern command. Following Tacitus' death at Tyana in 276, Probus refused to accept the elevation of FLORIAN, declaring that he himself was the man to whom Tacitus had bequeathed the throne – and after two or three weeks he was acclaimed emperor by his troops. When the armies confronted each other near Tarsus, Probus' avoidance of a pitched battle successfully caused Florian's heat-stricken soldiers to murder him and come over to his rival.

Probus proceeded to Rome, where the senate confirmed his imperial powers; at all times he remained meticulous in showing it respect, though the tradition that it actually took a leading part in his government is hard to accept. Vengeance was carried out on those of Aurelian's murderers who had survived. Meanwhile, his death had encouraged or accentuated a new series of German threats which had already become apparent in Tacitus' short reign. Probus' generals defeated the Franks, and he, in the course of more than a year's hard campaigning, captured Semnon, the chief of the Longiones, but subsequently allowed him and his people to return to their own country on condition that they surrendered their prisoners and their plunder.

Then Probus mounted successful attacks on further German tribes, the Burgundians and Vandals who had come to their compatriots' help. Although his army was numerically much inferior to theirs, he skilfully contrived to defeat their various forces separately and in detail. Conditions similar to those accorded to the Longiones were granted, but when they withheld the Roman prisoners of war whose return they had promised, Probus returned to the attack, capturing their chieftain Igillus and assuming the title Germanicus. Hostages were demanded and handed over, nine enemy chiefs knelt together at his feet, and sixteen thousand Germans were taken into the Roman army and distributed among different units. Sixty major Gallic cities had been liberated by the successful outcome of the war, and forts were re-established on the far bank of the Rhine to prevent the resumption of hostilities.

In 278 Probus repelled a further German invasion, this time by Vandals, describing himself on his coins as the Restorer of Illyricum (RES-TITVTOR ILLVRICI). In the next year he set out for the east, where various additional troubles were reported. In the first place, a high officer named Julius Saturninus had usurped the purple in Syria, issuing gold coins in his own name at Apamea; but he was killed by his own soldiers, or by men sent by Probus. Next, a gang of brigands had barricaded themselves inside the mountain fortress of Cremna in Isauria (southern Asia Minor), where they resisted a long and ferocious siege until their leader Lydius (or Palfuerius) was slain. Then the tribe of the Blemmyes broke through Egypt's southern frontier and captured the towns of Coptos and Ptolemais, but the governor was able to eject them.

Probus' ultimate purpose was to recover the former Mesopotamian province from the Persians. However he did not, for the present, think it advisable to embark on hostilities, and indeed, although rejecting their offer of gifts, he seems to have agreed upon a truce. This suited both parties: the new Persian king, Bahram II, was not yet sure of his position, and Probus himself was eager to return to Europe, where serious problems awaited him. As he passed through Thrace, he settled one hundred thousand Bastarnae (Scythians) inside the Empire. However, it was in Gaul and Germany that his presence was specially needed, since two of his commanders in those regions, Proculus and Bonosus, had raised the standard of revolt. The *Historia Augusta* rises to new heights of prolix inventiveness in explaining who they were and what they did. But it appears likely that both rebelled (possibly in conjunction) at Colonia Agrippinensium, where they may have shared the command of an imperial army. Whether Proculus also gained support from the citizens of Lugdunum, as one report stated, remains uncertain. Bonosus, for his part, seems to have been in close touch with the Germans. Before long, however, both met their deaths – Proculus, it was said, after betrayal to the emperor, and Bonosus by suicide when the military situation went against him. An inscription from Valentia in Spain, on which Probus' name is seen to have been erased, suggests that the unrest had spread to that country as well. Moreover, an imperial governor revolted in Britain; a Mauretanian named Victorinus, who had recommended him to the emperor and was anxious to remove the stigma, was sent to put him down.

Returning to Rome at the end of 281, Probus celebrated a magnificent Triumph, notable for the number and variety of the conquered enemies who adorned the procession. Now at last he was free to act against the Persians, and set about mobilizing an army for this purpose. However, he had evidently miscalculated in his treatment of his soldiers. They had fought many wars on Rome's behalf, and even when not fighting they had been made to work hard, for example in clearing the land for new vineyards. Moreover, the *Historia Augusta* quotes Probus as declaring that in a short time armies would not be needed any longer. Although the source is suspect, the remark, coming from a ruler proud of having pacified the Empire, may well be authentic. Such an opinion would not have endeared him to the senior officers, whose jobs might thus seem at risk; it was not long, therefore, before news reached him at Sirmium that the army in Raetia and Noricum had proclaimed CARUS, the praetorian prefect, as emperor in his place. The contingent sent by Probus to suppress him deserted, and he himself, while supervising a land recovery project, was compelled to take refuge from his own troops inside a tower, into which, however, they forced their way to kill him.

Although we must discount the exaggerated encomia of the literary authorities – for one thing, there was no senatorial 'restoration', and for another, the number of rebellions in the reign bore witness to an unhealthier situation than they admit – Probus was evidently a military ruler of a calibre scarcely inferior to his Danubian compatriot Aurelian, whose efforts to reconstitute the shattered Empire he so imposingly continued. His own view of his programme and achievements is displayed eloquently on the coinage. As in earlier reigns, stress is laid on the hoped-for harmony among the troops (CONCORD*ia* MILIT*um*), and the new Golden Age of peace (FELICIA TEMPORA) brought about by the emperor who is Restorer of the World (RESTITVT*or* ORBIS). But the most noteworthy feature of the coins and medallions of Probus is an extraordinary diversity of obverse types, which display many different versions of the emperor's portrait and numerous, varying combinations of his titles, thus testifying to a new enlargement of the imperial personality cult.

CARUS
282–3

CARUS (Marcus Aurelius Numerius [?]) (*c.* September 282–December [?] 283) was of uncertain origin: the *Historia Augusta* makes various conjectures but in fact he probably came from Narbo in southern Gaul. In 276 PROBUS made him praetorian prefect. Six years later, however, while he was mustering troops in Raetia and Noricum for that emperor's Persian expedition, the soldiers invested him with the purple, despite his alleged protestations of unwillingness. A force sent against him deserted, and Probus was assassinated by his own troops. The *Historia*'s assurance that Carus had no hand in this deed must be regarded with suspicion.

On receiving the news of Probus' death, he sent a dispatch to the senate announcing his own elevation by the army. His decision to report this as a *fait accompli* without even requesting the formality of the senate's approval was regarded as nonchalant and untraditional; it pointed the way to a time when autocracy would be completely undisguised. However, Carus did consider it advisable to propose, or agree to, his predecessor's deification. He then took what steps he could to establish his personal dynasty. His forerunners had often made similar attempts; but Carus, unlike so many of them, was fortunate to possess two sons of adult years whom he could call upon to help govern the Empire and fight its wars. First the older of the two, CARINUS, and then his brother NUMERIAN, were given the titles of Caesar and Prince of Youth (Princeps Iuventutis).

The first crisis of the reign was an incursion by the Sarmatians and Quadi, who crossed the Danube and ravaged Pannonia. But Carus, apparently without any prior visit to Rome, set out to repel them and hit them hard, killing (it was asserted, probably with some exaggeration) no less than sixteen thousand of the enemy and capturing twenty thousand of both sexes. Specimen prisoners are depicted on a coin later issued by Numerian showing his father and himself in a chariot, accompanied by the inscription TRIVNFV (s) (*triumphus*) QVADOR (*um*). Next, at the turn of the year, once again taking Numerian with him, and leaving his elder brother in charge of the west, Carus set out in the direction of Asia, to carry out Probus' plans for the recovery of Mesopotamia. This enterprise, he declared, was his principal ambition; his purpose in coming to the throne was to do the Persians damage. The prospects were promising, because the Persian king, Bahram II, was hampered by internal strife with his brother Hormizd. The mint of Cyzicus honours the arrival (ADVENTVS) of Carus and Numerian on their way to the east. In 283, entering Mesopotamia without opposition, the emperor inflicted a defeat on the Persians and captured first Seleucia on the Tigris and then the royal capital Ctesiphon itself. Rome's Mesopotamian province was duly reoccupied, and Carus assumed the title Persicus Maximus and raised his elder son Carinus to the rank of Augustus.

Next he planned to exploit this success by penetrating even more deeply into Persian territory, and this project, we are told, was encouraged by his praetorian prefect Arrius Aper. But then towards the end of July, not far from Ctesiphon, Carus was found dead in his tent during the night. There had been a violent thunderstorm, and some declared that he had been killed by lightning – a divine act of retribution, according to Victor and Festus, because he had tried to overstep the limits of success. Others believed he had died of an illness. But his death was, more probably, the work of Aper, who was the father-in-law of Numerian and saw a greater future for himself once the young man's father was out of the way.

The *Historia Augusta* describes Carus as 'a man of middling qualities, one might say, but one to be ranked with the good rather than with the bad emperors'. Elsewhere, however, the same writer calls him a 'good emperor', and his military achievements, during a reign that lasted scarcely more than a year, had been by no means unimpressive.

CARINUS
283–5

CARINUS (Marcus Aurelius) (joint emperor, December [?] 283– early 285) was the elder son of Carus, who on assuming the purple in 282 raised him to the rank of Caesar. When, in December or January, his father and younger brother NUMERIAN departed to fight against the Persians, Carinus was left in Rome, with a carefully selected staff of advisers, to direct the affairs of the west. Unlike more juvenile Caesars earlier in the century, he was saluted as Imperator and crowned with a laurel wreath on the coins that were issued in his name; and in the wake of his father's Persian victories in 283, he was elevated to the rank of Augustus and co-emperor. Their heads appeared together on coins issued at Lugdunum to celebrate the peace.

When Carus died, his two sons succeeded jointly to the throne without opposition, Carinus in the west and Numerian in the east. Numerian soon began to move homewards, but met his death in mysterious circumstances in autumn 284. His eastern army however refused to accept Carinus as sole ruler, and instead proclaimed a senior member of their own staff called Diocles, better known under his future name of DIOCLETIAN.

Meanwhile Carinus had claimed military successes against the Germans and Britons, assuming the titles Germanicus Maximus and Britannicus Maximus. Nevertheless, he was not in a position to deal with Diocletian immediately, because another commander Marcus Aurelius Julianus, the governor of Venetia, had risen in revolt in the Danubian region. He controlled the mint of Siscia, and issued coinage there assuming the title of Augustus, claiming the two Pannonias as his own (PANNONIAE AVGusti) and offering the traditional promise of freedom for all (LIBERTAS PVBLICA). But at about the beginning of 285 Carinus, moving southwards, suppressed him in the neighbourhood of Verona, taking over his troops. Carinus was now free to deal with Diocletian, and the rival armies confronted one another near Margum on the Danube. The battle was fierce, but when victory for Carinus seemed at hand he was assassinated by one of his own senior officers, and his army went over to Diocletian.

The man who murdered him, people said, was carrying out an act of vengeance because Carinus had seduced his wife. This forms part of a literary tradition that was thoroughly hostile to Carinus. No unfriendly tale is too extravagant (or trivial) for the *Historia Augusta* to omit.

His plunge baths were always cooled by means of snow. . . . He appointed as city-prefect one of his own doorkeepers, a baser act than which no one can conceive or relate. . . . Carinus was the most polluted of men, an adulterer and constant corrupter of youth (I am ashamed to relate what Onesimus has put in writing), and he even made evil use of the enjoyment of his own sex. . . . He filled the palace with actors and harlots, pantomimists, singers and pimps. . . . By marrying and divorcing he took nine wives in all, and he put away some while they were still pregnant.

Whatever the truth of these final statistics, his coinage only honours one single wife: she is Magnia Urbica, identifiable as Carinus' spouse because a coin shows her in his company. Towards the end of his reign he also issued coinages in honour of three deified members of his own family: Carus, Numerian and a boy named Nigrinianus, whom an inscription calls the grandson of Carus, so he is likely to have been the son of either Carinus or Numerian. Evidently Carinus was preoccupied with the idea of publicizing the new imperial house.

The last phase of his reign, when the clouds were gathering fast, is characterized by coin types conventionally stressing the loyalty of the troops and the peace that it was their function to bring. And the coinage is also filled with the other features of a beneficent imperial programme – an emphasis that was particularly needed because Rome in 283 suffered from an extremely destructive fire, which devastated huge areas of the city. How much relative weight is to be assigned to all his favourable self-publicity on the one hand, and the venomous literary tradition on the other? The latter attitude, it must be appreciated, was prompted by the dynasty of Diocletian, who overthrew him and was therefore biased; but it is supported, at least to some extent, by the fact that when Numerian was found dead his soldiers proved extremely unwilling to have Carinus as their emperor.

NUMERIAN
283–4

NUMERIAN (Marcus Aurelius Numerius Numerianus) (joint emperor, *c.*
July 283–November 284) was the younger son of CARUS, who elevated him to
the rank of Caesar and Prince of Youth very soon or immediately after the
same honours had been conferred on his elder brother CARINUS in 282. Carus
took Numerian, but not Carinus, with him on his expedition against the
Persians, and after victory'had been won the youth was allowed to participate
in their father's salutation as Imperator.

When Carus died, Numerian succeeded to the throne as the colleague of
Carinus (who had already been proclaimed joint Augustus in their father's
lifetime). Although Numerian is described on some coins by the juvenile title
of Prince of Youth, others display the united and equal portraits of the two
rulers, and a bronze medallion depicting Numerian as consul – in resplendent
court costume of oriental style – offers a scene of the imperial colleagues
haranguing their troops side by side (ADLOCVTIO AVGG. [*Augustorum*]), although they were, in fact, separated by many hundreds of miles. At
first Numerian attempted to pursue the Persian War, under the guidance of his
praetorian prefect Arrius Aper, although the latter had been suspected of
responsibility for the death of Carus. But Zonaras records that Numerian's
military efforts were not attended by success; a coin describing him as 'Pacifier
of the World' only reflects wishful thinking. The fact was that warfare did not
appeal to him; and so he began to march homewards through Asia Minor.

The *Historia Augusta*, like other sources, takes up the story. Numerian, still in
the company of Aper, had reached the neighbourhood of Nicomedia when he
began to suffer from a disease of the eyes – a kind of ailment, we are reminded,
from which those exhausted, as he was, by too much loss of sleep are likely to
suffer; he was being carried in a litter. There Aper put him to death. But for
several days the soldiers continued to ask after the emperor's health, while
Aper reported that Numerian could not appear in public because he had to

protect his weakened eyes from the wind and the sun. Finally however the stench of his corpse revealed what had happened. Aper had hoped that Numerian's death would be ascribed to natural causes, and that he himself would succeed to the vacant throne. But the troops were not of the same mind; nor did they favour Carinus (although he promptly deified his dead brother).. The man they preferred was DIOCLETIAN (see next entry), whose first act was to charge Aper with the murder and strike him down with his own hand.

Numerian, according to the *Historia*, was a young man whose tastes did not equip him for the task of emperor, especially in the exacting times of the later third century; for his interests were primarily of a literary nature. His oratorical talents, and written speeches, earned much admiration. He was also a poet of considerable reputation, ranking, people said, with the leading poet of the day, Olympius Nemesianus, whose work *On Hunting* (*Cynegetica*) – of which 325 lines survive – was composed during the joint reign of Carinus and Numerian and includes a passage in which he promises to write an epic on the deeds of the imperial brothers.

PART VII

THE
TETRARCHY AND
THE HOUSE OF CONSTANTINE

The Tetrarchy and the House of Constantine

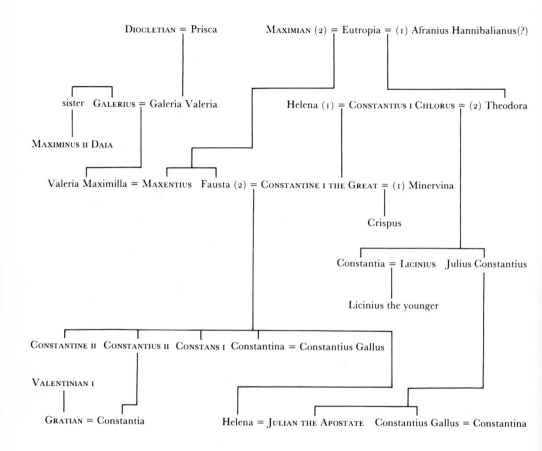

DIOCLETIAN
284–305

DIOCLETIAN (284–305; joint emperor from 286 onwards), originally named Diocles, was born in about 240 of a poor Dalmatian family, but rose in the military hierarchy until Numerian made him commander of the élite officer cadet unit attached to the imperial staff known as *protectores domestici*. In 284, near Nicomedia, he was selected by the soldiers to avenge NUMERIAN'S death, which he did by killing the praetorian prefect Aper who was suspected of having killed the young man.

Hailed as emperor, Diocletian, as he now began to be called – assuming the additional names of Gaius Aurelius Valerius – marched into Europe and defeated Numerian's elder brother CARINUS near Margum on about 1 April 285. Though he retained Carinus' praetorian prefect, Aristobulus, in office, he appointed his own comrade MAXIMIAN as Caesar, and then in the next year made him his full imperial colleague with the rank of Augustus. Next followed, for Diocletian, a number of years of energetic frontier fighting, first in Moesia and Pannonia, earning him the title Germanicus Maximus in about 286, and subsequently against Sarmatians in 289 and 292 and Saracens, an Arab tribe living in the Sinai peninsula who had launched an invasion of Syria, in 290.

In 293 Diocletian converted his dual régime into the Tetrarchy, founded on rule by merit – a system envisaging the joint rule of two Augusti (himself and Maximian) and two Caesars. These Caesars, once again of Danubian origin, were CONSTANTIUS I and GALERIUS, serving as junior colleagues to Maximian (in the west) and himself (in the east) respectively. Each of the tetrarchs had his own separate capital city, adorned with splendid buildings. The Empire had been divided between rulers before, but this new arrangement possessed a more systematic and far-reaching character; and Diocletian intended it to be permanent. It was planned both to satisfy military requirements and to ensure, when the time came, an orderly progress of joint successions to the imperial office. Nevertheless, while multiplying the ruling authorities, the Tetrarchy did not formally partition the Empire, which remained a single constitutional unit. Legislation was in the name of all four men, and both Caesars were required to obey both Augusti.

Diocletian put down the revolt of Domitius Domitianus and Achilleus in Egypt in about 296, and his lieutenant Galerius, after a setback, was victorious over the Persians. In 303 Diocletian visited Rome for the first time, to celebrate the twentieth anniversary of his reign. Then, after a serious illness in the following year, he took the unprecedented step of abdicating from the throne on 1 May 305, inducing the reluctant Maximian to act likewise. From his place of retirement at Salonae in Dalmatia, Diocletian briefly and temporarily returned to the political scene in 308, to help Galerius restore order among the various imperial contenders at the Conference of Carnuntum. But then, once again, he withdrew to Salonae, where he died in 316, saddened by the collapse of the tetrarchic system which he had so meticulously founded.

In other respects, however, he had left a truly imposing heritage, for he was the most remarkable imperial organizer since AUGUSTUS. One of his reforms was the doubling of the number of the provinces, which were increased from fifty to a hundred: it was intended that the governors of these relatively small areas – whose posts were not completely detached from military commands – would thus lack the resources necessary to start a rebellion. Italy was included in the system. Another innovation was the grouping of these provinces into thirteen larger units named dioceses. Their governors-general were subordinated to the four praetorian prefects (one attached to each tetrarch) who became the principal lieutenants of the Augusti and Caesars in the civil, financial and judicial administration of the Empire.

Diocletian also presided over a complete reconstruction of the Empire's military system. The army was divided into two distinct branches. One was a mobile field force, the *comitatenses*, 'soldiers of the retinue'. Its four formations, one for each ruler, contained a proportion of infantrymen but were particularly strong in cavalry, including a new mounted guard or retinue, the *scholae palatinae* (whose existence reduced the praetorian guard to little more than a metropolitan garrison). The second major division of the army consisted of frontier units, later known as *limitanei*, men of the borders, or *riparienses*, men of the river-banks. This corps, presiding over greatly strengthened fortifications, was maintained by annual drafts of conscripted Roman citizens. But numerous Germans and highlanders from Asia Minor, and other barbarian tribesmen of warlike temper and specialized skills, likewise found employment in these border units. (Diocletian also turned his attention to expanding the Roman fleets.)

In order to pay this large military establishment amounting to half a million men or more – a big increase on a century previously – Diocletian had to raise enormous taxes from the civilian population, increasing payments in cash and kind to the very utmost that the resources of the Roman world permitted. Yet he did try to ensure that these burdens were distributed as equitably as possible. One of his major endeavours in this direction was the issue of an edict fixing maximum prices for all saleable goods and costs of transportation, and the edict also, in 301, stipulated maximum salaries for every worker throughout the entire Empire. This edict, preserved in the most important economic document surviving from ancient times, was something entirely new in Roman imperial history, though much smaller endeavours along the same lines had from time to time been made by certain Greek states.

Since, however, Diocletian and his colleagues did not control the means and levels of production and consumption, they found it impossible to enforce their regulations. All that happened was that foodstuffs and other objects vanished from the markets, and inflation, which had been afflicting the Empire for so long and so disastrously, resumed its uncontrollable course. In an attempt to check this tendency, Diocletian had already in about 294 instituted a radical reform of the coinage, and it was in terms of this new and stable currency that the edict was framed. But he lacked the quantities of bullion needed to stabilize the relation between his gold and silver coins on the one hand and token base metal issues on the other, so that prices in terms of the latter denominations continued to display alarmingly steep rises.

Nevertheless, Diocletian instituted a further attempt to mitigate the taxpayers' lot. In the foregoing decades they had been gravely affected by the irregular suddenness and unpredictability of the demands made by the imperial exchequer. To remedy this, the entire tax-collecting process was unprecedentedly placed on a regular basis: a new and revised announcement of the imperial requirements began to be issued, every year, by the four praetorian prefects. As in the past, the taxation system was predominantly founded on agriculture. But now for the first time variations between harvests and between qualities of soil were given due consideration, by a new method of assessment deliberately calculated to take these inequalities into account. This new system, however, for all its fair aims, contained a repressive feature, because it accentuated the already existing tendency to compel the populace to stay at work exactly where they were, in the places where their presence was registered, and the compulsion was even extended from one generation to another. The tenants of large estates found themselves included in the freeze, and so were members of guilds and corporations unconnected with agriculture, and employees of the government in every field. Thus, on paper, a thoroughgoing totalitarian State was brought into existence – although there was, in practice, no means of bringing this mass of rules and prohibitions into total effect.

All these coercive measures were aimed at raising enough funds to pay the greatly enlarged army. The rulers had to be able to deal with internal rivals and external foes, often at one and the same time. Imperial publicity said nothing directly about the former, since the soldiers were ostensibly assumed

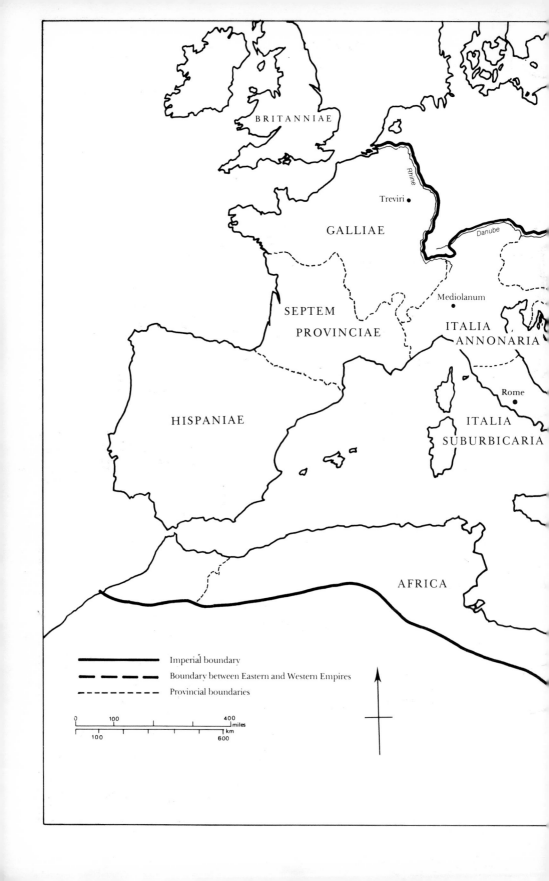

BRITANNIAE

Rhine

Treviri

GALLIAE

Danube

Mediolanum

SEPTEM
PROVINCIAE

ITALIA
ANNONARIA

Rome

HISPANIAE

ITALIA
SUBURBICARIA

AFRICA

——— Imperial boundary

– – – Boundary between Eastern and Western Empires

- - - - Provincial boundaries

0   100   400
                                    miles
                                    km
     100   600

8 The Administrative Dioceses of Diocletian (AD 284-305)

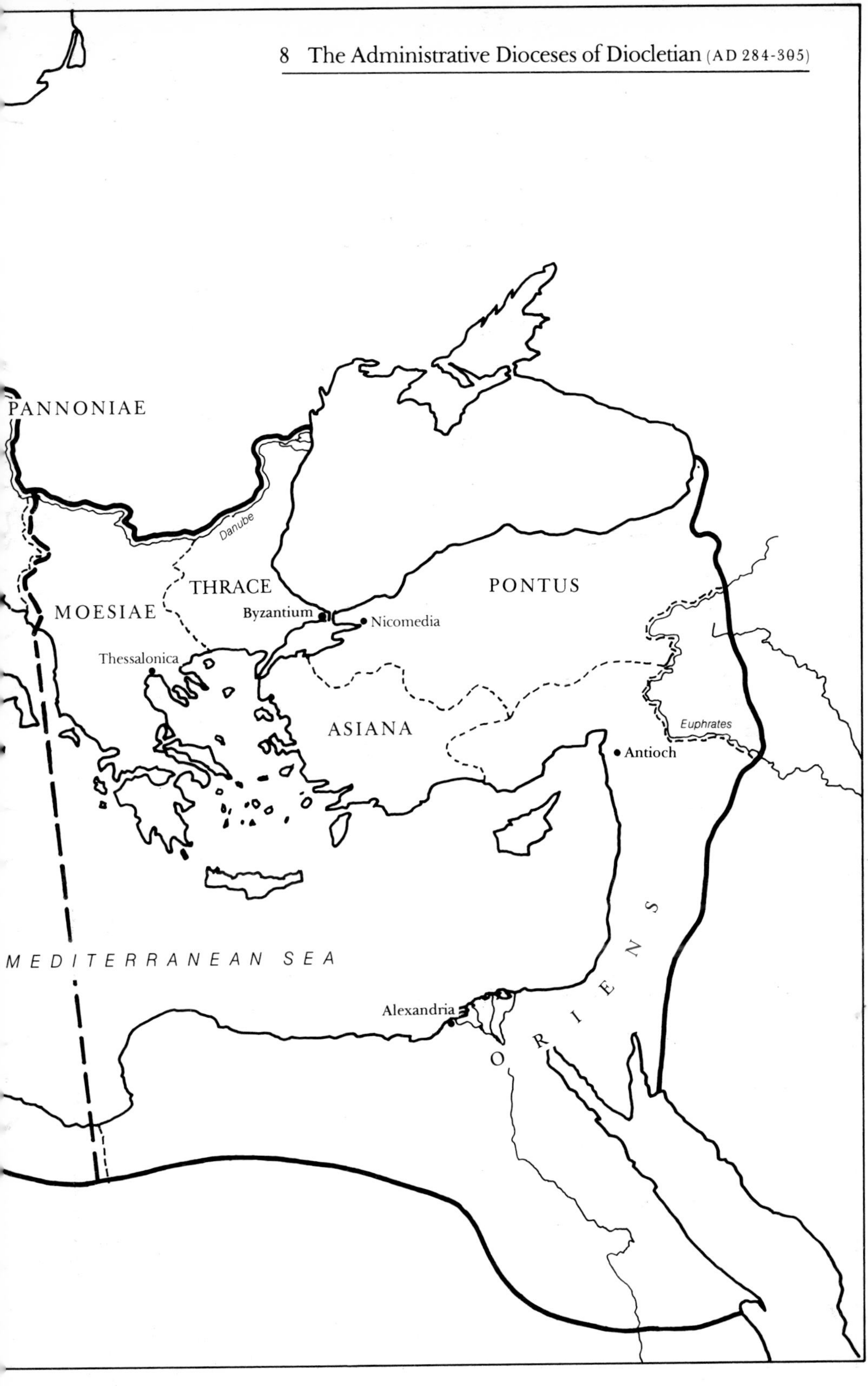
PANNONIAE
Danube
THRACE
MOESIAE
Byzantium
Nicomedia
PONTUS
Thessalonica
ASIANA
Euphrates
Antioch
MEDITERRANEAN SEA
Alexandria
ORIENS

to be loyal. But the designs and inscriptions on the coins concentrated remorselessly on victory over foreign enemies – with unceasing emphasis upon the rulers' role as triumphant military leaders. Diocletian and Maximian were raised to a new level of potent, more than human, conquering grandeur under the designations of Jovius and Herculius: that is, they were thought to enjoy the special protection and companionship of Jupiter and Hercules respectively (see also MAXIMIAN). Moreover, this exaltation was reflected in court ceremonial, which evolved an elaborate pattern far removed from the simpler practices of earlier Roman times and closer in spirit to the contemporary institutions of Persia.

However, the eternal State of Rome received ample glorification, and millions of coins celebrated the Genius of the Roman People (GENIVS POPVLI ROMANI). In pursuance of this appeal to traditional patriotic feeling Diocletian, encouraged by his Caesar Galerius, returned to the harassment of the Christians which had been in abeyance for four decades – although his own wife, Prisca, belonged to their faith. As never before, the motive of the Great Persecution which began in 303 was the total extirpation of Christianity: it was a struggle to the death between the old and new orders. The first of Diocletian's edicts directed to this end prohibited all assemblies of Christians for purposes of worship, and commanded that their churches and sacred books should be destroyed. Then two further edicts, in the eastern provinces, ordered that clergy, unless they sacrificed to the pagan divinities, should be placed under arrest. Finally, in 304, a fourth proclamation extended the application of the three previous edicts to all Christians.

At the outset of his reign Diocletian had rebuilt the Curia, the senate-house, beside the Roman Forum, a building which had been severely damaged in the fire of 283. His reconstruction, which has survived, followed very closely the traditional lines and proportions of the earlier versions of the edifice. Its interior was a plain rectangular hall with a coffered timbered ceiling, lined on either side by low steps to provide seats for the senators. The severely plain upper walls, lit by single large windows, presented a piquant contrast with the elaborately columned niches that were to be seen at a lower level, and with the rich multi-coloured marbles covering the floor.

It was not at Rome, however, but at Nicomedia in Bithynia, that Diocletian established his first headquarters. Very few traces of his extensive building programme there have survived, but a little more can be said about his reconstruction of Antioch, where he set up his residence after the foundation of the Tetrarchy, creating a new capital equipped with temples, granaries, baths, a stadium and a factory for making weapons. And in the same city he completed and expanded an imperial palace, within the framework of a fortress built half a century earlier; Libanius describes this palace quarter, with its four colonnaded streets.

Diocletian's Antioch now lies buried deep beneath the silt of the Orontes.

Extensive remains, on the other hand, have survived of the palace at Spalatum near Salonae, to which he retired after his abdication. This remarkable blend of civil and military architecture united the public rooms of an imperial residence, the personal quarters of a great Dalmatian villa or commander-in-chief's dwelling, and the strong defences of an inward-looking fortress, protected by a wall studded by square and polygonal towers. The design of the whole massive complex is rigorously axial, centred upon an avenue which proceeds through a colonnaded courtyard or *atrium* (flanked by an internally circular, externally octagonal mausoleum) to a domed and apsed vestibule. This in turn leads to the throne-room or Hall of Audience (Aula Palatina), of which the three-bayed columnar façade, crowned by a gabled Pediment of Glorification, can still be seen. Over the middle columns soars an arch beneath which the bejewelled and haloed ex-emperor would appear, as if framed by the vault of heaven, to receive the homage of the vast assembled throng. The south front of the Hall of Audience looked directly upon the Adriatic Sea. Flanked by two square towers, its surface is broken by an immense gallery with loggias at the centre and at either extremity. Between the gallery's forty-two arched windows stand engaged columns, resting upon corbels or consoles – blocks projecting from the wall – according to a Syrian fashion.

MAXIMIAN
286–305, 307–8

MAXIMIAN (joint emperor, 286–305 and 307–8) died in 310. He came of a peasant family living near Sirmium. Born in about 240, he received little or no education, but performed distinguished service in AURELIAN's armies on the Danube, Euphrates and Rhine, and then in Britain, and successfully continued his military career under PROBUS. He was on friendly terms with his compatriot DIOCLETIAN, who, a few weeks after his victory over CARINUS in 285, named him Caesar, whereupon Maximian assumed the names Marcus Aurelius Valerius. It was probably at this time, also, that Diocletian and Maximian assumed the titles of Jovius and Herculius, emphasizing their roles as supreme controller and man of action respectively.

Maximian's appointment was given urgency by events in Gaul, where gangs of displaced people and deserters known as the Bagaudae, driven from their homes by invading barbarians and Roman tax-collectors, had embarked on guerrilla warfare under two chieftains who may even have claimed imperial rank, Aelianus and Amandus. By the spring of 286, in a series of minor engagements, Maximian had effectively crushed these marauders; and shortly afterwards he was advanced to the rank of Augustus by his troops, on Diocletian's initiative.

Although there was as yet no formal geographical delimitation between the two colleagues, Maximian remained in the west. The years that followed saw him fighting repeatedly around the German frontier. In 286 and 287 he had to repel incursions of Alamanni and Burgundians on the Upper Rhine. Then CARAUSIUS, his fleet commander at Gesoriacum, set himself up as an independent Augustus and transferred his fleet across the Channel to Britain. Maximian attacked the usurper but was heavily defeated, and had to acquiesce, for the time being, in Carausius' autonomy. He met and conferred with Diocletian at Mediolanum in 291.

After the establishment of the Tetrarchy in 293 (see DIOCLETIAN) Maximian's sphere included Italy – where he set up his capital at Mediolanum – in addition to Sicily, Spain and Africa, where a new mint was established at Carthage in 296–7. The former praetorian prefect CON-STANTIUS I CHLORUS, who was already married to his step-daughter Theodora, became his Caesar. While Constantius was putting down the British secessionist régime, Maximian brought a Danubian corps to Gaul to watch the German frontier; but in 297 he moved east to the Danubian provinces, where he gained an important victory over the Carpi. Later in the same year, however, he was obliged to leave for north Africa, to suppress a Mauretanian tribe known as the Quinquegentanei who had penetrated the Numidian border. Having done so, he strengthened the African frontier defences all the way from Mauretania to Libya.

In 303 the persecution of the Christians (agreed upon by the four rulers) was launched by Maximian in Africa with particular severity. In late autumn of the same year he and Diocletian came to Rome to celebrate, in anticipation, the twentieth anniversary of the former's elevation to the purple, presiding over festivities which lasted for a month. But when, early in 304, Diocletian decided that both he and his colleague should simultaneously abdicate, Maximian was most unwilling to concur. Finally however he agreed to swear, in the Temple of Capitoline Jupiter, that he would lay down power after celebrating his own twentieth anniversary in 305. On 1 May of that year, therefore, both Augusti formally resigned their offices, conducting abdication ceremonies at Nicomedia and Mediolanum respectively, and withdrawing to their respective country palaces. Coinage was dedicated to each of them, to celebrate their new status as 'the Most Happy Senior (Elder) Emperors' (FELICISSIMO SE*Niori* AV*Gusto*).

Maximian's first reign, which was thus brought to a formal conclusion, had witnessed extremely important architectural achievements. In particular, when he came to Rome in 298, for the first time during his reign, he began to construct an unprecedentedly palatial thermal establishment, on raised ground north of the Viminal Hill; the work was completed in about 305. The design of these Baths of Diocletian, as they were called, followed the general plan of the Baths of Caracalla, but the enormous central block was more tightly designed, opening up a vista throughout the whole length of the transverse axis. While the exterior of the Baths relied on the massive structure of its masonry, their interior, on the other hand, was richly elaborate. It is possible to admire today the grandiose simplicity of the huge triple-vaulted cold room (*frigidarium*), subsequently converted, after Michelangelo's designs, into the church of Santa Maria degli Angeli; the façade of the church is provided by an apse of Maximian's rectangular, cross-vaulted hot room (*caldarium*), which replaces the domed rotunda of CARACALLA's building. Other important parts of the Baths of Diocletian have survived to house the Museo Nazionale Romano (delle Terme). They include remains of the elaborate columnar recesses which formed the front of the *frigidarium* facing the swimming-pool, as well as larger recesses in the walls of the enclosure. One of the rotundas at the corners of the perimeter is now the church of San Bernardo.

However, despite this adornment of Rome, the effective centre of power in Italy had by now been transplanted northwards to the Po valley; and Mediolanum, where Maximian established his capital, had become, and was long to remain, the most important political and military centre in the European west. The poet Ausonius, writing later in the century, refers to some of the buildings that Maximian created or extended in the city, including a theatre, a circus, a palace, temples, a bath building and a mint. Very little of all this splendour has survived, since medieval and modern Milan has been built over the ruins. But a stretch of the city wall is still visible together with a twenty-four-sided brick-faced tower (the Torre di Ansperto), erected by Maximian to bring a portion of the new palace quarter, including its baths and the adjacent circus, within the defences.

When Diocletian, on abdication, retired to Spalatum, Maximian also withdrew to a country palace – or perhaps to more than one. Some authorities indicate Lucania as the region of his retirement, but there are certain artistic, iconographic and literary reasons for conjecturing that he might instead, or as well, have been the builder and occupant of a sumptuous residence discovered near Philosophiana (and near the modern Piazza Armerina) in the interior of Sicily.* Instead of the compact planning of Diocletian's palace, here is to be found the unsymmetrical, single-storeyed sprawl of an old-style Italian

*On balance, however, this is not likely.

country villa – but magnified many times over, and adorned with the most spectacular series of floor mosaics that have been discovered anywhere in the Roman world. Some of these fifty polychrome pavements, skilfully blending naturalistic and schematic tendencies, have become famous, notably a representation of girls wearing what look like two-piece bathing suits; though many other designs dwell monotonously on the imperial sport of hunting, and the massacre of animals that was its inevitable accompaniment. One such picture includes what has tentatively been identified as a portrait of Maximian himself. Such an enormous range of mosaics and buildings must have taken years, if not decades, to complete. Nevertheless the whole design displays a kind of unity which suggests that it was more or less planned in its present form from the outset.

When Diocletian and Maximian abdicated, Constantius I Chlorus and GALERIUS became Augusti, and SEVERUS II and MAXIMINUS II DAIA (Galerius' nephew) took their places as Caesars. But this left Maximian's son MAXENTIUS (by his Syrian wife Eutropia) out in the cold, and when Maxentius decided to remedy this by carrying out a *coup* at Rome in October 306, he dispatched the imperial insignia, with the senate's approval, to his father, who gladly came out of retirement to begin a second reign, resuming the rank of Augustus in February 307 and issuing coins which prayed for thirty years of rule. Maximian still exercised sufficient influence to compel first Severus II and then Galerius to abandon successive invasions of Italy. Thereafter, his next enterprise was to leave for Gaul, where he sealed a useful alliance by converting the engagement of his daughter Fausta to Constantius' son CONSTANTINE (later the Great) into a marriage; coins were issued in her name as *nobilissima femina*. But then Maximian decided to turn against Maxentius after all, either disbelieving in the eventual success of his cause, or motivated by a restless ambition to take his place. So he reappeared dramatically, in person, in Rome; but his bid to win Maxentius' soldiers over to himself proved a dismal failure, and he was driven back to the court of Constantine in Gaul.

A conference called by Galerius at Carnuntum in 308, and attended by both retired emperors, resulted in disaster for Maximian, whose abdication Diocletian adamantly confirmed. He recoiled to his Gallic refuge, but soon decided to turn against Constantine as well, proclaiming himself Augustus for the third time, while his host was campaigning on the Rhine. When Constantine speedily returned, Maximian fled to Massilia, where he was besieged but forced to surrender by his own men. Shortly afterwards he was found dead. According to the official account he had committed suicide; but Constantine may have put him to death.

Despite occasional setbacks, Maximian had evidently been a general of considerable strategic ability – otherwise Diocletian would never have selected him as his colleague. However, as Eutropius suggested, he was also thoroughly coarse, savage, brutal, impatient and impossible to get on with. His coin-portraits, showing him enveloped in the head-dress of his divine patron Hercules, are at pains to emphasize this ferocious toughness of character. It was combined with a remorseless hankering to return to the power he had been induced to abdicate, supported by an infinite capacity for treacherous intrigue to secure that end – shown, for example, in his willingness to betray both his son Maxentius and his son-in-law Constantine. The former, however, forgivingly dedicated coins to the Eternal Memory of his father (AETER-NAE MEMORIAE), and even proclaimed his deification.

CARAUSIUS
286/7–93

CARAUSIUS (Mausaeus) (breakaway emperor in Britain and portions of northern Gaul, 286/7–93) originated from a humble family in Menapia, a district of seafarers which lay between the rivers Rhine and Scheldt.

After fulfilling an important role in MAXIMIAN's campaigns of 286 against the Bagaudae of Gaul, he was appointed to command the Channel fleet, now based at Gesoriacum, in order to clear the seas of Frankish pirates who had been launching attacks on the southern coasts of the Channel. This task he performed in a series of successful naval actions. However, he came under suspicion of keeping a personal grip upon the extensive plunder he had thus collected and utilizing it to pay the pirates whom he had captured and enrolled in his fleet. Maximian, fearing preparations for a rising, sent orders that he should be put to death, but Carausius learnt of this instruction in time and retaliated by proclaiming himself Augustus in late 286 or 287. He moved his fleet to Britain, which welcomed him as a deliverer; but at the same time he retained control over parts of the south Channel coast, and enjoyed the support of some of the Franks.

An attempt by Maximian in 289 to dislodge him was frustrated by inexperienced pilots and unfavourable weather. In consequence, Maximian was reluctantly obliged, for the time being, to acknowledge his independent authority; and at least Carausius seemed competent to deal with the warlike nations that threatened the shores and frontiers of Britain. There is evidence, for example, that he repaired gaps and weaknesses in Hadrian's Wall caused by barbarian ravages some years earlier; and he may have developed favourable relations with the 'Picts' (a generic term applied to tribesmen beyond the Wall). Carausius hoped that such activities would ingratiate him with DIOCLETIAN and Maximian. Furthermore, he not only assumed their names Aurelius and Valerius, but also issued coins in their honour, uniting their heads with his own with the inscription 'Carausius and his Brothers' (CARAVSIVS ET FRATRES SVI). But this was a good deal further than his 'brothers' were prepared to go, and none of these issues were reciprocated in any way by their own mints; nor, when he issued medallions displaying himself in consular robes, could he have worn these with their approval.

On the contrary, at their instigation CONSTANTIUS I CHLORUS, the western Caesar, was preparing a decisive onslaught to bring this Gallo-British empire down. At a period when rulers were devoting considerable attention to the expansion of their fleets, he began by stationing small naval units in the rivers of northern Gaul, in order to drive Carausius' adjacent flotillas out to sea. The usurper's main fleet however did not come to their help but remained close to the shores of Britain, in order to defend them from invasion by Constantius. But instead of attempting such an assault immediately, he preferred to blockade the northern Gallic port of Gesoriacum, which was held by Carausius' forces, in 293. A huge dam across the harbour mouth prevented Carausius from sending reinforcements, and he could do nothing to save the city from falling; though he was only defeated by the narrowest of margins, because the first tide after the capture of the fortress burst the dam and reopened the harbour.

Even after this success, Constantius still did not invade Britain, but instead attacked Carausius' allies among the Franks, driving them out of the Batavian coastal territory and islands which they had occupied. Carausius' dominion was now reduced to Britain, and his command of the Channel, too, was impaired. At this unsuccessful point of his fortunes, he was murdered by his finance minister Allectus, who declared himself emperor of the island kingdom in his place.

The extensive coinage of Carausius was mainly issued in Britain, at Londinium and at least one other city. The coins issued at this second centre, bearing the mint mark 'C', have been variously attributed to Camulodunum, Corinium Dobunnorum and Clausentum. Since, on some coins of Allectus, the mint mark appears in the form 'C L', Clausentum should perhaps be favoured. A further series inscribed 'RSR' seemed to suggest the existence of an additional British mint at Rutupiae, but it is more likely that these letters do not represent a mint mark at all, but stand instead for *rationalis summae rei*

(Allectus), the official responsible for the coinage. The theory that Carausius also coined at two mints in northern Gaul is not now regarded as acceptable. His first coinage included pieces of high-quality silver, which did not reappear on the central issues of the Empire until Diocletian's currency reform several years later. Carausius seems to have minted these coins because of his lack of gold, terminating the issue when that metal became available.

The reverse types of his coinage provide remarkable designs and inscriptions. Britannia is shown clasping hands with Carausius, to the accompaniment of a tag from the *Aeneid* of Virgil, 'O Come, Awaited One' (EXPECTATE VENI). However, his further type of the she-wolf suckling Romulus and Remus, inscribed 'the Renewal of the Romans' (RENOVAT*io* ROMAN*Orum*), makes it clear that his eventual ambition and programme extended far beyond his own Romano-British state. The legions which were serving (or had detachments serving) in his forces are also recorded by number. But by far the dominant theme of the coinage is peace – the Peace of Carausius Augustus (PAX AVG.), or the Peace of the Three Augusti (PAX AVGGG:).

Carausius' principal asset was his considerable talent as an admiral, but he must also have possessed qualities capable of rallying people to his cause. He was not however strong enough to stand up for ever against the central emperors, and the loss of Gesoriacum, preceding his murder, indicated that his breakaway state, in the shrunken form it had now assumed, could not continue to exist for very much longer. In fact in 296 his successor Allectus was overcome by Asclepiodotus, the praetorian prefect of Constantius.

CONSTANTIUS I CHLORUS 305–6

CONSTANTIUS I (Flavius Julius) (joint emperor, 305–6) was of humble Danubian origin; the assertions that he was a nobleman from Dardania (Upper Moesia) and descended from the emperor CLAUDIUS II GOTHICUS only originated after his death, when his son CONSTANTINE THE GREAT wanted to manufacture for himself a more impressive genealogy. Byzantine sources knew him by the nickname Chlorus 'the pale'.

In the early 280s, during a successful career in the army, he formed an association, perhaps a legitimate marriage, with Helena, an inn-keeper's daughter at Naissus, who bore him Constantine. Not later than 289 he repudiated Helena and married Theodora, the step-daughter of DIO-CLETIAN's co-emperor MAXIMIAN, by whom he had three further children. Rising to the rank of praetorian prefect, Constantius was chosen by Diocletian as one of the Tetrarchy established in 293. The senior of the two Caesars assisting the Augusti, he was adopted by Maximian and assumed his adoptive father's name Valerius (in place of his own family name Julius) and Maximian's additional designation 'Herculius'.

The provinces allocated to Constantius were those of Gaul and Britain, of which the former to some small extent, and the latter wholly, remained in the hands of CARAUSIUS, whom Maximian had failed to eliminate; and it was Constantius' first and most urgent task to repair this omission. He rapidly blockaded the usurper's cross-Channel base Gesoriacum by erecting a mole across its harbour mouth, and soon the town fell into his hands. It was this blow that caused the downfall of Carausius. However, his secessionist kingdom did not collapse, but was maintained by his murderer Allectus. Before attempting to deal with him, Constantius spent more than two years in further preparations, including the systematic suppression of whatever supporters Allectus might still have possessed in northern Gaul and Batavia.

Finally, however, in 296, he was ready to act. Two squadrons sailed across the Channel, one under his personal command from Gesoriacum, and the other led by his praetorian prefect Asclepiodotus from the mouth of the Seine. A fog enabled the prefect to evade Allectus' principal fleet and land at Dubrae or Rutupiae or Lemanae, whereupon he burnt his ships in order to commit his troops to the fighting that must inevitably follow. Allectus hastened to meet Asclepiodotus with his entire available force, thus providing Constantius himself with an opportunity to land in Kent. This, however, he could not do, because in a fog some of his transports failed to join his main body of ships, and sailed away instead towards the mouth of the Thames. Constantius subsequently returned to the southern coast of the Channel, but somewhere in north Hampshire or Berkshire Allectus was routed by Asclepiodotus, and lost his life. A number of his Frankish mercenaries, however, escaped from the battlefield to Londinium, where they were slaughtered by a band of Constantius' soldiers – the men who had not managed to effect a junction with him off the coast of Kent, and who had now come to the capital by a devious route.

Encouraged by the timely arrival of these troops, which offset his own failure to be present, Constantius took the credit for the recapture of Britain by the issue of large commemorative gold medallions. On one such piece, inscribed 'the Dutifulness of the Emperors' (PIETAS AVGG. [*Augustorum*]), Constantius, wearing the lionskin of Hercules, depicts himself offering his hand to a kneeling Britannia, while Victory places a crown on his head. An even larger medallion, bearing the inscription 'Restorer of Eternal Light' (REDDITOR LVCIS AETERNAE), shows the Caesar riding up to a city wall, in front of which a suppliant kneels; while a warship appears in the waters nearby. The city is identified as LON (*dinium*). It now became a new imperial mint, and the two Roman provinces in the island were divided into four.

On returning to the continent, Constantius repopulated the Batavian territory by Franks (Salii) from Frisia, replacing the expelled allies of Carausius and Allectus in 297. The following year the Alamanni suddenly attacked him near Andematunum; protected, however, by the town's new fortifications, he repelled the onslaught and chased them back to the Rhine.

Following the abdication of Diocletian and Maximian in 305, Constantius became Augustus of the west and senior emperor, although his territories only comprised Gaul, Britain and Spain, and his eastern colleague Galerius outstripped him in effective power. Moreover, Constantius' son Constantine was at Galerius' court, virtually held as a hostage. When, however, news of an invasion of Roman Britain by the Picts (see CARAUSIUS) necessitated Constantius' presence on the island, he used this emergency as an excuse to request the presence of his son, and Galerius complied. Constantine found his father still at Gesoriacum in the early months of 306 and crossed over with him to Britain, where Constantius, we are told, penetrated to remote coastal regions, and won notable victories over the Picts. But then, on 25 July, at Eburacum, he died – leaving an explosive succession problem as his heritage.

The capital and principal mint of Constantius I had been Augusta Trevirorum on the River Moselle, the city which had formerly been the residence of the Gallo-Roman Empire established by POSTUMUS, but which suffered severe damage from German incursions in 275/6. From about the time of Constantius it came to be known as Treviri or Treveris. He started to lay out a palace complex (completed by his son), which occupied the entire north-eastern part of the city. A so-called 'Basilica', 280 feet in length and a hundred feet in height, has now been recognized as the Hall of Audience or throne-room of the palace, like Diocletian's Aula Palatina at Salonae. The spacious, timber-roofed hall at Treviri displays an aisle-less, box-like simplicity. The classical orders only survive non-functionally as the frames for large niches; a chancel arch, anticipating those of Christian basilicas, divides the nave from an elevated apse. These massively dramatic internal effects are matched by a novel grandeur of external design, strengthening and diversifying the outer walls by powerful arcade-like projections which frame the two tiers of massive rounded windows, establishing a strongly articulated vertical pattern of light and shade.

The literary sources present a favourable picture of Constantius I. They include a highly laudatory *Panegyric*, while other praises emanate from the Christian tradition, because of its desire to glorify his son Constantine the Great and vituperate against his anti-Christian colleague Galerius; moreover Constantius himself, after enforcing the first joint edict of the persecution, does appear to have left the Christians alone. There are few independent means, however, of deciding how far his other eulogies are justified. But resourceful statesmanship did, apparently, earn him popularity in Gaul, and his military achievements were considerable – even if the most celebrated of these successes, his reconquest of Britain, was mainly the work not of himself but of his praetorian prefect. He has been complimented for not engaging in open opposition to Galerius, which would have plunged the Empire into civil war; but since Galerius possessed greatly superior resources, he had little alternative, and, indeed, it was probably only his own premature death that prevented a take-over attempt by his eastern colleague.

GALERIUS
305–11

GALERIUS (joint emperor, 305–11) was born in about 250. According to the anonymous *Epitome* (which is to be preferred here to an alternative account of Eutropius) he came from a village near Florentiana in Dacia Ripensis (Upper Moesia). His father was a peasant, and his mother Romula, after whom he named his birthplace Romulianum, had immigrated to the region from across the river.

He himself began life as a herdsman, but served as a soldier under AURELIAN and PROBUS, and became a senior officer in the reign of DIOCLETIAN. When the Tetrarchy was established in 293, Galerius was named Caesar (as colleague of CONSTANTIUS I) at Nicomedia, and assumed the nomenclature Gaius Galerius Valerius Maximianus. He also adopted Diocletian's designation of Jovius and married his daughter Galeria Valeria, divorcing a previous wife for the purpose. The area assigned to Galerius comprised Illyricum and the remaining lands of the Balkans, in addition, apparently, to the western provinces of Asia Minor.

Following upon his appointment as Caesar, he was sent to the Danubian frontier without delay. In 294 and 295 he had to keep a watchful eye on the Goths who were moving westwards; the two years that followed witnessed fighting against the Sarmatians and Marcomanni, and the entire tribe of the Carpi was transferred within the imperial frontiers, to live in Pannonian territory. Forts were constructed at Aquincum in Lower Pannonia and Bononia Malata in Dacia Ripensis, and the northern part of Lower Pannonia was made into a new province named Valeria, after his wife. This was enriched by land reclamation involving the construction of a channel from Lake Pelso to the Danube. But it was said that Galerius derived little pleasure from this useful task, for he saw his colleagues gaining greater glory from less laborious activities.

However, in 296 his opportunity was at hand, when Diocletian summoned him to the east to deal with a major Persian menace. The Sassanian monarch Narses, who had succeeded to the throne three years earlier, took advantage of Diocletian's preoccupation with an Egyptian rebellion by declaring war and invading the Roman province of Syria. Galerius crossed the Euphrates at Nicephorium Callinicum with insufficient forces and suffered a severe defeat, causing the loss of Rome's entire Mesopotamian province. The tradition, however, that Diocletian punished Galerius with public humiliation by making him walk for a mile in front of his chariot wearing the imperial purple is likely to be fictitious.

Be that as it may, Galerius, in the following year, was given an opportunity to repair his setback. Equipped with strong reinforcements, he marched into Armenia and routed the Persians; a huge amount of plunder was captured, including the king's harem, which was lodged at Daphne near Antioch. Then he moved on and captured their capital Ctesiphon itself. The king sent him an envoy who appealed for mutual acceptance of one another by Rome and Persia, as equal great powers. Galerius commented that this was a very different tale from Persia's earlier aggressive talk and behaviour. Nevertheless, shortly afterwards in 298, an imperial minister, Sicorius Probus, arranged a meeting with Narses in the middle of a river, and concluded a treaty. Mesopotamia, augmented by lands across the Tigris, was recognized as imperial territory, and Armenia, too, secured recognition as a Roman protectorate; in return, Narses' harem was sent back to him. As for Galerius, however, it was believed that he had been eager to press further forward into Persian territory, and in consequence did not welcome the treaty.

However, from this time onwards he seems to have exerted a stronger influence on the policies of Diocletian. In particular, there is every reason to accept Lactantius' opinion that the edicts launching the persecution of the Christians were published upon his initiative. His peasant mother Romula had been a fanatical devotee of local pagan cults; and his own attacks on Christianity enjoyed the enthusiastic support not only of the priests who served Apollo's oracle, but of neo-Platonist philosophers as well. After the first edict had been proclaimed, two fires broke out in quick succession within the imperial palace at Nicomedia, where Galerius was staying; whereupon he ostentatiously left the city – in order to protect his life, he announced, from such acts of arson perpetrated by the Christians (although they for their part declared that it was he himself who had set the building alight). Subsequently, it was believed to have been Galerius who enforced upon the enfeebled Diocletian the fourth edict of persecution of 304, insisting on compulsory pagan sacrifice and libation by every member of the faith.

During his tenure of the office of Caesar, Galerius established his capital (and a new mint) at Thessalonica, strategically located on the Via Egnatia, the main Roman land route from Italy to the Thracian Bosphorus and Asia Minor. To the city that already existed, Galerius added a new palace quarter.

Two large halls that formed part of the palace have been revealed by excavation. One is octagonal in shape, with apsidal niches in each of its eight angles. The other hall, which is rectangular, serves as a vestibule to a colonnaded processional street. This begins at a crossroads surmounted by the triple Arch of Galerius, which was a domed structure upon four piers ornamented with reliefs celebrating his victory over the Persians. From that point, the processional way leads up to an enclosure containing a circular building which is now the church of St George but was originally, it would seem, planned as Galerius' own mausoleum, and was sumptuously decorated with veneer marbles and mosaics. Excavations have also now revealed another of his palaces in Dacia Ripensis (Upper Moesia), on a site now known as Gamzigrad (in eastern Yugoslavia).

When Diocletian and MAXIMIAN abdicated in 305, Galerius was elevated to the rank of Augustus, and in consequence moved his capital from Thessalonica to Nicomedia. He was junior to his colleague Constantius I Chlorus in rank but superior in power, since the Balkans and Asia Minor came under his direct control, and both the new Caesars, SEVERUS II and MAXIMINUS II DAIA, were among his supporters. He agreed to hand Constantius' son CONSTANTINE, who was with him, back to his father; but in 306 Constantius died. Thereupon Galerius raised Severus to the rank of Augustus in his place, and granted Constantine the rank of Caesar. However MAXENTIUS, the son of Maximian, refused to accept the arrangement, declared himself Augustus at Rome, and repulsed first Severus and then Galerius himself, who marched into Italy as far as Interamna but then, in the face of desertions, was obliged to retreat. These failures cost Severus his life, and deprived Galerius of his final foothold in the west in 307 – though in the following year, when the various imperial personages met at the Conference of Carnuntum, he was still able to arrange that his own protégé LICINIUS should be given the rank of Augustus in Severus' place.

In 311 Galerius, planning to hold his twentieth anniversary celebrations, was busily engaged in levying taxes to pay for their costs; and he intended, when the time came, to abdicate (with an eye, it was said, to the elevation of his illegitimate son Candidianus, betrothed to the little daughter of Maximinus II Daia). But suddenly he was attacked by a serious illness – perhaps cancer of the groin. While on his sick-bed at Nicomedia, on 30 April, he and his fellow-emperors issued an edict cancelling the persecution of the Christians for which he had been so largely responsible. Under specific conditions, notably that 'they will be bound to entreat their God for our well-being and for that of the State and for their own', Galerius and his colleagues instructed their provincial governors to grant members of the Church freedom of worship and legal tolerance and recognition – including the right to assemble together for common worship. Various reasons have been sought for this momentous *volte-face* by Galerius. Christian writers gave God the credit for his grave illness, of which they described many gruesome details. Others have attributed the sponsorship of the edict to Licinius or Constantine or Galerius' own wife Galeria Valeria, who was known (like her mother, Prisca, the widow of Diocletian) to profess the Christian faith. But the most plausible explanation is that Galerius himself knew the persecutions had failed. Far from creating a unified state by destroying the autonomy of the Christians, they had hardened and strengthened their will to pursue their own beliefs and ways of life – to the detriment of national unity and harmony. And besides, the sufferings of individual Christians had not inspired enthusiasm among the pagan population as a whole.

Only a few days after this total reversal of policy, the emperor died, and was deified; he was not, however, buried in the mausoleum he had built at Thessalonica, but his remains were taken back to Romulianum, his birthplace which he had embellished and enlarged. His death gave the *coup de grace* to the already much damaged tetrarchic system of Diocletian, which only the survival of Galerius had hitherto prevented from collapsing.

It is hard to sum up his character, since Christian writers, despite his death-bed recantation, assailed him with all manner of abuse as the principal instigator of the persecutions. This they did with some justice, since the coercive measures in question had not only been brutally inhumane but misconceived and counter-productive as well. Because he saw this in the end, and acted accordingly, he deserves credit. His own personal morals, it appears, were strict. He was essentially an uncultivated, ambitious man of action. He was also, like all the leading tetrarchs, an excellent general: he failed at first against the Persians, but perseveringly converted his reverse into triumphant success.

SEVERUS II
306–7

SEVERUS II (joint emperor, 306–7), a friend of GALERIUS, came from the Danubian region; his origins were undistinguished. When DIOCLETIAN and MAXIMIAN abdicated in favour of Galerius and CONSTANTIUS I CHLORUS respectively in 305, Maximian, at Mediolanum, nominated Severus to be the western Caesar. Assuming the names Flavius (as an adoptive son of Constantius) and Valerius (as an adoptive member of Diocletian's house), Severus received Italy and Africa as his sphere of action. Pannonia, too, was transferred to his jurisdiction from the territories of Galerius, with the approval of the latter, who effectively exercised control over Severus as well as over his own eastern Caesar, MAXIMINUS II DAIA.

Both these promotions, according to Lactantius, caused some bewilderment among the soldiers, since they had little knowledge of either of the two new appointees; they were much better informed about Constantius' son CONSTANTINE, who, in common with MAXENTIUS the son of Maximian, had found himself passed over. Part of the reason why Constantine, when Galerius allowed him to rejoin Constantius on the Rhine, travelled with secrecy and caution was that he had to pass through the Pannonian territory of Severus, who distrusted him as a discontented rival.

When Constantius died in the following year, Galerius, who had now officially become the senior emperor, elevated Severus to be the Augustus of the west, appointing Constantine as Caesar simultaneously. This latter step, taken from diplomatic motives in order to keep Constantine quiet for the time being, exacerbated Maxentius' feeling that he himself had been left out, and prompted him to launch a *coup* at Rome. This was facilitated by the praetorians, who were angry because Severus had ordered that their corps – already reduced to a mere city garrison by Diocletian – should be completely abolished. On learning of Maxentius' revolt, Galerius requested Severus to march against the rebel, and early in 307 he obediently set out from his capital

Mediolanum. Northern Italy supported Severus' cause, but on arriving before the gates of Rome his troops mutinied. Loyalty to their former general Maximian, who had come out of retirement, made them unwilling to fight against the old man's son, and while secret agents further sapped their allegiance Severus' praetorian prefect Anullinus turned treacherously against him and distributed bonuses encouraging the soldiers to desert. Severus was obliged to fall back rapidly to the north with such troops as remained to him. Maximian pursued him to Ravenna and there arranged terms. Severus agreed to abdicate from the rank of Augustus – on the condition that his life should be spared. He was taken to Rome as a prisoner, and after being paraded through the streets was incarcerated at Tres Tabernae on the Via Appia, to provide a hostage in case Galerius invaded Italy. Indeed such an attack materialized very soon afterwards; but when, like the expedition of Severus that preceded it, it proved unsuccessful, Maxentius put Severus to death.

Severus, as far as we can tell, resembled his enemy Maxentius in granting toleration to the Christians; or at least, like Constantius he did not enforce the persecutions severely. Apart from this, however, little can be said about him. Although his army failed to take Rome, he was presumably regarded as a good soldier, since otherwise he would not have been appointed to the offices first of Caesar and then of Augustus. However, the historian known as Anonymus Valesii, justifiably or otherwise, described him as a man whose character was as degraded as his birth, and declared that the greatest asset he possessed, his friendship with Galerius, was owed to an impressive capacity for imbibing strong drink.

MAXENTIUS
306–12

MAXENTIUS (Marcus Aurelius Valerius) (breakaway emperor, 306–12) was born in about 279, the son of MAXIMIAN and his Syrian wife Eutropia (the report that he was a bastard was spread by his enemies).

Although granted senatorial rank, and awarded Galerius' daughter Valeria

Maximilla as a bride, he was not given a consulship or a military command. However, following the death of CONSTANTIUS I in 306, when GALERIUS raised SEVERUS II and CONSTANTINE to the rank of Augustus and Caesar respectively, Maxentius refused to acquiesce, and a rebellion was launched in his favour at Rome. Led by three military tribunes – one of whom commanded the urban cohorts (and directed the pork market) – the revolt won the active backing of the praetorian soldiers, whose guard had been abolished by Severus II. Most of the ordinary inhabitants of Rome, too, were in favour of the rising, because they resented a recent decree making them liable to taxation. So on 28 October 306, Maxentius was invested with the purple. The acting prefect of the city lost his life, but otherwise there were scarcely any casualties.

Central and south Italy declared for Maxentius, and so did Africa, the source of the capital's grain supply. But apart from the reconstituted praetorian guard, he possessed very few troops; and northern Italy remained loyal to Severus. Maxentius therefore proceeded with caution. This caution was displayed, for example, by a coin he issued at Carthage describing himself only as CAESAR; while other pieces, with equal modesty, omitted to ascribe him the title of Augustus, defining him as PRINC (*eps*) instead, and referring in honorific terms to the Augusti and Caesars elsewhere (AVGG. ET CAESS. NN. [*Nostri*]). Among these Maxentius numbered his father Maximian, whom he brought back from retirement; and he even issued coins which hailed Constantine as Prince of Youth, hoping for the support of the man whose preferment he had earlier resented.

What Maxentius particularly wanted, however, was recognition from Galerius, the senior Augustus, but this was not forthcoming, for Galerius objected, among other things, to his revival of the old, politically powerful praetorian guard. So he called upon Severus II to march on Rome and unseat Maxentius; although Severus' army, unsettled by Maximian's agents, failed and had to withdraw. Maxentius now assumed the title of Augustus and was recognized by Constantine. However, Galerius himself then proceeded to march down into the Italian peninsula in order to suppress him. But after he had reached Interamna unopposed, his expedition, too, ground to a halt, for the same reason as the invasion of Severus. Content to have become master of Italy, Maxentius did not attempt to pursue the retreating force. But news of his success caused Spain to declare in his favour, and this alienated Constantine, who regarded the country as part of his own sphere. Maximian, too, decided to turn against his own son, but on his arrival at Rome in 308 he was disarmed.

When all the Augusti and Caesars met at Carnuntum later in the year, they pronounced Maxentius a public enemy. This did not succeed in destroying his position inside Italy, but the acting praetorian prefect in Africa, Lucius Domitius Alexander, seceded and declared himself emperor on his own account. The consequent stoppage of the African grain supply caused famine in the capital, and fighting broke out between the privileged praetorians and the underfed population, reputedly causing the loss of six thousand lives. Finally, in 311, Maxentius sent his other praetorian prefect, Gaius Rufius Volusianus, to Africa, and Alexander was killed; Carthage suffered severely for its secession, and its mint was transferred to Ostia. Maxentius celebrated a Triumph, and issued coins inscribed 'Eternal Victory' (VICTORIA AETERNA). Other pieces display unexpected consecrations. One of them attributes divinity to his father Maximian, now deceased – forgetting how they had eventually become enemies; for the fact that he was son of the former Augustus was, after all, Maxentius' principal claim to imperial status. Another coin honours the deified Constantius I, describing him as a relative (*cognatus*) of Maxentius (whose sister Constantine had married). This homage to the late Constantius, emperor of the west, was meant to indicate that Maxentius, too, laid claim to the entire western Empire. It was not therefore a gesture of reconciliation with Constantine but implied the reverse, because it had now become clear that a clash between the two of them was no longer avoidable.

Indeed, in 312 Constantine moved into Italy across the Mont Genèvre pass, with an army of forty thousand men. Maxentius' troops outnumbered them at least four times over, although their quality and discipline were inferior; and so was Maxentius' capacity as a general. Constantine surprised the garrison at Segusio – refraining from sacking the place, which created a good impression – and defeated an army sent by Maxentius near Augusta Taurinorum, successfully trapping his mail-clad cavalry, of which much had been expected. Verona and Mutina and a large part of Italy were soon in Constantine's hands. Maxentius relied on the walls of Rome, which he had strengthened; but as the enemy troops approached, for fear of treachery within the city he decided, after all, to send his generals to meet them outside, himself following behind. After an initial engagement on the Via Flaminia, the final battle took place at the Milvian Bridge across the Tiber. Hemmed in between the hills and the river, Maxentius' soldiers were driven back in total confusion; their bridge of boats collapsed and thousands were drowned, including their leader himself.

The battle was subsequently seen by Christian historians as a decisive victory of their faith over paganism; and so it was. For although Maxentius, in order to win popularity, had shown leniency towards the Christians, even restoring confiscated property to the Church, his coinage struck a resolute pagan note. But its most remarkable feature was a determined emphasis on the city of Rome itself, Maxentius' capital and, despite the shift of power to the north, still the repository of all the Empire's most revered traditions. It was fitting, therefore, that Maxentius' young son and heir was called Romulus; his death in 309, which must have been a blow to his father's dynastic hopes, was followed by deification, proclaimed on coins depicting a circular temple which was dedicated to his 'eternal memory' (AETERNAE MEMORIAE), and can still be seen beside the Forum.

Not far from the temple stood Maxentius' most splendid contribution to the grandeur of Rome. This was the Basilica Nova, named after him (though finished and altered by Constantine). It was a huge, secular, pagan edifice, the heir to the old market basilicas which had served as meeting places for social, judicial and commercial purposes alike. Yet this was a basilica with a difference, based on the bold idea of isolating the central, apsed, cross-vaulted hall – familiar, for example, from the Baths of Caracalla – and converting it into an independent, free-standing structure. Like the central hall of those Baths, it consisted of only three bays, separated one from another by piers and surmounted by curving, intersecting barrel vaults. The Basilica Nova, of which three mighty spans still rise aloft today, represented the climax of Rome's most imaginative architectural achievement: the use of concrete (beneath the brick coverings and marble facings) to exploit the significance of interior space.

Maxentius also erected a complex of buildings on the outskirts of the city, beside the Via Appia. They included an imperial villa, a circus and a massive family mausoleum. The villa has so far scarcely been excavated; but the circus, we can see, could accommodate fifteen thousand spectators. The mausoleum was apparently a domed, circular structure with a deep, gabled, columnar porch, like Hadrian's Pantheon; but unlike the Pantheon, it was built so as to be viewed from all angles, and the porch and the rotunda were integrated by continuous lines.

CONSTANTINE I THE GREAT 306–37

CONSTANTINE I THE GREAT (Flavius Valerius Constantinus) (joint emperor, 306–23; sole emperor 323–37) was born at Naissus in Dacia Ripensis (Upper Moesia) in about 285. His father was CONSTANTIUS I CHLORUS, and his mother was Constantius' wife or concubine Helena, an inn-keeper's daughter, who died in 328 and was later declared a Christian saint.

When Constantius received the office of Caesar in 293, his son was admitted to DIOCLETIAN's court. He became known as a promising officer, serving against the Persians under his father's fellow-Caesar GALERIUS, to whose entourage he still belonged when Diocletian and MAXIMIAN abdicated in 305. Galerius and Constantius I were made Augusti in their place. In the following year, however, Constantius asked Galerius to release him to serve in Britain. This was conceded (although with such reluctance that Constantine took many precautions on the journey), and when Constantius died at Eburacum, his troops, with the encouragement of the king of the Alamanni, hailed his son Augustus. Galerius refused to accept this *fait accompli*, but felt unable to deny Constantine the title of Caesar, which the young man decided to accept. When he married Fausta, his title of Augustus was re-confirmed by her father Maximian – to whom in consequence he gave protection in Gaul after Maximian had broken with MAXENTIUS and left Rome.

At the Conference of Carnuntum in 308, however, Constantine was required to relinquish the rank of Augustus and become Caesar again, with the designation of 'son of the Augusti'; but he refused. Shortly afterwards, he successfully defended the Rhine frontier against the incursions of German tribes (Franks, Alamanni and Bructeri), but returned to Gaul when he heard that Maximian had turned against him and captured Massilia. Constantine compelled him to surrender and perhaps killed him; and, since the link with the dead man's Herculean dynasty (of which Constantine had earlier boasted) was now seen as discreditable, he invented for himself, instead, a genealogy going back to the emperor CLAUDIUS II GOTHICUS (268–70).

When Galerius died in 311, Constantine became involved in open warfare with Maxentius. Invading Italy, in the following year, he won major victories near Augusta Taurinorum and Verona and then marched on Rome, where Maxentius was defeated and killed at the battle of the Milvian Bridge. The victorious Constantine was welcomed by the senate and recognized as the senior Augustus. LICINIUS, who had supported his cause and married his sister Constantia, asserted his own domination of the east, counterbalancing Constantine's control of the west. But the harmony between the two rulers soon collapsed. A first war in 316 resulted in Constantine's victory at Cibalae in Pannonia, followed by an indecisive battle at Campus Ardiensis in Thrace. On the basis of renewed mutual tolerance, eased by a rectification of frontiers, the quarrel was patched up. But it soon erupted once again. First, Constantine's transfer of his headquarters to Serdica in 317/18, in the vicinity of their mutual border, seemed provocative to Licinius. Next, in 323, during a campaign to repel a Gothic incursion, Constantine violated territory in Thrace that belonged to his colleague. In the following year, therefore, a second wave of hostilities broke out between the two rulers. Constantine moved to the attack, and overwhelmed his enemy in major battles by land and sea – near

Hadrianopolis and Chrysopolis (on the Thracian Bosphorus) and at the mouth of the Hellespont.

Constantine continued Diocletian's reorganization of the army, which was honoured by ever-increasing commemoration on his coins and medallions. He also continued to expand the German element in his forces, since he appreciated the tribesmen's special qualifications for dealing with their hostile compatriots across the frontier. Privileged status, therefore, was conferred on German military units, and generals of that race received special favours. In addition, many Germans (as well as Sarmatians) who had been permitted to settle in the provinces were drafted into new cavalry and infantry units which Constantine now brought into being. These units, together with detachments taken from the imperial frontiers, were incorporated in the mobile field force, so that its legions of one thousand infantrymen and five hundred cavalrymen constituted a central striking force and strategic reserve considerably more substantial than anything that had existed before. To take command of this mobile army, Constantine created two new posts: Master of Horse (*magister equitum*) and Master of Foot (*magister peditum*).

The praetorian guard, which had fought for Maxentius against Constantine, was abolished once again, this time finally, after three centuries of turbulent existence, and replaced by the mainly German mounted guard, which Diocletian had founded. The post of praetorian prefect, however, still remained in existence. The number of prefects in office was still usually four; but their functions – and this applied to the city prefect as well – were now of a civilian character, relating mainly to financial and judicial affairs.

The second main branch of the army, the frontier troops consisting of static formations, were not so well paid as the field force. Nevertheless they continued to fulfil an essential role, since Constantine, intent on restoring the eroded Danube and Rhine lines, reorganized and increased their garrisons. Retired soldiers of the frontier army received privileges which were inheritable by their sons – whose initial compulsory recruitment was however enforced by stringent penalties, which caused widespread fear, especially in the provinces of a less militarized character.

While the peoples of the Empire remained in the grip of inflation and oppression, Diocletian's financial reforms were keenly followed up and extended. A new and lighter gold coin (at 72 to the pound) was successfully established; taxes – mainly in kind – were increased; and the bureaucracy needed to handle these tasks, and enforce tighter regimentation in general, was substantially enlarged. Constantine's administrative changes included the appointment of a *magister officiorum* to control the imperial ministries (*scrinia*), a *quaestor sacri palatii* who became the emperor's principal legal adviser, and two financial functionaries (the *comes rei privatae* and *comes sacrarum largitionum*) who controlled revenue and expenditure, including free distributions. These were permanent officials sitting on the emperor's council (*consistorium*). Constantine was also lavish in the bestowal of senatorial rank, and awarded many official posts to senators, who thus began to recover some of the political influence that they had lost in the course of the previous century.

Yet Rome did not play a central part in his thoughts and plans. With military needs in mind, it was perfectly clear to him – and a number of his predecessors had already felt the same – that Rome had ceased to be an appropriate capital for the Empire, since it was hard for an emperor operating from there to control the vital Rhine–Danube and Euphrates frontiers at one and the same time. After residing for a while at a number of different centres, both in the west (at Treviri, Arelate, Mediolanum and Ticinum) and in his native Balkans (Sirmium and Serdica), Constantine decided that the ideal location for his capital was the ancient Greek city of Byzantium on the strategic Bosphorus strait between Europe and Asia; and there he founded Constantinople, the modern Istanbul, from 324–30. The site possessed an excellent harbour, the Golden Horn. It could also be defended by land and sea, and was accessible to the vital industrial centres of heavily populated coastal Asia Minor and Syria, and within reach of grain-producing Egypt and south Russia as well. Although Rome lost none of its ancient privileges, and at first Constantinople and its newly created senate held lower rank, Constantine intended that his new foundation should become the metropolis of the Empire – as it very soon did. This set the scene for the Byzantine empire which dominated the ensuing Middle Ages, for many hundreds of years – eventually adopting Greek as its official language, so that Augustus' determination that Latin, the language of dominant Rome, should take first place was eventually frustrated.

Constantine also put into effect a second and even more momentous revolution, the conversion of the Empire from paganism to Christianity. Diocletian and Galerius had launched the most severe persecution of all time against the Christians, but it had failed, and in 311 Galerius in his terminal illness, along with Constantine and Licinius, had issued the Edict of Serdica granting freedom of worship to all Christians. Then Constantine's victory at the Milvian Bridge was won – as he later asserted, after he had seen a cross of light superimposed upon the sun, whereupon he ordered the monogram of Christ to be painted on his soldiers' shields. In the year after this victory he and Licinius reiterated the pronouncement of tolerance towards the Christians known as the Edict of Milan (which was, in fact, an agreement at Mediolanum, incorporated into an edict issued at Nicomedia). Constantine felt a persistent and overpowering need for a divine companion and sponsor. For a while the Sun-god, widely worshipped throughout the Empire at this time and long revered by Constantine's own forebears, had seemed to fulfil this role. But he himself, at the time of the Edict of Milan, had already left no doubt of his own personal leaning towards Christianity, which he described as 'the most lawful and most holy religion', increasingly identifying the One Supreme Power with Jesus Christ.

And so Constantine initiated, over a number of years, a whole series of measures favouring the Christians. Church and State were to work together in the closest association. Meanwhile, as the emperor became more and more convinced of his divine mission as God's champion, victorious by the divine grace, the successive Councils of Arelate of 314 and Nicaea of 325 made it very apparent that it was he who held the reins. The latter conference, attended by two hundred and twenty bishops, formulated the Nicene Creed declaring that the Son was 'of one substance' with the Father, and condemned Arius and other advocates of the Son's subordination to the Father (see CONSTANTIUS II).

Constantine's decision to Christianize the Empire was a highly personal and at first sight astonishing step. For despite the pressures brought to bear upon him by bishops, and the unquestionable recent expansion of local Christian communities, unchecked by successive imperial persecutions, the Church was not conspicuous for political, economic, social or cultural power. Moreover, although Constantine himself was deeply superstitious, he seems to have possessed only the most elementary understanding of theological problems; and his religious feelings and views appear to have changed radically on several occasions. Nevertheless, he and his advisers must have concluded that in a deeply divided society the Christians alone possessed the comprehensive purpose and efficient, coherent organization which in the long run could weld the various conflicting elements of the populace into the all-embracing unity required by imperial policy. Yet he himself, like many of his co-religionists, was only baptized at the very end of his life – when he could sin no more.

To serve his Church, Constantine became one of the outstanding imperial builders in the history of Rome and the world: the founder of an architectural revolution which was derived from its religious counterpart and stimulated by munificent official encouragement. In general, the remarkable constructions that now emerged assumed two alternative shapes, centralized (round, polygonal, cruciform) or rectangular. As for the centralized buildings, Diocletian's palace at Salonae had shown what could be done, and it now became clear that edifices of this kind provided an appropriate setting not only for churches and baptisteries but for the burial-places of Christian martyrs. Thus at his new capital of Constantinople the emperor built a church of the Holy Apostles, a conically roofed structure in the form of a cross, which combined the functions of a Martyrium of the Apostles and his own mausoleum (as their thirteenth member); here, for a time, his remains were lodged, beneath the central drum. Another great centralized building, which has likewise not come down to us, was begun, and nearly completed, by Constantine at Antioch. This was the Golden Octagon, standing next to the palace upon an island in the River Orontes, near the centre of the city. The

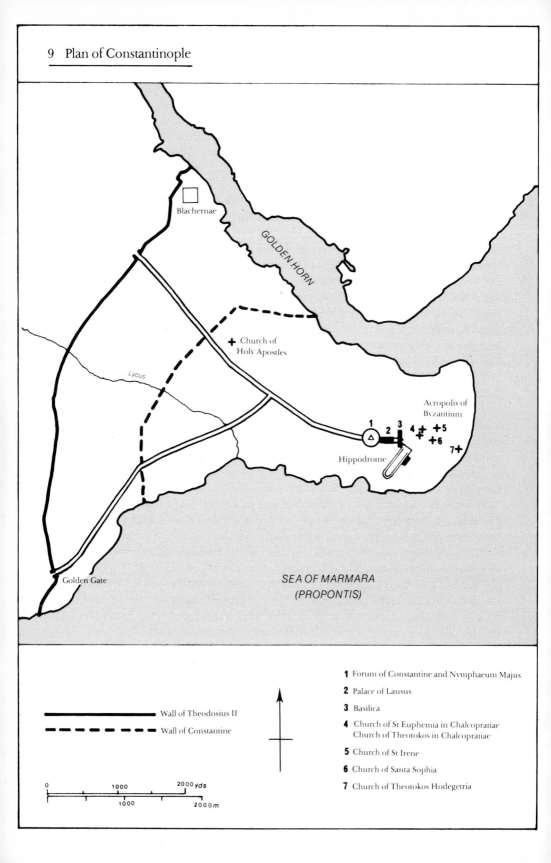

Blachernae

GOLDEN HORN

Church of
Holy Apostles

Lycus

Acropolis of
Byzantium

1 2 3 4 5
         6
      7

Hippodrome

Golden Gate

SEA OF MARMARA
(PROPONTIS)

Wall of Theodosius II

Wall of Constantine

0   1000   2000 yds

1000   2000 m

1 Forum of Constantine and Nymphaeum Majus
2 Palace of Lausus
3 Basilica
4 Church of St Euphemia in Chalcopratiae
   Church of Theotokos in Chalcopratiae
5 Church of St Irene
6 Church of Santa Sophia
7 Church of Theotokos Hodegetria

Octagon was an imperial church dedicated to Harmony, the divine power uniting Universe, Church and State. Its central area, beneath a gilded, wooden, domed or pyramidal roof, was surrounded by a circular colonnaded aisle in two storeys.

Equally remarkable were the rectangular buildings which housed a novel sort of building: the Christian basilica. These grandiose successors of the humble house-churches of the past were longitudinal structures entered from spacious courtyards and containing side-aisles separated from the loftier nave by arched colonnades. Above these arches rose brick walls, pierced by a series of windows which illuminated the nave. This was normally flat, roofed by a wooden ceiling; the great curving cross-vaults, like those of the recent Basilica of Maxentius, seemed too earthly and pagan, and would not have sufficiently drawn the eye to the east, where the rising sun descended on a celebrant at the altar as he stood facing his congregation. Yet pagan models helped to create these Christian basilicas all the same; for their east ends, containing the bishop's throne in their great curved apses, strongly recalled the Halls of Audience at Treviri and Spalatum: the altar beneath its canopy was like an emperor's throne, and the triumphal chancel-arch struck the same note.

Of Constantine's many spectacular basilicas, however, abounding in colourful gilding and other brilliant decoration, very few traces have survived. Nothing is left, for example, of his reconstruction of the church of St Irene (Holy Peace) at Constantinople (later rebuilt by JUSTINIAN I) or of his Basilica of St Peter at Rome, which was demolished in the sixteenth century to make room for its successor. Between the long, tall nave and towering apse of the Constantinian building, a massive transept, lit by sixteen windows, extended crosswise on either side, to help accommodate the great crowds who came to venerate the martyred St Peter. The rectangular Basilica Constantiniana at Rome, which was dedicated at first to the Saviour but later bore the name of St John Lateran, had small lateral wings or sacristies instead of transepts, but was resplendent with huge silver screen and yellow, red and green marble columns. More frequent were combinations, in one and the same building, of the two major formulae of the centralized and rectangular church. At Constantine's Grotto of the Nativity at Bethlehem, for example, an octagon was attached to the east end of an oblong structure, and his original Church of the Holy Sepulchre at Jerusalem comprised a circular martyrs' shrine (on the site of a Jewish tomb chamber) in the middle of an apsed basilica.

Constantine's reign was blackened by a domestic tragedy in the year 326, when, overcome by suspicions of treason (whether justified or otherwise), he ordered the execution of his wife Fausta and his eldest son Crispus, son of Minervina to whom he had probably been married before. Crispus was suffocated in a bath building at Pola in Istria, and Fausta, not long afterwards, met her death at Treviri. Constantine's three remaining sons (CONSTANTINE II, CONSTANTIUS II and CONSTANS I) were elevated to the rank of Caesar in

317, 323 and 333 respectively. This meant that they were being groomed for the succession; and two of the emperor's nephews, Delmatius and Hannibalianus, received preferment with the same intention. It was a strange miscalculation, however, to believe that all five of these young men would rule amicably together once he was gone.

Constantine was a man of deep and impulsive emotions. He was also extravagant, eager for popularity, vulnerable to flattery, and disconcertingly capricious and ruthless. He suffered from a ferocious temper, but could often be mollified. His ambition and energy were unbounded. He was a general of the highest order; and the two greatest decisions of his life – to found Constantinople, and to base his policy on Christianity – reverberated through the centuries that lay ahead, so that his reign was of supreme importance for the future of the Empire, the Church, and western civilization.

At the Council of Nicaea, reported his biographer Eusebius, 'he proceeded through the midst of the assembly like some heavenly Angel of God, clothed in a garment which glittered as though radiant with light, reflecting the glow of a purple robe, and adorned with the brilliant splendour of gold and precious stones. . . .' In his youth, Eusebius had seen him as 'matched by none in grace and beauty of form, or in tallness, and so surpassing his contemporaries in personal strength that he struck terror into them'. Later in life he put on weight, and was nicknamed 'bull-neck'. Through the impersonal, hieratic grandeur of his colossal portrait in the Conservatori Museum in Rome emerges a man with vigorously marked features, heavy eyebrow ridges and a forceful chin: a man it would be better not to have as an enemy.

LICINIUS
308–24

LICINIUS (joint emperor, 308–24) was born in about 250 and died in 325. He was the son of a peasant from Dacia Ripensis (Upper Moesia). He became the friend and military associate of GALERIUS, in whose Persian expedition of 297 he distinguished himself, subsequently holding a senior command on the

Danube. Adopted by DIOCLETIAN, he assumed the latter's designation 'Jovius', and henceforward bore the names Valerius Licinius Licinianus.

Before Galerius invaded Italy in 307 in his unsuccessful design to unseat MAXENTIUS, one of the two officers he had sent to Rome in a vain attempt to negotiate was Licinius. At the Conference of Carnuntum in the following year, Licinius was made Augustus, and allotted a territory comprising the Danubian provinces and the Balkans (in addition, theoretically, to Italy, north Africa and Spain, which were under the control of MAXENTIUS). His promotion flouted the claims of MAXIMINUS II DAIA and CONSTANTINE, and in 310, fearing a hostile move from Maximinus, he decided to appease Constantine by betrothing himself to the latter's sister Constantia. But in the following year, when Galerius died, Maximinus seized Asia Minor before he could do so himself. The two men reached an agreement, demarcating the continental boundary as their border; but it did not last. In the winter of 312/13 Maximinus crossed over into Thrace, but was defeated by Licinius at Campus Serenus and retreated to Tarsus, where he died. Thereupon Licinius took the opportunity to eliminate any imperial personage who might have become the figure-head for future subversion. Those who succumbed to his executioners included Maximinus' son and daughter, Galeria Valeria the daughter of Diocletian and widow of Galerius, Diocletian's widow Prisca, and Candidianus the son of Galerius.

The Roman world was now divided between Constantine (who had meanwhile eliminated Maxentius at the Milvian Bridge) and Licinius. At the beginning of 313 Licinius' marriage to Constantia was celebrated at Mediolanum, and in June of the same year, Licinius, having returned to Nicomedia, published a letter granting complete freedom of belief and worship to the Christians, on terms agreed upon earlier by the Edict of Milan (see CONSTANTINE). Licinius also began to claim descent from the emperor PHILIP, who had reputedly been pro-Christian (as a counterblast to Constantine's assertion that he was descended from CLAUDIUS GOTHICUS). He found the Edict of Milan a useful weapon against Maximinus, and accepted Constantine's claim to be senior Augustus in exchange for the right to legislate in his own portions of the Empire.

However, Constantine's plan to appoint his brother-in-law Bassianus as Caesar in charge of Italy and the Danubian provinces was unwelcome to Licinius, who believed the man would merely be Constantine's tool and in 314 incited him to revolt. But the treachery was detected, and war between the two emperors broke out two years later. Defeated at Cibalae in Pannonia by a numerically inferior force, Licinius retreated to Hadrianopolis where he defiantly proclaimed Aurelius Valerius Valens the frontier commander of Lower Moesia as Augustus of the west, in competition with Constantine. Following a second, indecisive battle at Campus Ardiensis, a treaty of partition was arranged. Valens was left stranded and put to death, and

Constantine won control of the Danubian and Balkan provinces, except Thrace. On the other hand Licinius retained full freedom of action in the eastern portion of the Empire.

To mark the apparent reconciliation, three new Caesars were created at Serdica in 317: Constantine's sons Crispus and the infant CONSTANTINE the younger, and the infant son of Licinius and Constantia, who bore the same name as his father. Further civil war was averted for a number of years, but relations between the two emperors soon began to deteriorate once again. In particular, while Constantine went ahead with his measures in favour of the Christians, Licinius instead came to the conclusion that the union of the State with the Christian community, as envisaged by Constantine, was a disastrous mistake. Accordingly he decided to suppress the power of the Church, and in the years 320 and 321 took a comprehensive series of measures directed to this end, forbidding synods, restricting the activities of the clergy and expelling Christians from official positions.

While these differences between the two régimes were making themselves felt, problems also arose about the annual consulships, which, although entirely honorary in character, provided useful opportunities to advertise the emperors' sons and train them for public appearances. These appointments were supposed to be a matter of agreement between the two rulers, but by 321 Licinius had formed the conviction that Constantine was weighting them unfairly in favour of his own sons. By way of retaliation, therefore, he unilaterally declared himself and his sons consuls in the eastern provinces for the following year. This amounted to an open declaration of estrangement; it had become clear that a new civil war was at hand.

A *casus belli* was soon found. In 322, to repel a Gothic encroachment, Constantine entered the territory of Licinius; although, in the event of an alien incursion, such action was allegedly permitted by the treaty of 314, Licinius chose to regard his move as a contravention of their agreement. Hostilities were therefore declared in the spring of 324. Licinius, establishing himself at Hadrianopolis, had 150,000 infantry and 15,000 cavalry at his disposal, while a fleet of 350 ships, under his admiral Abantus, lay off the mouth of the Hellespont. Constantine advanced on him from Thessalonica with 120,000 foot and 10,000 horse, leaving behind 200 war vessels and 2,000 transports under the command of his son Crispus. On 3 July Licinius suffered a severe defeat in a land battle, and fell back on Byzantium; soon afterwards his fleet, too, underwent serious losses. Byzantium had now been cut off, and Licinius retreated across the Bosphorus to Chalcedon. There he promoted Martinianus, the controller of his ministries, to be his fellow-Augustus (just as he had appointed Valens eight years earlier), with the task of preventing Constantine from crossing the strait; coins were issued in his name at Nicomedia. But Constantine, with a flotilla of light transports, evaded him and landed on the Asian bank. On 18 September the battle of Chrysopolis went decisively against Licinius, who fled to Nicomedia with the 30,000 survivors of his army but was captured soon afterwards.

Constantine's sister Constantia appealed to him to spare the lives of Licinius and Martinianus, and they were interned in Thessalonica and Cappadocia respectively. Licinius, however, was soon accused of plotting a come-back with the help of the Goths, and Constantine, either secretly or with senatorial approval, gave orders for his execution; and the same fate befell Martinianus in 325. Licinius the younger lost the title of Caesar, and two years later was put to death at Pola. Another son of Licinius, a bastard whom he had legitimized, was heard of in 336, reduced to his mother's slave status and working with women at an imperial weaving-mill at Carthage.

It is difficult to assess the merits of the emperor Licinius because his opposition to Constantine's pro-Christian measures earned him such violent opprobrium. Thus a modern writer has called him the most detestable of all the hard men of his age, self-seeking, unimaginative and coldly cruel. His religious policy, to say the least, seems inconsistent and unreliable, either because some of his pronouncements were insincere or because he could not make up his mind. His cruelty was displayed by his slaughter of the families and followers of his fellow-tetrarchs after the downfall of Maximinus II Daia. Throughout his long-drawn-out, worsening relationship with Constantine, although both sides were to blame, Licinius appears the more blameworthy of the two, because of his treacherous dealing with Bassianus in 314, his unscrupulous over-sensitivity a decade later, and perhaps also continued intriguing after all had been lost. Yet like other rulers of the day, he proved a competent general. It was this that earned him Galerius' support, gained him a great victory over Maximinus II Daia and earned him a longer reign than most of his contemporaries achieved. But, however good a soldier he may have been, he met more than his military match in Constantine, and that was the reason why he fell.

MAXIMINUS II DAIA
310–13

MAXIMINUS II DAIA (joint emperor, 310–13) was the son of a sister of GALERIUS; and it was Galerius who arranged his rapid promotion in the army, culminating in appointment as military tribune, and adopted him as his own son. When DIOCLETIAN and MAXIMIAN abdicated in 305, Daia was elevated to the rank of Caesar, and invested by Diocletian with the same purple robe which he had worn himself. He assumed the names Gaius Galerius Valerius Maximinus, betrothed his young daughter to Galerius' son Candidianus and was allocated the easternmost provinces and Egypt as his sphere of action.

Maximinus continued Diocletian's persecution of the Christians, with particular severity. In his first edict, in early 306, provincial governors were called upon to insist that every man, woman and child should sacrifice to the pagan gods. He himself, at Antioch and in Syria Palaestina (Judaea), presided personally over the enforcement of this demand. Thereafter the persecutions seem to have been temporarily halted, but in 309 Maximinus returned to the attack, launching an unprecedentedly stringent campaign against Christian believers. Everyone, even babies at the breast, had to attend the public sacrifices and eat the flesh of the sacrificial victims, whose blood must be sprinkled on every object sold in the markets.

But during the period between these two edicts Maximinus Daia had received a severe disappointment; for at the Conference of Carnuntum of 308, attended by all the recognized imperial personages, he had hoped for elevation to the rank of Augustus. This however was denied him by his uncle Galerius, who instead raised his military associate LICINIUS to that position. Like CONSTANTINE, he protested against this promotion over his head. Galerius attempted to console them with the newly invented title of 'Sons of the Augusti' (*filii Augustorum*), but Maximinus refused to be placated and in 310 had himself proclaimed Augustus by his troops.

Galerius was obliged to acquiesce, and in the following year he died. Thereupon Maximinus gained an advantage on Licinius by occupying Asia Minor and marching north-westwards as far as the Thracian Bosphorus. Licinius confronted him on the other bank of the straits, but then the two rivals laid down their arms and agreed for the time being to delimit their territories on the basis of the status quo. Meanwhile both plunged into feverish diplomatic activity, designed to win support among the various other contenders to the throne; and at the same time Maximinus embarked on a new phase of his religious policy. This did not involve any softening of his attitude to the Christians. For despite his initial compliance with Galerius' death-bed edict of toleration, six months later he had returned to a repressive policy, aided by the judicious distribution of forged, anti-Christian documents, including the notorious *Acts of Pilate*. Now, however, a more positive programme was adopted as well, seeking to match and outbid Christianity by the creation of a new, reconstructed pagan church, served by a universal network of priests who were divided into grades similar to the hierarchy of the Church he so hated.

Yet Constantine's victory over Maximinus' fellow-pagan MAXENTIUS at the Milvian Bridge subjected these plans to a sharp check. For on the very day after the battle, the victorious Constantine sent Maximinus a message insisting that all repression of the Christians must cease; he grudgingly complied, directing his governors that violence should not be employed to enforce worship of the Olympian gods.

The winter of 312–13 was another bad time for Maximinus, owing to failed harvests, severe famines and widespread epidemics in his eastern dominions. Moreover, military expeditions were needed to put down plundering robber bands who had caused a shortage of food in Caria; and the Armenians, too, who were in rebellion against his efforts to impose pagan worship, had to be suppressed. Nevertheless, if he could not frustrate Constantine he was at least determined to strike at the earliest possible moment against his other rival, Licinius, who was so much nearer; and it seemed best to do so at once, while Constantine, who might otherwise have come to Licinius' help, was away fighting in Germany. So in 313, before the coming of spring, Maximinus advanced through snow-bound Asia Minor by forced marches, crossed the Bosphorus and compelled Byzantium to capitulate. Licinius came to meet him, and on 1 May the decisive battle took place at Campus Serenus (Tzirallum) in Thrace. Although Maximinus' seventy thousand soldiers outnumbered the enemy by more than two to one, they were physically exhausted, and suffered a total defeat. Maximinus himself got away disguised as a slave. Pausing at Nicomedia, he punished the pagan priests who had so mistakenly promised him victory by rescinding his edicts against the Christians and restoring confiscated property to the Church. Soon afterwards, in order to escape the pursuing army of Licinius, he rapidly retreated behind the Taurus range. But at Tarsus, in the August heat, he fell ill and died.

The Christian writers describe with great satisfaction how, before perishing, Maximinus became blind and wasted away to a skeleton. They also accuse him of unparalleled boorishness, cruelty and inebriation – in addition to lust, for he was said to have had a passion for Galerius' wife. His activities as a persecutor, however, were at least accompanied by a realization, apparently unique among pagan contemporaries, of the impressive organization of the Christian Church – which paganism could have imitated. Besides, although an uneducated man himself, he appreciated the importance of pagan literature and learning. Nor would he have reached the positions he occupied had he not been a man of ability; and it is some tribute to his character that the relatives of Galerius and SEVERUS II preferred to live under his rule than under that of Licinius, who subsequently murdered them – along with Maximinus' own son and daughter.

CONSTANTINE II
337–40

CONSTANTINE II (Flavius Claudius, or sometimes Julius, Constantinus) (joint emperor, 337–40) was born at Arelate. He was CONSTANTINE THE GREAT's second son, and was stated to be the child of the empress Fausta; but if his birth was correctly dated to February 317, this cannot have been so, since she is known to have given birth to CONSTANTIUS II in August of the same year. In this event, Constantine II was the son of another woman, and therefore illegitimate. The alternative is to suppose that he was born to Fausta not, as reported, in 317 but in the previous year.

However this may be, before the end of 317 he was declared Caesar by his father at Sirmium, together with his older half-brother Crispus; and at the same time LICINIUS declared his son of the same name, a year or two older than Constantine II, to be Caesar in the east. By these promotions of a teenage boy and two infants, DIOCLETIAN's idea of rule by merit ceased to have any reality and the principle of inheritance by birth was re-established. The appointment of the infant Constantine II to consulships in 320 and 321 (in association first with his father and then with Crispus, who had been consul once before) contributed largely to his father's estrangement from Licinius, who felt that his own son had been passed over, and acted unilaterally to rectify this omission. In about 322, Constantine II was already able to sign his own name, amid rejoicings at court, and in 324 (the year of Licinius' final defeat), Crispus and he became consuls for the third time. But two years later Crispus was executed for alleged treason, so that Constantine II (although his own mother or supposed mother Fausta likewise fell into fatal disgrace) became the senior heir; for he was older than his surviving brothers (or half-brothers) CONSTANTIUS II and CONSTANS I.

In 332 he was sent to take titular command of fighting against the Visigothic ruler Alaric I on the Danube, in response to an appeal from the Sarmatian and Vandal tribes to whom Alaric posed a threat; and the Roman force won an important victory, inflicting heavy casualties (multiplied by hunger and cold) and taking hostages, including the king's son. In 333 Constantine II was transferred to Treviri in order to guard the Rhine front. Two years later his father, in anticipation of his own death, proclaimed the eventual division of the Empire between his sons (and two nephews, Delmatius and Hannibalianus). In this distribution of territories the emperor allotted the youth Gaul and Spain and Britain. When their father died in 337, his three sons were proclaimed joint Augusti. After deifying their father according to imperial tradition (despite the Christianity to which they all piously adhered), they agreed to the elimination of his two nephews; and many other men were killed as well. Very soon, however, friction began to arise between the brothers. In particular, when the famous but highly controversial bishop Athanasius, after taking refuge at Constantine II's capital Treviri, received his permission to return to Alexandria, Constantius II, within whose territories that city lay, was angry, because he did not want him there at all.

In 338 these growing dissensions prompted the three sons of Constantine the Great to hold a meeting, either in Pannonia or at Viminacium. Their principal business was to finalize their respective borders, and whereas the dominions of Constantine II remained unchanged, Constans I succeeded in gaining additional territory. This decision sharpened a dispute over the relative precedence of the brothers, since although at first Constans I issued medallions on which he and Constantius turned deferentially to their elder brother, the former became increasingly unwilling to accept Constantine II's claim to be the senior Augustus. In 340, therefore, Constantine II took advantage of Constans' absence from Italy (which formed part of his sphere) to march into the peninsula. But the vanguard of the force that Constans sent from Illyricum to confront his invading army ambushed and killed him at Aquileia.

Very little can be said about his character; but it is perhaps significant that although he was the oldest surviving son of Constantine the Great (and a married man, who might produce a dynasty), his father evidently did not think him able enough (or perhaps old enough, at nineteen) to bequeath him the entire Empire.

CONSTANTIUS II
337—61

CONSTANTIUS II (Flavius Julius Constantius) (joint emperor, 337–50; sole central emperor, 350–61) was the third son of CONSTANTINE THE GREAT, and the second (or perhaps first) son of his empress Fausta. He was born in Illyricum in 31, and proclaimed Caesar in 324. The massacre of relatives which followed his father's death in 337 was rumoured to have taken place at his instigation, though the responsibility was carefully obscured.

In the partition of the Empire between himself and his two brothers, Constantius II was allotted the east (though Constantinople itself was temporarily under CONSTANS I); his selection for this powerful role may indicate their father's high regard for his abilities. Almost at once the Persian king Shapur (Sapor) II the Great broke the peace which had been concluded four decades earlier, and the hostilities which ensued were destined to last for twenty-six years. The conflict focused upon the Mesopotamian fortresses. Although Constantius II did not conduct the war with outstanding vigour, Shapur II undertook three sieges of Nisibis without success. Moreover, and fortunately for Rome, the appearance of new tribal enemies in the east obliged him to move away and campaign against them in Khorasan for five years, from 353–8.

By this time, Constantius II had become sole Roman emperor, but it had been a long process. After his younger brother Constans I had overthrown their elder brother CONSTANTINE II in 340, he in turn was killed by a usurper, MAGNENTIUS, in 350. For a time, the Danube legions could not decide whether to support Constantius II or Magnentius. Constantina Augusta, Constantius' elder sister, who was living in Illyricum, persuaded the

Danubian and Balkan legions to hail a third party, their Pannonian Master of Foot, Vetranio, as Augustus, a title he proclaimed on his coinage at Siscia and Thessalonica. Since Constantina was still in favour with her brother at a later date, it is probable that she was working in his interests, believing that her move would hamper Magnentius.

At any rate Vetranio himself, after first accepting the overtures of Magnentius, subsequently changed direction and declared his loyalty to Constantius II instead. This is indicated by coins bearing the inscription 'By this sign you shall conquer' (HOC SIGNO VICTOR ERIS), a version of the divine injunction granted to Constantine the Great before the Battle of the Milvian Bridge. Subsequently Vetranio handed over his troops to Constantius II at Naissus, withdrawing into honourable retirement at Prusa in Bithynia. As for Magnentius, he suffered a heavy defeat from Constantius II in a great battle at Mursa Major in Lower Pannonia in 351, and committed suicide two years later.

While the war was still in progress, Constantius II had decided to appoint his twenty-six-year-old cousin Constantius Gallus as Caesar. After proclaiming the youth's new rank at Sirmium, and giving him Constantina Augusta as his bride, the emperor sent him to the east, where he suppressed rebellions in Syria Palaestina and Isauria (Asia Minor), and kept the Persians at bay. However, his administrative methods were tactless and tyrannical. There were complaints to Constantius II, who summoned him to Mediolanum to respond to them. But in 354, while still on his journey westwards, in Istria, he was arrested, tried, condemned and put to death.

Constantius II next had to deal with a Frankish leader named Silvanus, who had usurped the title of Augustus at Colonia Agrippinensium. His murder quickly followed, but in the confusion the city was sacked by Germans from across the Rhine. Constantius II mobilized Gallus' half-brother JULIAN (the future emperor) to deal with the situation, proclaiming him Caesar and giving him his younger sister Helena in marriage.

While Julian was still in the west, engaged in successful campaigns, Constantius II visited Rome, in the spring of 357. 'The emperor', reported the historian Ammianus Marcellinus (who was twenty-seven years old at the time),

was greeted with welcoming cheers, which were echoed from the hills and river-banks, but in spite of the din he exhibited no emotion, but kept the same impassive air as he commonly wore before his subjects in the provinces. Though he was very short he stooped as he passed under a high gate; otherwise he was like a dummy, gazing straight before him as if his head were in a vice and turning neither to right nor left. When a wheel jolted he did not nod, and at no point was he seen to spit or to wipe or rub his face or nose or to move his hand. All this was no doubt affectation, but he gave other evidence too in his personal life of an unusual degree of self-control, which one was given to believe belonged to him alone. As for his habit throughout his reign of never allowing any private person to share his carriage or be his colleague in the consulship, as many deified emperors have, and many other similar customs which his towering pride led him to observe as if they had all the sanctity of law, I will pass them by because I am conscious that I have reported them as they occurred.

After his visit to Rome Constantius II attacked the Sarmatians, Suevi and Quadi on the Danube. But before long he was urgently recalled to the east, where the Persian king Shapur II, after enforcing peace on his eastern borders, had renewed his attacks on the Romans. In 359 he stormed Amida in Mesopotamia, an event vividly described by Ammianus; and in the following year another fortress in the region, Singara, fell to him as well. In the course of these and other operations, which were accompanied by complex diplomatic negotiations, Constantius II sent a message to Julian requesting reinforcements. But Julian's soldiers in Gaul were unwilling to comply, suspecting that the demand was motivated by a jealous desire to weaken their own popular leader. In consequence, they proclaimed him Augustus; and he accepted the offer. Constantius II assembled an army to put down his treasonable cousin and moved westwards. By the winter of 361 he had got as far as Cilicia; but there he suddenly contracted a fever, and at Mopsucrene he died.

Constantius II was profoundly interested in theological matters, and set the Christian Empire on a new religious course by supporting Arianism, a doctrine initiated by the Alexandrian priest Arius and propagated by apologists reflecting Greek philosophical attitudes. Arius (d. 337), brought up on Origen's doctrine of the singleness of God, regarded Christ as distinct from Him in essence and, although created before all time, nevertheless a creature and changeable like other creatures. This was a view which duly stressed his humanity – on which Christianity's claim to a concrete place in history so strongly rested – but which invited criticism for seemingly depreciating his godhead. The result of Constantine the Great's Council of Nicaea had been the excommunication of Arius; but he was posthumously rehabilitated by Constantius II, whose consistent aim it remained, despite personal attacks on himself, to discover some compromise on which at least a large number of churchmen might be able to agree. To this end, in 341, ninety-seven Greek bishops assembled with the emperor at Antioch, where they dedicated the new cathedral begun by his father. While denying that they were Arians, or opponents of the Nicene Creed, they drew up another, supplementary, document; but its hostility to Arius' enemies meant that it failed to achieve the emperor's purpose.

The fact was that the controversy was developing into a rift between the western and eastern sections of the Church. The west regarded the Greeks as over-clever, and believed they were heretical Arians at heart, while the east (although it too contained its anti-Arians) resented dictation from the papacy.

In the hope of healing the threatened schism the emperors Constantius II and Constans I urgently called a council of both west and east at Serdica in

342, but it split into two rival bodies which assailed one another with curses. After the deadlock, however, a measure of reunion was achieved – under powerful imperial pressure, and at the cost of tacit but painful theological compromises on either side.

However, when Constantius II defeated the usurper Magnentius at Mursa Major, the Arian bishop of that city, Valens, was one of his most fervent supporters, so that from then onwards he enjoyed ready access to the ruler's ear. From successive, compliant synods at Arelate (in 353) and Mediolanum (in 355), Constantius extracted a condemnation of the arch-enemy of Arianism, Athanasius, bishop of Alexandria, and in 356 he was ousted from his see (not for the first time) by a military force. Fleeing to the desert, he poured out a torrent of pamphlets violently attacking the emperor and his Arian advisers. He was succeeded at Alexandria by a radical Arian, George of Cappadocia; and another prelate of the same persuasion obtained the vital bishopric of Antioch in 357.

Supporting them, an Antiochene logician, Aetius, went so far as to declare that the Son's essence is unlike the Father's. This position meant not only an abandonment of the Nicene assertion that the essence of the Father and Son is identical, but also a denial of the belief – held by most of the Greek bishops – that the Son's essence is 'like' the Father's, as a perfect image mirrors its archetype. Shocked, therefore, by this 'dissimilarian' doctrine, Basil, bishop of Ancyra, hastened to the court of Constantius at Sirmium to lodge a vigorous protest, and succeeded in persuading the emperor that the definition of 'likeness' was the only formula capable of maintaining the unity of the Church.

Then Valens of Mursa Major asserted his influence once again. This became increasingly clear in 359 when Constantius decided to hold another major Church council, divided for convenience into two parts, meeting at Ariminum in Italy and Seleucia ad Calycadnum in Cilicia. Avoiding the trouble-making word 'essence' (*ousia*), and merely claiming that the Son was 'like' the father, Valens was able to coerce the western representatives into this slightly disguised Arian approach; Basil of Ancyra, who still disagreed, failed to secure any support from the emperor, and many others of the same opinion lost their bishoprics and were sent into exile. For the emperor favoured the broad and imprecise definition put forward by Valens, proposing a simple creed of wide appeal, in contrast to his father's Nicene formulation which had produced so many acrimonious misunderstandings. But acrimony continued all the same, and in 360 Basil, and the Arians' most famous enemy Athanasius, agreed to work together – a pact which contributed to the ultimate defeat of Arianism, though not until two decades after the death of Constantius II. So the religious events of his reign, even if nothing was finally decided at the time, eventually proved decisive. True, things did not work out in the way that the emperor had planned. Nevertheless, it was he who taught the Church to accept its new role as the official religion of the Empire; and he signalized the achievement, in 360, by his dedication of the church of Santa Sophia, or Holy Wisdom, at Constantinople (later rebuilt by Justinian I.)

Constantius II inspired personal loyalty among those who worked for him – while scrupulously maintaining the dignity of his office, and without demeaning himself by an excessive regard for his own popularity. Ammianus Marcellinus, who was one of his officer cadets, subjected his complex character and behaviour to a detailed analysis.

Constantius was industrious and had aspirations to learning, but he was too dull-witted to make a speaker, and when he turned his mind to versifying produced nothing worth while. His style of living was frugal and temperate, and he ate and drank only in moderation; in consequence his health was so robust that he was rarely unwell, though such illnesses as he had were dangerous. When necessary he could do with little sleep, and for long periods of his life he was so exceptionally chaste that even his most confidential servants could not suspect him of behaviour which malice invents in those who enjoy the freedom of supreme power, even when it can find no grounds for it. In riding, throwing the javelin, and above all in archery, as well as in the various skills of the infantry, he was thoroughly expert. . . .

Although in most respects he was comparable to other emperors of average merit, yet if he discovered any ground, however false or slight, for suspecting an attempt upon the throne he showed in endless investigations regardless of right or wrong a cruelty which easily surpassed that of Gaius and Domitian and Commodus. Indeed, at the very beginning of his reign he rivalled their barbarity by destroying root and branch all who were connected with him by blood and birth. The sufferings of the wretched men accused of infringing or violating his prerogative were increased by the bitter and angry suspicions nourished by the emperor in all such cases. Once he got wind of anything of this kind he threw himself into its investigation with unbecoming eagerness, and appointed merciless judges to preside over such trials. In the infliction of punishment he sometimes tried to prolong the agonies of death, if the victim's constitution could stand it.

As to his appearance and build, he was rather dark, with staring eyes and sharp sight. His hair was soft and his cheeks regularly shaven to give him a trim and shining look. From the base of the neck to the groin his body was unusually long, but his legs were very short and bowed, which made him a good runner and jumper. . . . He enclosed the little building in which he used to sleep with a deep ditch crossed by a collapsible bridge; when he went to bed he dismantled the planks and pins, which he reassembled when he was going out at daybreak.

CONSTANS I
337–50

CONSTANS I (Flavius Julius) (joint emperor, 337–50) was born in about 320. He was the fourth son of CONSTANTINE I THE GREAT, by legitimate union with Fausta; the story that his mother was a concubine probably resulted from confusion with derogatory stories about Crispus or CONSTANTINE II. Constans I was educated at the court of Constantinople, and studied Latin under Aemilius Magnus Arborius. Proclaimed Caesar in 333, he was betrothed to the daughter of the powerful Cretan minister Ablabius (though she later married the king of Persia instead).

When Constantine I died in 337, Constans became joint Augustus with Constantine II and CONSTANTIUS II, receiving Italy and Africa as his sphere, and at their meeting in Pannonia or at Viminacium during the following year he was granted additional territories: not only the Danubian countries and Macedonia and Achaea (earlier allocated to Constantine I's nephew Delmatius, who had now been suppressed), but also Thrace and Constantinople, which Constantius II rather surprisingly allowed him to take over. Yet as relations between Constans I and Constantine II began to deteriorate – because the latter's claim to be senior Augustus now seemed objectionable – in 339 Constans gave Constantinople and its Thracian hinterland back to Constantius II as a bribe to win his support in this dispute. In 340, while Constans was away quelling trouble among the Danubian tribes, Constantine II invaded Italy, but was killed by his brother's troops at Aquileia. Constans now shared with Constantius II the control of the Roman world.

However, religious differences divided them. Both were very devoted Christians; but while Constantius, in common with most easterners, shared some sympathy with the Arian cause, Constans – the only one of the three brothers to receive baptism in 337 – distanced himself from the Arians, and became, like the majority of western Christians, a supporter of Catholic orthodoxy based on the Nicene Creed. This divergence became clear at the

247

Council of Serdica in 342, when Constans strongly took the side of Athanasius, the arch-enemy of the Arians; to many western Christians, who regarded them as heretics, he remained the hero who had saved the Church. However, after a serious threat of war between the emperors in 346, the two sides temporarily patched up their differences. Constans endowed ecclesiastical foundations with great generosity, and lavished favours upon the clergy. Moreover, acting, as he declared, in the interests of Church unity, he took strong measures against the Donatist heresy in Africa; and he sponsored persecutions directed against pagans and Jews.

After gaining considerable victories over the Franks in 341–2 and on the Danube, Constans became the last legitimate emperor to visit Britain (in 343), where he conducted operations on Hadrian's Wall. However, he was not popular among the troops, and it was this that finally caused his downfall. The historian Victor – who spoke harshly of his depraved, dissipated and avaricious character, with what degree of justice we cannot tell – described him as 'outstandingly contemptuous of the soldiers'. The result, in 350, was a military uprising led by an officer named MAGNENTIUS, a former slave of Constantine the Great. Magnentius declared himself Augustus at Augustodunum, and Constans fled towards the border of Spain, where Gaiso, an agent of the rebel leader, caught up with him and put him to death.

MAGNENTIUS
350–3

MAGNENTIUS (Flavius Magnus) (breakaway emperor in the west, 350–3) was born *c*. 303, in or near Ambiani (Samarobriva), reportedly of a British father and a Frankish mother. His wife (later married to VALENTINIAN I) was Justina. Magnentius served in a barbarian contingent in the reign of Constantine the Great, becoming a staff officer (*protector*) and then a field army commander (*comes rei militaris*) under his sons, who put him in charge of the élite legions known as the Joviani and Herculiani.

On 18 January 350, Marcellinus, financial minister of the emperor

CONSTANS I, held a birthday party for his sons at Augustodunum, at which Magnentius appeared in purple robes and was acclaimed as Augustus. The imperial army deserted to his cause, and Constans I, fleeing towards Spain, was killed by one of his adherents. In June Nepotianus, the son of CONSTANTINE THE GREAT's sister Eutropia, refused to accept Magnentius' rule and declared himself emperor, defeating a levy raised by the praetorian prefect Anicetus, but after twenty-eight days he and his mother, and other members of his family, were killed by Marcellinus, who had by then become Magnentius' chief administrative controller.

The whole of the west, including Africa, then recognized Magnentius, whose coins honour him as 'Restorer of Liberty' (RESTITVTOR LIBERTATIS), to point a contrast with the unpopular régime of Constans I. On the Danube, however, another usurper, Vetranio, after first supporting his cause, went over to CONSTANTIUS II, who in the meantime prompted the Germans on the Rhine to harass Magnentius; while he for his part, believing an attack from Constantius himself to be imminent, nominated Flavius Magnus Decentius, who was his relative and probably his brother, as Caesar.

Meanwhile an exchange of envoys had been taking place. Already in 350, while Vetranio was still Augustus, Magnentius sent a senator named Nunechius (perhaps his governor of Gaul) and his principal commander (*magister militum*) Marcellinus – not the same man as the chief administrative officer (*magister officiorum*) of that name – to Constantius, who placed them under arrest. Then the other Marcellinus met Constantius' representative Flavius Philippus and escorted him to Magnentius. Philippus' purpose was ostensibly to negotiate a peace settlement with the pretender, but his real objective was to find out his military dispositions on Constantius' behalf. Addressing Magnentius' army, he rebuked them for disloyalty to the house of Constantine and proposing that Magnentius should limit his territories to Gaul. His oratory caused the troops to waver, but Magnentius, after reminding them that it was the oppressive government of the imperial house that had prompted them to revolt in the first place, refused to allow Philippus to return to Constantius and placed him under arrest.

In 351 the inevitable hostilities between the two rivals broke out. Magnentius had raised large forces in Gaul, including numerous Germans, and in consequence outnumbered Constantius II, who as he advanced westwards was defeated with heavy losses at Atrans, on the border of Italy and Noricum, and compelled to retreat. Rejecting his offer of a compromise, Magnentius left his headquarters at Aquileia to march into the Danubian provinces. There, despite an initial lack of progress, he established himself at Mursa Major in the rear of Constantius' army, thus forcing him to fight back; but after a prolonged engagement Magnentius' right wing was routed by the opposing cavalry and he suffered a total defeat – the first reverse, it would appear, that heavy cavalry had ever inflicted on legionaries. Magnentius reportedly lost twenty-four thousand men and Constantius thirty thousand; this was the bloodiest battle of the century, and inflicted irreparable losses upon the Empire's military strength. Magnentius recoiled to Aquileia and endeavoured to rebuild his army. But in the summer of 352, unable to withstand Constantius II's invasion of Italy, he was obliged to withdraw to Gaul. There in the following year he was defeated again, and lost control of the Rhine frontier (which was temporarily overrun by barbarians). Next he retreated precipitately to Lugdunum, where, seeing that his position was hopeless, he committed suicide, leaving the entire Roman Empire in Constantius' hands.

Magnentius had made himself unpopular with the upper classes by rigorous taxation, so that the literary authorities offer an unfavourable view of his régime, ignoring whatever military, administrative or diplomatic gifts he may have possessed. He was a pagan and favoured the pagans, but was forced by political necessity to set this preference aside owing to the need to rally the orthodox Catholic (Nicene) party to his cause against the Arians who supported Constantius. These endeavours were displayed by a remarkable coinage of 353 which, for the first time in the history of Rome, devoted the principal part of its design to a Christian emblem, the Chi-Rho sign (XP in a monogram, standing for Christos) flanked by Alpha and Omega and inscribed 'The Well-Being of our Lords the Augustus and the Caesar' (Decentius) (SALVS DD. NN.AVG.ET CAES. [*Dominorum Nostrorum Augusti et Caesaris*]). These issues were made at the mint of Ambiani (Samarobriva). Magnentius and Decentius had also coined at Rome, Aquileia and Treviri; and after the loss of Treviri, towards the end of his reign, Lugdunum and Arelate became mints instead.

JULIAN
361–3

JULIAN (Flavius Claudius Julianus, generally known as Julian the Apostate) (361–3) was born at Constantinople in 332. He was the son of Julius Constantius, a half-brother of CONSTANTINE THE GREAT, and of Basilina, daughter of a governor of Egypt. His mother died shortly after he was born, and his father perished in the massacre of many of his relatives after Constantine's death in 337.

Placed by CONSTANTIUS II, two years later, in the care of the eunuch Mardonius, who inculcated in him a passion for literature and the old gods, Julian was educated at Constantinople, where he studied grammar and rhetoric. In about 342 the emperor transferred him to Nicomedia, but very soon afterwards he and his half-brother Constantius Gallus were sent away to the remote fortress villa of Macellum in Cappadocia, where they were given a pious Christian education and even ordained as readers, though Julian avidly continued reading the pagan classics. After six years of this exile, however, Julian was allowed to return to Constantinople; but the suspicious ruler quickly moved him out of the city, and in 351 he was sent to Nicomedia once again. From there he was able to visit Pergamum and Ephesus to continue his studies, sitting under the leading neo-Platonist Maximus, who converted him, secretly, to a form of paganism associated with mysticism and magical practices.

After the downfall and death of Constantius Gallus (who had been appointed Caesar) in 354, Julian was summoned to the court at Mediolanum; however, through the influence of the emperor's first wife Eusebia, he was soon permitted to move to Athens instead, to complete his higher education. But then he was called back to Mediolanum, created Caesar, and given Constantius' sister Helena in marriage in 355. Shortly afterwards he received orders to leave for the northern frontiers in order to repel dangerous invasions by the Franks and Alamanni. In 356 he recovered Colonia Agrippinensium and other centres, and during the following year defeated a greatly superior force of Alamanni near Argentorate. This success was followed up by a raid across the Rhine, and leaving his winter quarters at Lutetia (Parisii) he inflicted further reverses on the Germans in 358 and 359. Even if these victories were somewhat exaggerated by his eulogists, they constituted a substantial achievement, particularly since he had never received any military training. Moreover, Julian earned appreciation among his troops for sharing their hardships; and a large tax reduction (in face of opposition from the praetorian prefect Flavius Florentius) delighted the civilian population of Gaul.

Such signs of increasing popularity were not welcomed at the court of Constantius II. When news of Julian's doings arrived, according to Ammianus Marcellinus

all the most influential courtiers, past masters in the art of flattery, made fun of the Caesar's well-conceived plans and the success which had attended them. Endless silly jokes were bandied about, such as 'he is more of a goat than a man' (an allusion to his wearing a beard); 'his victories are becoming a bore', it was declared. 'Babbling mole', 'ape in purple', 'Greek dilettante', and other such names were applied to him, and by ringing the changes on these in the ears of the emperor, who was eager to hear this kind of talk, his enemies attempted to smother his good qualities under their shameless words. They attacked him as slack and timid and sedentary, and accused him of dressing up his reverses in fine language.

Nevertheless, Constantius' jealousy had been fully aroused; and he decided to withdraw some of Julian's best troops and summon them back to his own army. But the soldiers at Lutetia refused to accept the order, and proclaimed Julian as Augustus in February 360. After attempting in vain to negotiate with Constantius, he concluded that war was inevitable, and in 361 marched rapidly eastwards. Soon afterwards, however, he learnt that the emperor was dead. Julian, unchallenged, reached Constantinople in December.

A few of Constantius' supporters were executed, and others sent into exile. During the course of his journey, at Naissus, Julian had openly declared his adherence to paganism; now he immediately granted freedom of worship to all pagans, endowing their cults with substantial subsidies and providing them with an organization intended to compete with that of the Christians. His upbringing and youthful experiences impelled him in this direction – Christianity had not, he noted, prevented Constantius and his colleagues from committing many crimes, especially against Julian's own family. When, therefore, he himself came to the throne, while proclaiming toleration of any and every religion, he deprived the Christian Church of its financial privileges, and amid the disorders that inevitably followed, its members were penalized more rigorously than pagan offenders. An especially controversial measure excluded them from teaching posts. And to undermine their position still further Julian offered encouragement to the Jews, even projecting the reconstruction of the Temple at Jerusalem. Yet this plan to elevate the Jewish faith at the expense of Christianity came to nothing. Indeed the same may be said of his whole vehement anti-Christian campaign. Julian believed he was entrusted with a divine mission to heal a sick society. But his character, an unusual blend of idealism, pedantry and opportunism, found any sort of diplomatic compromise unacceptable; and his deep involvement in the antique classical traditions made it hard for him to reach out and understand the ordinary man and woman of his day. His archaistic attempt to roll back the Christian tide, which earned him the name of Apostate in posterity, was doomed to failure.

He was a more prolific author than any other Roman emperor, and exceeded all of them (except only MARCUS AURELIUS) in literary distinction. His admiration for pagan culture emerges strongly from his surviving speeches, essays and letters, in which he uses the Greek language of the day with confidence and skill. While Constantius II was still alive, Julian had written two insincere orations in his praise, in addition to a more heartfelt eulogy of the empress Eusebia. He also composed a commentary, now lost, on his own German campaigns. After he came to the throne, he began composing works propagating his personal and spiritual ideas. They included a prose hymn to the Sun-god, dedicated to Sallustius, the principal contemporary theologian of paganism – in whose honour he also penned a *Consolation to Himself*, when Sallustius, to his regret, departed from his court in Gaul. A further composition is addressed to the Mother of the Gods, and two others are directed against contemporary Cynic philosophers, who, according to Julian, were failing to live up to their founder Diogenes. His *Beard-Hater* is a satirical retort to the frivolous people of Antioch, who had mocked his old-fashioned beard and simple way of life. Another piece of satire that has survived is *The Caesars*, passing each of the earlier Roman emperors in turn under sardonic review: Marcus Aurelius wins the prize, while Constantine's Christianity is derided for its easy absolution of sins, however often one repeats them. Only excerpts from Julian's famous anti-Christian work, *Against the Galileans*, have come down to us. But his *Letters* (though hard to distinguish from numerous forgeries) contain valuable historical material and revelations of Julian's thinking; one fragment, *To a Priest*, recommends the pagan priesthood to emulate the Christians in their teaching of morality.

Outside the sphere of religion he had more to show for his efforts, since he was a hard-working and conscientious administrator. He did all he could to revive the decaying fortunes of the city-states in the eastern provinces – from whose impoverished gentry, displeased with court lavishness and theological confusions, he derived much of his political backing. He took steps to reduce the damaging monetary inflation, and, above all, he made a courageous attempt to cut down the ever-growing and all-encroaching imperial bureaucracy. His cultural interests were shown by the foundation of a great library in the Basilica at Constantinople, containing one hundred and twenty thousand volumes.

Although so unusual in other respects, he nourished the traditional hope of defeating the Persians in battle. In July 362 he entered Antioch to make his preparations. During his stay the temple at Daphne was burnt to the ground, and a famine occurred in which the city council responded in his relief measures with obstruction. In March 363, at the head of sixty-five thousand men, he marched eastwards, and by June, after an initial victory, he was outside the enemy capital Ctesiphon. However, he did not feel able to attack the city, and instead retreated, in order to effect a junction with a reserve force that was coming up behind him. His army was continually harassed by the forces of the Persian monarch Sapor (Shapur) II, and ran short of supplies; and on 26 June, in a region named Maranga, he was wounded in a skirmish with their armoured cavalry – though the word soon got about that he had been stabbed by one of his own Christian soldiers. The wound did not heal, and he died. His body, in accordance with his instructions, was buried outside Tarsus, but was subsequently taken to Constantinople.

Ammianus Marcellinus saw and recorded Julian's many remarkable qualities, but went on to list what seemed to be his defects. 'His temperament', he recorded,

was impulsive, but he compensated for this by the excellent habit of allowing himself to be corrected when he went wrong. He was a copious talker and very seldom silent. He was too much given to divination, and seemed in this respect to rival the emperor Hadrian. He was superstitious rather than genuinely observant of the rites of religion, and he sacrificed innumerable victims regardless of expense; it was reckoned that if he had returned from Parthia there would have been a shortage of cattle.

He liked the applause of the mob and was excessively eager to be praised for the most trivial reasons, and his desire for popularity often led him to converse with unworthy persons. He sometimes acted arbitrarily and in an uncharacteristic way. The laws which he enacted were not oppressive, and what they enjoined or prohibited was precisely stated, but there were a few exceptions, among them the harsh decree forbidding Christians to teach rhetoric or grammar unless they went over to worship of the pagan gods. An equally intolerable grievance was that he allowed some persons to be wrongfully conscripted into town councils, though they were either foreigners or else exempt by privilege or birth from liability to serve such bodies. . . .

He was of middle height, his hair was smooth as if it had been combed, and he wore a bristly beard trimmed to a point. He had fine, flashing eyes, the sign of a lively intelligence, well-marked eyebrows, a straight nose, and a rather large mouth with a pendulous lower lip. His neck was thick and somewhat bent, his shoulders large and broad. From head to foot he was perfectly built, which made him strong and a good runner.

JOVIAN
363–4

JOVIAN (Flavius Jovianus) (363–4) was born in 330 at Singidunum; he was the son of Varronianus, commander of the élite officers' cadet corps (*comes domesticorum*) of CONSTANTIUS II. Jovian himself served as a member of the same corps (*protector domesticus*) under Constantius and JULIAN. The story that the latter dismissed him because he was a Christian appears to be unfounded, since by 363 he had become commander of the force. In June, after Julian's death in the east, the throne was first offered to the praetorian prefect Saturninius Secundus Salutius. But after he had declined the honour on grounds of old age and ill-health, the troops proclaimed Jovian emperor.

The news of this unimpressive appointment encouraged the Persian king Shapur (Sapor) II to redouble his attacks on the retreating Roman army. The harassed Jovian rapidly made peace, exchanging hostages and conceding that the Romans should evacuate the five provinces beyond the Tigris annexed by DIOCLETIAN, together with the fortresses of Nisibis and Castra Maurorum and Singara; while the Persians also seized a substantial tract of Armenia. This agreement was regarded by contemporaries as unnecessary and disgraceful, but at least it enabled Jovian to bring his army, which was famished, back to safety. In the course of the march a senior notary (*primicerius notariorum*), a man with the same name as the emperor who had fought with distinction during the campaign, was charged with disloyalty and put to death.

As soon as Jovian returned to Roman territory, he publicly announced his repudiation of his predecessor's paganism and the return of the Empire to Christianity. Constantine's subsidies to the churches were revived, and although the distinguished pagan thinker Themistius paid a tribute to the new emperor's religious tolerance and moderation he took steps to close certain temples and prohibit sacrifices. A small Chi-Rho ('Christos') once again makes its appearance on military standards displayed on his coins.

Jovian spent some time at Antioch, conducting various business affairs, but was so anxious to move westwards that he left the city in mid-winter to continue his march. When he reached Tarsus, he paid tribute to Julian's temporary tomb. At Tyana he was told that there had been trouble at Durocortorum in Gaul, where two senior officers had been killed; this was followed by a second, more favourable, piece of news indicating that the army of Gaul had nevertheless declared in his favour. On arriving at Ancyra he assumed the consulship, taking as colleague his elder son (named Varronianus after his grandfather); he was only a very small child, and howled loudly on being placed in the curule chair. This behaviour was soon looked back upon as an unfavourable omen; for from this moment onwards, reported Ammianus Marcellinus,

fate drove Jovian rapidly on to meet his appointed doom. After arriving at Dadastana, on the border between Bithynia and Galatia, he was found dead in his bed. There are a number of conflicting accounts of the circumstances of his death. It is said that he was overcome by the noxious smell of fresh plaster in his bedroom, or that the fumes of a huge fire brought on cerebral congestion, or that he died of indigestion after eating to excess. He died in his thirty-third year. His death was like that of Scipio Aemilianus, and I have not heard of a serious investigation in either case.

Jovian had a dignified gait and a cheerful expression. His eyes were grey, and he was enormously tall, so tall that for some time no royal robe could be found to fit him. He modelled himself upon Constantius. He sometimes continued with serious business till after midday, and he was in the habit of jesting in public with his suite. He was no more than moderately well-educated, but he was of a kindly disposition and careful in his choice of officials, as was clear from the few appointments that he made. But he was greedy and given to wine and women, faults which regard for the dignity of his position might have led him to correct.

Elsewhere, however, Ammianus emphasizes his laziness and weakness. Christian writers, notably Theodoretus and Augustine, naturally approved of his reversal of Julian's apostasy; but they found it hard to explain why he had not received a longer reign as a divine reward for this praiseworthy course of action.

PART VIII

THE
HOUSE OF VALENTINIAN

The House of Valentinian

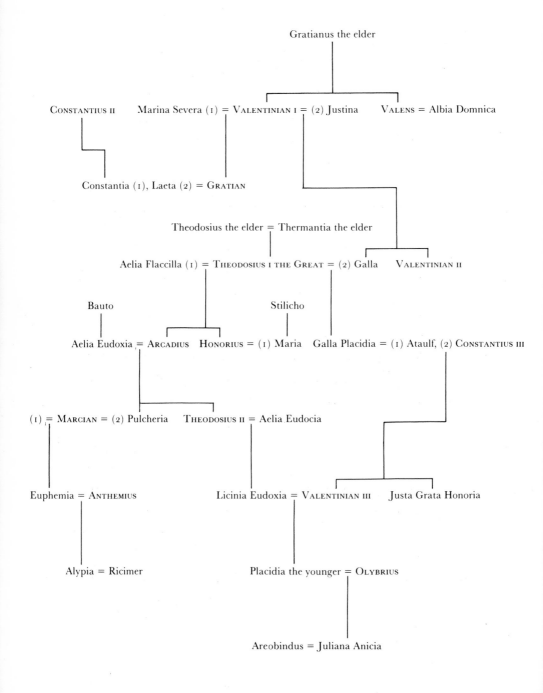

Gratianus the elder

Constantius II   Marina Severa (1) = Valentinian I = (2) Justina   Valens = Albia Domnica

Constantia (1), Laeta (2) = Gratian

Theodosius the elder = Thermantia the elder

Aelia Flaccilla (1) = Theodosius I the Great = (2) Galla   Valentinian II

Bauto   Stilicho

Aelia Eudoxia = Arcadius   Honorius = (1) Maria   Galla Placidia = (1) Ataulf, (2) Constantius III

(1) = Marcian = (2) Pulcheria   Theodosius II = Aelia Eudocia

Euphemia = Anthemius   Licinia Eudoxia = Valentinian III   Justa Grata Honoria

Alypia = Ricimer   Placidia the younger = Olybrius

Areobindus = Juliana Anicia

VALENTINIAN I
364–75

VALENTINIAN I (Flavius Valentinianus) (joint emperor in the west, 364–75) was born in 321, the first son of Gratianus the elder, a native of Cibalae in Pannonia. Valentinian was in Africa with his father, perhaps as a boy, and later served as a senior officer (*tribunus militum*) under CONSTANTIUS II in Mesopotamia *c.* 360–1 and commanded a division of spearmen for JULIAN. In 362, however, that emperor banished him to Thebes in Egypt because of his Christian allegiance. But JOVIAN recalled him and sent him to help win over the army of Gaul, a task only achieved after disturbances had compelled him to take refuge in the house of a friend. Subsequently, he was given command of a unit of targeteers (*scutarii*), a branch of the household troops.

On the death of Jovian, after the army had marched westwards as far as Nicaea, its commanders, following considerable discussion, decided to appoint Valentinian, then at Ancyra, as his successor. Immediately afterwards, he elevated his brother VALENS to rule in the eastern provinces, while he himself took over the government of the west. There had been divisions of territory between joint emperors before, but this new collegiate arrangement proved definitive and, except for the briefest intermissions, permanent: although the Roman world remained, formally speaking, an indivisible unit, the domination of the Mediterranean by one single power, which had lasted for so many centuries, was in fact at an end. The western Empire consisted of Roman Europe (with the exception of Thrace), together with north Africa as far as, and including, Tripolitana. Valentinian selected this western sphere for himself because, although it disposed of smaller resources, its frontiers were in far greater external peril. For the same reason he chose, like some of his forerunners, to reside not at Rome but at Mediolanum, in closer touch with the danger zone.

Indeed, very soon after his accession Valentinian was plunged into a series of grave military emergencies. First of all, the Alamanni broke over the Rhine, capturing the key fortress of Moguntiacum. But they suffered three defeats from Roman armies, commanded by Valentinian's influential Master of Horse, Flavius Jovinus. The emperor himself, after setting up his head-quarters at Lutetia, transferred it in 367 to Ambiani (Samarobriva) in order to direct cross-Channel operations in Britain, which had been invaded by Saxons from the continent and by Picts from the north. Later in the same year, however, he moved once again, establishing himself at Treviri; and from there he marched up the valley of the River Neckar and won a fierce battle in the Black Forest. He continued to reside in German lands for seven years, building a complex system of fortifications on the Rhine and a fortress at Basilia. He also did his best to divide the various German peoples by enlisting the help of the Burgundians, who were hereditary enemies of the Alamanni. At the same time, numerous Germans continued to secure admission within the boundaries of the Empire as settlers.

However, in 374 an easterly section of the frontier in Raetia was breached when a host of their compatriots, together with Sarmatians, erupted across the Danube. In the following year Valentinian took up his residence at Sirmium on the River Save, and reconstructed the strong-points on the Danube, which he crossed in order to devastate the German territory on the north bank. Later in the same year the insolent attitude of delegates from the German tribe of the Quadi, who came to interview him at Brigetio, so greatly enraged him that he broke a blood-vessel and died.

Valentinian I had made huge efforts to strengthen the army. He was likewise, according to Ammianus, 'the first to magnify the importance of the soldiers by increasing their status and property, to the disadvantage of the common interest'; for instance, it was he who presented them with agricultural stock and seeds and equipment, permitting them, in their spare time, to double as farmers and land-workers (who were difficult to find). This was regarded as over-indulgent by the senatorial class, which, in any case, resented its own political eclipse by the army; but in fact the soldiers had never been paid on a very lavish scale, and the changes inaugurated by Valentinian I merely served to raise their earnings towards a tolerable level.

Nevertheless, in order to pay for these increased military costs, more oppressive taxes had to be imposed on the general public than ever before: for example, Sextus Claudius Petronius Probus, the much criticized praetorian prefect in Italy, Illyricum and Africa, resorted to very severe impositions. Towards the end of the reign, in particular, taxation increased steeply. Yet Valentinian remained reluctant to take measures of this kind, unless they seemed absolutely necessary, and sought to allow the provincials whatever financial relief was possible. Indeed, certain of his measures reflected a genuine and profound concern for the well-being of the underprivileged classes; thus he endeavoured to ensure that tax concessions should no longer be accorded to favoured persons.

Moreover, with the same aims in mind, during the years 368–70 he appointed functionaries known as Defenders of the People, whose office was designed to assist the less prosperous members of the community. In each and every town of the western Empire, the praetorian prefect of the region was required to appoint such a Defender, and Valentinian himself required that all their names should be made known to him personally. They were empowered to deal with grievances, whenever possible, without reference to higher authority, and it was their task to ensure that the poor got fair treatment in all respects. Earlier rulers had experimented along similar lines, but it was Valentinian I who developed such experiments into a comprehensive scheme. As a Danubian soldier from outside the magic social circle, he was partly motivated by a strong dislike of the political and financial preponderance of the Roman landowners and senators. Indeed, their influence suffered substantially at his hands, and for a time a serious breach opened up between his administration – staffed from the military territories – and the senatorial class.

Like many other emperors before him, Valentinian I intended to establish his own dynasty, turning the army's preference for heredity to the advantage of this scheme. Thus in 367 he promoted his elder son GRATIAN to be his fellow Augustus in the west, and took pains to stage a ceremony that was wholly military in character, at which he commended the young man to the troops, declaring that his promotion was taking place 'by my will and that of our fellow-soldiers'. This attempt to create a new ruling house, with army backing, was to prove exceptionally successful, for the new dynasty lasted for no less than ninety-one years – one of the longest of such sequences in imperial history, and an impressive example of continuity in such a turbulent period.

Valentinian inherited a religious situation in which Christianity and paganism were severely at odds. Valentinian, however, although a Christian believer himself, decided in 371 to launch a policy of universal toleration 'never troubling anyone', in the words of Ammianus, 'by ordering him to adopt this or that mode of worship'. Pope Damasus possessed links with the pagan aristocracy which assisted the emperor to overcome the intransigence shown by other churchmen. This was a rare and notable display of broad-mindedness, and, combined with his strong sense of duty to the lower classes, entitles Valentinian to rank as a ruler of outstanding vision. Moreover, he was a fiercely energetic administrator, and an excellent soldier.

His qualities were not always appreciated by writers such as Ammianus, who echoed the values and criticisms of the senatorial class and felt little sympathy for a family, like Valentinian's, brought up to drink the wretched barley-wine of its native Danubian province. Yet the emperor had received a considerable education, and was a painter and sculptor of some merit. However, his character, as summed up by Ammianus, presented a disconcerting blend of virtues and faults. 'In the belief', he announces,

that posterity, being free from the constraints of fear and shameful servility, is usually an impartial judge of the past, I will enumerate Valentinian's defects and follow them by an account of his good qualities. He occasionally feigned mildness, though his naturally hot temper made him more prone to severity; he forgot that the ruler of an empire should shun all extremes as he would a precipice. He was never content with a slight punishment, and often ordered a proliferation of bloody trials, in which some people were brought to death's door by grim tortures. His propensity to inflict injury was so excessive that he never commuted the sentence of anyone condemned to death, though even the cruellest of rulers have occasionally done so. . . .

Furthermore, this emperor in his inmost heart was consumed with envy, and, knowing that most vices can generally masquerade as virtues, was apt to say that jealousy is the inseparable associate of the severity inherent in lawful power. Men in supreme positions, believing that they are above the law, are inclined to suspect those who oppose them and to remove from their neighbourhood anyone better than themselves. So Valentinian hated the well-dressed, the educated, the rich, and the highly-born, and disparaged the brave, wishing to monopolize all good qualities himself, a fault which we are told was glaringly apparent in the emperor Hadrian.

This same prince was in the habit of abusing timid persons, calling them dirty rascals for whom no degradation was bad enough. Yet he himself sometimes turned abjectly pale at the thought of imaginary terrors, and was inwardly afraid of non-existent bogeys.

It is fitting to turn next to those of his actions which deserve the approval and imitation of right-thinking men. He treated the provincials indulgently and everywhere lightened the burden of tribute. He met a longstanding need by building towns and fortifying frontiers. He was admirably strict in enforcing military discipline; his only defect was that while he punished even trivial offences in the rank and file he allowed grave faults in their superiors to grow unchecked, and often turned a deaf ear to the complaints brought against them. This led to disturbances in Britain, disaster in Africa, and devastation in Illyricum.

He was entirely chaste in his personal life both at home and abroad, and kept himself unspotted by any taint of obscenity or impurity. In consequence he kept a tight rein on the wantonness of the imperial court, which he was able to control the more easily because he never showed indulgence to his own relations. They were either kept in retirement or given posts of no great importance. The sole exception was his brother, whom the exigencies of the time compelled him to take as his colleague in supreme power.

He was most careful in making appointments to high positions. In his reign no one engaged in finance governed a province, and no office was put up for sale – except in his early days, a period when some crimes are often committed in the hope that the emperor will be too busy to punish them.

In wars both offensive and defensive he showed great skill and caution, being steeled to endure the dust of battle. He was prudent in urging the right course and deprecating the reverse, and he kept a keen eye on all ranks in the service. He wrote a good hand, was an accomplished painter and modeller, and invented new weapons. His memory was good and his speech vigorous, though it seldom approached eloquence. He loved elegant simplicity and took pleasure in tasteful but not profuse entertainments.

His frame was strong and muscular, and he had gleaming hair and a high complexion. His eyes were grey, with a stern sidelong glance. He was of a good height and perfectly well-built, and all in all presented a splendid figure as an emperor.

Valentinian's first wife was Marina Severa, the mother of Gratian; then he married Justina, who bore him another son (VALENTINIAN II) and three daughters.

VALENS
364–78

VALENS (Flavius Julius) (emperor in the east) (364–78) was the second son of Gratianus the elder of Cibalae in Pannonia, and was born in about 328. Under JULIAN and JOVIAN he served as a member of the household guard (*protector domesticus*), but his early career does not seem to have prospered. When his elder brother VALENTINIAN I became emperor, he initially appointed Valens to be the director of his stable with the rank of tribune, but very soon afterwards, at Sirmium, declared him joint emperor instead, with the east as his sphere, thus taking a decisive step towards the separation of the western and eastern (Byzantine) Empires.

The wife of Valens, Albia Domnica, who presented him with three children, was the daughter of a certain Petronius, a high official who was hated almost as much as his namesake Petronius Probus (see VALENTINIAN I) for his cruelty and avarice. The unpopularity of the new emperor's father-in-law prompted the rebellion of Procopius, a former senior commander who declared himself rival Augustus at Constantinople in 365, securing widespread support. In the following year, however, during a battle against Valens' forces at Nacolea in Phrygia, Procopius' German generals deserted him, and he had to flee, but was betrayed once again and put to death. Next Valens turned to face the Visigoths. They had sent assistance to the pretender and were now threatening to invade the eastern Empire's Danubian provinces; but in 367 and 369 Valens crossed the river and ravaged Visigothic territory. For the next seven years he was occupied in the east. First he had to suppress a conspiracy of Theodorus, a notary of the second rank, at Antioch in 371–2; then, declaring himself senior Augustus after his brother's death, he renewed the struggle against the Persians, gaining a victory in Mesopotamia which was not, however, conclusive enough to prevent an unsatisfactory peace in 376.

In that year the Visigoths burst into the eastern Empire in alarming numbers. Hitherto there had been two large Gothic states in eastern Europe, the Ostrogoths ('bright Goths') in the Ukraine, and the Visigoths ('wise Goths') centred upon what is now Rumania. But the frightening horsemen of the Huns had overrun the territories of both these peoples, destroying the Ostrogothic kingdom and driving two hundred thousand Visigoths before them across the Danube into the Empire of Valens, whose governors permitted them to settle. However, these new Visigothic settlers protested, with ample justification, that they were being exploited and oppressed by the east Roman administration, and in consequence they broke into open revolt. Under the leadership of their chieftain Fritigern, they ravaged the Balkan peninsula, while at the same time further waves of German invaders erupted across the Danube behind them.

Valens hastened from Asia to confront the crisis, and after an initial success by his general Sebastianus (at Beroe Augusta Trajana in Thrace) moved to the attack near Hadrianopolis in 378. No assistance came from his fellow-emperor Gratian; it was variously asserted afterwards, by easterners and westerners respectively, that Gratian (who was in ill-health – and resented his uncle's claim to be senior Augustus) deliberately delayed, or that Valens had joined battle so quickly on purpose, so that his colleague would not have time to arrive and share the credit. Be that as it may, Valens, whose generalship seems to have been incompetent, moved against the Visigoths with premature haste; they reacted by launching a successful mounted onslaught against his flank, and gained a crushing victory. The Romans' cavalry were routed, and their infantry suffered total annihilation. Valens himself evidently perished in the battle, but his body was never found. Saint Ambrose saw the catastrophic battle as 'the massacre of all humanity, the end of the world'; and indeed it foreshadowed the termination, or transformation, of the ancient Mediterranean political structure and way of life at the hands of the Germans – though in fact it turned out that the western, and not the eastern, Empire was destined for demolition.

Valens' religious policy had by no means shared his brother's toleration, since he was a determined Arian who launched persecutions against the Catholic Church, even putting some of its members to death. He also exiled certain Catholic bishops, although public outcry soon compelled him to recall their eminent leader Athanasius to his see at Alexandria, and eventually he let others, too, return to their posts. Catholics such as the historian Sozomen saw his death in battle as divine retribution for his Arian sympathies.

The most important monument of his reign was the great aqueduct he started to build in 368 to serve the needs of Constantinople, completing a project initiated by CONSTANTINE THE GREAT and utilizing stones from the walls of Chalcedon – a city that had been involved in the rebellion of Procopius. This majestic work, of which a portion still remains, spanned the valley between two of the city's hills, carrying water to an extensive reservoir, the Nymphaeum Majus.

Ammianus offered a comprehensive analysis of Valens' somewhat complicated character.

He was a faithful and reliable friend, and repressed ambitious intrigues with severity. He maintained strict discipline in the army and the civil service, and took particular care that no one should gain preferment on the score of kinship with himself. He was extremely slow both to appoint and to remove officials. In his dealings with the provinces he showed great fairness, protecting each of them as he would his own house. He was especially concerned to lighten the burden of tribute, and allowed no increases in taxation. He was mild in his assessment of what was due, and a harsh and bitter enemy of embezzlers and of officials detected in corrupt practices. In matters of this kind no emperor is more kindly remembered in the east. He also combined liberality with economy; of this one example out of the many available will suffice. Courts always contain people eager to enrich themselves at the expense of others. When anyone put in a claim to lapsed property or something of that kind he drew a clear line between right and wrong, and gave anyone who wished to protest an opportunity to state his case. If he allowed the claim he often added the names of three or four absentees as sharers in the grant. As a result men of restless greed behaved with more restraint, seeing that the profit they had their eye on was diminished by this device. . . .

He was insatiable in the pursuit of wealth, and unwilling to endure fatigue, though he affected enormous toughness. He had a cruel streak, and was something of a boor, with little skill in the arts of either war or peace. He was quite willing to gain advantages for himself from the sufferings of others, and his behaviour was particularly intolerable when he construed ordinary offences as *lèse-majesté*. Then his rage could be satisfied only by blood and the spoliation of the rich. What was also unendurable was that, although he pretended to leave all suits and trials to the operation of the law, and put their investigation into the hands of judges appointed for the purpose, he in fact allowed nothing to be done contrary to his own pleasure. In other ways too he was unjust and passionate, always ready to lend an ear to the charges of informers without sifting truth from falsehood. This is a shameful fault, and greatly to be dreaded even in private and everyday matters.

He was dilatory and sluggish. His complexion was dark, and the sight of one eye was impaired, though this was not apparent at a distance. He was well-made, neither tall nor short, bow-legged and with a somewhat protruding stomach.

GRATIAN
367–83

GRATIAN (Flavius Gratianus) (emperor in the west, 367–75; joint emperor in the west, 375–83), the son of VALENTINIAN I and Marina Severa and grandson of Gratianus the elder, was born at Sirmium in 359. Named consul in 366, he was proclaimed Augustus in the following year – at the age of eight – by his father in a military ceremony at Ambiani. Coins issued in Gratian's name at Arelate hailed him as 'the Glory of the New Age' (GLORIA NOVI SAECVLI).

After Valentinian's death on 17 November of the following year, he was declared sole emperor of the west. However, only five days later his four-year-old brother VALENTINIAN II was proclaimed Augustus at Aquincum, without the knowledge of Gratian and his advisers, who nevertheless accepted the declaration. A struggle for the power behind Gratian's throne followed, in which Theodosius the elder, Master of Horse in the west, and Maximinus, praetorian prefect in Gaul, played prominent parts; but both soon succumbed to their enemies, and were executed in turn. The government was now in the hands of the poet Ausonius, who held the offices of legal minister (*quaestor sacri palatii*) from 375–6, and then praetorian prefect, first in the Gallic provinces and subsequently in Italy and Africa as well. Regarding the ideals of the pagan majority of the senate with some sympathy, Ausonius showed eagerness to establish good relations with that body, which had become alienated in the previous reign; under the new dispensation Danubians were no longer in the ascendancy, and a policy of mildness towards senators was introduced, including amnesties for men under a political cloud. Moreover, when Gratian visited Rome in 376 he took further measures to secure as wide a degree of favour as possible.

But his principal residence was at Treviri, which he used as a base for operations against the Alamanni during the two years that followed. Then Gratian, leading a lightly armed force, moved down along the Danube to

Bononia Malata, Sirmium and Castra Martis (a small town in Dacia Ripensis, formerly Upper Moesia), where, while suffering from an intermittent fever, he lost a few men in a skirmish with the Sarmatian Alans. On learning that VALENS was confronting a large Visigothic army at Hadrianopolis, he sent word that he would soon be there to help him, but either through his own fault or that of his eastern colleague failed to arrive in time to prevent the latter's destruction (see VALENS). At Sirmium, in January 379, Gratian raised THEODOSIUS I (his cousin by marriage, and the son of Theodosius the elder) to the rank of Augustus in Valens' place – to govern the east, while he himself presided over the defences of the west – and in the following year they conducted combined operations which resulted in the settlement of Goths and Alans in Pannonia.

In winter 382/3 Gratian resided for a considerable period at Mediolanum, whose Bishop Ambrose had already for the past four years exerted an ever-increasing influence over the youthful emperor, contradicting the more moderate ideas of Ausonius. From his earliest days Gratian had been a very pious Christian, keenly interested in theological questions, and in 379 he not only proscribed all heresy but dropped the ancient pagan title *pontifex maximus* (chief priest) from his title – the first emperor to take such a step. In addition he withdrew the public funds that had hitherto been devoted to pagan worships. Another profoundly symbolic act was his command that the pagan altar of Victory should be eliminated from the senate-house of Rome, to which it had been restored by JULIAN THE APOSTATE after an earlier removal. This new order, interpreted by the numerous pagan senators as a decisive menace to their traditional faith, prompted them to dispatch a deputation to the emperor, under Quintus Aurelius Symmachus, the leading pagan of the day, but Gratian would not even grant them an interview.

In Raetia, during the year 383, while preparing further operations against the Alamanni, he learnt that MAGNUS MAXIMUS had been proclaimed Augustus by his soldiers in Britain, and had crossed the Channel. Gratian marched hastily to Lutetia to confront him but his troops, jealous of the privileges granted to Alan mercenaries, deserted to the usurper. With a small group of friends Gratian attempted to reach the Alps, but in August 383, at Lugdunum, he met his death, assassinated by Andragathius, a senior officer who was pretending to be one of his supporters.

At the age of seven Gratian had married Constantia, the twelve-year-old posthumous daughter of CONSTANTIUS II. She died in 383 (and their son did not outlive his father). After her death Gratian married a certain Laeta, who outlived him by more than twenty years. He was an agreeable and cultivated youth, a fluent orator with a keen interest in literature as well as religion, and Ammianus was impressed by the soldierly campaigning vigour he showed as an eighteen-year-old. He was also kind to his junior colleague Valentinian II. But Gratian's gifts were accompanied by an excessive preoccupation with sport (and the parade-ground) that distracted him from his administrative duties. 'He was a young man of remarkable talent,' concluded the historian, 'eloquent, controlled, warlike and merciful, and seemed likely to rival the best of his predecessors while the down was still spreading over his cheeks. But he had an innate tendency to play the fool which his intimates made no attempt to check, and this seduced him into the frivolous pursuits of the emperor Commodus, though he was never bloodthirsty.'

VALENTINIAN II
375–92

VALENTINIAN II (Flavius Valentinianus) (joint emperor in the west, 375–92) was born in 371 (not 366 as stated by certain authors) at Treviri. He was the son of VALENTINIAN I and Justina, and GRATIAN's younger half-brother. When Valentinian I died in 375, and Gratian was pronounced sole Augustus in the west, the four-year-old Valentinian II was declared his co-emperor by the soldiers at Aquincum; the motive was resentment among the Danubian troops because of the German legions' propensity to decide everything for themselves. The guiding spirits behind his elevation were two of his father's former leading advisers, the German Flavius Merobaudes, infantry commander on the headquarters staff (*magister peditum in praesenti*), and Flavius Equitius, the principal general in the Danubian provinces. Valentinian II, at the time, was a hundred miles away from Aquincum, living with his mother at a country house near Murocincta. After Merobaudes and Equitius had arranged his proclamation they sent his mother's brother Cerealis, director of the royal stable, to the villa, placed Valentinian in a litter and brought him to the camp; and only five days after his father's death he was proclaimed joint Augustus in the west.

It was feared that Gratian would resent this action taken without his permission. However he accepted the situation, and continued to regard the child with affectionate favour, keeping an eye on his education (against the wishes of Justina). The young Valentinian II was allotted, theoretically, a territory comprising Italy, Africa and western Illyricum (the Pannonias). A coin issued by Gratian at Treviri shows the imperial pair seated side by side; but Valentinian II is shown as considerably the smaller of the two, and for the time being the coins issued in his name described him as the 'junior' Augustus. He was still much too young to play an active part when their eastern colleague VALENS, defeated and killed by the Visigoths, was replaced in 379 – at Gratian's instigation – by THEODOSIUS I, and Gratian himself was eliminated by MAGNUS MAXIMUS four years later. Theodosius, fearing for the boy's safety at the usurper's hands, entered into negotiations with Magnus Maximus, who also made an uneasy peace with Valentinian II himself.

Gratian, shortly before his death, had ordered the removal of the altar of Victory from the senate-house. The dispute provoked by this action led to a famous series of appeals launched by the leaders of the two sides, Quintus Aurelius Symmachus and Saint Ambrose, in 384, during the reign of Valentinian II. At this juncture conditions at court seemed more favourable to the pagan cause, because the relations of the youthful emperor's advisers with Ambrose had deteriorated owing to the increasing influence of Justina (an Arian), supported by the Frankish Master of Soldiers, Flavius Bauto. In addition, Symmachus occupied an important power-base as city prefect, while the praetorian prefecture of Italy, Illyricum and Africa was in the hands of a like-minded personage, Vettius Agorius Praetextatus. The argument was conducted with responsible dignity. 'Everyone', declared Symmachus, 'has his own custom, his own religion. The love of habit is great. We ask for the restoration of the cult in its former condition, which has been beneficial to the Roman state for so long. One cannot reach so great a secret by one way alone.' However, this explicit denial of the Christian claim to universality was repudiated by Ambrose, who insisted that the emperor should 'do what he knew would be profitable to his salvation in the sight of God'; and Ambrose was also the man who told Valentinian II: 'if one reads the scriptures, one sees that it is bishops who judge emperors: a good emperor does not spurn the assistance of the Church – he seeks it'. Some counsellors at court, it is true, listened to Symmachus' address with greater sympathy. But under pressure from Ambrose the senate's petition was once more rejected. This had been the pagans' last important public stand; Symmachus resigned his office, and Praetextatus died in the same year. It was at about this time, or soon afterwards, that the magnificent Basilica of St Paul Outside the Walls of Rome was erected (on the site of a church of Constantine) – a huge, lavish replica of St Peter's. Nevertheless, Ambrose's triumph was not complete, for an edict of tolerance towards the Arians was published in 386; Ambrose, however, protested strongly, and his objections were shared by Theodosius I.

The following year Magnus Maximus felt sufficiently emboldened by his control of western Europe to launch a sudden invasion of Italy, where he found the Alpine passes undefended. Valentinian II and his mother fled to

Theodosius' dominions. Theodosius, after overthrowing Maximus, laid aside his grievances against Valentinian II's religious leniency and recognized him as emperor of the west, although in practice (since Theodosius himself stayed in Italy until 391) Valentinian's sphere of action was restricted to Gaul.

At this time he was almost entirely under the influence of Arbogast, an arrogant and overbearing Frank, the idol of the troops, who had been his Master of Soldiers since the death of Bauto in 388. The young emperor, dismayed by Arbogast's power, tried to hand him a letter of dismissal, but the Frank threw it to the ground. Shortly afterwards, on 15 May 392, Valentinian was found dead within his palace at Vienna in southern Gaul. Either he committed suicide or, more probably, he was murdered on the orders of Arbogast; who thereupon made a bid to raise his own nominee, Eugenius, to the throne. At Valentinian's funeral at Mediolanum, Ambrose delivered a eulogistic oration – although the dead youth, in fact, however high-spirited and conscientious, had never reached a mature enough age to enjoy freedom of political action.

THEODOSIUS I
379–95

THEODOSIUS I THE GREAT (Flavius) (joint emperor, 379–92; contested, 392–4; sole emperor, 394–5) was born in 347 at Cauca in north-west Spain. His father, Theodosius the elder, was from 368–9 granted a special field army command, and then became supreme cavalry commander (*magister equitum*), first at imperial headquarters and subsequently in Africa, from 369–75. The future emperor campaigned on his father's staff in Britain in 368, later returning to the continent to fight against the Alamanni. In about 373–4 he was governor of Moesia Prima (Upper Moesia) and conducted operations against the Sarmatians. After his father's conviction for high treason by VALENTINIAN I in 375, followed by his execution by the government of GRATIAN in the following year, the younger Theodosius retired to his Spanish estates. After the battle of Hadrianopolis, however, in which the eastern emperor VALENS lost his life against the Visigoths in 378, Gratian summoned him from Spain to take charge of the Danube front, perhaps in the capacity of Master of Soldiers. After considerable initial successes there, he was raised to the rank of Augustus at Sirmium on 19 January 379.

For the first few years of his reign Theodosius I continued to battle against Visigothic invaders and immigrants; but he failed to expel them and instead, in 382, concluded a treaty with their leaders, accepting them *en bloc* as federates within the imperial borders – the first of a number of German nations to be granted this federate, allied status. By virtue of this novel arrangement they were given lands in Thrace and permitted to live under their own laws and rulers, on the condition that they provided soldiers and farm-workers to the Romans. These men were no longer merely individual recruits but whole tribes under their own chieftains, who recovered from Theodosius an annual sum, in cash and kind, to pay the troops they continued to command as his lieutenants. These Visigothic soldiers serving under the Romans enjoyed very favourable terms, and were permitted, at any time, to withdraw their services, provided that they offered a substitute.

Once introduced, this new federal participation in the army – not only by Germans, but also by the Huns who played a large and helpful part in Theodosius' military establishment – rapidly assumed larger dimensions; and the process gained particular strength because the battles between Theodosius and rival contestants to the throne were fought between forces including numerous German and other non-Roman soldiers. The mobilization of all these foreigners, which thenceforward became a regular and widespread feature of the life of the Empire, incurred severe and widespread censure from Roman critics. Yet since the problem of obtaining other recruits had become so desperate it was probably the most effective practical remedy available; and it provided favourable opportunities for racial partnership – though Roman prejudice and German turbulence meant that these chances were not exploited, despite some Roman leaders, including Theodosius I himself, who found certain German chieftains personally likeable.

Meanwhile, in order to pay for this enlarged Roman army, the laws of Theodosius I, even more than those of Valentinian I, showed a passionate determination to augment the influx of tax revenue by every conceivable means. 'No man', Theodosius pronounced in 383, 'shall possess *any* property that is exempt from taxation.' A torrent of regulations and edicts extended this principle almost to breaking point. For example, tenants could not move from their place of residence without their landlord's consent; for although the private prisons which these landowners sometimes maintained were declared illegal, their tenants were considered 'slaves of the land itself to which they are born', so that anyone who tried to leave was committing a criminal act of theft: 'he is stealing his own person'.

Nor could victims of oppression any longer appeal to Defenders of the

People (see VALENTINIAN I), for Theodosius I cut the ground from under these functionaries by transferring their selection and appointment to city councillors – the very men who were themselves responsible for the collection of taxes. And yet the councillors, too, were liable to be flogged by agents of the central government if they failed to levy taxes with efficiency: when a law of Theodosius exempted them from blows of a whip loaded with lead, his words showed that this was the treatment they had been receiving.

Theodosius did not enjoy a happy relationship with his western colleague Gratian; but Gratian soon met his end, murdered by a usurper from Britain, MAGNUS MAXIMUS, in 383. Magnus Maximus overran Gaul and secured initial recognition from Theodosius, but when in 387 he suddenly invaded Italy that emperor, making skilful use of the German and Hun troops at his disposal, marched west, defeated him at Siscia and Poetovio, and beheaded him at Aquileia. Theodosius remained in Italy for three years but then, under severe pressure, was obliged to evacuate the western extremity of the Upper Danube frontier, and leave it wide open for German occupation. On the other hand the dioceses of Dacia (Upper Moesia) and Macedonia, together with the mint at Thessalonica, were transferred from now onwards – if not a little earlier – from the western to the eastern empire, under the new name of the praetorian prefecture of Illyricum. Thus, thenceforward the European frontier between the western and eastern Empires ran from Sirmium and Singidunum due south to the Adriatic.

Next Theodosius returned to Constantinople, leaving the *de facto* rule of the west in the hands of his German Master of Soldiers, Arbogast. Arbogast tried to assert his independence, creating a puppet western emperor in the person of Flavius Eugenius, a former teacher of Latin grammar and rhetoric who had risen to be the director of an imperial secretariat (*magister scrinii*) and had Frankish support. But Theodosius defeated their army on the River Frigidus in 394 and put Eugenius to death. He was now ruler of the entire Empire, east and west alike. Yet this reunification of the two realms proved transient and fleeting, for five months later, in January 395, Theodosius died.

He had earned the title 'the Great' because of his devout Christianity. At a very early point in his reign, during a grave illness, he accepted baptism. In 380 he pronounced that the faith professed by Pope Damasus and the bishop of Alexandria, based on the Catholic Nicene Creed, was the only true religion. In the following year he ordered that every church should be placed in the hands of Catholic bishops – whose claim to be regarded as Catholics he himself would define. Nevertheless, things did not go altogether smoothly: the one hundred and fifty bishops whom he summoned to a meeting at Constantinople refused to accept his nominee for the patriarchal see of that city, and he had to make another appointment from a short-list which they themselves drew up.

Meanwhile, however, Theodosius was taking severe action against heretics, who from 380 onwards found themselves attacked by a continuous series of repressive laws. One edict actually prohibited the discussion of any religious question whatever – thus endeavouring to deprive the people of one of their favourite pursuits. Manichaeans (dualists accepting the power of Darkness as well as the power of Light), who had already been attacked by Theodosius' predecessors, were classified among those professing heretical faiths, and driven underground; only the Jews were for a time treated with greater liberalism, because the emperor became a friend of their patriarch, Gamaliel VI. Towards the pagans his policy was at first ambiguous. They were not forbidden to offer sacrifice, but divination, on the other hand, was virtually prohibited. Although Theodosius omitted to prevent the destruction of their temples by hostile Christians, he did not at first actually close down any shrines. But in 391 this closure abruptly took place, and every form of pagan worship was banned, under the threat of the direst penalties. In a spirit of deliberate vengeance – sharpened by the revolt of Eugenius, who, although nominally Christian, sympathized with the pagan revival – Theodosius interpreted his role as the exact counterpoint and reversal of the former pagan persecutions of Christians.

These measures were largely prompted by Ambrose, bishop of Mediolanum, who had exercised great influence over Theodosius since 387. In the following year he compelled the emperor to allow the bishop of Nicephorium Callinicum in Mesopotamia, who had burnt down a synagogue, to remain unpunished. He did this by refusing to enact the Mass until the bishop's punishment (and an order to rebuild the synagogue) had been revoked. Then in 390, Theodosius ordered a massacre at Thessalonica to avenge the lynching in the circus of the Illyrian Master of Soldiers, Butheric, who had imprisoned a popular charioteer; but Ambrose refused the emperor communion until he had done penance. These were two historic victories of Church over State. Not surprisingly, the very anti-Christian priest and philosopher Eunapius declared that, under Theodosius I, 'our age has risked being wholly kicked about by jackasses'; and another pagan, Zosimus, looked back upon the emperor's compulsory Christianization of the Empire as the direct cause of the downfall of Rome which followed soon afterwards – being the retribution of the Olympian gods, provoked by the emperor's policy.

Theodosius I was married first, from 376–86, to a fellow-Spaniard, Aelia Flavia Flaccilla (in whose name he issued coins), and then to Galla, one of the sisters of VALENTINIAN II. The offspring of his first marriage included ARCADIUS and HONORIUS (whom he elevated to the rank of Augustus in 383 and 393 respectively). His daughter by his second marriage was Aelia Galla Placidia (born c. 388), who became the wife of Ataulf the Visigoth and then of CONSTANTIUS III.

With his blond hair and aquiline nose, Theodosius cut an elegant figure. But his behaviour veered disconcertingly between opposites – febrile activity and indolent sluggishness, a simple soldierly life and the splendours of the court.

He liked to award grim sentences and punishments, but was equally ready to cancel them and grant pardons; for he liked to please. His knowledge of Roman history was noted and admired. If he made a promise he tried to keep it – and yet, all the same, he could not be trusted as a friend or a leader. He was also rapacious. And the historian Zosimus (admittedly biased because he was a pagan) deplored his liking for mimes and dancers, and his general addiction to pleasure and luxury; though he admitted that Theodosius, when necessary, could prove capable. His rule brought a Spanish group, linked with the aristocracy of southern Gaul, into the most powerful positions.

MAGNUS MAXIMUS 383–8

MAGNUS MAXIMUS (rival emperor in the west, 383–8) came from a poor Spanish family, perhaps living in Callaecia and related to (or dependent upon) the house of THEODOSIUS I, under whose father of the same name he served in Britain in 369. He also fought in Africa against the rebellion of Firmus from 373–5. Later he became commander-in-chief (*comes*) in the provinces of Britain, where he operated successfully against the Picts and Scots. But the troops of the British garrisons were dissatisfied with the régime of GRATIAN, who occupied the western throne at the time, and instead proclaimed their allegiance to Magnus Maximus, who accepted their call (reopening the mint of Londinium).

Gratian moved up to Lutetia on the way to confront him, but his troops deserted, and after retreating to Lugdunum he was overtaken by the usurper's cavalry commander (*magister equitum*) Andragathius, and put to death. With the support of Flavius Merobaudes, Master of Infantry in the west, Magnus Maximus extended his territorial possessions to the German frontier and Spain, establishing his capital at Treviri. He also entered into negotiations with the emperors VALENTINIAN II and Theodosius I, in both cases with successful results; for Valentinian II, reluctantly, acknowledged his *coup*, and Theodosius, anxious for Valentinian's safety and preoccupied with his own eastern frontier, felt obliged to do the same. Meanwhile Maximus, for his part, assumed the name Flavius as a link with the imperial house.

He was an orthodox Catholic who took his religious duties very seriously; for example, sanctions against the dualist Manichaeans (see THEODOSIUS I) were vigorously resumed. Indeed, they led to a tragedy. Its victim was Priscillian, a Hispano-Roman layman whose discourses attracted a substantial following. Although he proclaimed himself a Christian, and even secured election to the bishopric of Abula, his extreme, ascetic dualist contempt for our sordid physical existence caused the hierarchy to suspect him of Manichaean allegiance. In 384, therefore, Priscillian found himself condemned by a Church synod at Burdigala. When he appealed to Maximus, an additional accusation, involving witchcraft, was brought against him at Treviri, and on this charge, despite protests from the great churchman Saint Martin of Tours (Caesarodunum) he was found guilty and put to death. As far as we know this was the first Christian execution of a man for his religious beliefs. The condemnation also created an ominous precedent for future handings-over of supposed heretics to the secular power, in contradiction to Martin's opinion that both Church and State should occupy themselves with their own affairs. Nor was Martin the only protester, since Priscillian's accusers were excommunicated by Pope Siricius and Bishop Ambrose of Mediolanum. As for Maximus himself, he displayed hostility not only to heresy but to classical paganism as well, accepting the suggestion of his brother Marcellinus that a fine should be inflicted on supporters of the pagan leader Symmachus. On the other hand, despite Ambrose's disapproval, he ordered the rebuilding of a Jewish synagogue that had burnt down.

In 387 Maximus promoted his infant son Flavius Victor to be his fellow Augustus, and to celebrate the dynastic occasion the mint of Treviri issued coinage in the child's honour, depicting him seated with his father, and reviving a traditional assurance that they were 'Born for the Good of the State' (BONO REIPVBLIC[a]E NATI). In summer of the same year, leaving Victor behind in Gaul, Maximus suddenly invaded Italy, crossing the Alpine passes unopposed but meanwhile offering conciliatory gestures to his fellow-emperors. However, Theodosius I, to whom Valentinian II fled to escape capture, was ready to counter-attack in the following year. While Maximus himself remained at Aquileia, his army, under the command of Andragathius, advanced into Illyricum. The imperial troops however did not desert to him in the numbers he had hoped for, and he suffered a reverse in the neighbourhood of Siscia. His brother Marcellinus succeeded in rallying the army, but it was decisively defeated again at Poetovio on the Drave. Maximus threw himself on Theodosius' mercy, but this did not save him from the capital penalty. Nor was his son Victor, captured by Arbogast, allowed to survive.

Theodosius pronounced that Maximus' reign had constituted an illegal usurpation, and that all measures taken by his government were consequently null and void. Some modern authorities, however, have described him as an able and far-sighted ruler.

ARCADIUS
395–408

ARCADIUS (Flavius) (emperor in the east, 395–408), was born in Spain in about 377. He was the eldest son of THEODOSIUS I THE GREAT and Aelia Flavia Flaccilla; his father proclaimed him Augustus in 383. His education was entrusted first to his mother, then to the deacon Arsenius, and finally to a famous pagan man of letters, Themistius. When Theodosius I set out in 394 to suppress the usurper Eugenius, he left Arcadius as the titular head of the government in Constantinople.

Theodosius died the following year, and the eighteen-year-old Arcadius succeeded him on the eastern throne, while his brother HONORIUS took titular charge of the west. This division proved a decisive event. Although the Roman world had sometimes, on earlier occasions, been divided into two territorial spheres, one of the emperors had generally been regarded as senior to the other – so that a certain measure of unity could be preserved. But the pressing political and military circumstances of the new age meant that this was no longer likely to be possible: by then, each of the two governments was more likely to go its own way. It is true that the legislation promulgated by the eastern and western emperors alike was still supposed to apply to his colleague's realm as well, and that each issued numerous coins with the name and head of that colleague. Yet the new division was more real than any previous sharing of the power, and, indeed, political relations between the two administrations were often severely strained. It is a matter of opinion when one should date the replacement of 'the eastern Roman Empire' by the concept of 'the Byzantine Empire', but many have regarded Arcadius as the first Byzantine ruler.

However, the real ruler of the east was not the youthful Arcadius himself but Flavius Rufinus, a shoe-maker's son from Aquitania who had been Praetorian

Prefect of the east for the past three years. True, he did not succeed in his plan to marry his only daughter to Arcadius, for the young man was instead persuaded to marry Aelia Eudoxia, the daughter of the Frankish general Bauto and protégée of the bald old eunuch Eutropius, who held the post of court chamberlain (*praepositus sacri cubiculi*). So Rufinus was not quite supreme at the court of Constantinople. Yet he enjoyed a position of great power. He was an enthusiastic Christian, who passed severe laws against pagans, heretics and adulterers, and founded a monastery on his estate near Chalcedon.

Rufinus also gained a name for unscrupulous ambition and avarice. As for his political designs, they brought him into sharp collision with Stilicho, who had been left by Theodosius to direct the affairs of Arcadius' ten-year-old brother Honorius in the west – and claimed that the late emperor had requested him to exercise some powers of supervision or guardianship over Arcadius as well. This suggestion, however, was entirely distasteful to Rufinus, and conflict between the two ministers proved impossible to avoid. It was brought to a head by the Visigoths whom Theodosius I had settled in the provinces now known as Dacia, bounded by the Danube to the north and the Balkan (Haemus) mountains to the south. Under the leadership of Alaric, these settlers now rebelled, devastating Macedonia and Achaea. The personal property of Rufinus, however, was mysteriously spared by the assailants, and the western poet, Claudian, declared that he had treacherously withdrawn his troops; easterners on the other hand believed that Stilicho had deliberately diverted the barbarians from the west, setting them against the east.

Whether or not this was true, Stilicho was certainly eager to readjust the borders between the two Empires fixed by Theodosius I. His aim was to recover the prefecture of Illyricum, so rich in manpower, for the west, which would have meant reoccupying the Balkan peninsula and leaving the eastern Empire virtually nothing in Europe except Thrace. So Stilicho marched into northern Greece – ostensibly to confront Alaric's Visigoths; but Rufinus, acting for Arcadius, resented his interference and peremptorily commanded him to withdraw. This order, to the surprise of many, Stilicho obeyed, leaving his Gothic general Gainas behind, in charge of some legions which were due to be restored to Arcadius. Gainas marched to Constantinople, where he and his troops were met and saluted by Arcadius and Rufinus. At the meeting Rufinus, as his enemies subsequently noted, was more sumptuously dressed than his master, and expected to be created Augustus on the spot. Instead, however, he was attacked, and stabbed to death. It is almost certain that this act was instigated by Stilicho, with or without the complicity of Gainas; indeed, Claudian publicly congratulated Stilicho on the murder. Yet it created a fatal breach in the unity between the eastern and western Empires.

Eutropius then took over Rufinus' post as the most influential minister in the east. He kept Arcadius' praetorian prefects under close and suspicious control. But any hopes of collaboration with the western Empire that might at

10 The Provinces of the
Two Empires, AD 395

Abbreviations

FLAVIA CAES.	FLAVIA CAESARIENSIS
MAXIMA CAES.	MAXIMA CAESARIENSIS
NARB.	NARBONENSIS
FLAMINIA et P.ANN.	FLAMINIA et PICENUM ANNONARIUM
PICENUM SUB.	PICENUM SUBURBICARIUM
NORICUM RIP.	NORICUM RIPENSE
NORICUM MED.	NORICUM MEDITERRANEUM
DACIA RIP.	DACIA RIPENSIS
DACIA MED.	DACIA MEDITERRENEA
MAURET. SITIF.	MAURETANIA SITIFENSIS
AM.	ALPES MARITIMAE
APeG	ALPES POENINAE et GRAIAE
PHRYGIA P.	PHRYGIA PACATANIA
PHRYGIA S.	PHRYGIA SALUTARIS
GALATIA S.	GALATIA SALUTARIS

VALENTIA

BRITANNIA II

FLAVIA CAES.

BRITANNIA I

MAXIMA CAES.

BRITANNIA I

Rhine

GERMANIA II

GERMANIA I

BELGICA II

Treviri •

LUGDUNENSIS II

LUGDUNENSIS III

BELGICA I

Danube

RAETIA II

NORICUM RIP.

LUGDUNENSIS SENONIA

MAXIMA SEQUANORUM

RAETIA I

NORICUM MED.

AQUITANIA I

LUGDUNENSIS I

APeG

LIGURIA

VENETIA et HISTRIA

CALLAECIA

NOVEM POPULI

AQUITANIA II

Rhône

VIENNENSIS

AM.

ALPES COTTIAE

• Mediolanum

AEMILIA

FLAMINIA et PICENUM

TARRACONENSIS

NARB. I

Arelate

NARB. II

TUSCA et UMBRIA

VAL.

LUSITANIA

CORSICA

Rome

SAMNIUM

CAMPANIA

CARTHAGINENSIS

APULIA et CALABRIA

BAETICA

SARDINIA

LUCANIA et BRUTII

BALEARES

TINGITANA

Carthage •

MAURETANIA CAESARENSIS

MAURET SITIF.

AFRICA

SICILIA

NUMIDIA

BYZACIUM

TRIPOLITANA

━━●━━ Imperial boundary

━ ━ ━ Boundary between Eastern and Western Empires

------- Provincial boundaries

0   100   400
|_____|_____| miles
     100   600   km

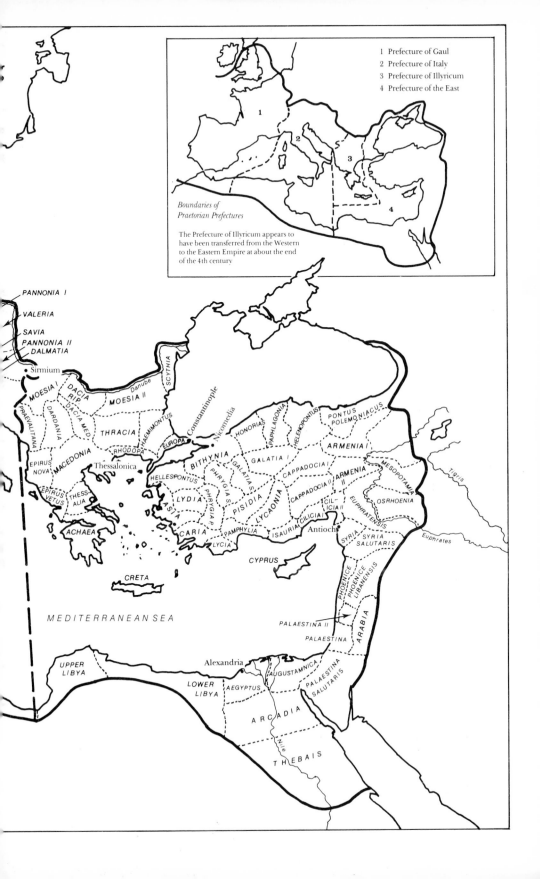

1 Prefecture of Gaul
2 Prefecture of Italy
3 Prefecture of Illyricum
4 Prefecture of the East

*Boundaries of
Praetorian Prefectures*

The Prefecture of Illyricum appears
to have been transferred from the Western
to the Eastern Empire at about the end
of the 4th century

PANNONIA I

VALERIA

SAVIA
PANNONIA II
DALMATIA

• Sirmium

MOESIA I
DACIA RIP.
DARDANIA
DACIA MED.
MOESIA II
SCYTHIA
Danube

PRAEVALITANA
THRACIA
HAEMIMONTUS
RHODOPA
EUROPA

EPIRUS
NOVA
MACEDONIA
Thessalonica

EPIRUS
VETUS
THESS-
ALIA

ACHAEA

Constantinople
Nicomedia

BITHYNIA
HONORIAS
PAPHLAGONIA
HELLESPONTUS
PONTUS
POLEMONIACUS

ARMENIA I

GALATIA I
GALATIA SAL.
CAPPADOCIA I
ARMENIA
II
MESOPOTAMIA

Tigris

HELLESPONTUS
PHRYGIA S.
PISIDIA
LYCAONIA
CAPPADOCIA II
CIL-
ICIA II
EUPHRATENSIS
OSRHOENIA

LYDIA
PHRYGIA P.

ASIA
CARIA
PAMPHYLIA
ISAURIA CILICIA I
Antioch
SYRIA
SYRIA
SALUTARIS
Euphrates

LYCIA

CYPRUS

CRETA

MEDITERRANEAN SEA

PHOENICE
PHOENICE
LIBANENSIS

PALAESTINA II
ARABIA

PALAESTINA

Alexandria

UPPER
LIBYA

LOWER
LIBYA
AEGYPTUS
AUGUSTAMNICA
PALAESTINA
SALUTARIS

ARCADIA

Nile

THEBAIS

first have been entertained were very soon to vanish once again. First, when the east, after all, invited Stilicho to renew his intervention against Alaric in Greece in 397, he mysteriously allowed the Visigoth to escape from his grasp. Shocked by this inexplicable behaviour, Eutropius declared the western general a public enemy; yet at the same time he himself felt it necessary to appease Alaric by appointing him Master of Soldiers in the Balkans – a step which caused considerable consternation in the west.

In the same year, a fresh cause for mutual embitterment between the two Empires was provided by the provinces of north Africa, where an uprising broke out. Its leader was Gildo, who, although the brother of an earlier rebel Firmus, had been made the principal military commander in the area. Gildo proceeded to revolt against the western government, declaring his allegiance to Arcadius instead. This presented a catastrophic prospect for the west, for Africa was the source of Rome's principal grain supply. Eutropius, on the other hand, connived with the rebel, thus incurring violent personal abuse from Claudian, who deplored the elevation of a eunuch to such a position, and urged Stilicho to launch a military onslaught upon the régime at Constantinople. Stilicho however did not act openly, preferring a more surreptitious form of subversion; for the overthrow and banishment of Eutropius which followed in 399 can confidently be ascribed to his agency, or indirect support.

The eastern government now came into the hands first of Gainas, in 400, for six months, and then of Arcadius' forceful and impulsive wife Aelia Eudoxia, who was proclaimed Augusta. In the following year she felt strong enough to retaliate against Stilicho. It was now, with her encouragement, that Alaric transferred his hostile activities from the eastern to the western Empire, and even appeared within the borders of Italy itself. Eudoxia had good reason to damage Stilicho in this way, for she detected his ambition to retake Illyricum. In 405 and 406 this design was momentarily interrupted by German invasions; but in the following year Stilicho actually made the final plans for an invasion of the Balkan provinces, instructing Alaric to occupy the Greek sea-coast on behalf of Honorius. But once more his project had to be postponed, this time owing to a rebellion in Britain.

During these years the outstanding development in the eastern capital had been the clash between the personalities of the empress Aelia Eudoxia and Saint John Chrysostom ('golden-mouthed'), the uncompromising bishop, or patriarch, of Constantinople. Concerned with people's practical behaviour rather than with theological niceties, John passionately attacked the rich and powerful, and Eudoxia soon felt that her own luxurious living was the real target of much of his invective. They became sufficiently reconciled for the bishop to perform the baptism of her and Arcadius' son, THEODOSIUS II, in 401, but the following year she objected strongly to a violent sermon he preached against women, during which she was implicitly compared to Jezebel, the supreme villainess of the Bible. Under her influence, John's numerous enemies succeeded in prompting the eastern emperor to establish a commission to enquire into charges against his conduct. The commission condemned and deposed him, and Arcadius pronounced his banishment. John left for Asia Minor in 403, but not before specifically identifying the empress with Jezebel or Herodias in a further sermon. He and Eudoxia were once more persuaded to mend their relations, and he was able to return, but not for long. Soon, in 404, John went into exile once again, and it was learnt that he had died after spending three years in remote places.

Eudoxia, meanwhile, had also succumbed – to a miscarriage; and thus Arcadius' government passed into the hands of his praetorian prefect of the east, Anthemius, who was raised to the rank of patrician. Anthemius directed the suppression of Isaurian brigands in the southern and eastern provinces of Asia Minor; and he had to keep a watchful eye on Alaric and Stilicho.

In 408 Arcadius died a natural death. He had done little to make himself known to the people, although crowds had flocked to see him, according to the church historian Socrates Scholasticus, on one of the rare occasions when he had appeared in the streets. Another ecclesiastical chronicler, Philostorgius, mentions his dusky complexion, and describes him as a short and thin young man of unimpressive appearance. His heavy-lidded, somnolent eyes reflected a sluggish, stupid personality. His public life, therefore, amounted to little more than the careers of the persons who successively directed his government. Yet the fact that the throne, upon his death, passed without a hitch to his seven-year-old son Theodosius II – who had already been nominated Augustus at the age of one – was a remarkable tribute to the prolonged stability of the dynasty to which they belonged.

HONORIUS
395–423

HONORIUS (Flavius) (emperor in the west, 395–423) was born in 383, the second son of THEODOSIUS I THE GREAT and Aelia Flavia Flaccilla. He was promoted to the rank of Augustus at Constantinople in 393, and when his father died two years later, he became emperor in the west, while his elder brother Arcadius assumed the same position in the east.

Since Honorius was only twelve, the effective rulership of the west devolved upon his enigmatic Master of Soldiers, Flavius Stilicho, half-Vandal, half-Roman, who was married to the boy-ruler's cousin Serena: their daughter Maria became the wife of Honorius himself in 395. Stilicho's exceptional talent and energy failed, in the long run, to save the Roman Empire, because of two features of his policy. In the first place, he behaved in a cool and finally hostile manner towards the rulers of the eastern Empire, because he wanted to seize from them the Balkan territories (the prefecture of Illyricum) which Theodosius I had taken over (see ARCADIUS). In the pursuit of this aim, Stilicho even had Arcadius' principal minister and praetorian prefect Rufinus assassinated. The second, and related, damaging aspect of Stilicho's conduct was his unwillingness to maintain a sufficiently formidable opposition to his German compatriots, the Visigoths, and Alaric, their able leader from 395 to 410. In 397, after Stilicho had accepted the eastern government's plea to repel them in Greece, he let them get away. When they turned against the west in 401 (prompted by Constantinople), he summoned troops from the Rhine and Britain and succeeded in repelling their invasions of Italy during the two years that followed. Again, however, Alaric was not prevented from effecting his escape.

This did not deter Honorius from making a triumphal entry into Rome, to celebrate the defeat of the Visigoths. Nevertheless he no longer felt that his residence, Mediolanum, was safe from invaders, and in 404 decided to move to Ravenna. Protected by marshes, and easy to escape from by sea, it remained the capital of the western Empire throughout the three-quarters of a century that remained before Italy passed under barbarian control.

But meanwhile another group of German tribes, the Ostrogoths, had been encroaching on the territory of the Middle Danube, driving a large part of the Roman population from the Hungarian plain. In 405 these Ostrogoths and others, under the leadership of Radagaisus, flooded into the Italian peninsula itself, but were overwhelmed by Stilicho at Faesulae. Stilicho next intended to put into effect his longstanding desire to attack the Empire of the east; but his plans were interrupted by the most damaging of all the German invasions of the western provinces that had so far occurred. This took place on the last day of 406 (or over a longer period), when a mixed mass of Vandals, Suevi, Alamanni, Alans and Burgundians crossed the ice of the frozen Rhine. Moguntiacum and Treviri were among the numerous frontier cities that succumbed to them, often almost without a fight; and the invaders then proceeded to fan out across the provinces of Gaul, spreading devastation wherever they went. 'The barriers', declared Edward Gibbon, 'which had so long separated the savage and the civilized nations of the earth, were from that fatal moment levelled to the ground.'

Stilicho, still preoccupied by his hostility towards Constantinople, took few effective measures to stem this tide. Seeing the apparent impotence of the western imperial government, a usurper named CONSTANTINE (III) seized control of Britain, Gaul and parts of Spain, and other similar *coups* followed not long afterwards. Meanwhile, when Alaric demanded four thousand pounds of gold from Honorius, Stilicho compelled an unwilling senate to comply. But soon afterwards, through the machinations of the same senatorial class, which regarded such military chiefs as alien to its interests, he himself was accused of conspiring with Alaric to place his own son Eucherius on the imperial throne. The troops at Ticinum were prompted to mutiny against him, and in 408 he surrendered to Honorius at Ravenna and was put to death. A powerful reaction against the influence of the Germans then followed; there would not be another commander-in-chief of that race in the west for half a century to come. The German soldiers who had served under him, facing a massacre of their wives and children by men belonging to Roman units, went over to Alaric. He for his part, deprived of his lucrative contacts with Stilicho, proceeded to march on Rome, and was only deterred from entering the city by the receipt of another huge bribe, which Honorius and his new chief adviser, Olympius, had reluctantly consented to hand over, after an initial refusal. Then in the following year Alaric approached Rome again, occupied Portus Augusti and compelled the senate to set up a puppet emperor, Priscus Attalus, who issued coins and a huge medallion inscribed 'Unconquerable Eternal Rome' (INVICTA ROMA AETERNA).

The inscription was peculiarly ironic because the next year witnessed the famous and catastrophic fall of Rome to Alaric. Before it happened, the

Visigoth had disowned Attalus, and arranged to have a personal interview with Honorius near Ravenna. But when his camp was attacked by a hostile compatriot, Sarus, Alaric broke off negotiations, suspecting that his assailant had acted with the emperor's knowledge. And so there followed the Visigoths' third and last march on Rome. The gates were treacherously opened to admit them, whereupon Alaric and his soldiers moved in and occupied the ancient city, which had not been captured by a foreign enemy for nearly eight hundred years. Jerome and Augustine were among the many throughout the Roman world who felt appalled, and it was to meet the charge that nothing so awful had ever happened under pagan rule that Augustine wrote *The City of God*. 'Blessed', declared the abbot Gerontius in more practical terms, 'are those who perceived, and sold their property before the arrival of the barbarians.' Nevertheless, although Alaric's soldiers burnt a few buildings and seized some plunder, they did not stay in the city for more than about three days. After that, taking with him the emperor's twenty-year-old half-sister Aelia Galla Placidia, Alaric moved on to the south of the peninsula. His intention was to invade Africa, but before he could do so, at Consentia, he died.

Honorius' dominant military leader during the decade that followed was CONSTANTIUS (III), who soon dealt effectively with usurpers in Gaul. In 414, however, Alaric's successor Ataulf married Galla Placidia at Narbo. But Honorius withheld his consent, and Constantius drove Ataulf into Spain, where he was murdered. His successor Wallia allowed the Romans to take Placidia back, and in recompense was permitted to return with his Visigoths to Gaul, where in 418 they were granted federal status, with Tolosa as their capital.

After the death of Constantius (by now joint-emperor) in 421, Honorius, who had always been fond of his half-sister, displayed his affection by caresses and embraces which, besides causing public scandal, turned her against him. This estrangement prompted skirmishes in the streets of Ravenna between their respective entourages. One of her enemies was Castinus, the Master of Soldiers, who, although he had been heavily defeated by the Vandals in Africa, nevertheless hoped to succeed to Constantius' position. Finally Placidia was exiled from Ravenna, and sought refuge at Constantinople in 423, taking her two children with her, including the infant VALENTINIAN (III). But in the same year the emperor himself was struck down by dropsy and died.

Paradoxically, the reign of the insignificant Honorius witnessed the towering achievements of Saint Augustine, bishop of Hippo Regius, and Saint Jerome. Yet the thinking of the imperial court on the one hand and of the great theologians on the other was not unconnected, because Honorius was very devout; and Augustine for his part finally came to the regrettable conclusion that religious dissidents – first pagans and then heretics – should be made subject to coercion by the State. First, after religious riots had broken out in Africa among the pagans whose shrines had been closed in 399, Augustine joined his fellow-bishops in 401 in asking the government for new laws to 'extirpate the last remnants of idolatry'. Stilicho, although he felt it necessary to burn the Sibylline books, the most sacred documents of paganism, was inclined to favour a certain measure of toleration. But his death was immediately followed by a law excluding pagans from the army. In 407–8 heresy, too, was once again declared a public crime, 'because offences against the divine religion are injuries to the whole of the community'. At the same time, all non-Catholics were excluded from court – although the following year Honorius was compelled to relax these regulations, because it proved impossible to turn out every Arian German. But further threatening edicts very soon followed; and it was at this stage that Augustine, after prolonged meditation, abandoned his earlier tolerance towards heretics, and wrote to Vincentius, bishop of Cartennae, in 408 that they too, like pagans, should be subject to governmental compulsion. Moreover, penal measures were taken against the last of the Jewish patriarchs, Gamaliel VII, in 415.

Since the emperor had by now reached adult years, he presumably played some part in these happenings. It is also legitimate to blame a certain obstinacy in his otherwise soft and gentle character for the failure of the negotiations with Alaric which led to the sack of Rome; perhaps Alaric was even right in supposing that Honorius had incited the treacherous attack on him which caused the talks to be broken off. Honorius was also believed to have tried to assert his will in order to prevent Constantius III from becoming his colleague, but if so, his wishes did not prevail. One detects, in his dealings, a certain tendency to treachery. He was also not very bright. There was even a story, recounted by Procopius, that when he was told Rome had fallen he misunderstood, and concluded that it was his pet cock, which bore the name of Roma, that had succumbed: 'and I was only just feeding him', he remarked.

Many grievous wounds, declared Philostorgius, had been inflicted on the state during Honorius' reign. In particular, the western field army had lost at least half, and perhaps two-thirds, of its total strength in the various military disasters. His own personal contribution to the course of events had been negligible.

CONSTANTINE III
407–11

CONSTANTINE III (Flavius Claudius Constantinus) (rival emperor in the western provinces, 407–11) was a private soldier in Britain; nothing more is known of his origins. In 406 the legions in Britain, discontented with the failure of HONORIUS and Stilicho to protect the island, proclaimed a certain Marcus as emperor, followed after his assassination by the equally unknown pretender Gratianus, who after four months, in 407, suffered a similar fate. They then set up yet another would-be ruler, a soldier named Constantine – the third of that name to wear the purple.

His first act was to cross over to the continent, taking with him a large part of his field army – whose removal contributed greatly, and perhaps terminally, to Britain's detachment from the Empire. Then the legions in the Gallic provinces likewise deserted to Constantine III, and he extended his dominions throughout many parts of that country, evacuated by the representatives of Honorius who fled to Italy. Establishing mints at Arelate (his capital), Lugdunum and Treviri, he guarded the Rhine frontier with considerable efficiency, and won victories over certain of the Germans in Gaul, while arriving at agreements with other German groups. The government of Ravenna sent a force against him commanded by the Visigoth Sarus, who defeated his generals but failed in an attempt to besiege him at Valentia in southern Gaul. But Constantine's son Constans, appointed Caesar and accompanied by a general named Gerontius, moved into Spain and defeated Honorius' forces, establishing his headquarters at Caesaraugusta; before long, however, he was recalled to Gaul and promoted to the rank of Augustus.

Constantine III then sent envoys to Ravenna to demand recognition by Honorius, who felt compelled to agree owing to the proximity of Alaric, and Constantine claimed the consulship of 409 as his colleague. The government of Theodosius II at Constantinople did not follow Honorius' lead, but that did not deter Constantine and Constans from celebrating the 'Victory of the Four

Augusti' (VICTORIA AAAVGGGG.) on their coinage – that is to say, the two central emperors and themselves. Constantine also agreed to help Honorius against Alaric, probably with the intention of seizing Italy for himself if he got the chance; the imperial Master of Cavalry, Hellebich, was suspected of favouring these designs, but Honorius arranged to have him murdered.

Constantine's military chief Gerontius, whom he had left in Spain, was weakened by rivalries among his troops, and could not prevent a large number of Germans (Asling and Siling Vandals, Suevi and Alans) from entering the country. Thereupon Constantine sent his son Constans back to Spain to supersede him. But Gerontius, refusing to accept this dismissal, abandoned his allegiance to Constantine III and in 409 set up an emperor on his own account, an officer cadet (*protector domesticus*) named Maximus, who was possibly his son. At Tarraco (his headquarters) and Barcino, Maximus issued coins which spoke of three Augusti, meaning, presumably, himself and the emperors at Ravenna and Constantinople. Next Gerontius moved into Gaul, where he was joined by German allies who helped him to kill Constans and besiege Constantine III and his second son Julian in Arelate. However, CONSTANTIUS III (representing the government of Honorius) intervened at this point, and forced Gerontius to go back to Spain, where the house in which he had taken refuge from his mutinous troops went up in flames, and he and his Alan squire committed suicide. Maximus was deposed by his own troops but survived to live in exile among the Spaniards. The imperial forces now turned against Constantine III and besieged him in Arelate, which his general Edobich, reinforced by Alamanni and Franks, failed to relieve. Constantine, facing imminent capture, stripped off his imperial purple and fled to a sanctuary, where he hurriedly had himself ordained as a priest. Honorius' commanders guaranteed his safety, and when Arelate surrendered he and his son were sent back to Ravenna. But the emperor, remembering that Constantine had killed certain of his cousins, repudiated the guarantee and in 411 had them executed outside the city. Of Constantine's qualities as a ruler little is known; but the ancient writers described him as wayward and gluttonous.

His death did not mark the end of the western provincial dominion, for it survived briefly, and in an attenuated form, as a puppet state sponsored by the Germans on the Rhine. The titular emperor of this régime was a Gallo-Roman nobleman named Jovinus, who was proclaimed Augustus at Mundiacum near the River Meuse, at the instigation of the Burgundian king Gundahar and a certain Goar, a chieftain of the Alans. Jovinus, describing himself as 'Restorer of the State' (RESTITVTOR REI P*ublicae*), coined at the same mints as Constantine III had employed. Constantius III, who had been commanding the forces of the central government in Gaul, was no longer available to deal with this new pretender, since he had returned to Italy; and the question arose, which side Ataulf and his Visigoths in southern Gaul would take. Ataulf at first seemed not unfavourable to the cause of Jovinus, but became less enthusiastic when his compatriot Sarus, whom he hated, transferred his loyalty to that quarter. Then in 412 Jovinus proclaimed his own brother Sebastianus as his fellow-Augustus, thus further alienating Ataulf, who by now had had enough of such a proliferation of pretenders.

In consequence, Ataulf got in touch with the praetorian prefect in Gaul, Dardanus, who had remained loyal to Honorius, and after an exchange of communications with Ravenna defeated Sebastianus and put him to death. Jovinus fled to the Gallic city of Valentia and was pursued there by Ataulf, so that the town underwent its second siege in only five years. This time it fell to the imperial troops, and Jovinus was captured and taken to Narbo, where Dardanus had him put to death. Authority in Gaul, once again, was now divided between the Ravenna government on the one hand and the various German states and tribes on the other, without the intervention of puppets or usurpers.

THEODOSIUS II
408–50

THEODOSIUS II (emperor in the east, 408–50) was born in 401. He was the son of ARCADIUS and Aelia Eudoxia. In January of the following year his father proclaimed him joint Augustus; and a curious but not impossible story told how Arcadius, fearing that upon his death the boy would be deposed, appointed the Persian king Yezdegerd I as his guardian.

At all events, when Arcadius died in 408 the seven-year-old Theodosius II succeeded peacefully to the eastern throne. He was entrusted to the care of Antiochus, a palace eunuch, but his first regent was Anthemius, whom he had inherited as praetorian prefect. With the assistance of his friend Troilus, a pagan sophist of Side who had become prominent in the literary circles of the capital, Anthemius ruled with energetic efficiency. Faced immediately with a serious shortage of grain, which caused the infuriated population of Constantinople to burn down the city prefect's house, he adopted useful measures to improve both short-term and long-term supplies. Good relations with the court of Ravenna, facilitated by Stilicho's death, were firmly established. A new treaty was arranged with the Persians, and tax arrears in the eastern provinces were cancelled. The relief of the Danubian and Illyrian cities, ruined by the Visigoths, received careful attention. An invasion of Moesia by Uldin, King of the Huns, was repelled, and a very large number of German prisoners of the war (members of the tribe of the Sciri, in Uldin's employment) were transferred to landowners in Asia Minor to work on the soil.

Steps were also taken to provide against future Hun or German invasions. To this end, the fleet stationed on the Danube was substantially improved and increased. Above all – after noting how Rome had fallen to Alaric – Anthemius fortified the city of Constantinople itself. CONSTANTINE THE GREAT had built a wall round his new foundation, but by this time the eastern capital had far outgrown those original limits. So in 413 the new Wall of Theodosius was constructed, extending from the Propontis to the Golden Horn; and this was the outstanding achievement of Anthemius' tenure of power.

In 414, however, the emperor's sister Aelia Pulcheria, although only two years older than himself, was proclaimed Augusta and assumed the regency in the place of Anthemius, of whom we hear no more. He was succeeded as praetorian prefect by a functionary named Aurelianus, who evidently became Pulcheria's principal adviser. She also dismissed Antiochus from his post as tutor to her brother, to whom, it was said, she thenceforward gave personal instruction in deportment. Soon after her assumption of her new responsibilities, serious religious rioting broke out at Alexandria, where Hypatia, a pagan woman famous for her philosophical learning, was lynched by a band of Christian lay brethren. Cyril, patriarch of Alexandria, was believed to have been involved, but his influence at Pulcheria's court prevented the commissioner whom she sent to investigate the matter from producing a satisfactory report.

For Pulcheria was, above all else, a devoted Christian. Such was her asceticism that she decided to remain chaste, and induced her sisters Arcadia and Marina to make the same resolve, with the encouragement of their spiritual counsellor the patriarch Atticus, who wrote a eulogy of the virgin state for their benefit. Evidently Theodosius, on the other hand, had to marry, and it was Pulcheria who arranged his wedding to Athenais, daughter of the Athenian sophist Leontius, in 421. The bride was baptized under the name of Aelia Eudocia and was proclaimed Augusta two years later. Coinage was issued in her name, as it had already been issued for Pulcheria. Aelia Eudocia gave birth to a daughter Licinia Eudoxia (who subsequently became the wife of VALENTINIAN III) and to a son (who died young). She was also a versatile author: her works ranged from a poem celebrating a military victory over the Persians to a paraphrase of the prophecies attributed to Daniel and Zechariah.

In about 416, when he was fifteen years of age, Theodosius II was declared to have attained his majority. But for a considerable time thereafter Pulcheria still presided over the government, assisted by Monaxius, who succeeded Aurelianus as praetorian prefect. The principal event of the ensuing years was the decision of the government to place the emperor's boy cousin, Valentinian III, on the western throne, and this was duly achieved in 425. As a preliminary, the eastern authorities had occupied Salonae in Dalmatia, thus making it clear that they wanted that country (and its hinterland) back from the west as a *quid pro quo*; and this was later arranged. Meanwhile, once Valentinian had been established at Ravenna, Theodosius II himself set out for Italy to crown him with his own hand. But he fell ill at Thessalonica so that Helion, his Master of Offices (*magister officiorum*), had to act as his deputy.

In the same year a decisive step was taken to provide Constantinople with a university. Constantine the Great had founded a school in the Stoa, and CONSTANTIUS II transferred it to the Capitol. JULIAN THE APOSTATE attached a valuable public library to its premises. Now Theodosius II created Chairs for ten Greek and ten Latin grammarians or philologists, five Greek and three Latin rhetoricians, two jurists and a philosopher. The preponderance of Greek over Latin rhetoricians marked a stage in the gradual process by which the official language of the eastern Empire was changing from Latin to Greek.

The outstanding event of the reign, however, was the compilation of the Latin Theodosian Code of laws, which was drawn up by order of the eastern emperor and published in 438, after eight years' labours, in association with his colleague Valentinian III. The Code, which consists of sixteen books, contains a collection of imperial enactments extending back for more than a century. It played a great part in supplying the foundation for the Code of Justinian which followed a century later; and it also exerted a vast influence upon the legislation of the rising German peoples. For example, the 'Roman Law of the Visigoths' or 'Breviary of Alaric' (the sixth-century monarch Alaric II), which became the principal source of Roman law in the west, is basically an abridgement of the Theodosian Code, supplemented by other collections.

As a source of historical information regarding many imperial epochs, Theodosius' compilation is of unparalleled importance. For one thing, since the measures which it embodies cover the period when Christianity became the official cult of the State, they provide a kind of summary of what the new religion accomplished – and changed – in the field of law. However, the general message that emerges is in many respects a sad one. We find emotional confusions between sin and crime which the classical Roman lawyers of earlier times would never have perpetrated. Moreover, the imperial pronouncements are often not only verbose but repetitive. The monotony of their reiterations makes it clear that these successive, repressive measures, each promulgated in

more strident language than the last, were circumvented and disobeyed with
equally continuous regularity. Some of the legislation, it is true, was humane
and enlightened. There were laws, for example, safeguarding the conditions of
slavery, saving debtors from unjust hardship and prohibiting infanticide.
However, a great deal of judicial inhumanity is also to be found. Nor was there
even a pretence of equal rights before the law. 'If a man be poor', declared
Bishop Theodoretus, 'his terror of the judge and law-courts is doubled.' As for
the privileged, however, when the Code of Theodosius II was presented to his
senators in 438 they cried out in unison, not once but twenty-eight times in
succession, 'through you we hold our honours, our property, everything!'

During the final years of the reign, despite the efforts of the emperor's
generals Ardaburius and his son Aspar, the Danubian provinces suffered
grievously at the hands of the Huns, from whose devastations even Constantinople itself was not believed to be safe. Moreover, in the winter of 447–8,
Anthemius' historic land-wall, together with its coastal extension erected in
439 by the city prefect Cyrus, was shattered by a series of earthquakes, which
knocked down fifty-seven towers. Two months of desperate hard work,
directed by the praetorian prefect Constantius, repaired the damage; and in
addition a new wall, equipped with ninety-two towers, was built between its
predecessor and the adjoining moat. 'Even Pallas Athene', declared an
inscription on one of the gates, 'could scarcely have built such an unshakeable
citadel.' Indeed, for ten centuries to come, one invader after another found
these ramparts impossible to penetrate.

During the 440s the decisive personality at court was the eunuch
Chrysaphius Zstommas, who for a time succeeded in overriding even
Pulcheria's influence. His policy was to pay off the Huns by massive subsidies.
But this made him enemies among the east Roman generals, and at the turn of
the decade he lost favour and Pulcheria succeeded in reasserting her power.
Very soon afterwards, however, the emperor Theodosius himself, while out
riding near the River Lycus not far from the city, fell off his horse and suffered
an injury to his spine, from which he died.

Theodosius had been Augustus for forty-nine years (since the first year of his
life), and sole emperor of the east for forty-two – the longest reign in the whole
course of Roman history. During this prolonged period his chief advisers were
generally competent men, laying the foundations for the stability of the
Byzantine Empire during the millennium that lay ahead. But the emperor
himself, who was neither a statesman nor a warrior, did not play a prominent
part. In his final years, it was said, he used to sign official papers without even
troubling to read them. His character was gentle and kindly, and he disliked
inflicting capital punishment. Living a secluded life, he studied the sciences,
including astronomy, and encouraged historical research: it was to him that
Olympiodorus and Sozomen dedicated their chronicles. But his principal
interest was theology. He formed an outstanding collection of books in this

field, and was himself an accomplished calligrapher, copying numerous old religious manuscripts in his own hand. The court, people remarked, bore a strong resemblance to a monastic institution, devoted to pious observances and charitable works. In these high-minded activities the emperor's sisters took the lead: the virtuous Pulcheria, for example, bestowed ceremonial honours upon the alleged relics of forty-two martyrs. Orthodox Catholic Christians such as Theodoretus and Socrates Scholasticus saw their ruler as a gentle priest king intervening personally with God. Supposed heresies, on the other hand, received severe treatment, and the Arian, Philostorgius, listed a series of dread and destructive happenings which he blamed on this policy. Moreover, the Jewish patriarchate in Syria Palaestina was abolished, and its financial resources annexed by the State, in 429.

The wider literary interests of the empress Aelia Eudocia may have somewhat mitigated the austere atmosphere of the court. For a long time she lived on good terms with Pulcheria, until quarrels between churchmen in their respective entourages caused a rift to develop between the two women, creating upheavals which eventually forced first Pulcheria and then Eudocia to withdraw into exile. Eudocia spent the rest of her life in the Holy Land engaged in works of piety and charity, and was buried in Jerusalem in the church of St Stephen which she herself had built. Pulcheria, however, despite a second period of eclipse, was back in power at the time of the emperor's death.

CONSTANTIUS III
421

CONSTANTIUS III (joint emperor of the west, February–September 421) was a Roman, born at Naissus. As HONORIUS' Master of Soldiers (*magister militum*) from 411 to 421 (and as a patrician from 415), he was virtually in control of the western Empire. He had emerged on the political scene shortly after Alaric's sack of Rome in 410, when CONSTANTINE III and his son Constans were proclaimed joint Augusti at Arelate, only to find that Gerontius, their general in Spain, had broken away from their allegiance and set up another emperor, Maximus, in that country. Gerontius moved into Gaul, but Constantius, with his Gothic lieutenant Ulfilas, advanced on Arelate from Italy, and forced him to return to his Spanish base; thereupon he proceeded to move against Constantine III in Arelate, causing his downfall and death.

However, when a further usurper, Jovinus, arose in the Gallic and German provinces in 411, Constantius did not try to deal with him, probably because he was engaged in suppressing a further rebel, Heraclianus, in Africa. Meanwhile Jovinus also had fallen, but his supporters, the Burgundians, proved strong enough to resist expulsion, and were instead permitted in 413 to form a kingdom of their own beside the Rhine, with their capital at Borbetomagus, where they enjoyed the status of allies or federates.

The subjugation of Jovinus had been the work of the Visigoths under Ataulf, who, in response for this assistance, was allowed to establish his own federate state in south-western Gaul. Nevertheless, in defiance of the emperor and Constantius, he refused to give back Honorius' half-sister Galla Placidia (whom his father Alaric had abducted), and instead – contrary, it was said, to her wishes – married her at his capital Narbo in 414. Ataulf issued a second challenge to Ravenna by turning to Priscus Attalus, who had been his father's puppet at Rome, and setting him up as rival emperor again, on Gallic territory. Constantius marched on Arelate once more, and forced Ataulf to withdraw to Spain, capturing Attalus who was obliged to adorn the emperor's subsequent triumphal entry into Rome.

A year after the murder of Ataulf in 414, his brother Wallia handed Placidia back to the Romans, in exchange for a large subsidy of grain. After five years spent among the Visigoths she returned to Italy, and was induced (again despite considerable reluctance) to become the wife of Constantius. They were married on 1 January 417, the day on which he entered upon his second consulship. After the Visigoths had made themselves useful by suppressing Rome's barbarian enemies in Spain, Constantius recalled Wallia to Gaul, where his federal state was re-established in 418 on a larger scale than before, with Tolosa as its capital city. It was no doubt also on Constantius' initiative that Honorius, in the same year, proclaimed a measure decentralizing the imperial authority in Gaul by the establishment of a regional administration and assembly at Arelate, in which Romans and Visigoths would collaborate. However, the new creation never became very effective.

After Constantius had been virtual ruler of the west for ten years, and the emperor's brother-in-law for four, Honorius was persuaded – reportedly against his wish – to declare him his fellow-Augustus in the west: the third Constantius to occupy this rank. Placidia, despite her original unwillingness to become his wife, had presented him with two children; and immediately after the proclamation of Constantius III she was raised to the rank of Augusta. However, the eastern ruler, THEODOSIUS II, refused to recognize the

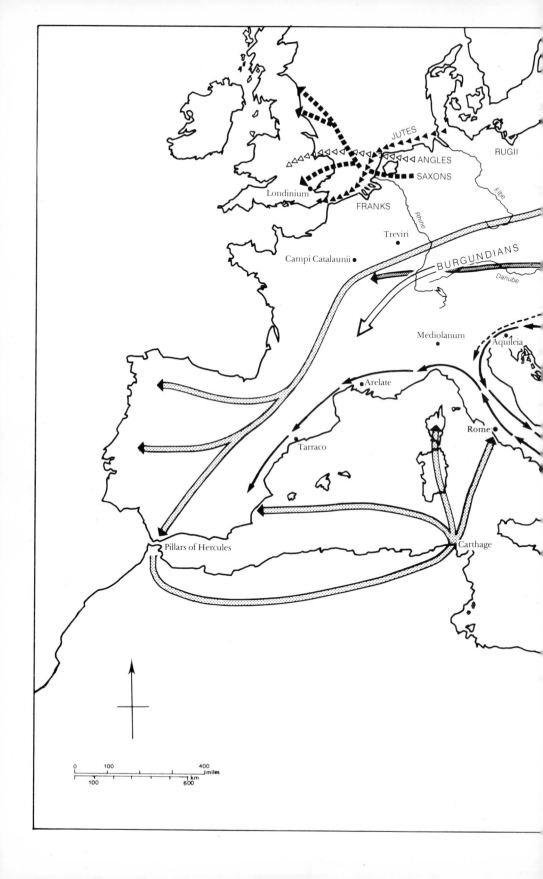

JUTES

ANGLES

SAXONS

RUGII

Londinium

FRANKS

Elbe

Rhine

Treviri

Campi Catalaunii

BURGUNDIANS

Danube

Mediolanum

Aquileia

Arelate

Rome

Tarraco

Carthage

Pillars of Hercules

0   100   400
                     miles
   100   1 km
        600

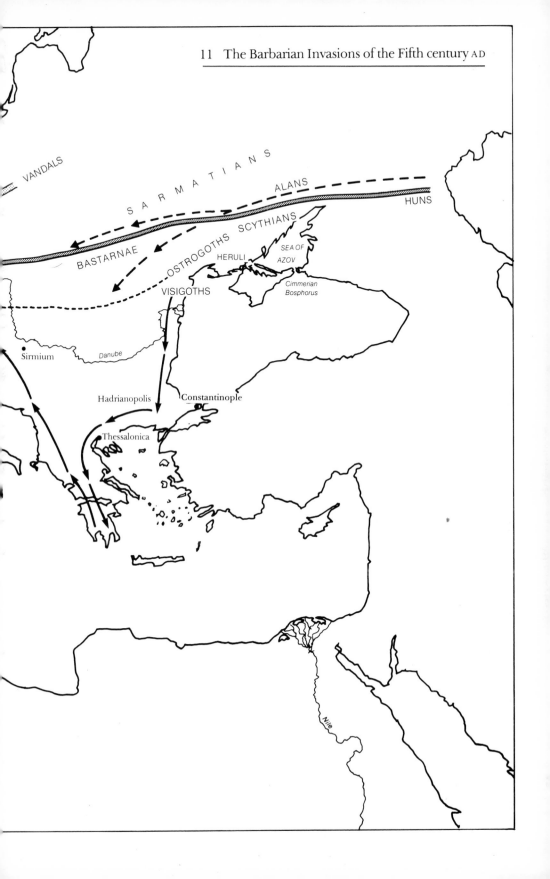

VANDALS

S A R M A T I A N S

ALANS

HUNS

BASTARNAE

OSTROGOTHS   SCYTHIANS

HERULI

SEA OF
AZOV

VISIGOTHS

Cimmerian
Bosphorus

Sirmium

Danube

Hadrianopolis   Constantinople

Thessalonica

Nile

elevation either of Placidia or her husband – perhaps because his government hoped to reunite the whole Empire under its own control, once Honorius was dead. Constantius was outraged, and spoke of extorting recognition from the east by force; so that the co-operation between east and west, which alone could have saved the western Empire, was further away than ever. But meanwhile his health had begun to fail, and after a joint reign of only seven months he died.

'On his progresses', wrote the contemporary historian Olympiodorus,

> Constantius went with downcast eyes and sullen countenance. He was a man with large eyes, long neck and broad head, who bent far over towards the neck of the horse carrying him, and glanced here and there out of the corners of his eyes so that he showed to all, as the saying goes, 'an appearance worthy of an autocrat'. At banquets and parties, however, he was so relaxed and witty that he even contended with the clowns who often played before his table.

He was said to have found his new position as emperor irksome, because he could no longer come and go as he pleased. It was also reported that he successfully resisted financial temptations until this last stage of his life, when he became greedy and extortionate, and his popularity consequently declined.

JOHANNES
423–5

JOHANNES (emperor in the west, 423–5) was a civil servant (of Gothic origin, according to a late source), who rose to the rank of senior notary (*primicerius notariorum*). He entered history because of the estrangement that had arisen between HONORIUS and his formerly much loved half-sister Galla Placidia, who was banished from Ravenna in 423 and took refuge with the eastern ruler THEODOSIUS II at Constantinople, accompanied by her four-year-old son VALENTINIAN (III) and a daughter.

In this dispute the western Master of Soldiers (*magister militum*) Castinus had opposed Placidia, so that he was now determined to prevent her and her family from returning to Italy and proclaiming the infant Valentinian as emperor. To anticipate such a step, he invested Johannes with the purple in September 423. Johannes issued a small series of bronze coins in Rome, where his proclamation had taken place, and produced a regular gold coinage at Ravenna. It not only displayed his own portrait but showed the head of Theodosius II as well, in the hope of securing recognition from the eastern régime. But this was not forthcoming; and when Johannes' envoys arrived at the court of Constantinople to request approval for his *coup*, they were refused admittance and dismissed to the Propontis.

In the diplomatic manoeuvring that followed, a prominent part was taken by two youthful military personages who were destined to play a large part in later years. One of them, Bonifatius, the field army commander (*comes*) in Africa, had given Placidia financial help, and could be relied upon to reserve African grain supplies to assist any move she might make to return to power. The second general, Aetius, on the other hand – son of a certain Gaudentius from Durostorum in Moesia Secunda (Lower Moesia) – accepted the elevation of Johannes, who appointed him director of his imperial residence (*cura palatii*). However, when it became clear that the government of Theodosius II was dispatching an army to depose Johannes in favour of Valentinian III, he sent Aetius to secure assistance from his friends among the Huns.

The invading force from the eastern Empire, led by Theodosius' ablest general Ardaburius the elder, and his son Aspar, set sail from Salonae but suffered dispersal by a storm, and Ardaburius himself, washed ashore near Ravenna, was taken prisoner by supporters of Johannes. Aspar, on the other hand, got as far as Aquileia, but Johannes, instead of proceeding promptly against him, decided to stay where he was until the arrival of the Hun reinforcements which he hoped Aetius was bringing from central Europe. Meanwhile Ardaburius occupied his captivity at Ravenna in undermining the allegiance of Johannes' officers; and he also contrived to get a message through to Aspar urging him to advance. Guided through the marshes round the city by a shepherd (who was later reported to have been an angel of God), Aspar's troops entered the gates of Ravenna unopposed. Johannes was placed under arrest and conducted to Aquileia, where Placidia condemned him to death. His captors cut off his right hand, and he was placed on a donkey and exhibited in the circus. Then, in May or June 425, he was killed.

The acts of his reign were declared invalid. But the historian Procopius recorded that he had ruled with moderation and gentleness – although Socrates Scholasticus describes jubilation at Constantinople when news came of his fall. His interruption of the dynastic rule of the Valentinians and Theodosii had only lasted for a year and a half.

VALENTINIAN III
425-55

VALENTINIAN III (Flavius Placidus) (emperor in the west, 425–55) was born in 419. His father was the emperor CONSTANTIUS III and his mother Aelia Galla Placidia, the half-sister of Honorius. Since HONORIUS himself had no children, he designated Valentinian as his heir, in 421 or shortly afterwards, with the title of *nobilissimus puer*. In 423, however, when Honorius fell out with Placidia, she and her son and daughter took refuge at the court of THEODOSIUS II at Constantinople.

But Honorius had died shortly afterwards, and a public functionary JOHANNES was elevated in his place; thereupon Theodosius II proposed to return the exiles to power at Ravenna. With this in mind, he recognized Placidia as Augusta, her late husband as Augustus, and her son as heir presumptive – all titles which the Constantinople court had failed to acknowledge when they had originally been conferred in the west. Placidia and her children accompanied Ardaburius and Aspar who were dispatched from the east to set them up in Johannes' place, and at Thessalonica, in 424, the five-year-old Valentinian was promoted to the rank of Caesar. The eastern army, after adventurous vicissitudes, captured Ravenna in May or June 425. Johannes was put to death, and Placidia with her children left for Rome, where Valentinian was installed as Augustus.

During the first twelve years of his reign Placidia acted as regent. Although strengthened by her links with Theodosius II and the great western senatorial houses, her power became increasingly limited by the personality of the greatest western general of the age, Flavius Aetius (see JOHANNES). Aetius, who had accepted Johannes and been honoured by him, brought a large army of Huns to Italy in support of his cause, only to find that his nominee had already perished. Placidia was obliged to offer him terms, and gave his Huns large sums of money to persuade them to return home. Aetius was then sent away to Gaul as Master of Cavalry (*magister equitum*), where he fought against the Visigoths and Franks in 427–8, gaining successes which Placidia, remembering his earlier hostility, learnt about with mixed feelings.

Nevertheless, Aetius' prestige now enabled him to secure appointment as Master of Soldiers (*magister militum*) in 429. But in the same year, Bonifatius, the army commander in Africa, estranged from Placidia after his initial support for her cause, returned to Italy and became reconciled with her. Their renewed friendship prompted her to hope that he might strike Aetius down, but when the two men clashed in 432 Bonifatius was wounded, and later died. Aetius' pre-eminence was now unchallenged, and it was said that envoys from the provinces no longer reported to the teenage emperor or his mother, but that it was he who granted them audiences instead.

The most significant feature of the age was the rise of Gaiseric, leader of the Vandals. In 429 this unprecedentedly formidable German transported his people from Spain to north Africa, where ten years later he occupied Carthage, the western Empire's second city, and the source of its grain supply. There he declared himself an independent ruler, owing no allegiance to Valentinian III or to anyone else; and in 431 and 441 he heavily defeated Ravenna's attempts to bring him to order. Gaiseric contributed more than any other single man to the downfall of the Roman west.

Aetius was unable to stop him. Elsewhere, however, he enjoyed certain successes. The Germans were temporarily forced back beyond the upper Danube; peasant resistance movements in Gaul were overcome; and when, in about 437, the Burgundians tried to break out from the Rhineland into Gaul, Aetius crushed them, and transplanted their entire federal state to Sabaudia. Any such military success at this late date was a considerable achievement; for edicts of 440 and 443 show that shortage of manpower and reluctance to serve in the western Roman army had become so acute that recruits were only called up in the most serious emergencies. Indeed, in a further pronouncement in 444, Valentinian III openly admitted the failure of his mobilization plans – this time owing to a shortage of funds.

Moreover, these were also the years when the Huns, who had hitherto provided Aetius with many of his troops, began instead to turn against the Ravenna régime. By the 430s their rulers had built up an enormous dominion in eastern and central Europe. In 434 this was inherited by Attila and his brother, whom Attila then proceeded to murder, thus becoming sole ruler. The government of Constantinople paid him large subsidies until in 450 Marcian refused to do so any longer, whereupon Attila turned against the western Empire instead in order to renew his supplies of plunder. At this point Justa Grata Honoria, the sister of Valentinian III, played a part in events. Resenting her brother's order that she should marry a Roman whom she found distasteful, she sent her signet ring to Attila, urging him to come to her rescue. Attila professed to interpret this appeal as an offer of marriage, and demanded that Valentinian should give him half his Empire as his dowry.

When this proposal was turned down, Attila marched into Gaul, where Aetius and his allies the Visigoths confronted the Huns and their numerous German subjects on the Catalaunian Plains (perhaps between Châlons and Troyes). Although the Visigothic king Theoderic I fell during the battle, Attila was decisively defeated; it was the one and only military setback of his lifetime, and the greatest victory of the reign of Valentinian III. Frustrated in Gaul, the Huns moved into Italy instead, where they captured and sacked Mediolanum; but somehow Pope Leo I persuaded them to turn back. In 453 Attila, after his marriage banquet, burst a blood-vessel and died in the night, and his empire abruptly fell apart.

In the same year Aetius' son was betrothed to the emperor's daughter; he himself attained the exceptional honour of a fourth consulship in 454. Yet he had made very powerful enemies, including both PETRONIUS MAXIMUS, twice praetorian prefect of Italy and twice prefect of Rome, and the court eunuch Heraclius, who was Valentinian's chamberlain. When Aetius threatened their lives, they persuaded the emperor to kill him, and in September 454, while the general was making a financial report, Valentinian, with Heraclius at his side, leapt at him and stabbed him to death. Thus fell the man who for nearly two decades had given unequalled support to his throne, and had propped up the failing western Empire. 'With your left hand', someone was reputedly bold enough to tell the emperor, 'you have cut off your right hand.'

At this juncture Petronius Maximus expected to become the chief power at court, but Heraclius persuaded the emperor that this would be a mistake; so Petronius commissioned two Scythians (or Huns), Optila and Thraustila, who were eager to avenge their former commander Aetius, to carry out a murderous plot. On 16 March 455, shortly after Valentinian had celebrated his thirtieth anniversary and eighth consulship by the issue of gold coins and medallions, they were among his company when he dismounted to practise archery in the Field of Mars. While Thraustila disposed of Heraclius, Optila struck the emperor in the face and on the temple, inflicting fatal wounds.

Like his mother, Valentinian III, in his later years, had resided at Rome. He greatly appreciated the city's many available luxuries, but he also found time to publish harsh edicts denouncing the Manichaean heresy; and he took a historic step by recognizing and increasing the authority of the Pope. This was the theme of his famous decree of 444, issued in conjunction with Pope Leo I the Great, to whom he assigned supremacy over the provincial churches that many ecclesiastics had hitherto been reluctant to concede.

It is also reasonable to suppose, in the light of his keen interest in matters of religion, that Valentinian played an encouraging part in the architectural 'Sixtine Renaissance', named after Pope Sixtus III, which took place from 432–40. This movement, aimed at reviving ancient forms, found its most resplendent expression in the Roman church of Santa Maria Maggiore (also known as the Basilica Liberiana, although the foundation of Pope Liberius, built from 352–66, had in fact stood elsewhere). The vast interior of the Basilica still preserves its original form, divided by forty columns into a wide nave and flanking aisles. Between the clerestory windows were forty-two rectangular mosaic panels (of which twenty-seven still remain intact). Each mosaic offers a lively, classical rendering of a scene from the Old Testament – the earliest cycles of such a kind to survive, probably derived from illuminated books. On the triumphal arch dividing the body of the church from the chancel, further mosaics illustrating Jesus' infancy place special emphasis on the role of the Virgin, whose title 'Mother of God' had just been solemnly reaffirmed by the Third Ecumenical Council at Ephesus.

However, the capital of the Empire was no longer Rome but Ravenna, and the transformation of that city, too, into an imperial residence worthy of the name, adorned with distinguished architecture and art, was initiated by Galla Placidia in this reign, under the influence of the great metropolitan artists of Constantinople. Her major Church of the Holy Cross, built in about 425, cruciform in accordance with its name, is only known from excavations. To the side of the long narthex, however, there still stands a small, domed, barrel-vaulted structure which combines the features of an imperial tomb and martyr's chapel and is known as the Mausoleum of Galla Placidia. In fact, it contained not only her own remains, but those of her husband Constantius III and of her half-brother Honorius as well. The interior of the building is adorned with mosaics, against a serene blue background. Over the entrance is the Good Shepherd with his flock, the opposite lunette shows the martyrdom of St Laurence, and at the side are stags quenching their thirst at the Holy Fount. Like the mosaics of Santa Maria Maggiore at Rome, these scenes point the way to what became the major Byzantine decorative art, but at the same time still retain a plastic quality firmly rooted in the realism of the Greco-Roman tradition.

A further development of the style can be seen in another religious edifice at Ravenna, the Baptistery of the Orthodox, an octagonal building that had been constructed or reconstructed in about 400 but was given its dome during the bishopric of Neon which ran from about 449 to 460. Here, richly coloured, brilliantly imaginative mosaic decoration, which covers the whole of the interior, concentrates on the importance of baptism. Once again the treatment of the figures is classical, as their drapery swings freely with their movement; but their feet are no longer in contact with the ground, and the acanthus spikes which separate one saint from another are stylized: the naturalism of the Hellenistic tradition is gradually blending with formal, eastern motifs to create the full Byzantine style that would shortly become manifest.

There was important humanitarian legislation during the reign of Valentinian III; for although sympathy was tactfully expressed with the fiscal burdens that had to be endured by the wealthy, steps were taken to protect the rights of the poor from their encroachments. Taxation was remitted to stop rural hardship and depopulation; and the oppressiveness of tax collectors, too, was denounced. Indeed, an edict even conceded that certain bureaucrats 'put out a smoke-screen of minute calculations involved in impenetrable obscurity'. But few such edicts could be effectively enforced. As for the emperor himself, it remains very uncertain to what extent he himself had a hand in these measures. For apart from questions of religion, and his one indubitable intervention in state affairs – the catastrophic assassination of Aetius – he showed little or no desire to take part in the affairs of government.

His principal concern, instead, was to have an enjoyable time. He was a fast runner, and a skilled horseman and archer – or so we are told by Vegetius, who dedicated to him a study of military science. Valentinian III liked the company of astrologers and magicians, and in spite of the spectacular good looks of his wife Licinia Eudoxia (whom he married at Constantinople in 437), he was said to indulge repeatedly in affairs with other men's wives.

Yet Valentinian remained on the throne for no less than thirty years. Moreover, light-weight though he was, his death proved a disaster, because it brought to an end the dynasty which, for so long, had given the western Empire such stability as it still managed to possess. With the dynasty gone, the Empire's end was in sight.

PART IX

THE
SURVIVAL OF THE EAST AND THE FALL OF THE WEST

The Family of Leo i the Great

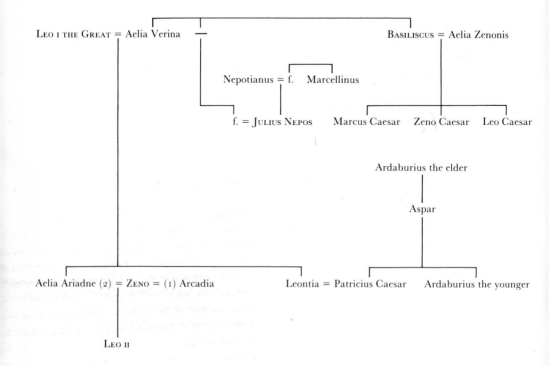

MARCIAN
450–7

MARCIAN (Marcianus) (emperor in the east, 450–7) was born in 392. He was the son of a Thracian or Illyrian soldier, and became a soldier himself, enrolling in a unit at Philippopolis. In 421 he took part in military operations against the Persians (during which he fell ill), and subsequently became an officer cadet (*protector domesticus*). Thereafter he served, for fifteen years, as a regimental commander under Ardaburius the elder and his son Aspar, the principal generals of THEODOSIUS II; in 431–4 he was one of Aspar's officers in Africa, where he was captured by the Vandals but released.

When Theodosius died, because he possessed no male heir and had not co-opted a colleague or successor, the government at Constantinople should, constitutionally speaking, have passed into the hands of the western emperor VALENTINIAN III; but this would have been unwelcome to the eastern court and population. It was also, supposedly, not the wish of Theodosius himself, since on his death-bed, in the presence of Aspar – who was by now Master of Soldiers (*magister militum*), but debarred by his Arian religious leanings from himself seeking the throne – he was reported to have said to Marcian, 'It has been revealed to me that you will reign after me.' And that is what happened – with the approval of Theodosius' powerful sister Pulcheria. Moreover, Marcian being a widower, Pulcheria agreed to become his second wife, though in name only because of her oath of virginity; thus the dynasty founded by VALENTINIAN I was formally preserved in the east, if only for the duration of one more reign.

Marcian's first act was the execution of Theodosius II's unpopular adviser Chrysaphius Zstommas. His own principal counsellors, apart from his strong-minded wife, were Euphemius, the Master of Offices (*magister officiorum*), and Palladius, the praetorian prefect. But a very prominent part was also payed by Anatolius, the patriarch of Constantinople. It was he who, together with Pulcheria, was mainly responsible for convening the Fourth

Ecumenical Council of the Church at Chalcedon in 451, which proved to be of fundamental importance to subsequent religious and political history. The attendance at the Council was very large, and included delegates representing the Pope. Departing from the decisions of recent Councils, and reverting to previously formulated doctrines, the Council of Chalcedon pronounced Christ to be perfect God and perfect man, consubstantial with the Father and his Godhead, and with ourselves in his manhood; and made known in two natures, divine and human, without confusions, change, division or separation. These definitions satisfied Marcian and Pulcheria, and became the basis of the religious teaching of the Eastern Orthodox Church. However, they alienated the oriental provinces, Syria and Egypt, where the majority of the population were Monophysites – believers that Christ possessed one nature, not two.

Although the Council's decisions tactfully incorporated the Tome (doctrinal statement) of Pope Leo I, they nevertheless widened the already existing rift between the eastern and western Churches. For the principal sponsor of the conference, together with Pulcheria herself, was the patriarch Anatolius, who intended to reassert the claims of his Constantinopolitan see to be the second in Christendom, and brought these claims forward in terms that the Papacy felt unable to accept. In particular the Council, while voting to confirm the patriarch's precedence over eastern bishops, took the opportunity to enlarge his jurisdiction as well. The papal envoys, and subsequently the Pope himself, objected to this aggrandisement of the patriarch, whose residence at Constantinople, where he could enlist the support of the eastern emperors, seemed to make him a serious rival of Rome. Moreover, Pope Leo I was displeased because the offending clause made no explicit reference to the unique Apostolic, Petrine character of the Roman see, which his delegates had continually emphasized. All in all, a large step had been taken to increase the already growing breach between Catholic and Orthodox which has constituted the largest division in the Christian Church ever since.

Pulcheria died in 423, leaving her possessions to the poor. In addition to her foundation at Chalcedon, she had sponsored the construction of a number of important buildings in Constantinople itself. One was the octagonal church – now almost vanished – of the Theotokos (Mother of God), in the bronze merchants' quarter, Chalcopratiae. Her other church of the Theotokos Hodegetria, Our Lady who leads to Victory, housed a sacred shrine reputed to heal the blind, and the adjacent convent contained an icon of the Virgin Mary which was said to have been painted by Saint Luke and had been sent to the empress from Jerusalem by her sister-in-law.

Marcian's reign was so free of the military and political convulsions which accompanied the dismemberment of the western Empire that it was later looked back upon as a Golden Age. True, his relations with that Empire were not entirely happy, since Valentinian III at first failed to recognize his

accession (though he subsequently acquiesced). Moreover, after Valentinian's death, Marcian was discouraged by Aspar from intervening to prevent
the sack of Rome by the Vandals – an omission which caused a bad impression
in the west; and when he granted part of Pannonia to the Ostrogoths and the
Tisza region to another people, the Gepids, he was accused of encroaching
upon the borderland between the eastern and western Empires. Within his
own eastern realm, however, there were only minor disturbances, such as
those in the deserts of Syria and southern Egypt. Marcian cautiously preferred
not to tackle the Persians, and when the Armenians resisted pressure from that
quarter – designed to make them abandon their Christian beliefs – he assured
the Persian King Yezdegerd II that he need not fear hostile actions by Roman
troops.

This restraint was partly due to Marcian's anxiety about possible attacks
from another enemy – the Huns in the north. Towards that people and their
monarch Attila he took a new, strong line, discontinuing the tribute they had
been accustomed to receive from his predecessor's minister Chrysaphius. 'I
have iron for Attila,' Marcian observed, 'but no gold' (a decision which
launched the Huns against the western Empire instead). Marcian's refusal to
renew these subsidies formed part of a general tightening-up of expenditure:
for example the consuls, instead of distributing money to the population of
Constantinople, were directed to spend it on keeping the city aqueduct in
repair. On the other hand, tax arrears were remitted, and duties on the
property of senators abolished. They were also relieved from a regulation
refusing legal recognition to marriages they contracted with slaves, freed-
women, actresses and other women of low social class.

Early in 457, Marcian fell ill; and after five months of suffering he died, and
was buried beside Pulcheria in the Church of the Holy Apostles. He was
greatly regretted: 'Reign like Marcian!' shouted the crowd at the installation of
subsequent emperors. With Marcian, the dynasty of the Valentinians and
Theodosii – to which he had belonged by marriage – came to an end at
Constantinople, as it had ended at Ravenna two years earlier. But its
termination did not produce the same chaotic instability in the east as in the
west.

PETRONIUS MAXIMUS 455

PETRONIUS MAXIMUS (Flavius) (emperor in the west, 17 March–31 May 455) was born in about 396. Of unknown origin, Petronius served as tribune and *notarius* in about 415 and finance minister (*comes sacrarum largitionum*) from about 416–19. Subsequently he held the office of praetorian prefect in Italy on two if not three occasions, and was twice city prefect and consul, receiving elevation to the rank of *patricius* by 445. He became very wealthy, and built a Forum at Rome.

After the murder of VALENTINIAN III in 455 there had been no male heir of the imperial house, and no eminent general who could have nominated an acceptable successor. Opinion on the future occupant of the throne was therefore divided. Some leading figures supported the claims of a certain Maximianus, who was the son of an Egyptian merchant and had been the steward of AETIUS. The eastern ruler MARCIAN, if there had been time to consult him, might very well have favoured another well-known personage MAJORIAN (who became emperor later); and Valentinian's widow Licinia Eudoxia would have been likely to take the same view. But the choice fell on Petronius Maximus, and he was duly elevated to the throne.

He immediately married the late monarch's widow, Licinia Eudoxia, but she only complied with marked distaste, mainly because she held the new emperor responsible for the murder of Valentinian, who had allegedly seduced his first wife; certainly Petronius Maximus showed favour to his predecessor's assassins. In despair she appealed, not to the eastern court, but to Gaiseric, the Vandal king of Carthage. She had a further reason, too, for selecting Gaiseric as the recipient of her plea, since his son Huneric had been engaged to her own daughter Eudocia the younger, who was now, however, upon the initiative of Petronius Maximus, betrothed instead to his own son Palladius, created Caesar.

In May, news reached Rome that Gaiseric had responded to Licinia

Eudoxia's appeal and was sailing against Italy. Many of Rome's inhabitants hastily evacuated the city, and Petronius Maximus himself, far from organizing an effective resistance, concerned himself exclusively with plans for flight, urging the senate to leave in his company. He was abandoned, however, by his bodyguard and all his friends, and as he rode out of the city on 31 May he found himself assailed by a shower of stones. One of them struck him on the temple and killed him: a Roman and a Burgundian soldier later claimed the credit for this accurate aim. The crowd mutilated his body and threw it in the Tiber. On 2 June Gaiseric entered the city, and after ravaging it thoroughly for two weeks departed with an enormous quantity of loot. He also took with him Licinia Eudoxia and her daughters Placidia the younger and Eudocia the younger, who in the following year married the Vandal king's son Huneric in accordance with the earlier plan.

The reign of Petronius Maximus had lasted for seventy days. We learn something about him from a letter written by the Romano-Gallic nobleman and literary personage Sidonius Apollinaris. His friend Serranus, who is otherwise unknown, had hailed the emperor as Most Happy, because a distinguished series of official posts had been rewarded by the imperial throne. Sidonius, on the other hand, points the moral that 'uneasy lies the head that wears a crown', since he says of Petronius Maximus,

when by straining every nerve he reached the precarious peak of imperial majesty, he felt beneath his crown dizziness, the result of unlimited power. . . . When he received the title of Augustus and was imprisoned on this pretext behind the doors of the palace, he groaned before evening because he had reached his ambition. . . . For although he had passed through all the other high offices of the court in peace and quietness, his supremacy over that court, as emperor, was characterized by extreme violence, amid risings of the soldiers, and the citizens, and the federate peoples. And all this was revealed also by his end, which was strange, swift and terrible: after Fortune had long flattered him, her last treacherous act bathed him in blood, for like a scorpion she struck him down with her tail. A certain Fulgentius used to say that he had often heard from Petronius Maximus' very lips, when he was disgusted by the weight of empire and longed for the old tranquility, the cry: 'You happy man, Damocles [condemned to eat his regal dinner with a naked sword hanging over his head], who had not to submit to the obligation of kingship for more than the duration of a single meal!'

AVITUS
455–6

AVITUS (Marcus Maecilius Flavius Eparchius) (emperor in the west, July 455–October 456) came of a wealthy and distinguished family of the Arvernian territory in Gaul. His son-in-law, Sidonius Apollinaris, has left us a description of his remarkably palatial villa, Avitacum. 'A copious stream,' paraphrases Edward Gibbon,

issuing from a mountain, and falling headlong in many a loud and foaming cascade, discharged its waters into a lake about two miles in length, and the villa was pleasantly seated on the margin of the lake. The baths, the porticos, the summer and winter apartments, were adapted to the purposes of luxury and use; and the adjacent country offered the various prospects of woods, pastures and meadows. In this retreat Avitus amused his leisure with books, rural sports, the practice of husbandry, and the society of his friends. . . .

However, Avitus tore himself away from these amenities in order to pursue a long and respected career of public service, first studying law and then attaining the rank of Master of Soldiers (*magister militum*) in 437 and praetorian prefect in Gaul – a new honour for a man who was of Romano-Gallic origin himself, showing the importance the country had achieved at this last stage of the western Roman Empire. During the warfare of Aetius against the Visigoths, Avitus induced their king Theoderic I, over whom he enjoyed substantial influence, to accept terms of peace in 437; and in 451, after his retirement from office, he helped to persuade the same monarch to co-operate in resistance to Attila the Hun, culminating in the victory of the Catalaunian Plains. Theoderic was killed in the battle, but the second of his sons to succeed him, Theoderic II, was once again a close friend of Avitus (who had perhaps tutored him in Latin literature).

In 455 PETRONIUS MAXIMUS tried to persuade Avitus to come out of retirement and hold public office again, as Master of Soldiers on the headquarters staff. But when news came that Petronius was dead, Theoderic II, whose court Avitus was attending at the time, urged him to take the throne in his place, offering Visigothic support; and after a modest show of reluctance Avitus accepted. A hastily summoned gathering of senators met at Ugernum, and enthusiastically acclaimed him as the champion of Gaul and saviour of the Empire. On 9 July 455, he was also hailed as Augustus by the soldiers; and the mint of Arelate issued coins bearing his name and his portrait. The formal consent of MARCIAN, ruler of the east, was sought for and duly obtained.

Towards the end of the year Avitus crossed the Alps to assert his position in Italy. Sidonius Apollinaris, who had travelled with him, celebrated the new emperor's assumption of the consulship on 1 January 456 by a long panegyric (rewarded by a bronze statue in the Forum of Trajan) which accorded him every possible virtue. The detractors of Avitus, on the other hand, suggested that he led too luxurious a life and not only continued, even at his mature age, to pursue women, but showed bad taste by mocking the men whose wives he had slept with. Above all, however, the metropolitan senatorial class did not like having a Gallo-Roman on the throne, appointed without their consent. Another difficulty was that Gaiseric the Vandal, after returning home to Africa laden with the spoils of devastated Rome, had remained hostile and defiant, dispatching a fleet of sixty ships to harass the imperial coasts.

In response to these problems, Avitus entrusted his fortunes to a senior officer named Ricimer. He was to dominate the west for the next sixteen years. The son of two Germans – a man of Suevic origin and the daughter of the Visigothic king Wallia – he had risen high in the military hierarchy of the western Empire, and Avitus appointed him Master of Soldiers on the headquarters staff. Ricimer proceeded to Sicily to deal with the Vandals, repelling their attempted landing near Agrigentum and then winning a naval victory off the island of Corsica in 456. Meanwhile Rome's Visigothic ally, Theoderic II, crushed the hostile Suevi in Spain; while Avitus himself campaigned in Pannonia.

Nevertheless, these activities did not help him to establish himself in the capital, for now not only the senate but the bulk of the population, too, had become discontented with his rule. A failure of the grain supply was threatening famine. Avitus tried to lessen the number of mouths to be fed by dismissing the federate troops, Gallic and German, who had accompanied him from Gaul; but they had to be paid off by selling some of the city's bronze statues – an action which provided fuel for hostile propagandists – and their departure deprived Avitus' régime of essential backing. The result was that Ricimer, hailed on his return as Deliverer of Italy, decided, in conjunction with senatorial accomplices, to bring about a change. Avitus attempted to flee back to Gaul, but was defeated and captured near Placentia. Deposed from the throne, he was allowed to become bishop of that city in October 456. But when a report reached him that the senate had decided on his death, he hastened onwards towards the Alps in order to seek refuge in his native Gaul. On the way, however, he died either from plague or at the hand of a murderer; and his remains were buried at Brivas, not far from his birthplace.

LEO I THE GREAT
457–74

LEO I (Flavius) (emperor in the east, 457–74) was sometimes known as 'the Great', probably to distinguish him from his grandson Leo II; his contemporary, Pope Leo I (440–61), was also known as the Great. He was born in 401, and seems to have belonged to the tribe of the Bessi in Thrace.

When MARCIAN died, the obvious candidate for the succession was his distinguished son-in-law ANTHEMIUS; but Anthemius (who subsequently became the emperor of the west) did not enjoy the favour of the Alan Aspar, the Master of Soldiers (*magister militum*) at headquarters. Instead Aspar's choice fell on his own subordinate Leo, who was commander (*tribunus*) of the legion of the Mattiarii Seniores at Selymbria. The senate could not reject Aspar's protégé, and Leo was crowned by Anatolius, the patriarch of Constantinople, to the accompaniment of magnificent and complex ceremonial.

Aspar remained Master of Soldiers at headquarters, and his son Ardaburius the younger, a more frivolous character, held a similar post on the eastern frontier. Aspar remained the dominant influence in the state for six or seven years, though his nominee on the throne was not always as amenable to his suggestions as he had hoped; for example, Leo procrastinated over the promised promotion of another of the general's sons, Patricius, to the status of Caesar, and did not, as expected, give him one of his daughters, Aelia Ariadne or Leontia, as his bride. Moreover, to counteract the preponderant influence of Aspar's German soldiers, Leo recruited on a considerable scale from the Isaurian mountaineers of south-east Asia Minor, whom he drafted into a newly created Guard (*excubitores*) in 461. To carry out this task he mobilized the services of an Isaurian chieftain, Tarasicodissa (the future emperor

ZENO); and it was to him that he gave his daughter Aelia Ariadne in marriage in 466 or 467.

Leo himself was married to the energetic and ambitious Aelia Verina, and her brother Basiliscus secured the command of a great armada which was launched against the Vandals in 468 in a combined operation with the western Empire, on whose throne Leo I had recently placed Anthemius (after refusing to recognize his two predecessors). The total failure of the attack, followed by another expedition in 470 which likewise came to nothing, not only greatly harmed the west – by showing that the Germans were irresistible – but was also regarded as a humiliating catastrophe at Constantinople, where it nearly bankrupted the treasury (see also ANTHEMIUS and BASILISCUS).

Aspar was widely accused of having undermined the enterprise by treasonable conduct. Nevertheless, seizing his opportunity while Zeno, who in 469 was made Master of Soldiers at headquarters in his stead, was away fighting the Huns in Thrace, he finally succeeded in securing the rank of Caesar for his son Patricius – and arranged for the young man's marriage with the emperor's remaining unmarried daughter, Leontia, in 470. All the same, there was a public outcry against the elevation of a heretic, because Patricius, like his father, was an Arian. Aspar, anxious to counteract this hostility and outmanoeuvre Zeno's faction, tried to win over the Isaurian soldiery at Constantinople. But Zeno, learning of this, in 471 hastily returned to the city of Chalcedon, from which he could influence events in the adjacent capital. Aspar and the younger Ardaburius fled to the church of St Euphemia, where, despite a promise of safe conduct from the emperor, they were seized and assassinated, probably at Zeno's instigation; Patricius escaped with a wound.

In protest, a senior officer and supporter of Aspar named Ostrus, who had succeeded Zeno as Master of Soldiers at headquarters on the latter's appointment to the corresponding post in the east, broke into the palace with a party of soldiers; but he was driven back by the Isaurian guard and fled to Thrace, taking Aspar's Gothic concubine with him. Yet another reaction to Aspar's removal was the violent behaviour of one of his German relations, Theoderic Strabo ('squint-eyed'), chieftain of Ostrogothic federate troops in the Balkans, who now proceeded to devastate Philippopolis and Arcadiopolis (formerly Bergula) in Thrace, and was proclaimed king by his troops. Leo I felt obliged to recognize his royal title and possessions, and granted him a subsidy, on condition that he would fight for the Empire against all its enemies (except the Vandals). Leo also gave him the post of Master of Soldiers at headquarters, previously held by Ostrus; but he was not granted the power that had so often gone with this job, for as the emperor Leo had already shown by his establishment of an Isaurian guard, it was his intention to put a stop to German attempts to dominate the eastern Empire, and to rely on troops from his own provinces instead.

In October 473 Leo I had his grandson of the same name – a young boy who had been born to Zeno and Ariadne – proclaimed Augustus as Leo II; and shortly afterwards he himself fell ill of dysentery, from which he died on 18 January of the following year.

Always a fervent Christian, he gained great public enthusiasm by bringing a reputed Veil of the Virgin from Galilee for the Church of the Theotokos at Blachernae (Constantinople), where a special edifice was built to house the precious relic; it came to be relied upon by the population as the divine talisman of their city, protecting it from invaders. Leo I legislated harshly against surviving pagan practices, and against Christian heresies as well, prompting the bishops of Constantinople, Rome, Antioch and Jerusalem to censure the Monophysites, who had set up a rival patriarch in a move to reject the Council of Chalcedon, which had been the highlight of his predecessor's reign. The downfall of Aspar, to whom Leo owed his throne, was partly or largely due to the German general's Arian beliefs; it earned the emperor the designation of 'Macelles' (Butcher).

The historian Malchus, in about 500, accused Leo of religious bigotry, and described him as an evil and rapacious ruler. Yet he was a man by no means lacking in common sense, who knew how to attain his ends; and he took reasonable measures to alleviate hardship, for example after Antioch had been destroyed by an earthquake. Moreover, although lacking in formal education himself, he appreciated the importance of literature and science: when reproached by one of his courtiers for giving a pension to a philosopher he reportedly said, 'I wish to God scholars were the only people I had to pay!' It would also appear that he was punctilious towards his family, for he regularly visited his unmarried sister Euphemia once a week.

MAJORIAN
457–61

MAJORIAN (Julius Valerius Majorianus) (emperor in the west, 457–61) took his name from his maternal grandfather, who had served THEODOSIUS I as Master of Soldiers (*magister militum*) in Illyricum, fighting successfully against the trans-Danubian tribes, while the emperor's father had earned a good reputation as a financial administrator in Gaul, where he controlled the war-chest of the great general Aetius (see VALENTINIAN III).

Majorian himself, too, became one of the officers of Aetius, who allegedly dismissed him because his wife was jealous of the young man's increasing success. Majorian retired to his country estate, but was recalled to military service by VALENTINIAN III early in 455 (after Aetius' death), to become commander of the officer cadet corps (*comes domesticorum*). When Valentinian was murdered shortly afterwards, Majorian appeared a possible candidate for the succession, for he was favoured by the late emperor's widow Licinia Eudoxia and would probably have secured the backing of the eastern ruler, MARCIAN; but the throne went instead to PETRONIUS MAXIMUS and then to AVITUS.

The deposition and death of Avitus (in which Majorian seems to have had a hand) were followed by a period of six months during which there was no emperor of the west, though this cannot be accurately described as an interregnum since, legally speaking, the eastern emperor Marcian was the sole head of the Empire, and coins in his name were issued in the west. Then Marcian's death early in 457 meant that Constantinople's formal backing for the appointment of a new western ruler had to be postponed. But either Marcian or his successor LEO I, in February of that year, took advantage of the hiatus at Ravenna to honour Majorian (who had become Master of Soldiers in Gaul and was fighting the Marcomanni) with the title of patrician –whereupon Leo duly nominated Majorian as western emperor, no doubt on the recommendation of Ricimer, the all-powerful German Master of Soldiers on the headquarters staff. So Majorian was acclaimed emperor on 1 April, although it appears likely that he was not formally installed until 28 December. His address to the Roman senate complimented Ricimer on his patrician rank, and coins show the new western and eastern emperors seated side by side.

The first task of the new reign was to conciliate (or intimidate) the powerful and quasi-independent nobility of Gaul, disaffected owing to the downfall of Avitus, who had been one of their number. On his arrival in that country, leading an army which mainly consisted of German mercenaries, Majorian found that the population of the province of Lugdunensis Prima refused to accept him, along with the Burgundians who had placed a garrison in Lugdunum itself. But Majorian compelled the city to surrender and punished its inhabitants by increased taxes (which were soon mitigated, however, through the mediation of Sidonius Apollinaris). Another German threat to Roman territory came from Theoderic II, King of the Visigoths, who was besieging Arelate; but Majorian's Master of Soldiers in Gaul, Aegidius, repulsed them, and the two rulers came to an agreement, while the Romano-Gallic aristocracy received a lavish distribution of honours.

After these successes it remained to deal with Gaiseric's Vandals, who dominated the coastal waters of the central and western Mediterranean. Majorian confronted a band of Vandals and Mauretanians who had landed at the mouth of the Liris (Garigliano) and were ravaging Campania. Taken by surprise by the Romans, they found themselves deprived of their spoils, and driven back to their ships with severe casualties, including the brother-in-law of Gaiseric himself.

Next, during the winter, Majorian collected a substantial army in north Italy comprising German, Hun and Scythian contingents. An imperial fleet of three hundred warships, together with transports and smaller vessels, in 460 conveyed the force to Carthago Nova on the west coast of Spain. This was the most important military and naval enterprise which the western Empire had attempted for years – and it came to nothing at all; for while harassing the coasts of Spain, Gaiseric was enabled by his excellent intelligence (including information from disloyal Roman subjects) to surprise and destroy the unguarded fleet in the bay of Lucentum. Majorian was then compelled to accept an unfavourable treaty, according to which he had to recognize the possession of Mauretania and Tripolitana by the Vandals.

Lacking a fleet, Majorian returned to Italy by land, and after celebrating games at Arelate crossed the Alps. However, Ricimer – who had not accompanied the force to Spain, regarding his own presence in Italy as essential, in order to keep his various German enemies away – concluded that Majorian had ceased to be an asset. It was not, therefore, fortuitous that when the emperor reached Dertona in north Italy a mutiny broke out which compelled him, on 2 August, to abdicate; and five days later it was reported that he had died of dysentery, though he was presumably murdered.

It is difficult to sum up the qualities of Majorian, since Sidonius Apollinaris, although the son-in-law of his dethroned predecessor Avitus, lavishes upon him every kind of flattery. It is true that romantic stories gathered round the name of Majorian, such as the report that he had visited Carthage (with dyed hair) in order to see the condition of the Vandal kingdom for himself. The account given of this alleged event by Procopius is no doubt legendary; but his agreement with Sidonius that Majorian was a sort of compendium of all the royal virtues does suggest that, even if Gibbon went too far in asserting that his 'great and heroic character, in a degenerate age, vindicated the honour of the human species', he must still have been quite an imposing personage – as well as the possessor, we are told, of a considerable sense of humour.

He also passed impressive laws. Nine of his measures, long documents that can be found at the end of Theodosius II's Code, represent a serious attempt to remove abuses. True, his sanctions against celibacy (a traditional feature of Roman legislation) were unlikely to have much effect. But oppressed provincials found their tax arrears cancelled, and the Defenders of Cities, officials appointed to represent the grievances of the population, were revived. Another much needed law aimed to preserve the public buildings of Rome, which had suffered from Avitus' sale of their statues. Majorian also showed considerable energy in mustering an expeditionary force against the Vandals; but since the enterprise abysmally failed, his survival was out of the question – as Ricimer saw, and ensured.

LIBIUS SEVERUS 461–5

LIBIUS SEVERUS (emperor of the west, 461–5) was not chosen to be MAJORIAN's successor until more than three months after the latter's death – on 19 November. He came from Lucania in south-western Italy; apart from that, however, nothing can be discovered about his origins, and his early career, too, is unknown.

He was little but a figurehead, ostensibly presiding over the government dominated by the German Master of Soldiers (*magister militum*), Ricimer. This situation is illustrated on the coinage. The very small bronze coins of the period often display not only an emperor's head on the obverse but his monogram on the reverse. A coin issued at Rome by Libius Severus, on the other hand, bears his own head on one side but Ricimer's monogram on the other. The general's name, with the title of patrician, is also found coupled with the titles of the western and eastern emperors on a bronze weight bearing the stamp of the prefect of that city.

Libius Severus however did not succeed in obtaining recognition from the eastern ruler, LEO I. Indeed, his titular authority did not extend much beyond the borders of Italy. In particular, two generals in other western territories showed reluctance to accept his puppet régime. One of them was Majorian's general Aegidius, Master of Soldiers in Gaul, who possessed a considerable army and was praised for military skill and Christian piety; according to the historian Gregory of Tours, the Franks, who had temporarily exiled their young king Childeric I, paid Aegidius the singular honour of offering him their kingship, which he temporarily accepted, returning it to the Merovingian Frankish house eight years later. After learning of the accession of Libius Severus, Aegidius proposed to march on Italy, but was instead detained by hostilities against the Visigoths in Gaul, whose troops, under Frederic, the brother of Theoderic II, he defeated near Aurelianum. Meanwhile, however, he had been actively intriguing with Gaiseric, intending that, while he himself kept the Visigoths at bay, the Vandals should attack Ricimer in Italy. But in 464 he died, allegedly from poison.

Ricimer's other principal opponent was a certain Marcellinus, a pagan and an expert diviner, whose reputation as a man of learning, courage and literary talent may owe something to the partisanship of his co-religionists. Involved in the ruin of his patron Aetius (in 454), he had withdrawn to Dalmatia (now under the control of the eastern Empire), but was considered for the western throne before its acceptance by Majorian. His loyalty, however, was rewarded and encouraged – by the post of military commander (*comes*) in Sicily in 461, where his army consisted mainly of Hun auxiliaries, posted there in order to repel invasions by the Vandals. But when Ricimer's bribes tempted the Huns into his own service instead, Marcellinus returned to Dalmatia and was granted the novel title of *magister militum Dalmatiae* by Leo I, emperor in the east, who conceded his position as a virtually independent ruler and incited him to hostile acts against Libius Severus.

Meanwhile the Vandals, masters of Sardinia, Corsica and the Balearic Islands, continued to devastate the Mediterranean coasts all the way from Spain to Egypt, and Gaiseric persuaded the eastern court to connive in his encroachments on the western Empire, which were intended to provide a dowry for Eudocia the younger, wife of his son Huneric and daughter of

VALENTINIAN III. This meant that the Vandals now declared themselves openly against the régime of Libius Severus. Eudocia's sister Placidia the younger, who had been sent to Constantinople, was married to a nobleman named OLYBRIUS, and it was he whom Gaiseric now put forward as candidate for the western throne. Hastening back from a victory at Bergomum against the Alans – whose king, Beergor, he had killed – Ricimer found himself threatened by the Vandals and Marcellinus alike. He urged Leo I to persuade them to abandon their hostility. Marcellinus agreed, but Gaiseric rebuffed the request, and indeed became a greater menace than ever, launching a major expedition against Italy and Sicily. During these events Libius Severus died on 14 November 465. Ricimer was rumoured to have given him poison, and this may well be accurate, for it had become inconvenient to sponsor a western emperor whom the eastern ruler persistently refused to recognize.

ANTHEMIUS
467–72

ANTHEMIUS (Procopius) (emperor in the west, 467–72) was one of the most famous subjects of the eastern Empire. Gaiseric, the powerful king of the Vandals, had requested that LIBIUS SEVERUS should be succeeded on the western throne by OLYBRIUS, but the very fact that he was the Vandal candidate made him unacceptable to many others. As a result, for two months after Libius Severus' death there was no emperor at Ravenna at all; but a raid made by Gaiseric on the Peloponnese in 467 persuaded the eastern ruler LEO I that co-operation between the two Roman Empires had become an urgent necessity, so that a new western Augustus must be appointed – and selected by himself.

His choice fell on Anthemius, the husband of his daughter Euphemia. This man, who had been born in Galatia and was well-versed in Greek philosophy, claimed descent from Procopius, who in 365 had briefly occupied the eastern throne. Anthemius' father, likewise called Procopius, was Master of Soldiers (*magister militum*) and of patrician rank; and his maternal grandfather

Anthemius was the praetorian prefect who had successfully acted as regent during the boyhood of THEODOSIUS II. The future emperor himself was commander (*comes*) in Thrace in 453–4, Master of Soldiers in 454–67, consul in 455 and patrician from the same year. It had been regarded as possible that he might follow MARCIAN on the eastern throne, until Leo I received the appointment instead. Anthemius was said to have borne this setback with dignity, and thereupon proceeded to win two military victories on Leo's behalf, against the Ostrogoths in Illyricum from 459–64 and the Huns at Serdica in 466/7. In 467 Leo nominated him emperor of the west.

After enlisting the support of the western Master of Soldiers, Ricimer, by the bestowal of his daughter Alypia in marriage, Anthemius set out from Constantinople with a distinguished entourage and a considerable military force; and his appointment was confirmed not only by the Roman people and the barbarian federates but also by the senate. His coinage displays himself and Leo I standing together, each carrying a spear and jointly holding a globe surmounted by a cross; the inscription is SALVS REIPVBLICAE (the Welfare of the State). Leo, for his part, offered public statements declaring paternal affection and authority in relation to Anthemius, with whom, he declared, he had divided the government of the universe.

After the many debilitating rifts between the two Empires this collaboration offered encouragement; but it came too late to save the west. Indeed, its immediate practical manifestation proved disastrous. This took the form of a combined expedition against Gaiseric. Even if the reported totals of 1,113 ships and one hundred thousand men were exaggerated, it was a huge and ambitious enterprise. But the commander of the eastern contingent, Basiliscus, was unreliable, and the appointment of Marcellinus (warlord in Dalmatia) as the western Empire's admiral alienated Ricimer. Marcellinus attacked Vandal bases in Sardinia and another flotilla landed in Tripolitana, but as Basiliscus' eastern fleet approached Carthage, Gaiseric, helped by a favourable wind, set fire to many of his ships and destroyed others, and the rest fled to Sicily with Basiliscus and Marcellinus, who was murdered, perhaps at Ricimer's instigation.

Anthemius also had to face a worsened situation in Gaul, where the formidable Visigothic king, Euric, who had assassinated and succeeded his brother Theoderic II in 466, was believed to be aiming at the annexation of the whole of Gaul. The Gallo-Roman nobility, feeling themselves imperilled, sent a deputation to Anthemius in Italy. The party included Sidonius Apollinaris, who now had a third successive emperor to honour in his poetry, and responded in no uncertain fashion, fulsomely hailing the restoration of the unity of the Empire; he was rewarded with the city prefecture of Rome. Meanwhile in Gaul, Ricimer's forces maintained important links with the Suevi and the Burgundian king, Gundioc, who married his sister. On the basis of this connexion Anthemius granted the Burgundians considerable favours, in order to gain their help against Euric. But Arvandus, praetorian prefect of the Gauls, was found guilty of treason and embezzlement and put to death; and Euric totally defeated a Roman army on the left bank of the Rhone, killing the emperor's son Anthemiolus and his three principal generals.

Nor was Anthemius popular everywhere in Italy, where his Greek culture and way of life aroused distaste; he was rumoured to be lenient on paganism as well. Unsuccessful against Vandals and Visigoths alike, he began, like his predecessors, to inspire doubts in Ricimer, and their relations sharply deteriorated. The emperor was reported to have expressed regret that he had allowed his daughter to marry a barbarian like Ricimer, who, for his part, was heard describing his father-in-law as a 'Greekling' and a Galatian.

This mutual ill will meant that Italy was virtually divided into two hostile parts, with Anthemius reigning at Rome and Ricimer at Mediolanum. Epiphanius, bishop of Ticinum, patched up a reconciliation in 470, but it did not prove lasting, and in 472 Ricimer marched south to the gates of Rome with the intention of removing his former protégé. His candidate for the western throne was now Olybrius (husband of VALENTINIAN III's daughter Placidia the younger), who arrived in Italy from Constantinople. Anthemius had the support of a Visigoth force under Bilimer (probably the Master of Soldiers in Gaul), and the senate and people of Rome for the most part sided with him against Olybrius. A three-month siege of the city accordingly followed, accompanied by famine and epidemic. At length Ricimer made a violent onslaught on the Pons Aelius, the bridge opposite Hadrian's mausoleum (later the Castel San Angelo). Bilimer put up a vigorous defence but finally fell, whereupon Ricimer's troops broke into the centre of the city, assisted, it would seem, by treachery from within. Anthemius capitulated, but as plundering continued he disguised himself and hid among the beggars at the church of Saint Chrysogonus. However his identity became known and he was beheaded, on the orders of Ricimer's nephew Gundobad, in March or April 472. All that can be said about the reign which thus abruptly came to an end is that, although Anthemius was a Greek, he had enjoyed wider support in the city than his successful rival Olybrius.

OLYBRIUS
472

OLYBRIUS (Anicius) (emperor in the west, March or April–October 472) was a member of the great family of the Anicii. He was descended from Sextus Petronius Probus, the powerful minister of VALENTINIAN I, and married VALENTINIAN III's daughter Placidia the younger, whom Gaiseric the Vandal carried away from Rome with her mother and sister in 455. Olybrius himself fled to Constantinople at the same time – holding the consulship there in 464 – but retained the support of Gaiseric, whose son had married Placidia's sister. When, therefore, the western emperor LIBIUS SEVERUS died in 465, Gaiseric demanded that Olybrius should be appointed as his successor; but this Vandal backing attracted too much opposition, and in 467 the throne of the west went to the Greek ANTHEMIUS instead.

Five years later, however, when relations between Anthemius and his Master of Soldiers (*magister militum*), Ricimer, broke down, the idea of Olybrius' nomination came up again. What apparently happened is that the eastern emperor LEO I sent Olybrius to Italy to try to patch up a peace between the two men; but once he had arrived, he was raised to the purple himself. Leo is not very likely to have supported this move, because he must have agreed with those who did not want a candidate favoured by the Vandals on the western throne – indeed John Malalas relates that he secretly sent a letter to Anthemius requesting him to put Olybrius to death, but that Ricimer intercepted and suppressed the letter. Whether that is true or not, Ricimer gave Olybrius a triumphant welcome at his camp on the River Anio outside Rome, and proclaimed him emperor in April 472. Three months later Anthemius had lost the city, and his life. Olybrius now reigned unchallenged, though Leo still does not seem to have acquiesced in his elevation.

Only forty days after the completion of these bloody events, Ricimer himself, who had dominated the western imperial scene for so long, was dead, vomiting blood. His post as Master of Soldiers was taken over by Gundobad, the son of his sister and of the Burgundian king, Gundioc. But Gundobad only enjoyed a brief association with Olybrius, who died of dropsy some five or six months later.

One of the few records of Olybrius' brief reign is a gold coin issued at Rome which displays a frontal portrait, wearing a pearl diadem without the usual helmet or spear; on the reverse stands a large cross inscribed SALVS MVNDI, 'the Welfare (or Salvation) of the World' – one of the most specifically Christian allusions ever to appear on the Roman coinage.

Olybrius, by his marriage with the younger Placidia, left one daughter, Juliana Anicia, who married an officer named Areobindus (proclaimed emperor at Constantinople for a single day in 512), and is portrayed in a manuscript of a work on plants by Dioscorides.

GLYCERIUS
473–4

GLYCERIUS (emperor in the west, March 473–June (?) 474) did not succeed to the western throne until four months after the death of OLYBRIUS; for LEO I, emperor of the east, who was thus the sole ruler of the Roman world during this period, proved unable at first to find a suitable nominee. Instead Gundobad, the Burgundian Master of Soldiers (*magister militum*) in Italy, took matters into his own hands and arranged that Glycerius, recently appointed commander of the élite officer cadet corps (*comes domesticorum*), should be raised to the western throne. In March 473 he was duly proclaimed at Ravenna, and Gundobad's compatriot Chilperic, Master of Soldiers in Gaul, supported the nomination.

His short reign was dominated by a serious threat to Italy from the Ostrogoths. After the collapse of the Hun empire in 454, this people, under the rule of three brothers, Walamir, Theodemir and Widemir, had been allowed by the eastern emperor MARCIAN to settle in northern Pannonia with federate status, and after ravaging the Illyrian provinces and fighting other German tribes, they established control over the area of the Middle Danube in about

469. Theodemir was succeeded two years later by his son Theoderic, who led part of the Ostrogothic nation from Pannonia to a new home in Lower Moesia, and was destined to become King of Italy two decades later. Another of their groups, which likewise moved south from Pannonia – under the leadership of Theoderic's uncle Widemir – displayed their intention of invading the Italian peninsula. The new emperor Glycerius, however, handled them with diplomatic skill, and they refrained from entering Italy, moving onwards into Gaul instead.

But Glycerius had never been recognized by Constantinople, and Leo I determined to replace him on the western throne by his wife's nephew by marriage, JULIUS NEPOS, the more or less autonomous Master of Soldiers in Dalmatia. Nepos proceeded to Italy with a fleet, landed at Portus Augusti and declared himself emperor. The only man who might have opposed his claim successfully, Gundobad, had vanished from the Italian scene; for upon the death (perhaps by murder) of his two brothers, he became his father's sole successor to the kingdom of Burgundy, and at once made his way there to take up this heritage. Glycerius therefore surrendered to Julius Nepos without a struggle. He was deposed, and accepted ordination as bishop of Salonae in Dalmatia.

Although it is sometimes doubted whether he lived long enough to take up the post, the historian Malchus assures us that he did, and that he subsequently became archbishop of Mediolanum from where he arranged the murder of his successor Julius Nepos (see next entry) in 480.

It had become customary for these late western emperors to include among their reverse coin types the revival of a familiar design dating from the beginning of the fifth century, which displayed a frontal figure of the ruler holding a long cross-headed sceptre and Victory on a globe – regardless of whether any victory had actually been won. The coins issued by Glycerius at Ravenna follow an identical pattern, but their obverses go further still along this nostalgic path by portraying his profile in a style reminiscent of issues made more than a hundred years previously.

JULIUS NEPOS
474–5, 477(?)–80

JULIUS NEPOS (emperor of the west, June 474–August 475 and, in Dalmatia, 477 (?)–80) was the son of Nepotianus, Master of Soldiers (*magister militum*) under AVITUS; his mother was the sister of Marcellinus, commander in Sicily and Dalmatia. In about 468 Nepos had succeeded to his command in Dalmatia, which owed formal allegiance to the eastern Empire but in practice obeyed no master. He had married the niece of the empress Aelia Verina, wife of the eastern ruler LEO I; and Leo, after failing to recognize the accession of GLYCERIUS to the western throne in 473–4, provided military support to Nepos, who sailed from Constantinople and landed at Portus Augusti. There, in June 474, he was hailed emperor, relegating Glycerius to the bishopric of Salonae.

The accession of Nepos was acknowledged by the Roman senate and the Italian people, and Sidonius Apollinaris (by now accustomed to praising transient new emperors) acclaimed his character and military talents alike. Upon his accession, Dalmatia was briefly returned to western rule; but at the same time a large part of Gaul became detached from it, for the most significant event of Nepos' reign was the declaration of the Visigoth ruler, Euric, that his expanded Gallic kingdom was no longer a federate state, ostensibly dependent upon the western Roman Empire, but a fully independent nation, like that of Gaiseric's Vandals.

The former emperor Avitus' son, Ecdicius, whom Nepos appointed Master of Soldiers on the headquarters staff, and also patrician, was helped by his brother-in-law Sidonius Apollinaris, who was now bishop of the Arverni, in the defence of Arverna, the principal city of the region, against repeated sieges by the Visigoths over nearly four years. But Nepos, unable to send help (and no help came from the Burgundians either), felt obliged to enter into negotiations with Euric – negotiations which he entrusted to five bishops. After a number of diplomatic missions, in which territorial exchanges were vainly discussed, a treaty was arranged in 475 which ceded the entire Arvernian territory to the Visigoths, much to the indignation of Sidonius Apollinaris, whom they temporarily incarcerated near Carcaso. The treaty recognized the Visigoths' conquest not only in Gaul, where their kingdom now extended from the River Loire to the Pyrenees and the lower reaches of the Rhone, but also throughout the greater part of Spain.

Meanwhile Julius Nepos had replaced Ecdicius by Orestes (formerly Attila's secretary) as Master of Soldiers, and Orestes now decided to elevate his own son ROMULUS ('Augustulus') to the western throne, in place of his unsuccessful titular master. With this intention, Orestes led a force from Rome to attack Ravenna, where the emperor had taken up his residence; but he, distrusting the supposed impregnability of the city, escaped by sea and withdrew to his princedom of Dalmatia.

However, in the following year Romulus was forced to abdicate by Odoacer, whose troops proclaimed him king, so that it was not long before the eastern emperor ZENO had to receive two deputations. One was from Odoacer, requesting that his *de facto* control of Italy should receive formal recognition from the eastern Empire – in return for which he was prepared to acknowledge Zeno's supremacy. The other deputation came from Julius Nepos, recalling his marriage connexion with Constantinople, urging sympathy for a man who had been compelled to flee from his country (like Zeno himself, on a recent occasion), and appealing for support to regain the throne. Odoacer's request was granted, and he was promoted to the rank of patrician. As far as Nepos was concerned, Zeno reminded the Roman senate that it had dealt badly with both of the emperors it had received from the east, killing ANTHEMIUS and sending Nepos into exile. He therefore requested the senators to take Nepos back – and Odoacer, too, was bidden to do the same. Odoacer, in fact, predictably took no action to reinstate him in Italy, but the resumption of gold coinage in Nepos' name at Italian mints indicates that Odoacer (who controlled them) at least ostensibly accorded him the recognition that the eastern emperor had requested.

The tradition, therefore, that the western Empire ended with Romulus Augustulus needs at least formal modification; for the last man to be recognized as emperor of the west, though at this stage no longer residing in Italy, was Nepos. The exile lived on in Dalmatia until 9 May 480, when he was murdered by two of his retainers, Viator and Ovida, at his country house near Salonae, perhaps – though not certainly – on the orders of his predecessor Glycerius. After his murder Odoacer crossed over into Dalmatia, on the pretext of taking vengeance upon his assassins but in reality to annex the country and make it part of his own dominions.

ZENO
474–5, 476–91

ZENO (joint emperor in the east, February 474 until towards the end of the year; sole emperor in the east thereafter until January 475, and August 476–April 491) was originally named Tarasicodissa; he was an Isaurian from Rousoumblada in Isauria (south-eastern Asia Minor).

The emperor LEO I brought him to Constantinople, and, with the aim of counteracting the influence of Aspar the Alan's German troops, entrusted him with the leadership of a new palace guard (*excubitores*) composed of his fellow-Isaurians; he assumed the less uncouth name of Zeno, after a personage who had come from the same region. Leo I gave him his elder daughter Aelia Ariadne in marriage (replacing his previous wife Arcadia), and in 467–8 he was appointed Master of Soldiers (*magister militum*) in Thrace, in order to repel an incursion of Huns under Attila's son Denzic (Dengesich).

Prompted by Aspar, a party of soldiers planned to assassinate Zeno, but he received advance warning and escaped to Serdica. After holding the consulship in 469, he was transferred to the Mastership of Soldiers in the east, and left for Asia Minor, where he was needed to suppress the brigand activities of his Isaurian compatriot, Indacus. It was a blow to learn that Leo I had conferred the rank of Caesar on Patricius, the younger son of his rival Aspar, betrothing him to his own younger daughter Leontia; and Zeno also discovered that Aspar's elder son, Ardaburius, was trying to win over the Isaurian troops in the capital. When Aspar and Ardaburius, therefore, were murdered in 471, Zeno was believed to have been responsible. In 473 he was appointed Master of Soldiers on the headquarters staff.

In October of the same year Leo I raised his five-year-old grandson of the same name, the son of Zeno and Aelia Ariadne, to the position of joint Augustus, and when the emperor died on 18 January 474, the boy became the titular eastern ruler. But on 9 February his father, Zeno, was made his colleague. The initiative was taken by the senate, with the concurrence of

Leo's widow Aelia Verina. Coins were issued at Constantinople bearing the usual helmeted, cuirassed bust accompanied by the inscription 'Our Masters Leo [II] and Zeno the Perpetual Augusti'. The bust, being of adult appearance, presumably represents Zeno. But on the reverse of the coin, accompanied by the inscription 'The Welfare of the State' (SALVS REIPVBLICAE), are to be seen the seated figures of the two emperors; and Leo II, though of miniature size, sits on Zeno's right in the position of the senior Augustus. Before the end of the year, however, Leo II was dead. It was rumoured that he had been killed by his father. Whether this was so or not, Zeno now reigned as the only emperor in the east.

Zeno's relations with the west were good, because the occupant of its throne, JULIUS NEPOS (474–5), was his protégé (linked to his wife's family by marriage). But Gaiseric, the King of the Vandals, who had been deeply displeased by the assassination of Aspar, invaded Epirus by sea and captured Nicopolis; though in the end, a peace treaty between the eastern Empire and the Vandals was agreed upon (and proved unusually durable, lasting for more than half a century). Zeno's accession had also prompted Aspar's Ostrogothic kinsman, Theoderic Strabo, to renew hostile operations in Thrace. He succeeded in capturing the Master of Soldiers in the region, but was subsequently checked by Zeno's Isaurian general, Illus.

However, Illus was soon to prove unreliable; for he became involved in a dangerous subversive movement in Constantinople itself. The conspiracy was masterminded by Zeno's own mother-in-law Aelia Verina, who, although she had concurred in his elevation, did not like being outshone by her daughter the reigning empress, Aelia Ariadne. Her plan was to supersede him by her own lover Patricius, a former controller of the imperial secretariats (*magister officiorum*) – not the same man as Aspar's son of that name. Illus and his brother Trocundes were also brought into the plot, by her brother BASILISCUS. Zeno, forewarned that his life was in danger, fled to Isauria with many of his compatriots and abundant funds. The senate, as it turned out, rejected Patricius in favour of Basiliscus, but after twenty months' rule, he too had lost all his supporters, and Zeno returned to the capital in August 476.

One of his first actions thereafter was to preside over the termination of the western Empire. Only a few months after his flight from Constantinople in the previous year, his nominee Julius Nepos had been chased out of Italy and replaced by ROMULUS AUGUSTULUS, under the guidance of his father Orestes. But Romulus was never accepted in the east, and, in any case was soon compelled to abdicate by the German general Odoacer. The western Empire had ceased to exist in Italy, which was now controlled by Odoacer himself, ruling as king. He sent envoys to Zeno, and at the same time a deputation from Nepos likewise arrived in Constantinople to appeal for assistance in an attempt to recover the western throne. In response Zeno, while continuing to recognize Nepos as the rightful western emperor, did not go so far as to send him help, and indeed granted Odoacer the title of patrician and *de facto* even if not *de jure* independence; while Odoacer for his part (in addition to tactfully placing Nepos' head on his coinage) issued other coins in Zeno's name at Ravenna, Mediolanum and Rome (INVICTA ROMA). The remaining years of Zeno's troubled second reign – in which Illus led a rebellion, with the support of Aelia Verina, in 483–4 – do not fall within the scope of this book.

The historian Malchus, writing in about 500, showed vigorous prejudice against Zeno, but others, too, wrote about him in hostile terms. He emerges from these accounts as physically unattractive, morally degraded and cowardly in battle. Another chronicler, however, the *Anonymus Valesii*, was more complimentary, not only noting that a peculiar formation of the knee-caps made him an extremely fast runner, but suggesting that, as an emperor, he was in some respects an improvement on Leo I, both less avaricious (despite a growing lack of funds) and less cruel: regarding capital punishment, for example, as distasteful. Zeno was also clever and steadfast enough to stand up to Odoacer's successor in Italy, the forceful Ostrogoth, Theoderic. What turned public opinion against him, however, was a religious even-handedness which was interpreted as sympathy towards the Monophysites (denounced by the Council of Chalcedon for declaring that Christ only had one single nature). Also the reliance he placed, like Leo I before him, on Isaurian mercenaries, though it helped to create a national as opposed to a German army, seems to have made him unpopular; for many of his subjects did not like having these uncouth men around, and could not forget that Isaurians, not so long ago, had violently devastated Asia Minor.

BASILISCUS
475–6

BASILISCUS (rival emperor in the east, January 475–August 476) was the brother of Aelia Verina, wife of the emperor LEO I. From about 464 he was Master of Soldiers (*magister militum*) in Thrace, where he was said to have won successes against invaders, although Verina may have magnified their importance. Next, in 468, she secured him the Mastership of Soldiers on the headquarters staff and the command of a massive expedition launched jointly by the eastern and western Empires against the Vandals. The powerful German general Aspar concurred in the appointment, allegedly, it was afterwards said, because he thought Basiliscus was too inept to win a victory – and Aspar did not want any project of Leo I's to fare too well. No less than 1,113 ships reportedly sailed from Constantinople, carrying more than a hundred thousand men. The combined operation was launched successfully but off Carthage Basiliscus allowed himself to be surprised by a Vandal naval force including fireships, which destroyed half his fleet. After taking temporary refuge in Sicily he returned to Constantinople, where, under the protection of Aelia Verina, he fled for sanctuary to the church of Santa Sophia. Then he went into retirement at Heraclea in Thrace, having reduced the eastern Empire, by his failure, to the point of almost total insolvency (see also LEO I, ANTHEMIUS).

However, when Leo I died in 474, the unpopularity of his Isaurian son-in-law ZENO gave Basiliscus a further and greater chance, when a conspiracy launched by his sister Verina temporarily gained him the eastern throne in Zeno's place in 475–6 instead of her own candidate (and lover) Patricius – whom he proceeded to put to death. The coinage of Basiliscus confirms literary reports that he adopted an unusually elaborate dynastic policy. His wife Aelia Zenonis was raised to the rank of Augusta and portrayed on coins, and their son Marcus was proclaimed Caesar and shortly afterwards Augustus, in which capacity his name appears on pieces struck at Constantinople bearing the head of his father (*Dominorum Nostrorum* BASILISCI ET MARC*i* *Perpetuorum* A V*Gustorum*). Other *aurei* show the names of two new Caesars, Zeno and Leo. Attempts to identify these with the emperors Leo II and Zeno are frustrated by their description merely as 'Caesar'; moreover, these issues are overstruck on coins of Basiliscus and Marcus (who did not claim the purple until after Leo II was dead). It must therefore be supposed that Zeno Caesar and Leo Caesar were younger sons of Basiliscus who obtained the title when Marcus was elevated to the rank of Augustus.

Nevertheless, things were not going well at Constantinople. The outstanding event of the reign was a catastrophic fire which consumed a great part of the city. Among the buildings demolished was the Basilica in which the emperor JULIAN had founded his library, containing a hundred and twenty thousand volumes. In the Palace of Lausus, too (named after a court chamberlain of THEODOSIUS II), a unique collection of archaic and classical Greek sculpture was destroyed in the blaze.

Basiliscus also became involved in serious religious controversies. This was because he openly favoured the Monophysites, accused of heresy. His *Encyclical Letter* concurring in their view that Christ only had a single nature was regarded in orthodox Catholic circles as outrageous. In particular, the influence exerted over the pretender by Timothy Aelurus, the Monophysite bishop of Alexandria, greatly upset Acacius, the patriarch of Constantinople who, although himself a man of moderate views, felt obliged to protest against the *Encyclical*. And then Basiliscus distressed the patriarch still further by detaching the bishoprics of Asia from this metropolitan control. When Acacius learnt of this decision he appeared publicly in Santa Sophia, wearing mourning. As for Pope Simplicius at Rome, he regarded it as quite wrong for an emperor to think that he was entitled to pronounce on theological questions at all.

Basiliscus had also made an enemy of his former supporter Theoderic Strabo, who now held the rank of Master of Soldiers. This was because he had conferred a similar and equal appointment on a playboy named Armatus, who was the lover of the empress Aelia Zenonis and was known to the population as Pyrrhus ('pink cheeks'). Moreover, the Isaurian, Illus, who had helped to bring Basiliscus to the throne, decided to turn against him, encouraged by numerous complaints about the rapacity of his ministers. So Zeno felt encouraged to leave his Isaurian place of refuge; and he and Illus began to march on the capital. Basiliscus hurriedly cancelled his theological edicts, recanting in an *Anti-Encyclical* designed to conciliate the patriarch and the populace. But Armatus, who had been sent to stop the advancing army, was persuaded by its commanders to go in another direction, and avoid them. So Zeno re-entered Constantinople unopposed, in August 476. Basiliscus and his wife and the children whom he had made Augustus and Caesars were exiled to Cucusus in Cappadocia, where they were immured in a dried-up reservoir and starved to death.

He was said to have been a good soldier – though his failure against the Vandals scarcely confirms this assessment – but slow of understanding, and easily deceived.

ROMULUS
475–6

ROMULUS ('Augustulus') (emperor in the west, October 475–September 476) was the son of Orestes, a Roman from Pannonia who had been the secretary of Attila, King of the Huns, and had been sent by him on missions to Constantinople. Orestes married the daughter of a senior Roman officer (*comes*) Romulus, who came from Poetovio, and after Attila's death, he himself joined the service of the western Empire. His talents gained him rapid promotion, and in 474 JULIUS NEPOS appointed him Master of Soldiers (*magister militum*) on his headquarters staff (*in praesenti*), with patrician rank.

His longstanding connexions with central Europe endeared him to his German troops, who constituted, at this epoch, almost the entire Roman army in Italy; and they preferred him to the emperor Nepos, who had come to them in 474 from the Greek east. Orestes responded to the soldiers' desire for a rebellion, but decided – for some reason that we do not know – to elevate not himself, but his young son Romulus, to the western throne. Julius Nepos fled to Dalmatia in August 475; and Orestes robed Romulus in the purple on 31 October. The boy assumed, or already possessed, the designation Augustus not only as a title but also as a personal name (inscriptions show that this was not unprecedented, even among private citizens): his coins bear the curious style 'Dominus Noster Romulus Augustus Pius Felix Augustus'. His position, however, was not recognized in the eastern Empire, where Nepos continued to be regarded as the emperor of the west. Nevertheless, for ten months Orestes controlled Italy in the name of his son.

Their downfall was caused by a mutiny among their own troops. These consisted almost entirely of east Germans (mainly Heruli, but also Rugii and

Sciri). They knew that the government had made arrangements with Germans in other parts of the western Empire whereby local landlords were obliged to hand over a fixed proportion of their lands to the immigrants. This principle had not hitherto been extended to Italy, but now the German soldiers stationed in the country demanded that similar action should be taken for their benefit as well. They did not insist on receiving two-thirds of the land, which HONORIUS had granted the Visigoths in Gaul more than half a century earlier. They would be content, they said, with one-third, such as had been conceded, for example, to the Burgundians.

Orestes, it appears, had at first made them some such promise if they would help him dethrone Julius Nepos. Once that was achieved, however, he had changed his mind; for despite his long association with Germans and Huns, he was still Roman enough to feel that an arrangement of this sort, while permissible in the provinces, should not be applied to the soil of Italy itself, which ought to remain inviolate. His reaction inspired Edward Gibbon with a certain awe. 'The dangerous alliance of these strangers had oppressed and insulted the last remains of Roman freedom and dignity. . . . Orestes, with a spirit which, in another situation, might be entitled to our esteem, chose rather to encounter the rage of an armed multitude, than to subscribe to the ruin of an innocent people. He rejected the audacious demand.'

But this firm gesture came too late to have any chance of success, and the disaffected soldiers found a leader in one of Orestes' leading officers, Flavius Odoacer (Odovacar). Odoacer was a German (Scirian, or perhaps Rugian), whose father had served Attila as envoy to Constantinople. After Attila's death he had joined the army of the western emperor ANTHEMIUS, and subsequently helped Orestes to expel Julius Nepos. Now, faced with his hostility, Orestes barricaded himself within the walls of Ticinum. However, the stronghold was placed under seige, stormed and pillaged. Its bishop Epiphanites protected Church property and rescued women from rape, but could not save the life of Orestes himself, who was executed at Placentia in August 476. His brother Paul was killed fighting in the woods near Ravenna, and Odoacer, entering the city, compelled Romulus to abdicate from the imperial throne on 4 September. His life however was spared, and he and his family were assigned the palace of Lucullus on the promontory of Misenum (Campania) as their place of exile, together with an annual allowance of six thousand pieces of gold (it is possible that he was still alive in 507–11).

Odoacer's future fortunes have been mentioned in connexion with Julius Nepos, who lived on in Dalmatia, and did not die for another four years. But it was the year 476, and the abdication of Romulus, that was canonized by scholars of Byzantium, Renaissance Italy and the eighteenth century as the epoch-making final moment of the western Empire's decline and fall. Moreover much dramatic play has been made of its last inoffensive young monarch's name Romulus – the name of Rome's legendary founder, more than twelve hundred years earlier, mockingly perverted, in his own case, to Momyllus ('little disgrace'). And ironical attention was also accorded to his other name Augustus, transformed into the derogatory diminutive 'Augustulus' by which he is generally known.

In more recent years there has been a tendency to minimize the importance of the removal of Romulus Augustulus, because, after all, it was only one more in a long series of piecemeal disintegrations. Nevertheless, his demotion did signify that the last major territory of the west, and its metropolitan territory at that, had become, for good or evil, just another German kingdom. The western Roman Empire was no more. Its long-drawn-out demise, declared Edward Gibbon, 'will ever be remembered, and is still felt by the nations of the earth'.

KEY TO LATIN TERMS

Note: LE = 'Later Empire' (fourth and fifth centuries AD)

AERARIUM   The treasury of the Roman State; the *aerarium Saturni*, so-called from the Temple of Saturn (beneath the Capitol) in which it was located.

ALIMENTA   A scheme for providing allowances to poor and orphaned children, by the investment of capital in land mortgages.

AMICI PRINCIPIS   Friends of the emperor, a semi-official rank; there were many *amici* in the *consilium principis* (*q.v.*).

ANTONINIANUS   The name given to a base silver coin, weighing initially 1½ *denarii*, but probably valued at 2; named (unofficially) after its introducer CARACALLA (Marcus Aurelius Antoninus).

ASSEMBLY   See *Comitia*.

AUGURS   The official Roman diviners; the augurate was one of the four major Orders of Priesthood.

AUGUSTUS   The name selected by or for Octavian in 27 BC as his most distinctive appellation, and assumed by all the emperors who followed. Etymologically related to *augur* (*q.v.*) and *augere* meaning increase, i.e. the sanctified and 'augmented'.

AUREUS   The standard gold coin, replaced in the LE by the lighter *solidus*.

AUXILIA   Augustus, building on Republican precedents, established a permanent auxiliary army (supplementary to the *legions*, *q.v.*) probably numbering some one hundred and fifty thousand soldiers. The auxiliaries only became Roman citizens on retirement (at least from the mid-first century) but were officered by citizens. LE: CONSTANTINE I THE GREAT created new infantry units called *auxilia* to expand the *comitatus* (*q.v.*).

BASILICAS   The large columnar halls, for various meeting purposes, which were usually situated beside the *Forum* (*q.v.*) in a town of the western Roman world. LE: (1) huge vaulted structures, derived from the central halls of imperial Baths, e.g. the Basilica Nova of MAXENTIUS; (2) major Christian churches, closer in structural form to the earlier basilicas.

CAESAR   The name of the dictator Gaius Julius Caesar (d. 44 BC) which was assumed by Roman emperors as part of their nomenclature and was also granted (without the designation *Augustus*, *q.v.*) to imperial princes, subsequently with the implication that they were heirs to the throne. *LE*: The *Tetrarchy* (*q.v.*) of DIOCLETIAN comprised two Augusti and two Caesars.

CAPITOLINE GAMES   See *Ludi*.

CASTRA PEREGRINA or PEREGRINORUM   'Foreigners' Camp', on Rome's Caelian Hill. Constructed to house legionary detachments (or individuals) visiting Rome, it became the headquarters of the *frumentarii*, messengers and intelligence personnel.

CENSORS   Republican officials appointed every four (then five) years for eighteen months to draw up and maintain the roll of citizens and revise the list of senators. Practically defunct from the time of AUGUSTUS, who assumed censorial powers. CLAUDIUS had himself made censor (and DOMITIAN censor for life).

CENTURION   The principal professional officer in the Roman army; originally in charge of one hundred men (*centuria*). The centurions were divided into a number of different grades and ranks. AUGUSTUS' centurions received between 3,750 and fifteen thousand *denarii* a year.

CHIEF PRIEST   See *Pontifex maximus*.

CITY PREFECT   See *Praefectus*.

CLIENTS   (1) Individuals, the dependants of their *patroni* according to an ancient social institution; (2) (by an extension) client-states round the fringes of the Empire, dependent on the emperor.

COHORT   A military unit. There were ten cohorts in a *legion* (*q.v.*), and each was divided into six centuries. The infantry units of the *auxilia* (*q.v.*), five hundred or one thousand men strong, were also called cohorts, and the praetorian and city troops and *vigiles* (*q.v.*) were divided into units of the same name.

COLONIES   Cities and towns settled by Roman citizens; see also *Ius Latii*.

COMES   *LE*: a military commander or high civilian official ('count').

COMES SACRARUM LARGITIONUM   Count of Sacred Largesses (earlier, *rationalis rei summae*). *LE*: the financial minister controlling currency and mints, revenue and expenditure (in coin), mines and provision of uniforms to the army and civil service.

COMITATENSES   Units forming the emperor's *comitatus*. *LE*: mobile forces; one of the two main divisions in the imperial field army (see also *Limitanei*).

COMITIA (*tributa*).   This ancient Republican Assembly still elected magistrates and for a time passed laws under the Principate (see *Princeps*) but lacked real power.

CONSILIUM PRINCIPIS   The emperor's privy council, given greater formality in the second century and further formalized in the third; see also *Amici principis, Consistorium*.

CONSISTORIUM   *LE*: the name given to the *consilium principis* (*q.v.*) from the time of DIOCLETIAN, since the members no longer sat but stood. A general council of State and a supreme court of law.

CONSUL   The two chief annually appointed officials (magistrates) of the ancient Republic. Their appointment continued throughout the Principate (see *Princeps*), when *consules ordinarii* were the initially 'elected' consuls of each year, usually resigning after a few months in favour of substitutes known as *consules suffecti*.

CONSULAR ORNAMENTS   See *Ornamenta*.

CORRECTOR   *LE*: the title of certain governors from the later third century (notably of Italian regions).

CUBICULARII   See *Praepositus sacri cubiculi*.

CURA PALATII   *LE*: controller of the palace.

DENARIUS   The standard silver base coin (twenty-five to a gold piece [*aureus, q.v.*]). *LE*: a much smaller and largely theoretical denomination.

DIOECESES   Dioceses. *LE*: administrative groups of provinces created by DIOCLETIAN, originally thirteen and subsequently more; governed in most cases by a deputy praetorian prefect or vicar.

DIVUS   The term employed (rather than *deus*) for Julius Caesar and emperors after their posthumous deification by the Roman State.

EQUITES   The *equester ordo*, 'knights'. In the later Republic a class with a minimum property qualification immediately below that of the senators; one section developed important financial interests. Reformed by AUGUSTUS and others to provide holders of many important new administrative posts.

EXCUBITORES   *LE*: a new imperial guard created by LEO I, three hundred strong, recruited from his fellow-Isaurians (of south-central Asia Minor).

FORUM   The chief public square of a town, usually surrounded by important temples and halls. Beside the ancient Forum Romanum, Julius Caesar, AUGUSTUS, VESPASIAN, NERVA and TRAJAN constructed supplementary Fora in Rome bearing their names.

FREEDMAN, FREED SLAVE   See *Libertus*.

FRIENDS   See *Amici Principis*.

HIGH PRIEST   See *Pontifex Maximus*.

HONESTIORES   Men of higher birth (from the second to third centuries AD). At first a social but then also a legal distinction, in contrast with the underprivileged *humiliores*; lesser penalties were inflicted on the *honestiores* for crimes.

IMPERATOR   (1) General, commander; (2) after a victory a general was saluted Imperator by his soldiers; (3) Julius Caesar used the title permanently and it was assumed by emperors as part of their nomenclature, generally as a prefix.

IMPERIUM   The supreme administrative power, involving command in war and the interpretation and execution of law. AUGUSTUS, who frequently adjusted the definition of his *imperium*, instituted the custom of delegating it, in a superior form (*majus*), to others entrusted with important commands.

IUS LATII (Latin rights)   The status of Latin colonies in which the officials (magistrates), but not the remainder of the population, were Roman citizens.

KNIGHTS   See *Equites*.

LAETI   A German word. *LE*: barbarian prisoners of war or refugees allocated land, settled in small groups under Roman prefects and required to provide recruits for the army.

LATIN RIGHTS   See *Ius Latii*.

LEGATUS   Deputy, envoy, general. (1) Commanders of legions; (2) governors of 'imperial' provinces (depending directly on the emperor), except Egypt and small territories, were *legati Augusti propraetore*; (3) deputies of the governors of 'senatorial' provinces (proconsuls).

LEGION   A military unit. Under AUGUSTUS there were 28 and then 25 legions (each comprising 5,000 infantry and 120 cavalry); under SEPTIMIUS SEVERUS there were 33. Legionaries were Roman citizens. *LE*: the number of legions was considerably increased, but infantry legions of the field army (see *Comitatus, Limitanei*) were only 1,000 strong.

LIBERTUS (*libertinus*)   A freed slave. He still owed deference and service to his former master, as client to patron, but his son became a full citizen. As the households of the emperors gradually turned into State departments, freedmen – mostly Hellenized orientals – took charge of these bureaux, reaching the zenith of their power under CLAUDIUS and NERO. Originally a *libertinus* was the son of a *libertus*, but this distinction became blurred.

LIMITANEI   Border troops (or *riparienses, ripenses*: riverside troops). *LE*: the frontier forces, normally static; one of the two main divisions of the field army (see also *Comitatenses*).

LUDI CAPITOLINI (or Romani or Magni)   Annual Games, lasting for sixteen days in the later first century BC: the most ancient and important of the public Games. DOMITIAN instituted a Capitoline Competition (*agon*) or *Capitolia* based on Greek Games.

LUDI SAECULARES   Secular Games. A much venerated religious ceremony inherited from the Republic and revived by AUGUSTUS under a Board of Fifteen of which he was chairman. Horace wrote his *Secular Hymn* for the occasion. Thereafter the rites took place at irregular intervals, sometimes corresponding with centenaries of the alleged foundation-date of Rome, 753 BC. In AD 248 Millenary Games were celebrated by Philip the Arab.

MAGISTER EQUITUM   Master of Horse. (1) Deputy to a dictator in the Republic; both posts were abolished in the Principate (see *Princeps*); (2) *LE*: commander of cavalry in the *comitatus* (*q.v.*) with authority over generals on the frontier. There was often more than one *magister equitum*, in the western and eastern Empires alike. The *magister equitum in praesenti* or *praesentalis* was on the imperial headquarters staff.

MAGISTER MEMORIAE   *LE*: secretary of state for general petitions under the *magister scriniorum* (*q.v.*).

MAGISTER MILITUM   Master of Soldiers. *LE*: commander-in-chief, also known, especially in the eastern Empire, as *magister utriusque militiae* (Master of Both Services). For plurality and the term *in praesenti* (*praesentalis*) see *Magister equitum*.

MAGISTER OFFICIORUM   *LE*: imperial minister controlling the secretariats (*scrinia*, *q.v.*), the corps of imperial couriers (*agentes in rebus*) and the imperial bodyguard (*scholae palatinae*, *q.v.*), and regulating the emperor's audiences.

MAGISTER PEDITUM   Master of Foot. *LE*: commander of infantry in the *comitatus* (*q.v.*) with authority over generals on the frontier. For plurality and the term *in praesenti* (*praesentalis*) see *Magister equitum*.

MAGISTER SCRINII (or **SCRINIORUM**)   Master of the Secretariat (*scrinium*, *q.v.*). *LE*: Controller of the departments of general petitions (see *Magister Memoriae*), letters and rescripts and cases for the imperial court.

MARTYRIUM   *LE*: the place where a Christian martyr was supposedly buried.

MASTER OF FOOT, HORSE, SOLDIERS   See *Magister Peditum, Equitum, Militum*.

NOTARII   *LE*: members of the corps of notaries. They kept the minutes of the *consistorium* (*q.v.*). *Notarii* were often rapidly upgraded, rising to the highest offices of state. Their chief was the *primicerius notariorum* (*q.v.*) and a second-rank official was the *secundarius notariorum*.

NUMERI   Military units found from the time of TRAJAN onwards, formed from un-Romanized tribes which could not easily be assimilated into the *auxilia* (*q.v.*).

OFFICER CADETS   See *Protectores*.

ORNAMENTA   These conferred the status and rank of an office (*consularia, praetoria, quaestoria*) without its having to be held. Successful generals were also awarded the *ornamenta triumphalia*, the *Triumph* itself (*q.v.*) being the prerogative of the emperor.

OVATION   A minor form of *Triumph* (*q.v.*), last recorded in 47.

PATER PATRIAE   Father of the Country. Caesar accepted the designation 'Parens Patriae', and after AUGUSTUS had been pronounced 'Pater Patriae' in 2 BC, most, but not quite all, emperors incorporated this title sooner or later into their nomenclature.

PATRIARCH   (1) In the second century this became the title of the leaders of the Jewish community in Syria Palaestina (Judaea) (the term had been used by the Greek translators of the Septuagint); (2) *LE*: a title used by Christian bishops, especially in the eastern Church; the bishop of Constantinople was regularly described in this way.

PATRICIAN   (1) Since very early times the patricians were the higher class of Roman citizens, in contrast to the plebeians: fourteen patrician clans still survived at the beginning of the Principate (see *Princeps*); (2) *LE*: a title of honour revived by CONSTANTINE I THE GREAT and sparingly bestowed. The *magister militum* (*q.v.*) *in praesenti* of the western Empire came to be known as the *patricius*.

PEREGRINI   See *Castra Peregrinorum*.

PIUS   Meaning dutiful to gods, state or family. This was a title conferred on many emperors from ANTONINUS PIUS onwards. *LE*: the appellation became, with 'Felix', part of the normal imperial titulature.

PONTIFEX MAXIMUS   Chief priest. The head of the Pontifices, one of the four major Orders of Priesthood, he presided over the State cult generally; from 12 BC, emperors adopted the title. In Christian times, GRATIAN was the first to refuse it, in about 375, and it passed to the Popes.

PRAEFECTUS   A term used for the holders of a variety of military commands and civilian offices. The latter included the city prefect of Rome (*praefectus urbi*), the commander of the praetorian guard (*praefectus praetorio*, *q.v.*), the *praefecti annonae* (*q.v.*) and *vigilum* (see *Vigiles*) and a few governors of knightly rank (see *Equites*) including the prefects of Egypt and at first Judaea (the latter were subsequently *procuratores* (*q.v.*) and eventually *legati*, i.e. of senatorial status).

PRAEFECTUS ANNONAE   The commissioner of the grain supply at Rome.

PRAEFECTUS PRAETORIO   The praetorian prefect and commander of the praetorian guard (see *Praetoriani*). Originally appointed in pairs (a custom that was sometimes resumed later), they were often the most influential men in the Empire. During the second and third centuries they acquired extensive judicial powers and were, on occasion, not military men but well-known jurists. *LE*: under the *Tetrarchy* (*q.v.*) the praetorian prefects of each of the four rulers were their principal finance ministers, and when the guard was abolished they became civilian officials with increasingly comprehensive financial and judicial functions. From about 395 there were four prefectures, two in the western and two in the eastern Empire.

PRAEPOSITUS SACRI CUBICULI   *LE*: the court chamberlain and chief of the *cubicularii*, eunuchs of the imperial bedchamber.

PRAETOR   The praetors were the annually elected state officials next in importance to the consuls. Twelve in number in the early Principate (see

Princeps), they were often placed in charge of important state directorates. Most provincial governors were former praetors.

PRAETORIAN EDICT The edict formulated by a *praetor* (*q.v.*) when he took up office, indicating his intended courses of action. The edict acquired a permanent form when it was revised and standardized by Salvius Julianus under HADRIAN.

PRAETORIANI The praetorian guard, developed from the *cohortes praetoriae* of late Republican generals. A permanent corps of nine *cohorts* (*q.v.*), each of five hundred infantry and ninety cavalry, was established by AUGUSTUS, under joint *praefecti praetorio* (*q.v.*). Their size and composition fluctuated. *LE*: the *praetoriani*, now virtually the city guard of Rome, were abolished by SEVERUS II and then again, after temporary revival, by CONSTANTINE I THE GREAT.

PREFECT See *Praefectus*.

PRINCEPS The term, with sound Republican associations, which was selected by AUGUSTUS to indicate his own constitutional position as the inaugurator of the Restored Republic or Principate (imperial epoch).

PRINCEPS IUVENTUTIS (Prince of Youth) The *equites* (*q.v.*) pronounced AUGUSTUS' grandsons Gaius and Lucius to be the leaders of the youth movement he had dedicated to military training (*iuvenes, iuventus*), and the same honour was renewed for subsequent 'crown princes' – although reigning emperors, too, later claimed the title for themselves.

PROCURATOR Agent or representative. This became the distinctive term for the emperor's civil employees, mostly *equites* (*q.v.*) in rank. They included finance officers of imperial provinces (and governors of minor ones), directors of the emperor's private domains (*procuratores thesaurorum*), and holders of a rapidly increasing number of State directorates at home.

PROPRAETOR Official holding the rank but not the office of *praetor* (*q.v.*); see also *Legatus*.

PROTECTORES *LE*: a corps of officer cadets, subsequently divided into *protectores* and *protectores domestici* (who soon became regimental commanders). They were employed for miscellaneous staff duties. The *protectores divini lateris* were imperial bodyguards.

PROVINCIAE Provinces – of two main kinds: 'senatorial', governed by proconsuls (still elected ostensibly by the senate), and 'imperial', governed by *legati* (*q.v.*), the direct subordinates of the emperor and commanders of armies. *LE*: DIOCLETIAN doubled the number of provinces (to about a hundred) and divided them into groups (*dioeceses, q.v.*).

QUAESTOR The junior office of state in the senator's official career. From AUGUSTUS' time there were twenty quaestors, many of them attached as finance officers and assistants to the governors of senatorial provinces.

QUAESTOR SACRI PALATII *LE*: the empire's chief legal officer, a post created by Constantine I the Great.

RATIONALIS *LE*: a high finance officer, e.g. the *rationales rei privatae* who, under a *comes* (*q.v.*), controlled the imperial properties. For the *rationalis summae rei* see *Comes sacrarum largitionum*.

REPUBLIC The period of Roman history extending between *c.* 510 (legendary date) and 31 BC, i.e. between the Kingship and the Principate; although propaganda sometimes declared the latter a 'Restored Republic' and the term *respublica* continued to be employed to mean the Roman State.

RIPARIENSES See *Limitanei*.

SALII An ancient ritual organization found in many towns of Italy, usually in association with the war-god.

SATURNALIA The most jubilant festival of the Roman year (in honour of Saturn), celebrated on 17 December. *LE*: by the fourth century many of its elements were transferred to New Year's Day; among Christians, they became part of the traditional Christmas celebrations.

SCHOLAE PALATINAE *LE*: a bodyguard of household troops created by DIOCLETIAN, consisting of two (and later more) cavalry regiments, each five hundred strong; named after the palace portico where the units were stationed.

SCRINIUM *LE*: The department of a ministry and, in particular, those controlled by the *magister scrinii* (*q.v.*).

SECULAR GAMES See *Ludi Saeculares*.

SENATE The chief council of state in Republican times, preserved with limited powers (but additional judicial functions) by the emperors. AUGUSTUS fixed membership at six hundred. Acknowledgment by the senate was in theory the precondition of an emperor's legitimacy, though in practice the approval of the army or praetorian guard was decisive. *LE*: CONSTANTINE's new senatorial order, virtually incorporating the *equites* (*q.v.*), recovered much administrative authority, and subsequently became a body of great landlords leading the defence of paganism in Italy and often assisting the German generals to undermine imperial authority. Constantine created a senate at Constantinople as well.

SESTERTIUS The largest token coin of brass, representing four copper *asses* and one-fourth of the silver *denarius* (*q.v.*). *LE*: a much smaller and largely theoretical denomination.

TETRARCHY *LE*: the imperial system founded by DIOCLETIAN (but not long surviving his abdication), according to which the Empire was ruled by two *Augusti* (*q.v.*) and two *Caesars* (*q.v.*).

TREASURY See *Aerarium*.

TRIBUNICIA POTESTAS Ostensibly the power of a *tribunus* (*q.v.*) *plebis*. The ancient association of this power with the protection of the people induced AUGUSTUS, followed by his successors, to select this power (divorced from office) as the most distinctive prerogative of an emperor, marking the years of his reign by a numeral. The power was also conferred on the members of the imperial family who held important posts, and especially on the heir to the throne.

TRIBUNUS   (1) *Tribunus plebis*, in the Republic a step in the senatorial career (for plebeians). The tribune was empowered to 'protect the people' by intercession, veto and punitive action. This right vanished but was perpetuated in the *tribunicia potestas* (*q.v.*) of emperors. (2) *Tribunus militum*, a senior army officer assisting commanders of legions (*legati*, *q.v.*) or commanding cohorts of *auxilia* (*q.v.*). *LE*: a commander of a regiment or other unit.

TRIUMPH   The procession of a victorious Roman general to the Temple of Jupiter Capitolinus. Under the Principate (see *Princeps*) Triumphs soon became a monopoly of the emperor, or – with his permission – of his family, while other generals could be awarded triumphal *ornamenta* (*q.v.*).

TRIUMVIRATE   An association of three men governing the State: (1) 60 BC (Pompey, Caesar, Crassus – unofficial); (2) 43 BC (Marcus Antonius, Octavian [the future Augustus], Lepidus – official).

VESTAL VIRGINS   Women, in historical times usually six in number, tending the fire of the goddess Vesta in her temple beside the Forum Romanum, and subject to vows of virginity, generally for a duration of thirty years.

VEXILLATIONES   From *vexillum*, standard. Detachments taken from legions for special purposes and returned to them when these tasks had been completed. *LE*: *vexillationes* of cavalry were created by CONSTANTINE I THE GREAT to expand the *comitatus* (*q.v.*).

VIGILES   A corps of seven thousand ex-slaves (*liberti*, *q.v.*) was created by AUGUSTUS as a city fire-brigade for Rome under a *praefectus vigilum*. By the time of SEPTIMIUS SEVERUS they were regarded as part of the army.

INDEX OF LATIN AND
GREEK AUTHORS

Note: Dates given are A D unless otherwise stated.

LATIN

Alaric, Breviary of   See *Roman Law of the Visigoths*.

Ammianus Marcellinus   *c.* 330–95. Born at Antioch. Wrote a history (*Rerum Gestarum Libri*) of the years 96–378. (Books 14–31, about the years 353–78, survive.)

Anonymus Valesii (or *Excerpta Valesiana*, after the first editor, H. Valesius, 1636)   The name given to two unidentifiable authors, (1) of a *Life of Constantine the Great*, written in the fifth century and based on a fourth-century collection of imperial biographies; and (2) of a sixth-century study of the years 474–526, particularly relating to Theoderic the Ostrogoth.

Augustine, Saint   354–430. Born at Thagaste. Bishop of Hippo Regius. Ninety-three writings include *Confessions*, *On the Trinity*, *The City of God* and attacks on eight categories of heretics.

Ausonius   *c.* 310–95. Born at Burdigala. Consul in 379. His poems include the *Mosella* (Moselle) and twenty-five letters.

Breviary of Alaric   See *Roman Law of the Visigoths*.

Cervidius Scaevola, Quintus   See *Scaevola*.

Chronographer of 354   Unidentified author of an illustrated calendar, of which there survives an edition dated to 354, commissioned by a certain Valentinus and subsequently enlarged.

Claudian   Died *c.* 404. Born at Alexandria. Pagan. His poems include *Panegyrics*, *Invectives*, commemorations of the emperor HONORIUS' marriage, and *Rape of Proserpine*.

Codes of Euric, Justinian I, Theodosius II   See *Euric, Justinian I, Theodosius II*.

Epitome   A short history of the Empire (down to THEODOSIUS I) which purports to be an epitome of the *Caesars* of Victor (*q.v.*) but is really an independent work of which only the earliest part is in any way derived from Victor's writings.

Euric   King of the Visigoths in Gaul and Spain, 466–84, who gave his name to a collection of laws, the *Codex Euricianus*, of which the greater part survives.

Eutropius   Fourth century. Court official (*magister memoriae*) of VALENS.

345

Wrote a survey (*Breviarium*) of Roman history from its beginnings to 364.

Festus   Fourth century. Court official (*magister memoriae*) of VALENS. Wrote a survey (*Breviarium*) of Roman history from its beginnings to 364, of which the first half is lost.

Florus   Second century. Born in north Africa; probably identifiable with a friend of HADRIAN. Wrote *Epitome* of Roman history to the wars of AUGUSTUS. He is also probably the author of an imperfectly preserved dialogue about Virgil.

Fronto   *c.* 100–*c.* 166. Born at Cirta. Orator and tutor of MARCUS AURELIUS and LUCIUS VERUS. Wrote *Letters*.

Gregory, Saint, of Tours   *c.* 540–94. Born at Arverna, Bishop of Civitas Turonum. Wrote *History of the Franks* and religious writings.

Historia Augusta   Probably written towards the end of the fourth century. A collection of biographies of Roman emperors, Caesars and usurpers from 117–284 (the years 244–59 are missing). Many of the contents (such as the names of the six alleged authors) are fictitious, but personal descriptions and other details sometimes contain authentic features.

Horace   65–8 BC. Born at Venusia. Poet; wrote *Epodes, Odes, Secular Hymn, Satires, Epistles, Poetic Art (Ars Poetica)*.

Jerome (Hieronymus), Saint   *c.* 348–420. Born at Stridon (north-west Illyricum). Secretary to Pope Damasus; founder of monastery at Bethlehem. Numerous writings include Latin translation of Bible (the Vulgate) and attacks on heresies.

Julianus, Salvius   *c.* 100–69. Jurist and legal adviser of HADRIAN. Wrote *Digesta* (in ninety books; excerpts survive in codes). Responsible for the revision and arrangement of the praetorian edict (see Key to Latin Terms).

Justinian I the Great   Byzantine (east Roman) emperor 527–65. He conquered large portions of the former western Empire from their German occupants, and gave his name to a collection of laws (*Codex* [two editions], *Digest, Institutes*, 'Novels') brought together under the direction of Tribonian.

Lactantius   *c.* 240–*c.* 320. Born in north Africa. His works in defence of Christianity include *Divine Institutions* and *On the Deaths of the Persecutors*.

Lex Romana Visigotorum   See *Roman Law of the Visigoths*.

Livy   59 BC–AD 17. Born at Patavium. Wrote *History of Rome* in 142 books (thirty-five survive).

Lucan   39–65. Born at Corduba. Wrote an epic poem about the war between Julius Caesar and Pompey the Great: *Bellum Civile* ('Pharsalia').

Nemesianus   Late third century. Born at Carthage. Wrote pastoral and didactic poems; planned an epic on the deeds of CARINUS and NUMERIAN (283–4).

Notitia Dignitatum (*Record of Official Posts*)   List of senior offices of state and military posts (with their staffs) in the western and eastern Empires (395).

Orosius   Early fifth century. Born at Bracara Augusta. Church officer (presbyter). His works include a chronicle from the Creation to 417, attacking paganism (*Historiae adversus Paganos*).

Ovid   43 BC–AD 17. Born at Sulmo. Poet; wrote *Amores, Heroides, Art of Love* (*Ars Amatoria*), *Fasti, Tristia, Letters from the Black Sea* (*Epistulae ex Ponto*), *Metamorphoses* and others.

Panegyric to Constantius I   Written at Treviri, by an anonymous Gallic orator (296). The eighth of a series of twelve *Panegyrici Latini* extending from TRAJAN to THEODOSIUS I.

Papinian   Died 212. Perhaps born in Syria. Jurist and praetorian prefect. Author of *Quaestiones* (thirty-seven books), *Responsa* (nineteen books) and others; excerpts survive in codes.

Paulus (Julius)   Early third century. Jurist and praetorian prefect. Wrote 320 books; excerpts survive in codes.

Petronius 'Arbiter'   Died in 65. Courtier and minister of NERO; perhaps consul in 61. Novelist; wrote *Satyricon*, including *Feast of Trimalchio*.

Pliny the elder   23/24–79. Born at Comum. Wrote encyclopaedic work on natural history and other sciences, art etc. (*Naturalis Historia*) in thirty-seven books. His extensive writings on historical and other subjects are lost.

Pliny the younger   61/62–before 114. Born at Comum. Wrote ten books of literary letters (*Epistulae*) and *Panegyricus* to TRAJAN.

Propertius   54/48–after 16 BC. Born at Asisium. Elegiac poet (wrote four books).

Roman Law of the Visigoths (*Lex Romana Visigotorum* or *Breviary of Alaric* [*Breviarium Alarici*])   Drawn up by the Visigothic king, Alaric II, for his Roman subjects in Gaul (506). Laws from the *Codex of Theodosius II* and other Roman sources are included.

Salvius Julianus   See *Julianus*.

Scaevola (Quintus Cervidius)   Later second century. Jurist and legal adviser of MARCUS AURELIUS. Wrote extensive works, now lost.

Scriptores Historiae Augustae   See *Historia Augusta*.

Seneca the younger   *c.* 5/4 BC–AD 65. Born at Corduba. Minister of NERO and author of ethical treatises, scientific writings, tragedies, prose and verse satire (*Apocolocyntosis*) and literary letters.

Serenus Sammonicus the elder   Late second and early third century. Killed by CARACALLA in 212. Grammarian and antiquarian; author of *Res Reconditae* (lost), dedicated to SEPTIMIUS SEVERUS and probably CARACALLA.

Serenus Sammonicus the younger   Described by the *Historia Augusta* as a third-century poet who was esteemed by SEVERUS ALEXANDER and presented the library of his father (the foregoing) to his former pupil

GORDIAN II. But it is uncertain if he ever existed.

Sidonius Apollinaris   *c.* 430–88. Born at Lugdunum. Bishop of Arverna (469). Wrote panegyrics and other poems, and nine books of letters.

Suetonius   *c.* 69–130/140(?). Probably born at Hippo Regius. Secretary of Hadrian. Wrote biographies of the Twelve Caesars (*De Vita Caesarum*: Julius Caesar–DOMITIAN), grammarians and rhetoricians (part of a series *De Viris Illustribus*), poets and orators and historians (portions survive).

Tacitus   *c.* 55–*c.* 117(?). Probably of Gallic or north Italian origin. Consul and governor of Asia. Wrote *Histories* of the years 69–96 (the surviving portion is on the civil wars, 69–70); *Annals* of the years 14–68 (most of TIBERIUS, part of CLAUDIUS and most of NERO survive); *Agricola* (biography of his father-in-law); *Germania*; *Dialogue on Orators* (*Dialogus de Oratoribus*).

Theodosius II   Born 401. East Roman emperor 402–8 (joint) and 408–50 (sole). Gave his name to a collection of laws (*Codex Theodosianus*, 438).

Ulpian   Died 223. Born at Tyre. Jurist and praetorian prefect. Nearly 280 works are recorded; excerpts from almost one-third of JUSTINIAN's *Digest*.

Valesiana, Excerpta   See *Anonymus Valesii*.

Varro   116–27 BC. Born at Reate. The most famous Roman scholar. Author of numerous works, of which *Res Rusticae* and part of *De Lingua Latina* survive.

Vegetius   Late fourth century. Military historian; wrote manual of Roman military institutions (*De Re Militari*).

Victor (Sextus Aurelius)   Fourth century. Born in Africa. Governor of Pannonia Secunda (361) and prefect of Rome (389). Biographer; wrote *Caesars* (lives of the emperors from AUGUSTUS to CONSTANTIUS II).

Virgil   70–19 BC. Born at Andes near Mantua; died at Brundusium. Poet; wrote *Eclogues* (ten poems), *Georgics* (four books), *Aeneid* (twelve books).

Visigoths, Roman Law of the   See *Roman Law of the Visigoths*.

GREEK

Acts of Pilate   Forged documents circulated round the east by MAXIMINUS II DAIA (310–13) to discredit Christianity.

Arius   *c.* 260–336. Probably Libyan by birth. Christian teacher at Alexandria. Founder of Arianism. Three letters and fragments of *Thalia* (verse and prose popularization of his doctrines) survive.

Arrian   Second century. Born at Nicomedia. Governor of Cappadocia under Hadrian. Wrote *Anabasis* (history of Alexander the Great); history of Alexander's successors (fragments survive); *Indica*; the lost *Bithynica* and *Parthica* and *Alanica*, and a tactical manual and maritime guide of Black Sea.

Athanasius, Saint   *c.* 295–373. Bishop of Alexandria. His apologetic, dogmatic, ascetic and historical treatises survive (including *History of the Arian Heresy*); also letters.

348

Aurelius, Marcus   Emperor 161–80. Wrote twelve books of *Meditations*, following the principles of Stoicism.

Cassius, Dio   Second to third century. Born at Nicaea. Eighty books of Roman history from beginnings to AD 229, preserved partly in full but mainly in abbreviation and epitome.

Chrysostom, Saint John   See *John*.

Cyril, Saint   Died 444. Bishop of Alexandria. Author of a twenty-book work refuting the pagan views of JULIAN THE APOSTATE.

Dexippus   Born *c*. 210. Athenian sophist and statesman and commander. Wrote *Chronicle* (*Chronike Historia*) to 269–70; history of Alexander's successors; and *Scythica*, on the Gothic wars from 238 to AURELIAN. Fragments survive.

Dioscorides   First century. Born at Anazarbus. Served in NERO's army as a doctor. Wrote *Materia Medica* (*Pharmacology*).

Eudocia, Aelia (originally Athenais)   Born at Athens. Married THEODOSIUS II (421), died 460. Wrote poems on the martyrs Cyprian and Justina and New Testament themes. Fragments survive.

Eunapius   *c*. 345–after 414. Born at Sardis. Pagan philosopher and priest. Wrote *Lives of the Philosophers and Sophists* (*c*. 396) and a history (variously titled by himself) of the years 270–404 (later published in an expurgated edition omitting anti-Christian sentiments).

Eusebius   *c*. 260–*c*. 340. Born in Syria Palaestina (Judaea). Bishop of Caesarea Maritima. His works include *Church History* and *Life of Constantine the Great*.

Galen   129–99(?). Born at Pergamum. Gladiators' doctor in Asia Minor and MARCUS AURELIUS' court physician. Wrote 153 works, of which those on anatomy, physiology, pathology, therapeutics and psychology are most influential.

Gerontius   Early fifth century. Born at Rome in 383 and died at Jerusalem in 439. Abbot and writer of *Life of St Melania* (the younger).

Herodes Atticus   *c*. 101–77. Consul in 143 and friend of four emperors. Wrote philosophical treatises, speeches and letters; only one Latin translation of a (doubtfully authentic) speech survives.

Herodian   Born *c*. 180. Perhaps from Syria. Wrote *Roman History* from the death of MARCUS AURELIUS (180) to the accession of GORDIAN III (238).

John Chrysostom, Saint   *c*. 354–407. Born at Antioch. Patriarch (bishop) of Constantinople in 398. Wrote many treatises (e.g. *On the Priesthood*), sermons, commentaries and over two hundred letters.

John Malalas   *c*. 491–*c*. 578. Of Syrian origin. His *Chronographia*, in eighteen books, begins with the Creation and ends in 563 (originally it continued to 565 or 574).

Julian the Apostate   Emperor 361–3. Pagan. Surviving writings include eight speeches, the satirical *Misopogon* ('Beard-Hater'), the humorous

Caesars and eighty letters.

Leo I the Great   Pope 440–61. There are ninety-six extant sermons and 432 letters, including the *Tome*, an exposition of Catholic doctrine.

Libanius   314–*c.* 393. Born at Antioch. Pagan professor of rhetoric. Surviving writings include sixty-four speeches and 1,600 letters.

Malalas, John   See *John Malalas*.

Malchus   *c.* 500. From Philadelphia in Syria. Wrote *Byzantiaca* (a history of the period perhaps extending from CONSTANTINE I THE GREAT to Anastasius I, 493–518). It is uncertain if he was pagan or Christian.

Marcus Aurelius   See *Aurelius*.

Olympiodorus   Before 380–after 425. Born at Thebes (Egypt). Pagan. Wrote history or memoirs from 407–25, surviving in summaries.

Onesimus   Fourth century (attributed to the time of CONSTANTINE I THE GREAT). From Sparta (or possibly Cyprus). Writer of numerous rhetorical works.

Origen   185/6–254/5. Probably born at Alexandria. Christian writer of very many works of biblical criticism, exegesis etc. His tract *Against Celsus*, a vindication of Christianity against paganism, survives.

Philo Judaeus   *c.* 30 BC–AD 45. Born at Alexandria. Jewish author of numerous theological and philosophical works and of the *Legatio ad Gaium* describing his mission to GAIUS (CALIGULA) in 39–40.

Philostorgius   *c.* 368–430/440. From Cappadocia. Arian. Continued Eusebius' *Church History* to 425.

Philostratus   Born *c.* 170. His family came from Lemnos. Member of a philosophical circle patronized by Julia Domna, wife of SEPTIMIUS SEVERUS. Author of *Life of Apollonius of Tyana*, mysticizing first-century philosopher.

Plotinus   205–69/70. Born at Lycopolis in Upper Egypt; died in Campania. Neo-Platonist philosopher. His *Enneads*, essays based on seminars, were collected by Porphyry of Tyre (232/3–*c.* 305).

Procopius   *c.* 500–*c.* 565. Born at Caesarea Maritima. Wrote *History of the Wars of Justinian*, *Secret History* and *On Justinian's Buildings*.

Sallustius   Fourth century. Pagan. Praetorian prefect of the Gauls 361–3, consul in 363. Wrote *De Deis et Mundo* (*On the Gods and the Universe*) and a handbook of neo-Platonic doctrines.

Socrates Scholasticus   380–*c.* 450. Lawyer at Constantinople. Continued Eusebius' *Church History* to 439.

Sozomen (Salamanes Hermeias Sozomenos)   Fifth century. Lawyer at Constantinople. Wrote *Church History* from 324–439; his epitome of earlier periods is lost.

Themistius   *c.* 317–88. Born in Paphlagonia. Pagan philosopher and rhetorician; thirty-four speeches, mainly official addresses, survive.

Theodoretus   *c.* 393–466. Born at Antioch. Bishop of Cyrrhus. Numerous works include *Church History* to 428, *Religious History* comprising biographies of ascetics, and theological disputations.

Zonaras   Twelfth century. Commander of the Byzantine imperial body-guard, imperial secretary, and then monk. His works include *Epitome of Histories*, a universal history to 1118.

Zosimus   *c.* 500. Tentatively identified with a sophist from Ascalon or Gaza. Pagan. Wrote *New History*, from AUGUSTUS to 410.

Index to Maps and Plans (with modern equivalents of place-names)